DIALOGUE ABOUT LAND JUSTICE
PAPERS FROM THE NATIONAL NATIVE TITLE CONFERENCE

Edited by Lisa Strelein

First published in 2010
by Aboriginal Studies Press

© Lisa Strelein in the collection, 2010
© in individual chapters is held by the contributors 2010

All rights reserved. No part of this book may be reproduced or transmitted in any form or by any means, electronic or mechanical, including photocopying, recording or by any information storage and retrieval system, without prior permission in writing from the publisher. The Australian *Copyright Act 1968* (the Act) allows a maximum of one chapter or 10 per cent of this book, whichever is the greater, to be photocopied by any educational institution for its education purposes provided that the educational institution (or body that administers it) has given a remuneration notice to Copyright Agency Limited (CAL) under the Act.

Aboriginal Studies Press
is the publishing arm of the
Australian Institute of Aboriginal
and Torres Strait Islander Studies.
GPO Box 553, Canberra, ACT 2601
Phone: (61 2) 6246 1183
Fax: (61 2) 6261 4288
Email: asp@aiatsis.gov.au
Web: www.aiatsis.gov.au/asp/about.html

National Library of Australia Cataloguing-In-Publication data:

Title: Dialogue about land justice : papers from the National Native Title conference / editor, Lisa Strelein.

ISBN: 9780855757144 (pbk.)

Notes: Bibliography.

Subjects: Native title (Australia) Aboriginal Australians — Land tenure. Aboriginal Australians — Government relations. Aboriginal Australians — Politics and government. Aboriginal Australians — Legal status, laws, etc. Land tenure — Law and legislation — Australia — History. Australia — Colonization — History.

Other Authors/Contributors:
Strelein, Lisa.

Dewey Number: 323.119915

Printed in Australia by Ligare Pty Ltd

Cover art: Arrernte coolamon presented to the Indigenous Women's Talking Circle by Lhere Artepe representatives, Karen Liddle and Barb Satour, at the Native Title Conference 2007, Yidinji Country (Cairns, Qld).

The book has been printed on paper certified by the Programme for the Endorsement of Forest Certification (PEFC). PEFC is committed to sustainable forest management through third party forest certification of responsibly managed forests.

FOREWORD

In the years since Eddie's passing, I have attended quite a few of the Native Title Conferences around the country. Over the past ten years, AIATSIS has built on Eddie's work, bringing together more people every year to discuss progress, challenges and new ideas in native title.

We come to the conference and see old friends, new allies, and sometimes it feels like catching up with family. To stand back and see just how many people move in a field of work that Eddie started is sometimes overwhelming: the Traditional Owners, people from native title representative bodies, government and business.

My family and I are proud that so many respected leaders have spoken with such passion and insight over the past ten years at the annual national Native Title Conference. These men and women do justice to the legacy of Eddie's fight for title to his land, the land of the Mer people.

I am pleased to see the insights and dreams from leaders in all walks of life brought together in this historic book about native title. I think Eddie would be proud to see these contributors continue his fight. I hope it will be a valuable tool to inspire all those who come after us.

Mrs Bonita Mabo

CONTENTS

Foreword		iii
Preface		vii
Contributors		ix
Introduction: The legacy of Mabo's case		1
1.	Mabo Lecture: Asserting our sovereignty *Mick Dodson*	13
2.	Confessions of a native judge: Reflections on the role of transitional justice in the transformation of indigeneity *Joe Williams*	19
3.	Mabo Lecture: Where we've come from and where we're at with the opportunity that is Koiki Mabo's legacy to Australia *Noel Pearson*	33
4.	Native title is property *Greg McIntyre*	52
5.	A curious history of the *Mabo* litigation *John Basten*	69
6.	The role of the High Court and the recognition of native title: Address in honour of Ron Castan QC AM *Robert French*	78
7.	Hypothesising social native title *David Ritter*	115
8.	Symbolism and function: From native title to Indigenous self-government *Lisa Strelein*	127
9.	Societies, communities and native title *Kingsley Palmer*	139
10.	Self-determination and Indigenous nations in the United States: International human rights, federal policy and Indigenous nationhood *Christine Zuni Cruz*	159

11.	Legal personality and native title corporations: The problem of perpetual succession *Marcia Langton and Angus Frith*	170
12.	Native title, agreements and the future of Kimberley Aboriginal people *Wayne Bergmann*	183
13.	Achieving real outcomes from native title claims: Meeting the challenges head on *Graeme Neate*	198
14.	Who's driving the agenda? *Tom Calma*	253
15.	Mabo Lecture: A long journey to climb the mountain *Les Malezer*	267
16.	Mabo Lecture: Addressing the economic exclusion of Indigenous Australians through native title *Aden Ridgeway*	287
Notes		302
Index		336

PREFACE

Since its inception in 1999, the annual national Native Title Conference has established itself as the leading Indigenous policy conference in Australia and as a flagship event for the Native Title Research Unit (NTRU) and the Australian Institute of Aboriginal and Torres Strait Islander Studies (AIATSIS). The conference combines key note addresses and multiple streamed sessions, cultural events, stalls and exhibitions. A range of speakers is invited each year, representing the fields of law, anthropology and public policy, both domestically and internationally. The public program attracts a wide range of native title delegates.

Each year a different native title representative body co-convenes the Native Title Conference with the NTRU in consultation with the Traditional Owners of the town or city where the conference is held. The first day of the program is reserved for native title claimants, native title holders and their representatives. This closed day and Indigenous Talking Circles held throughout the program are an important part of the conference program. These sessions provide an opportunity for Indigenous delegates to talk among themselves about the impact of the native title process on their communities and to discuss strategies to reach their goals for land justice and self-determination.

Three protocols shape the Native Title Conference:
1. recognising Traditional Owners;
2. working with native title representative bodies/native title service delivery agencies; and
3. maximising the participation of Aboriginal and Torres Strait Islander people.

These protocols give the Native Title Conference standing as a legitimate and accessible forum for Indigenous people to have a voice in and lead national debates, think through ideas and share experiences from across the country. The high participation rate of native title representative bodies — and the many native title claimants and holders who have given presentations and engaged in discussion — provides a unique opportunity for the discussion of common concerns and the development of valuable networks. This also makes the event attractive to other stakeholders, who gain insight and access to Indigenous native title networks through their participation in the conference. All of the relevant state and Commonwealth ministers have addressed the conference, alongside the federal judiciary and industry leaders.

Following the inaugural meeting in Melbourne, the conference has now been held in Townsville, Geraldton, Alice Springs, Adelaide, Coffs Harbour, Darwin, Cairns and Perth, arriving back in Melbourne for the tenth anniversary in 2009.

A significant feature of the conference program is the annual Mabo Lecture. The lecture is a dedication to the late Koiki (Eddie) Mabo and his historical legacy of the *Mabo* case that established native title under Australian law. The lecture aims to provide a contemporary commentary on native title issues in the context of Indigenous peoples' struggle for recognition and control over their country and their lives.

It is hoped that this volume goes some way to capturing the spirit of dialogue and accumulated wisdom of the conference, and that it marks its importance as a national forum to move native title forward in the pursuit of Indigenous land justice.

Lisa Strelein

CONTRIBUTORS

Wayne Bergmann has been Executive Director of the Kimberley Land Council since 2001. Prior to this he worked in Chambers and private practice in Perth. Wayne has Nykina, Nyul Nyul, Greek and Sri Lankan ancestry, and grew up near Derby in the Kimberly region of Australia.

John Basten is a Judge of the Court of Appeal, Supreme Court of New South Wales. Before his appointment to this position, he argued many leading cases on land rights and the *Native Title Act 1993*. Justice Basten advised the National Indigenous Working Group in 1997–98 and participated in negotiations with the government over what became the *Native Title Amendment Act 1998*.

Tom Calma held the positions of Aboriginal and Torres Strait Islander Social Justice Commissioner between July 2004 and January 2010 and Race Discrimination Commissioner between July 2004 and July 2009. Tom is an Aboriginal elder from the Kungarakan tribal group and a member of the Iwaidja tribal group. From 1995 to 2002 Tom worked as a senior Australian diplomat in India and Vietnam. During his time in India, he also oversaw the management of the Australian international education offices in Pakistan, Nepal and Sri Lanka.

Mick Dodson is the Chair of the Australian Institute of Aboriginal and Torres Strait Islander Studies, Director of the National Centre for Indigenous Studies at the Australian National University, and 2009 Australian of the Year. Mick was Australia's first Aboriginal and Torres Strait Islander Social Justice Commissioner, serving between 1993 and 1998, and is presently a member of the United Nations Permanent Forum on Indigenous Issues. Mick is a member of the Yawuru peoples, the traditional Aboriginal owners of land and waters in the Broome area of the southern Kimberley region of Western Australia.

Angus Frith is a barrister at the Victorian bar, and has previously worked as a solicitor with native title representative bodies in Victoria and the Kimberley. Part of that work involved working for the National Indigenous Working Group on the amendments to the *Native Title Act 1993*.

Robert French is the current Chief Justice of the High Court of Australia. In 1986 Justice French was appointed to the Federal Court of Australia, having previously practiced as a barrister and solicitor, and he was the first President of the National Native Title Tribunal from 1994 to 1998. Justice French was also a founding member and Chairperson of the Aboriginal Legal Service (Western Australia) from 1973 to 1975. In 2003 Justice French was appointed as a permanent non-resident member of the Supreme Court of Fiji and in 2008 was appointed as the President of the Australian Competition Tribunal.

Marcia Langton in the Inaugural Chair of Australian Indigenous Studies at the University of Melbourne. Marcia is also Chief Investigator with the research project on Agreements, Treaties and Negotiated Settlements and is a descendant of the Yiman people of central Queensland.

Les Malezer is Gubbi Gubbi/Butchulla, from south-east Queensland, with more than thirty years of experience in Commonwealth and Queensland public services and Indigenous organisations. Les was founding President in 1977 of the Foundation for Aboriginal and Islander Research Action (FAIRA) and General Manager when FAIRA was appointed a native title representative body in 1994. For the past five years, Les has been a non-governmental organisation delegate to the United Nations and currently holds the position of Chairperson of the Global Indigenous Caucus to the United Nations.

Greg McIntyre has been a legal practitioner since completing his university degree and was instructed by Eddie Mabo to commence proceedings that culminated in the *Mabo* case in 1992. Greg was Principal Legal Officer of the Aboriginal Legal Service of Western Australia from 1988 to 1990, and was President of the National Environmental Law Association from 1992 to 1997. In 2002 Greg was appointed Senior Counsel.

Graeme Neate has held the position of President of the National Native Title Tribunal since 1999. Prior to this, Graeme was a part-time member of the Tribunal (from 1995) and was previously the Chairperson of the

Aboriginal and Torres Strait Islander Lands Tribunal in Queensland and a member of the Land Court of Queensland.

Kingsley Palmer was a Director of Research and subsequently Deputy Principal of the Australian Institute of Aboriginal and Torres Strait Islander Studies in Canberra between 1985 and 2001. Prior to this, he worked as senior anthropologist at the Northern Land Council, Darwin. He now works as a private anthropological consultant.

Noel Pearson is the co-founder of the Cape York Institute for Policy and Leadership. Noel is a member of Bama Bagaarrmugu from the Kalpowa and Jeanie River area in the south-eastern Cape York region. He is a history and law graduate from the University of Sydney and has recently published his first book, titled *Up from the Mission: Selected writings* (Black Inc., Melbourne, 2009).

Aden Ridgeway has long been involved in Indigenous affairs, and has worked in both the public and private sectors. In 2001 Aden was elected Deputy Leader of the Australian Democrats and remained in the Senate until 2005. Aden is a member of the Gumbaynggir people and, since leaving politics, he has been the host of ABC TV's *Message Stick* and is the chairman of the Indigenous Tourism Industry Advisory Panel (formerly Indigenous Tourism Australia).

David Ritter has held the position of Principal Legal Officer with Yamatji Land and Sea Council and teaches at the Faculty of Law at the University of Western Australia. He is currently working with Greenpeace in London. David is the author of two books on native title — *The Native Title Market* (UWA Publishing, Perth) and *Contesting Native Title* (Allen & Unwin, Sydney), both published in 2009.

Lisa Strelein is the Director of the Research Programs at the Australian Institute of Aboriginal and Torres Strait Islander Studies. Lisa's research and publications have focused on the relationship between Indigenous peoples and the state, and the role of the courts in defining Indigenous peoples' rights. Lisa is the convener of the annual national Native Title Conference. Lisa's book *Compromised Jurisprudence: Native title cases since Mabo* (2nd edn, Aboriginal Studies Press, Canberra, 2009) is the leading text on native title law.

Joe Williams was appointed to the New Zealand Supreme Court in 2009. Judge Williams was previously Chief Judge of the Māori Land

Court from December 1999 and also the Chairperson of the Waitangi Tribunal. He was a junior lecturer in law at Victoria University in Wellington from 1986 to 1987 before gaining a Master's degree with first-class honours in Indigenous rights law at the University of British Columbia in Vancouver in 1988. In 1999 he was awarded the Mäori Students Millennium Prize as a former student of Victoria University of Wellington. In 2001 he was appointed Fellow of Victoria University of Wellington Law Faculty.

Christine Zuni Cruz is a Professor of Law at the University of New Mexico, becoming a member of the law faculty in 1993. Professor Zuni Cruz is a member of Isleta Pueblo. A significant achievement of Professor Zuni Cruz was the establishment of the Southwest Indian Law Clinic. She has been a Tribal Court Judge with the Pueblo of Laguna and Pueblo of Taos, was Presiding Judge with the Isleta Court of Tax Appeals and an Appellate Judge with the Southwest Intertribal Court of Appeals. Professor Zuni Cruz is an Associate Judge on the Isleta Appellate Court and is Editor-in-Chief of the *Tribal Law Journal*.

INTRODUCTION: THE LEGACY OF MABO'S CASE

LISA STRELEIN

In Melbourne in 2009, on Wurundjeri Country, seven hundred Indigenous people, policy makers and practitioners met to discuss native title. It was the tenth annual national Native Title Conference. The Commonwealth Attorney-General and Minister for Indigenous Affairs presented a vision of land settlements that would go beyond native title to meet the broader aspirations of Indigenous peoples. The Victorian Government and the Aboriginal Land Justice Group revealed their alternative framework for land settlements. Judges, practitioners and claimant groups proposed significant reform to the requirements of proof of native title, and the representatives of all of the successful native title groups met to discuss the challenges of managing their responsibilities for their land within the existing governmental arrangements. At the same time the steering group for a new representative body for Aboriginal and Torres Strait Islander peoples held discussions on an appropriate national structure. The topics discussed at the conference placed native title within a much broader context, ranging across land and water management, economic development and corporate governance.

This broad agenda for the conference should not be seen as novel or surprising. For Indigenous peoples, native title is not isolated from other aspects of Indigenous relations with the state and their relationship with their country. Thus the conversation with policy makers across the institutions of government is not a debate simply about the law of native title. The conversation is rooted in the colonial encounter, the inter-cultural encounter and the struggle for self-determination that underpins debates about Indigenous land and wellbeing.

This book brings together a selection of the papers from the ten years of this conference. Over those ten years many of the leading thinkers and commentators on native title and Indigenous rights have regularly participated in this annual dialogue. Former Senator Aden Ridgeway, for example, notes in his paper that, in the absence of a representative voice, the conference took on greater significance after the abolition of the Aboriginal and Torres Strait Islander Commission. Indeed, during the ten years covered by this collection, many Indigenous voices were silenced and dissociated from policy debates. Even for Noel Pearson, whose views on education and welfare reform received a great deal of attention from the Howard Liberal Government, was ensconced in the same colonial battle when it came to land and autonomy.

The conference invites critical reflection on the state of native title and the observations are often confronting for a system that has its own dynamic, morass of legislation, institutions, processes and money. In particular, the Mabo Lecture at the conference each year prompts a consideration of the legacy of Eddie Mabo and the *Mabo* decision.[1] The Mabo Lecture often explores whether native title meets the expectations and the vision that Indigenous people had for native title and, importantly, whether it does justice to the struggle of Eddie Mabo and the radical advocacy that gave him the courage to challenge the state's assertion of ownership of his traditional land. Invariably, the answer is that it does not.

Pearson is critical of the conference itself for perpetuating a mythology that the state is supporting Indigenous aspirations for native title. Māori Judge Joe Williams describes in detail the gamesmanship involved in the type of transitional justice that native title represents. While the dialogue between Indigenous peoples and government at the conference has largely been a respectful and constructive engagement, with all parties publicly expressing their commitment to seeking a way forward that would build rather than destroy relationships, a number of the contributors in this collection draw attention to the divisive game that is played whenever Indigenous rights are at issue.

The complexity of the system that has emerged from the *Native Title Act 1993* (Cth) (NTA) is probably most evident in the paper by Graeme Neate, President of the National Native Title Tribunal, who looks at the barriers to the progress of claims within the system and some of the ways that key players can contribute to better outcomes. There is no doubt, as you read the papers in this volume, that the legal framework for native title and the interpretation by the courts of what is required to prove native title is problematic.

Justice John Basten of the New South Wales Supreme Court and former native title barrister highlights the original limitations of the *Mabo* decision and, in particular, the discriminatory aspects of the doctrine of native title. Justice Basten is critical of the use of emotive language by the Court, which obscures the critical compromises of Indigenous rights in the doctrine and the essentially mundane decision that the common law can protect an allodial, communal and inalienable title. Despite the High Court's references to justice and values of non-discrimination and equality, the principle of non-discrimination is not applied consistently. This is particularly true in relation to extinguishment and the revival of native title and rights to resources. In a similar vein, High Court Chief Justice Robert French, former Justice of the Federal Court and President of the National Native Title Tribunal, explores the limitations of the 'recognition' provided by the *Mabo* decision. He posits the recognition of native title as a metaphor, something more than merely the legal act of recognition, but also as an act of humanity. Terra nullius, he argues, was an act of racism that denied a shared humanity. Chief Justice French describes the *Mabo* case as not merely the simple legal discovery that Justice Basten identifies, but as a 'shock of awareness' for Australian society.

This theme is carried through from Greg McIntyre's paper on native title as property and into Noel Pearson's critique of the legacy of the *Mabo* judgment. Pearson embraces the original *Mabo* decision as a just compromise of the social and legal reality of colonisation. But he is highly critical of subsequent decisions, in particular the *Yorta Yorta* case,[2] in which the courts have reified the notion of Indigenous law and custom. Here again, Pearson argues that the courts have not grasped the mundane aspects of native title identified by Basten. Pearson is also critical of the Australian courts' failure to utilise comparative law and to appreciate native title as a possessory title.

Using the comparative traditions of native/aboriginal title and the leading jurisprudence and the decisions of the High Court itself, Senior Counsel Greg McIntyre advocates a proprietary model of native title, arguing that the law has the capacity to deal with property as both jural right and socially constituted fact. McIntyre is critical of the decision of the full Federal Court (ultimately upheld by the High Court) in the *Miriuwung Gajerrong* case,[3] which sought to apply a lesser conception of native title right or title than would be enjoyed under any non-Indigenous common law property right. Property, he argues, is not absolute, yet the readiness of the courts to 'extinguish' exclusivity and rights to control access would presume so. Exclusivity can be seen in a relative sense (like landlord and tenant or co-tenancy); that is, an interest can be exclusive except against those with better title.

Chief Justice French, like Justice Basten, notes the importance of the experiences of the members of the *Mabo* High Court with the Northern Territory and other land rights systems, as well as the *Racial Discrimination Act 1975* (Cth), to their decision in *Mabo*. Justice Basten also draws a comparison with the *Aboriginal Land Rights (Northern Territory) Act 1971* (Cth) (ALRA). The history of the ALRA shows the capacity of our legal system to accommodate exclusive communal rights to land (simple inalienable freehold) with rights to resources, and, more recently, exclusive possession of coastal waters. But native title does not enjoy the stronger elements of ALRA titles. In the NTA the legislature adopted some measures to strengthen the title; for example, sections 47A and 47B allow prior extinguishment to be disregarded in some circumstances. However, more needs to be done to improve the opportunities provided by native title, especially to increase its economic potential.

Both Justice Basten and Chief Justice French question why 'revival' of native title rights was precluded by the Court and is only remedied to a limited extent by the NTA. To this end Chief Justice French explores the limits of recognition or the withdrawal of recognition embedded in the concept of extinguishment, which, he argues, is apt to mislead. The courts make decisions about the existence of rights and the relative priorities to be accorded to them, but there is a human or social element to how relative rights and power are managed in society. The withdrawal of recognition by the colonial law does nothing to impact on the right to the land under the Indigenous legal or social reality. Chief Justice French thus concludes that native title is a poor reflection of the full cultural, historical and human reality from which it is derived.

This disjunction between legal doctrine and the fact of Indigenous peoples' connection to country permeates a number of the papers in this book. David Ritter has included a paper originally presented to the 2002 conference in Geraldton, Yamatji Country. Rather than rewrite the paper, a new prologue provides for the paper as an historical artefact. At the time, Ritter sought to capture both the limits of native title as jural right and the social reality of Indigenous peoples' rights to land under their own jural system. Picking up the themes of metaphor from Chief Justice French, Ritter sought to garner support for a notion of 'social native title'. He recalls the feeling that native title had failed to provide the foundation for greater things that many believed would be the legacy of Mabo's case. Ritter argues that social native title captures something of which all the actors in the system are cognisant, that is, the legitimate assertions and aspirations of Indigenous peoples for dominion over their traditional territories. Ritter uses an example of the assertion of rights over country by many groups in the Yamatji and Pilbara regions to illustrate that if the state fails to recognise native title as a jural right, relying on the constraints of the native title system as it has developed, then the claims of Indigenous peoples do not go away. There need to be transformative opportunities for the state, a chance to set things right and to achieve a legitimacy that is missing.

Without relying on the lexicography of social native title, my paper in this volume seeks to make a similar point. Drawing on my long participation in the dialogue on native title, I am frustrated by the inability of governments at both Commonwealth and state levels to understand the symbolic importance of native title for Australia as a nation. The language of agreement making is too often shadowed by fierce opposition in litigation. I share the view of Williams — what we do with the legacy of native title must remain a measure of our maturity as a nation. But it must not be the line in the sand; it should be the beginning of a process of renegotiating the relationship between Indigenous peoples and the state, one that creates space for Indigenous peoples to articulate a comprehensive vision of their future, to see and support sovereignty in action.

Instead, Pearson observes that for much of the history of native title, Indigenous people have been seen as antagonists. The recognition of the interests of Indigenous peoples is seen as antithetical to the national interest and is opposed on that basis. Pearson laments this lost opportunity and expresses puzzlement over the reluctance of non-Indigenous peoples to embrace native title in its original form, as both a creature of the colonial legal system and as one that was constructed in such a way as to ensure no-one's rights were affected. 'This was their law', he says; 'nobody was losing any legal rights; why the bitter opposition?'

Similarly, McIntyre calls for a right to possession, an interest in the land itself, consistent with international comparisons. Under this conception, the traditional law and custom of the group is only relevant to determining the group that is 'entitled' and from thence has only a role internal to the group. The courts have taken a property law notion — the 'bundle' of abstract rights and utilities that make up any title — to an absolute level. This is illustrated by the courts' propensity to narrow the interpretation of rights and interests under native title to particular uses of resources, such as minerals and water, and to actual historical uses rather than to a general right to the resources of the land as an incident of the right to the land itself. In large part, this has operated to strip native title of its economic value.

The legal search for 'absolutism' that McIntyre refers to in relation to the nature of native title is also evident in the debates within native title law about the nature of the society that holds title. Kingsley Palmer, a prominent native title anthropologist, looks at some of the words that have attracted special privilege or meaning within native title, in particular the notions of society and community. Palmer argues that the legal process of proving native title seeks bounded, absolute groupings to define a land-holding entity, whereas anthropology would see social relationships and social processes as never complete or absolute. Anthropology does not admit absoluteness, but the law requires it. This is not to say that it is impossible to identify a collective interest in land based on cultural cohesion and shared law and custom.

Pearson critiques the reliance on law and custom to prove native title in this way. It is interesting to compare this view with that of Christine Zuni Cruz, Pueblo Indian judge and academic, who has studied Indigenous legal systems extensively. Zuni Cruz argues that Indigenous legal traditions should be the guiding principle for Indigenous peoples seeking to utilise the legal doctrines and institutions to achieve any outcome. For Zuni Cruz, the integrity of the traditional legal system is the most important measure of the usefulness of any legal or political tool. These two perspectives are not inconsistent. Zuni Cruz speaks of the meaning of self-determination from within Indigenous nations — an internal perspective. Pearson, too, is cognisant of this internal dimension to native title. The operation of traditional laws and customs is a matter internal to the group and should not be the concern of the non-Indigenous legal system, especially not in determining the extent of the right of Indigenous peoples to occupation of their lands. Zuni Cruz warns of the dangers of externally imposed visions of self-determination, which, if they fail to understand and nourish the internal system, risk assimilating the Indigenous nation while believing that they are asserting or supporting self-determination.

In Darwin in 2007 Professor Marcia Langton brought these risks into sharp relief with an analysis of native title corporations under the NTA, which gives a 'prescribed' corporate form to the body that will be recognised by the courts to hold the title on behalf of an Indigenous people. Writing here with Angus Frith, a native title barrister, Langton argues that the legal entity must operate in a bijural environment, both as holding and managing native title under traditional law and custom, as well as conducting external dealings with government and commercial interests. Langton and Frith examine the risks to the long-term sustainability of such organisations from the idiosyncratic processes that bring the native title corporation into existence and the pressures of their operating environment, especially in the absence of financial resources. They argue that market pressure may result in the bijural nature becoming less significant as participation in the market increases if traditional legal structures are not robust enough to continue to instil principles and provide direction to the corporation.

Wayne Bergmann, Chief Executive Officer of the Kimberley Land Council, explores in more detail the economic leverage that native title has provided in the expanding economy of the region. The Kimberley is a region where settlement of non-Indigenous people and economic interests on any scale have occurred only within the past generation or two. With more than fifty percent of the Kimberley now recognised as native title land, some of the earlier antagonism has given way to a more cooperative engagement from government and industry. Bergmann attributes much of this difference in attitude to the fact that native title has been determined. But even for the native title holders, the NTA has significant limitations, not least that there is no right to refuse a proposal for development. However, the strategic use of the processes under the NTA, building on past experiences, and a clear expression of the principles upon which the group is prepared to negotiate (regardless of the limits of the law) has led to significant outcomes. As Langton and Frith also explain, Bergmann identifies that the challenge for the Kimberley native title holders is to effectively utilise the resources gained from negotiations to leave a positive legacy of cultural, social and economic strength for future generations.

While only touched upon briefly, Bergmann notes that the successful claims in the Kimberley were hard won. The opposition from the state government and other parties, particularly in the early years, was ferocious. Graeme Neate's paper traces this history, noting the slow progress of claims since the recognition of native title. In his estimation, based on current progress, remaining claims could take more than thirty years to resolve. The trajectory of claim resolution is sobering, considering that it could be argued that to date it is the 'easier' claims that have been resolved. Neate further explores the collaborative approach to the settlement of claims, identifying what he sees as the key challenges and actions required of each of the participants in the process if the native title system is to deliver 'win–win' outcomes. Neate tethers his argument for a new approach to the comments of the Commonwealth Attorney-General and Minister for Indigenous Affairs, who have given support to a new, more creative and flexible approach to native title settlements. The year after Neate presented this analysis, the conference in Melbourne saw the announcement of the new Victorian land justice model that would seek alternatives to the strict requirements of the NTA and look more broadly at seeking to meet the land justice aspirations of the Indigenous peoples in that state.

Both Tom Calma and Les Malezer's papers were part of the conversation in Melbourne, acknowledging the Commonwealth and the state governments' commitments against the backdrop of the United Nations Declaration on the Rights of Indigenous Peoples and the emerging new representative body for Aboriginal and Torres Strait Islander peoples. Les Malezer has fought tirelessly for recognition of the struggles of Indigenous peoples in Australia within the United Nations system. His paper draws on the strength of those, like Eddie Mabo, who have fought before him and draws hope from the recognition of the rights of Indigenous peoples within the United Nations through the Declaration. Malezer draws attention to the recognition by various human rights bodies of the discriminatory aspects of the native title doctrine and the operation of the native title system. He warns that the native title system can be distracting for both Indigenous peoples and the Australian Government; it expends human and financial resources but it does not meet the standards expected and required of Australia in the relationship between Indigenous peoples and the state. This is a failure not lost on those international bodies that have repeatedly called on Australia to strengthen its efforts to guarantee Indigenous peoples' rights to self-determination and the enjoyment of their identity and culture.

Human rights in the Indigenous context are not simply about overcoming individual disadvantage and eliminating personal experiences of discrimination, though these are important. Human rights also recognise and protect the distinct collective identity and experience of colonisation and the survival of Indigenous peoples as self-determining peoples. Malezer, like Zuni Cruz, warns against those elements of inadvertent assimilation that undermine the distinct identity and culture of Indigenous peoples. In a similar vein, Aden Ridgeway warns of the danger of the 'disadvantage' or deficit model of Indigenous identity that pervades this and previous government policies. For example, instead of seeking to privatise communal lands, Ridgeway puts forward concrete options for improving the economic power of communal lands, particularly in improving access to financing. For Ridgeway, the failure to embrace the cultural character and capital of Indigenous peoples limits participation and denigrates the strength of Indigenous peoples. Moreover, it burdens the psyche of the nation. Ridgeway sees native title as having left a gift: an opportunity to transform our national identity by forging a new and more inclusive Australia. In his vision, Australia's identity should be one that acknowledges the impact of past treatment and addresses the ongoing legacy of disadvantage, but also one that moves forward in a spirit of coexistence and commitment to a just settlement.

Pearson described Indigenous peoples' claims for land justice as one of those tenacious wounds that never heal if no honest justice is done. *Mabo*, he suggests, was an opportunity for a just compromise. This kind of compromise is what Judge Joe Williams calls transitional justice. Speaking from his experience as a Māori claimant, lawyer and judge, Justice Williams takes a frank look at the systems in which native title and aboriginal rights are negotiated within colonial states. He describes transitional justice as the process by which the new colonial order agrees to either uphold pre-existing rights recognised in the old, usurped order or to make good on those that were unfairly taken away. Justice Williams argues that doctrines such as native title are not to be mistaken; they are designed to affirm and provide legitimacy to the new legal order, not necessarily constitutionally (because the domestic and international systems support their statehood), but morally. Justice Williams argues that colonial states like Australia and New Zealand are at such a stage in their development as mature states that they should be able to address questions of transitional justice without fear of undermining their legitimacy. But the accommodation must be meaningful; without a real shift in resources and power to Indigenous peoples over time, the whole question of legitimacy remains open.

For Indigenous peoples, it is imperative in Williams' view not to undervalue the legitimacy that they provide by acceding to transitional justice measures. The negotiation of the price of legitimacy is a game of strategy; it depends on a number of factors of power, timing, vision and courage. In particular, he suggests it must be a price that, while realistic in its view, does not disrespect the elders' struggle and pain. It requires this generation to bear witness to the cruel legacy of colonisation and to transcend it. Transitional justice is explained as a bridge, not an end in itself. A bridge to where? This is where the true challenge lies. It requires leadership and courage to define a vision of Indigenous peoples' destiny, one grounded in identity, not simply in overcoming disadvantage but accenting advantage and celebrating uniqueness. For Williams, this requires practical personal commitments, an acceptance of interdependency and a willingness for both sides to be changed by the process.

A number of papers presented in this volume unapologetically speak to Indigenous people, to disengage from the dialogue with government to focus on an internal conversation about responsibility and self-respect, of leadership and authority. Mick Dodson, chair of AIATSIS and Professor of Law, opens the dialogue with a call to arms for authentic leadership as the essence of self-determination — that is, self-determination as an internal dynamic of Indigenous society. Les Malezer expresses grief for those Indigenous people within Australia who are separated from the strength of their societies and culture by homelessness, alcohol, incarceration or institutionalisation. The sense of identity and self-pride of every Indigenous person and the cohesiveness of families, communities and societies is critical to true self-determination. Tom Calma, in his address to the Indigenous delegates and their representative bodies, called on them to make use of the mechanisms that the human rights system provides, both domestically and internationally, to drive the agenda for justice. As politicians come and go and debate among themselves about what is right for Indigenous peoples, Indigenous people divide under native title laws designed by a different legal system. Indigenous peoples, he argues, must take control and develop a sustainable and just system for land settlements, again not solely as an end in itself, but because the recognition of Indigenous peoples' rights and connection to their lands is integral to the physical, mental and economic wellbeing of every Indigenous person.

These messages echo the opening paper by Dodson, which captures much of the conversation over ten years. Dodson argues that the *Mabo* decision does not recognise land rights as Indigenous people understand them. Dodson reiterates that the NTA is based on racial discrimination and neither the courts nor the legislature have adequately overcome the discriminatory aspects of native title. Active opposition to individual native title claims by state, territory and Commonwealth governments, Dodson argues, belies a deeper incapacity of the state to support Indigenous peoples' right to self-determination. The land and resources of Indigenous peoples have always been too valuable. Dodson argues that what is required is a space within the economy and society for the exercise of culture, language and community development, without interference. Dodson expresses a form of self-defence against colonial forces that, like Williams, looks inward to a vision of self-determination that requires Indigenous people to make personal choices to defend their identity and inheritance, including through the active practice of culture. He calls on Indigenous people to pull together to invest in the cultural authority and moral standing of Traditional Owner communities; to demonstrate a form of diverse, personal leadership, courage and strength within families and communities.

THE PATH FORWARD

Many of the threads of this volume express frustration and disappointment at the legacy of Mabo's case in a country where genuine settlement of land justice issues remains for most an elusive prospect. Native title itself has been moulded into a form that does not do justice to its purpose of reconciling sovereign peoples' competing claims over territory. Yet, throughout the volume there are consistent messages as to the path forward and a hopeful vision of what lies ahead.

Tom Calma argues that the connections between native title and broader Indigenous policy discussions are beginning to be understood by governments, and there is an appetite for change. He refers to parliamentary debates on amendments to the NTA in 2007 that showed a dawning awareness of a system in crisis. Neate has demonstrated that a broader, more flexible approach to settlement of land justice requires commitment from all institutions of government involved in the process in order to overcome substantive and procedural impediments. But as many of the voices in this volume make clear, governments will never be able to design a system that meets the aspirations of a new and just partnership; Indigenous people must drive this change.

The Indigenous contributors to this volume speak with a fierce honesty about the challenges for their own communities to achieve such a goal and work towards what Dodson describes as the 'abundant enjoyment of self-determination'. They recognise the need to overcome Indigenous dispute and greed and violence against their own communities to open up the opportunities provided by native title.

There is an imperative to address the challenges presented by the dialogue about land justice presented in this book; to take the advice of those who have discussed and considered the native title system for more than a decade. Many of the contributors agree that it is not simply a matter of finding alternatives to native title. The *Mabo* case and the concept of native title have symbolic importance in Australia's nation building. Pearson points out that the courts have failed to acknowledge the constitutional aspect of native title as a reconciliation of prior occupation with the assertion of sovereignty. The weight of legal opinion in this book suggests that in order to move forward the discriminatory aspects of the native title doctrine must be removed. In particular, there is consensus that change is needed in the requirements of proof that use traditional law and custom as a means to stratify Indigenous societies on a scale of authenticity; the limiting of the content of the title by focusing on defined rights and interests; unnecessarily prioritising the rights of others; the failure to recognise the 'revival' or continuity of native title; and limiting the economic potential of native title.

If the courts are no longer able to retreat from the discriminatory doctrine they have drawn for themselves, then there is clear support here for reforms to the NTA that reflect principles of international law and comparative best practice. Malezer and Pearson go so far as to suggest that if a new form of land title is required, then this should be explored.

Beyond the confines of native title law and policy, it is imperative that national Indigenous affairs policy be based on the value of Indigenous culture and identity, as well as on overcoming the legacy of the past. Self-determination of Indigenous peoples depends on the continued existence of their distinct culture, legal traditions and identity as peoples, including self-government. To achieve this, Indigenous peoples must have control over institutions that determine their future, as well as input into policies that affect them and access to economic structures that respect the contribution of Indigenous identity and traditions.

Valuing Indigenous institutions and cultures is also essential to Australia's own sense of national identity. To mature as a nation, we must embrace rather than exclude Indigenous peoples. This volume seeks a personal commitment from all Australians, particularly those of us who are involved in the process of native title and land justice, to honour the legacy of Eddie Mabo's struggle for a better and more just society.

1.
Native Title Conference, Gimuy Walubara Yidinji Country, 2007

MABO LECTURE: ASSERTING OUR SOVEREIGNTY

MICK DODSON

First, I acknowledge the Traditional Owners of Cairns, the Gimuy Walubara Yidinji people, and pay my respects to their elders and ancestors, and thank them for protecting and caring for this beautiful country. I also recognise and pay my respects to the other Traditional Owners here today, some who have travelled a long way to participate in this important conference. And I thank Mrs Bonita Mabo for her introduction to this lecture and, on behalf of AIATSIS, thank the Mabo family for their continued support for this lecture. I also wish to thank the North Queensland Land Council and AIATSIS for inviting me to speak at this important time in our continuing struggle.

This lecture is addressed primarily to Indigenous people. I want to highlight the paramount need for Indigenous people to assert our rights to self-determination. It is my view that:

> every issue concerning the historical and present status, entitlements, treatment and aspirations of Indigenous peoples is implicated in the concept of self-determination…The right to self-determination is the right to make decisions. And these decisions affect the enjoyment and exercise of the full range of fundamental freedoms and human rights of Indigenous peoples.[1]

And, we should be able to 'freely determine our political status and freely pursue our economic, social and cultural development'.[2]

On the anniversary of the High Court decision in the *Mabo* case, we should celebrate the hard work and achievements of Eddie Mabo and the other Meriam applicants.[3] But let us not pretend that the decision by the High Court recognised land rights as we understand them, as we understand our responsibilities for country and connections with each other. The High Court attempted to accommodate Indigenous law and custom with the colonial common law, but was only able to understand our law and custom from within the framework of the colonial legal and political systems.

In addition to the *Mabo* decision, we can also celebrate the achievements of the Wik and Thayorre peoples, the Miriuwung and Gajerrong peoples, the peoples of Croker Island, the Blue Mud Bay mob, and my family, the Yawuru people, among many others.[4] These great nations have struggled and won recognition as native title holders. And there are many others, some of you here, continuing to struggle within the native title system to gain acknowledgment of your rights.

But of course our struggles have been made more difficult by the compromised and complicated *Native Title Act 1993* (Cth) (NTA), which, right from the start, was based on racial discrimination. The High Court's decision in *Mabo* contained the fundamentally discriminatory doctrine of extinguishment, which denies Indigenous peoples the same rights and protections for our property as enjoyed by other people. In drafting the NTA, the federal government had the choice to overcome the discriminatory aspects of the common law or to reinforce them. They decided to build upon the racist extinguishment doctrine in both the NTA and the subsequent amendments. The NTA does only what is legally necessary and the courts have similarly made sure that the legal recognition of our land rights is contained and constrained to the greatest extent possible.

Both at the federal level and state and territory level, governments have actively opposed the recognition of native title, especially in Western Australia and Queensland, but also in the Northern Territory. The most recent example is the great victory by the Noongar nation, where the Western Australian lawyers argued that the colonisers had wrought such devastation upon the Noongar people — through dispossession of lands, killings, the removal of children, introduced diseases, suppression of culture — that the Noongars could not possibly have survived.[5] But the Noongars clearly demonstrated their strength and resilience in the face of continuing oppression. I just hope that the Yorta Yorta people get another opportunity one day to show their continuing cultural strength and capacity for resistance, and I know that you will fight on.

My point about the Noongar case is that the Western Australian Government, with encouragement from the Commonwealth, tried every dirty trick to oppose the recognition of native title in the south west, even trying to remove the judge when they thought they were beaten. This is not just political opposition for the sake of securing the redneck voters; it is structural and systematic opposition by governments at all levels to the recognition of native title, it is disrespectful to the first peoples of this country and it is clearly a rejection of our right to self-determination.

It has been ten years since the report on the Stolen Generations was released, the *Bringing Them Home* report,[6] which documented the deliberate theft of our cultural identity by removing the children from our families and, notably, by removing the next generations from their land. It is no surprise to me that the report has been largely ignored by the federal government but I have been saddened by the ongoing vilification of many of the Stolen Generation, who fight for recognition and compensation, only to be attacked by racist historians and bankrupt politicians.

It is also forty years since the referendum where the Australian people decided to include us in the census, so we were no longer part of the flora and fauna, and to empower the Commonwealth to make laws on our behalf. I think that the referendum was a symbol of hope that, finally, the government might use its powers to protect and support Indigenous people, but apart from the *Land Rights Act* of 1976[7] there is little evidence that the state has the capacity to support our aspirations, let alone recognise and respect our sovereign status. It is shameful that in this day and age, with the enormous wealth of this nation, that many Indigenous people struggle to find basic housing, to access quality education for our kids, to find jobs at the same rate of pay as other workers, and/or to exercise and enjoy our cultural wealth and diversity.

My argument is that we are getting slaughtered by the colonial imperative to steal our land, to strip our culture, and to demoralise us as peoples and nations. It's about self-defence — we must defend our identity and our inheritance in the land and sea. And as we resist — and we have always resisted in many different ways — I say that we must pull together as nations, forever connected to the land and fortified by our law and culture, to make decisions for ourselves in determining our futures. We must assert our sovereignty and, in so doing, we must prioritise the place of Traditional Owners and native title holders in our decision-making processes and our resistance strategies.

And this means that we need strong leadership, from men and women, young and old, city and country, all of us together. We need community leadership that is based on cultural authority and moral standing; leadership that displays courage and strength. Our leaders must tackle the problems of grog, drugs, gambling, corruption and the neglect of children. Indeed, we must reinstate the legitimacy of traditional leadership to make decisions about the land and law, which includes punishing those members of the community who act inappropriately, who are violent within our communities and families, and who disrespect the fundamental role of the Traditional Owners.[8]

Through this leadership, we will create space within the economy and society for the abundant exercise of our culture, languages and arts; land and sea management; political organisation; and community development. Governments need to get out of the way; they need to get out of our lives in order for us to make decisions; they need to stop designing policies and programs that they think will help us and, instead, pay us the respect that we deserve as sovereign people. But somehow I don't think that governments are able to get out of the way, especially in Indigenous affairs, where they think that they know better than us about our life decisions. It is more likely that we need to push governments out of our lives, to resist their cajoling and interfering, which requires strength on our part.

I was heartened and impressed by the example of the Tangentyere Council recently in not folding to the bullying by the Minister for Indigenous Affairs, who offered funding for housing in exchange for control over their land. First, this was a blatant attempt to privatise more communal land, which is how liberal governments leverage wealth from under Traditional Owners. Second, it is a government responsibility to provide housing and other basic services to the poorest people in society, without stealing their land for ninety-nine years, which probably means forever. And third, why not just offer the blackfellas some tea and blankets for their land? And while they're at it, why not offer us poisoned tea and infected blankets?

I don't want to be seen to simply be bagging a particular federal government or minister; that's not my argument. I want to be clear that all colonial regimes — all levels of government in Australia — are incapable of showing respect for Indigenous people because they need to subjugate us in order to steal our land, because that is the basis for their wealth accumulation — access to property rights in order to exploit our land.

I've been thinking about this since May 2008, when I was hopeful about a new dialogue with the federal government to focus on improving health and education outcomes for all Indigenous people — so I gave a speech in the company of Prime Minister Howard at the corporate lunch where I stuck my neck out to engage with the Prime Minister and his government on these important issues.[9] As was organised, the Prime Minister gave a speech in response to mine, and he'd had a copy of my comments in advance, where he proceeded to give a flaccid explanation of the government's record on education spending and his self-proclaimed achievements in Indigenous affairs, which were thin to say the least.[10]

The people in the audience, many corporate types sympathetic to the needs of Indigenous people, afterward expressed surprise that the Prime Minister didn't take the opportunity to at least acknowledge that a better dialogue might be possible on key issues; but, on reflection, I realised that the government as a whole was not just unwilling to support us, as some people were suggesting, but that the colonial state is fundamentally incapable of responding in a constructive way, and that the Prime Minister's speechwriters were not just unwilling to be positive for political reasons, but were unable to show respect to Indigenous people, or to engage with us with honesty or fairness. I should have known this from the Prime Minister's shameful display at the Corroboree 2000 meeting where he shouted at the dissenting voices in the audience.

Indigenous people all over the world understand that it is a constant and continuing battle to retain our land rights, to exercise our responsibilities for the land and waters, to practice our culture and languages, to build our families and communities, whether in the cities or the bush, because we are the first peoples — this is our country and we will defend it. The Traditional Owners ought to decide who comes onto our land, and we should say 'no' more often, because the consequences of sharing our country with the colonisers are devastating.

One of the positive outcomes from the native title process is the establishment of Prescribed Bodies Corporate (PBC), which are the recognised entities through which Traditional Owners and native title holders can and must assert their responsibilities for country and make decisions on land and water management.[11] These entities are a new vehicle for Traditional Owners to assert their authority and to exercise their right to self-determination.

I want to mention that PBC members from all over the country met at AIATSIS in April 2007, which was the first meeting of its kind — to recognise and support them as landholders and to facilitate their engagement with government departments. It was clear from this national meeting that Traditional Owners can and should be playing the central role in the management of their lands.

And further, the PBCs should be the basis for Indigenous representation in the future, as the point of reference for Traditional Owners to engage with governments and other parties, if they so choose. For example, if the Labor Party is talking about new national and regional representative structures, they should be prioritising the right to self-determination and engaging with Traditional Owners through the PBCs in thinking about appropriate ways to have a respectful dialogue between nations.

It is my argument that Indigenous peoples must use all of the tools at our disposal to create space in the economy and society for the exercise of our right to self-determination, for the protection and maintenance of our culture and languages, and for the development of our communities and families. This approach requires solidarity across our nations, courageous leadership and probably some sacrifice, which is not new to most Indigenous people.

I encourage all of the participants at this conference to use this opportunity to design strategies, forge new linkages and make plans to create space for the abundant exercise of our right to self-determination.

2.
Native Title Conference, Noongar Country, 2008

CONFESSIONS OF A NATIVE JUDGE
Reflections on the role of transitional justice in the transformation of indigeneity

JOE WILLIAMS

> *Tena koutou katoa e nga uri o te hunga kua mene ki tua o te pae o maumahara. Apiti hono tatai hono, te hunga mate ki a ratou. Tena hoki koutou e te manawhenua, e Ngati Noongar, na koutou te reo powhiri, te reo karanga. No reira mihi mai ra, whakatau mai ra.*

I bring greetings to you, the descendants of those who are gathered beyond the horizon of memory. May our ancestors join each other in greeting as we, their living faces, join each other this day. I offer my respect to the people whose fires of authority burn in this land. To the Noongar people, I come in answer to your invitation and your call. I ask that you bid me welcome and grant me hospitality in your land.

I want first to record what a privilege it is to be asked to give the Mabo Lecture this year. This for two reasons: first, because of the historic contribution that Koiki Mabo made to the cause of Indigenous people in Australia and around the world when he brought his application for native title on behalf of himself and his people — and I might add in this vein his contribution to the growing up of Australia. Second, because of the list of those who have given this lecture in the past — Indigenous leaders and philosophers whose impact is felt across national boundaries. It was indeed a surprise and an honour to be approached.

SOME COMMONALITIES

The Indigenous stories in Australia and New Zealand have been joined from the beginning of the colonisation story. The first Māori experience of British colonisation outside New Zealand was of Sydney and Melbourne. As an aside, the Māori names for those two cities are still Poihakena — Port Jackson — and Poipiripi — Port Phillip — even though those original names have long fallen out of use in English. This is good linguistic evidence of the depth of common experience.

The first experience of British treatment of Indigenous people outside of themselves was when Māori first saw the plight of Indigenous people in Australia — and they were appalled. This experience sparked Māori opposition to colonisation in the early years. And even amongst those who were not so disposed, there was, as a result, a high level suspicion of British motives towards Māori. It is true, of course, that there was a treaty in New Zealand in 1840 and that the British saw no need to engage in the same formality with respect to the Indigenous people of Australia. This difference is often used to show that the colonisation stories in the two countries have little in common. That idea is discredited. It must be remembered that for much of New Zealand's history after 1840, the Treaty of Waitangi was treated as a dead letter — a 'simple nullity' in legal terms. It did not return to the consciousness of politics, the law and the non-Indigenous majority until the 1980s.

From that decade on, the development of Indigenous rights law in Australia and New Zealand ran roughly in sync. Eddie Mabo won posthumously in the Australian High Court in 1992[1] and the *Native Title Act* was enacted the following year. In New Zealand the long-running Māori fisheries litigation was settled in 1992 with the enactment of the *Treaty of Waitangi (Fisheries Claims Settlement) Act* of that year. The *Wik* case was decided by the Australian High Court in 1996.[2] At the same time, New Zealand tribal leaders were bringing their land claims before the Waitangi Tribunal and to direct negotiations with the government. The first of the large tribal settlements — the Tainui raupatu settlement — had been concluded a year earlier. It settled claims relating to the confiscation of a million acres of Waikato land following the so-called 'rebellion' of the Māori King in 1863. The settlement of the Taranaki confiscation claims, the South Island claims of the Ngai Tahu people and others, would follow.

In the meantime, tribal leaders in New Zealand would bring proceedings to prevent the privatisation of radio and television in the absence of a guarantee of Māori language broadcasting in each medium. The proceedings would be brought by those leaders in their own names and at their own cost. They would ultimately lose the battle but in a sense win the war. Through negotiations in the course of the litigation, promises were made to fund twenty-two tribal radio stations and a single Māori television station. The radio stations were all operational within a short time, although Māori television would not finally be established until 2004. Despite the legal and political controversy surrounding the conception of Māori television, it would prove to be a runaway success with New Zealanders of all cultures.

So the great questions of the land, fisheries and other natural resources, as well as the place of indigeneity in post-colonial society, were being confronted by the systems in Australia and New Zealand. In each case, the anvil upon which results were hammered out was a transitional justice forum built for the relevant national context. I use the term 'transitional justice' in a particular way. I mean a process by which the new order agrees either to uphold pre-existing rights recognised in the old usurped order or to make good on those that were unfairly taken away. In Australia, because of longstanding legal and political reliance on the discredited notion of terra nullius, a 'surviving title' model was used. The forum would be the National Native Title Tribunal, augmented by pronouncements of the Federal Court and High Court of Australia. In New Zealand the existence of the Treaty of Waitangi meant a reparative model was necessary with a focus on the wrongful extinguishment of rights during the colonial period.[3] The forum would be the Waitangi Tribunal, augmented by strategic use of the New Zealand Court of Appeal and occasionally the Privy Council in London.

BEING SCHIZOPHRENIC AND REALISTIC

Throughout this time I have been a law student, a lawyer and then a judge, and for nearly thirty years my focus has been on the anvil of transitional justice. As a Māori, that focus has been both professional and personal. Personal in the way that criminal law is personal to the burglar. I have been in the difficult and interesting position of being both the subject and object of my work. I have both the challenge of objectivity and the gift of empathy. It is these two ideas in combination that provide me with the insights I now offer. They also keep me poised at the point of sanity between idealism and realism. Most of all, they tell me that this is not the place for yet another arid doctrinal analysis of the shades of possibility to be found in treaty and aboriginal rights law in our two countries. I think that if I am to satisfy my dual personality anywhere, it will be in looking past legal formalism to the ebb and flow of power underlying law. It is in the realistic assessment of the ebb and flow of power between the state and the Indigenous people that I want to spend a good part of this lecture.

Both Australia and New Zealand are independent post-colonial states and have been for at least two generations. They have reached the point in their development where they can address questions of transitional justice without fearing that to do so would undermine the legitimacy of the existing legal order. There are some tough but unsurprising realities for Māori and Aboriginal and Torres Strait Islander peoples that follow from this starting point. First, the prime and unstated purpose of transitional justice is to affirm that legal order. Affirmation is not required in law — no domestic court would find that it was itself illegitimate and none has ever done so in Australasia. But transitional justice is about moral legitimacy, not legality. So the first rule of transitional justice is that it must be achieved within the existing game and must have the effect of confirming the moral legitimacy of that game. As I have said, this purpose is usually unstated. It can remain unstated because of the prodigious weight and momentum of the political economy that now underlies the legal order. There is no need to require that its existence be formally accepted by Indigenous people as a precondition to participation in transitional justice. It has become, over time, like the air that we breathe. Yet, powerful though the status quo is, it still craves the absolution that transitional justice can provide.

The second reality is that, from the Indigenous perspective, transitional justice is about the price that can be extracted from the legal order in return for the offer of moral legitimacy. The price can have value that is easily quantifiable in modern economic terms such as the transfer of property rights or it can relate to less easily quantifiable structural change such as guaranteed access to decision-making power within the legal order. It will usually involve both in varying degrees. But the price cannot be so high as to fundamentally change or undermine the game. On the contrary, as I have said, the first purpose of transitional justice must be to affirm the game.

I call this the 'yes, but' principle. For example, is aboriginal title to be recognised? *Yes, but* only to the extent that Indigenous resources have not already been appropriated by the existing order; to the extent that if they survive they will be protected, but no more. Or in the New Zealand context, does the Treaty of Waitangi have legal force? *Yes, but* only where Parliament says it may be enforced, and only to the extent it says so. Beyond that, it may be relevant to the exercise of executive power but it does not bind. And it certainly does not provide a basis for leaving the final assessment of loss and damages as a result of colonisation anywhere other than with the executive — the apex of settler political power. This 'yes, but' principle is the means by which the status quo is protected while offering some recognition to the Indigenous circumstance. It ensures that the recognition of past wrongs or surviving rights does not go so far as to unravel, or even disrupt to any material extent, the status quo.

There is a possibility, as yet unexplored anywhere in the world as far as I know, that transitional justice can ultimately lead to the evolution — and note I say evolution, not revolution — of a subtly new game in which Indigenous modalities come to be introduced and participated in by all. But that requires additional ingredients. I want to come back to that idea at the end, but let me leave it to one side for now.

None of this analysis can be particularly surprising to anybody: transitional justice is inherently conservative in the sense that it is always predicated on the continuation of the post-colonial order and that must be particularly so when the transitional revolution occurred more than a hundred years ago. It is none the less very important to restate this idea so that we can focus on what can be achieved on the anvil of transitional justice, and what can't: that is, what objectives will require Indigenous peoples to adopt other strategies and techniques. This restatement also takes us to an even more important question — in fact the most important question: what is the ultimate goal for Indigenous peoples? I will come back to this, too.

My comments here have been intentionally realistic — some might say ruthless. I certainly don't shrink from this approach. But I do not mean to disrespect the agony of the ancestors. They paid so much more than can ever be won back. Whenever I feel in danger of becoming too clinical about these things, I think back to a particular story of the second Māori King, Tawhiao. He had waged a war against imperial forces between 1863 and 1864. He had fought to a standstill. While the result of the war was inconclusive, he lost the politics. His villages were destroyed, his people scattered and he retreated into the centre of the North Island, where British authority did not reach — thereafter called the King Country. A million acres of his traditional homeland was confiscated in punishment for the 'rebellion'. In the 1870s and 1880s a new movement arose in a village called Parihaka in southern Taranaki, a region that had suffered even greater confiscation because of opposition to the land-hungry settler government. The leaders of the village were the prophets Te Whiti o Rongomai and Tohu Kakahi. At a time when Gandhi was only ten years old, they pioneered the technique that later became known as passive resistance. When surveyors came to lay out settler townships and farms on confiscated land, the people of Parihaka were sent out to pull out the survey pegs and plough up the land in preparation for planting. They delayed the confiscation by a decade. Hundreds were arrested and transported to imprisonment and hard labour in the South Island.

As Parihaka reached the zenith of its political power, Tawhiao, now a fugitive, met with Te Whiti and Tohu. They invited him to join their movement. His reply is still remembered to this day as one of the most poignant descriptions of the pain he and his people had suffered through years of war and dispossession. He said:

> *E Whiti, e Tohu, rapua te mea ngaro. E hoki ake nei au ki te riu o Waikato he roimata taku kai i te ao, i te po.*
>
> Whiti, Tohu, I bequeath to you the search for that which has been lost. As for me, I will return to the valley of my birth and I will eat my tears from sunrise to sunrise.

It is impossible to forget such stories. But we must be conscious of the realities in which we operate, just as Tawhiao was, for even in his despair, he planned for the return of his people. He said to Te Whiti and Tohu:

> *Maku ano e hanga i toku whare. Ko tona tahuhu he hinau, ko ona pou he mahoe, he patate. Me whakatupu ki te hua o te rengarenga, me whakapakari ki te hua o te kawariki.*
>
> I will build my own house. Its ridgepole and support posts will be of humble soft-woods. Those who live within it will be raised on the thin gruel of the *rengarenga* and strengthened on the sour fruit of the *kawariki*.[4]

Using the architecture of the traditional carved meeting-house as his metaphor, his message to the prophets of Parihaka was that his first task was to be the shelter in which his people could survive and heal themselves. He was a tough realist and he knew the years to come would be hard. We do ourselves no favours if we fail to adopt the same approach today.

2. Confessions of a native judge

THE PRICE

How, then, is the price of legitimacy to be fixed? Within the parameters of the status quo, there will be a great deal of haggling over that question. Price parameters will be set in the design of the transitional justice system itself and individual prices will be arrived at case by case within it. Many factors will come into play, including:

1. The reality of majority rule and the level of nervousness that the (majority) electorate feels about the ramifications for their own primacy of recognising Indigenous rights. Most politicians when negotiating settlements will say that they cannot go any higher without alienating the electorate. Whether that is true or not in any particular case bears careful analysis.
2. Demographics and the relative size and importance of the Indigenous minority. In theory, the larger the Indigenous minority, the greater the leverage. This has to some extent been the case for Mäori who make up fifteen percent of the population but a much larger proportion of the young. To be effective, however, there must be some level of organisation and cohesion. Like all Indigenous people, this has proved a constant challenge for Mäori.
3. The perceived importance among the political elite of international credibility and standing. A country that is conscious of its international status will want to be seen to be doing the right thing, particularly if it is being led by an internationalist. In his famous 1992 Redfern speech about the need to uphold the *Mabo* decision, Paul Keating, then Australian Prime Minister, made the point:

   > We simply cannot sweep injustice aside. Even if our own conscience allowed us to, I am sure, in due course, the world and the people of our region would not. There should be no mistake about this — our success in resolving these issues will have a significant bearing on our standing in the world.[5]

4. Timing and the importance of symbols in politics. This is often a difficult factor to plan for. But it can be a very powerful force for change. Looking at it from a distance, the Stolen Generations apology by the incoming Rudd government appears to be such an example. It seems likely that the new administration needed a powerful symbol of a clean break from the style of the old. The apology provided such

a symbol at the right time. Whether it produces a systemic increase in price across the wider field of transitional justice remains to be seen, but it certainly creates a mood and expectation that needs to be lived up to.
5. Political vision and courage on all sides. This is obvious. Without it there will be no movement.
6. The ability of the Indigenous side to act consistently with the moral high ground it holds.
7. The nature of the legal or political process used to assess price, case by case.
8. If price is assessed by judges, the doctrinal principles they adopt.

These influences are generally in tension amongst themselves. They produce steady incremental change at best. At worst, they sometimes produce no change at all, although this state of affairs is unlikely to be allowed to last indefinitely. Without at least incremental shifts in resources and decision-making power to Indigenous peoples over time, the whole question of the moral and political legitimacy of the current legal order remains a stone in the shoe of the state.

This suggests something that Indigenous peoples often forget. The gift of legitimacy to the state is a powerful moral and political card. Just as the position of the West in the globalisation debate is undermined if its effect will be to entrench geographic disparity, so it is that nations with dispossessed Indigenous minorities remain deeply uncomfortable about the taint of an immoral past and its living consequences. The gift of legitimacy must not be given lightly.

UNINTENDED RESULTS

I think the right metaphor can be found in rugby league — although it may not be a metaphor with which you are familiar this far west of Sydney. Transitional justice is like a rugby league scrum: the side putting the ball in almost always wins it back. For the defending side, the limited objective is to do all they can to make the ball less useful to the attackers by slowing it down or making it untidy in some way. The only difference is that in transitional justice, the Crown always puts the ball in and the Indigenous group is always defending. Their objective is generally to make the Crown pay dearly for its ball.

I said the side putting in almost always wins it back. Sometimes, very rarely in the game of rugby league, the defending side unexpectedly wins the ball. Usually this is because someone on the attacking side takes his eye off it.

This can happen in transitional justice, too. For example, in 2004 a full bench of the New Zealand Court of Appeal decided unanimously that it was possible in law for Māori to make claims to the foreshore and seabed in the Māori Land Court. The government announced three days later that it would introduce legislation to explicitly extinguish any remaining Māori title (without compensation), while recognising the right of Māori to claim more limited-use rights. This was done on the basis of an assessment that the non-Māori electorate would not tolerate exclusion from New Zealand's beaches. That assessment was probably right, though just how many exclusive titles could have been granted by the Māori Land Court remains unknown. On the Māori side, there was great anger. A large-scale protest march was held in Wellington when the legislation was introduced. The march gained unprecedented national coverage. True to the government's perception of the majority will, the *Foreshore and Seabed Act 2004* was enacted but not before a Māori member of Cabinet resigned her ministry, her seat and her party membership and set about forming a new Māori party. She was re-elected in a by-election and in the next General Election the Māori Party took four of the seven Māori constituency seats.

In a sense the Indigenous community lost the foreshore and seabed battle but in doing so fundamentally changed the New Zealand political landscape. As a result, there is now genuine competition for the growing Māori vote. This has changed the game. Instead of Māori issues being on the political agenda because they are risks that must be mitigated, there is now competition for policies that are pro-Māori. Had it not been for the foreshore and seabed earthquake driving Māori to a collective expression of indignation, this change could well have taken much longer to manifest itself.

BEYOND TRANSITIONAL JUSTICE

Though transitional justice is seen both in Australia and New Zealand as an iconic component of general Indigenous policy, it cannot be the whole picture for Indigenous people. First of all, as I have said, its drivers are not exclusively Indigenous. It is as much focused on the legitimacy of the state as it is on outcomes for Indigenous people. There is also the problem of the adversarial format preferred in both countries. In an incisive critique of the native title process in Australia, Hal Wootten wrote:

> To leave the consequences of these policies to litigation in private actions based on existing rights, in courts designed to settle legal rights by an adversary system within a relatively homogeneous community, is at once an insult to the Indigenous people and a prostitution of the courts.[6]

He is essentially right. In Australia the surviving title approach to transitional justice requires the Indigenous community to prove in a court or tribunal that colonisation caused them no material injury. This is necessary because the greater the injury, the smaller the surviving bundle of rights. Communities who were forced off their land lose it. Those whose traditions and languages were beaten out of them at state-sponsored mission schools lose all of the resources owned within the matrix of that language and those traditions. This is a perverse result. In reality, of course, colonisation was the greatest calamity in the history of these people on this land. Surviving title asks Aboriginal people to pretend that it was not.

In New Zealand the reparative approach encourages Māori communities to argue that the policies and actions of the colonial Crown were responsible for every injury they have ever suffered. This just as unrealistically and unfairly places all of the incentives at the other end of the spectrum. It encourages claimants to paint their ancestors as victims for whom all choices were imposed by colonial authorities bent on their destruction. It patronises those Māori leaders in history who sought, sometimes rightly and sometimes wrongly, to make choices that might mitigate the worst effects of colonialism on their communities. It discourages pride in those aspects of Māori identity that have survived the trauma of colonisation. Both approaches contain the seeds of a potential future but the seeds struggle to grow because of an all-consuming focus on a traumatic, conflicted and caricatured past. Though that past is vitally important, it cannot define our present or our future. If we allow it to, we will inevitably become imprisoned by it and addicted to our own oppression.

How, then, do we survive and gain strength in the present? How do we conceive of a future when the term 'Indigenous' is not automatically followed by nouns like 'injustice', 'disparity', 'loss' or simply 'problem'? Transitional justice alone does not give us the answers. There is nothing we can do to change the last two and a half centuries. Our first task as

Indigenous peoples is to bear witness to its cruel legacy. But beyond remembering, the true work of this generation, here and now, is to transcend it. If we do not, we doom the next generation to a kind of ground-hog day of dispossession. What are we to do about the next two and a half centuries is where we must ultimately focus. In fact, what about the next two and a half decades!

And the transcendence must begin on the Indigenous side. Why? Perhaps it is because the settler cultures lack the ability to make the necessary leap of faith or imagination. Perhaps, ironically, the trauma of colonisation expands the mind and makes imagining easier for the peoples who suffered it. Perhaps it is just that the greatest incentives for breaking out are with Indigenous peoples rather than those with the greatest investment in the status quo. I don't know, to be honest. I just know that Indigenous people must take the lead and the settlers must be convinced to follow. The key to unlocking this thing is not with settlers, governments or the state. It is with us. And, of course, there is no way to guarantee success. But failure is inevitable if we do not begin to imagine and, in imagining, take ownership of a future that is different from our past.

I want to suggest four overlapping ideas that must be applied in the here and now to take us beyond transitional justice — indeed, to discipline us into using transitional justice as a bridge into the future rather than as an end in its own right. Those ideas are vision, identity, practical commitment and interdependence.

We must build a vision of our destiny — because without vision our future path will be that of the wanderer. It may well be a different vision for different peoples or communities, but it is this vision which provides us with our road map. Vision is the great challenge of leadership and it will be for Indigenous leaders to build the vision and convince the people to travel with them. Our vision must not be just that our land claims will be settled fairly. It is not to be found in transitional justice. It is to be found beyond transitional justice.

The vision must be grounded in our identity for it to have any meaning at all for our people. It must capture our highest ideals and greatest imaginings. It must not be just about removing disadvantage; on the contrary, it must accentuate our advantages. It must celebrate our separateness and our uniqueness. It must begin with the positive things that we bring to the great story of humanity. Thus our vision will be about protecting our unique relationships with the land, rivers, mountains and seas. It will be about the survival and growth of our languages and cultures, our strong sense of togetherness and community. It will be about the quiet wisdom of our elders and the sacredness of our traditional knowledge. It will be about how we intend to carry these forward as markers for the generations to come — how, far from being anachronisms, these markers will help those in the future to make greater sense of the world and their place in it than we have been able to. There will, of course, be more to it than that. For example, we will need to grapple with how we participate in modernity when building our vision. And we will need to heal our disadvantage in comparison to the wellbeing of the wider population. Different communities will seek different paths. But all must start with identity. That is how we choose to measure our performance against ourselves rather than against the settlers. That is how we avoid making their reality our vision.

This vision must then be backed up by practical commitments at individual and community level. This obvious element is as essential to transcending the past as is vision. It is the means by which we take personal and collective ownership of our future. It is, in some small way, the means by which we dispossess the bureaucrats and politicians of their mortgage on our futures. I practised for many years as a lawyer working for Māori communities in their land claims. It was important and challenging work at the interface between Māori and the government. It was a privilege to be given the opportunity to do it. But over the years I came to understand that although that work was important, it was not as important as my decision to accept personal responsibility for the survival of my language in my own home. Walk the talk as best you can in your own circumstances. This is important because it is the practical means by which we stop the government or the courts owning more of our future than we do.

And finally we must recognise in our vision that our future is not as some sort of isolated, idealised island. That while we must take responsibility for the future we wish to imagine, we cannot achieve that vision alone. Our world is far too complicated now. It is globalised, virtual and fragmented. Our people live within our traditional communities and outside them. They have inter-married with the settlers and raised families. They work within the bureaucracies that we complain about. In other words, we must recognise that we have become interdependent peoples and it is through our interdependence that we will ultimately transcend our past. We have interdependent relationships with bureaucracies, politicians and with settler communities for a start. These exist at local, state and (in Australia) federal levels. When you think about it, interdependence is a strength, not a weakness. It means that it is possible to call on capacity and ideas outside ourselves to help achieve visions we have grown from within. In theory, collaboration should produce a better and stronger result than isolation, even if it requires negotiation. I am aware that the past has not produced many successful models of collaboration but that does not mean that it is impossible. Remember that interdependence is a two-way street. It is true that we need them; but they also need us. They need the gift of moral legitimacy. They need to stop spending money on our dependence. They need the comfort of positive and healthy relationships with us. These are powerful incentives in anyone's book.

Earlier on, when talking about the 'yes, but' principle, I mentioned the possibility of a new game. The possibility that, rather than simply locking in the status quo, transitional justice could lead to the evolution of a new status quo. The concept of interdependence makes that possible. When partnerships are developed, both sides are changed. It is possible — indeed, I think likely — that over time Indigenous ways of doing will come to change 'the system' itself, but that will be for the future. I am aware of examples of this in New Zealand. There are cases where the creation of formal relationships between Department of Conservation regional offices and local tribes has changed the culture — and even the language — inside that department. I know that formal relationships with Indigenous communities at central and local government have led to the realisation that the adoption of Māori ceremonial norms lend weight and solemnity to important occasions in a way that settler cultures cannot. My sense is that through the incremental creation of strategic relationships with Indigenous leaders, organisations and communities, bureaucracies, political institutions and non-Indigenous communities are, indeed, being counter-colonised and transformed. The process is achingly slow, but it is a beginning.

ENDING ON A POSITIVE NOTE

The amazing thing is that, even as I write this, I realise that all over Australia and New Zealand Indigenous communities are already creating visions, strengthening identity, making practical commitments to the growth of culture and language and building partnerships of interdependence with the wider community. After all, this is hardly rocket science. If there is an element missing, it might only be the realisation that it is in doing these things we will transcend the cruel legacy of our past. It would be great if these efforts were better coordinated and if those engaged in them saw, as I do, that theirs is the great work of this generation. But it may be in real life things are just not that tidy. It may be that we will not understand the miracles they have created until long after these heroes have passed into memory.

E tau ana

3.
Native Title Conference, Arrernte Country, 2003

MABO LECTURE
Where we've come from and where we're at with the opportunity that is Koiki Mabo's legacy to Australia

NOEL PEARSON

On the occasion of the tenth anniversary of Australia's decision in the *Mabo* case, a widespread sense that the native title system was not working was articulated. Then, later in the year, the Gleeson High Court delivered its tragic decisions in *Miriuwung Gajerrong* and *Yorta Yorta*,[1] and if governments — states, territories and Commonwealth — were uncertain about making consent determinations on native title when the law according to the High Court was uncertain, they are now certainly opposed to making such determinations now that the law has been made more certain and the Court has foreclosed on issues. Of course, the bind faced by native title claimants is this: it is only where a legal issue has been foreclosed upon that governments are prepared to accept that there is sufficient clarity to make decisions. Where a legal issue remains unsettled, governments are unwilling to negotiate the settlement of claims.

One of the most remarkable features of the original *Mabo*[2] litigation was that it had taken ten years of bitter perseverance and struggle for the claim of the Meriam people to their traditional homelands of the Murray Islands to be finally determined. Ten years is an incredibly long time and Eddie Mabo had died at the end stage of that long struggle for recognition. Next year, 2004, will be the tenth anniversary of numerous claims under the *Native Title Act 1993* (Cth) (NTA) that are a long way off from delivering any sort of recognition to the Indigenous peoples who have made them. On eastern Cape York, the Yalanji people's claim to their remnant homelands in the rainforests of the wet tropics of North Queensland will enter its tenth year of long suffering and patience on the part of the Traditional Owners.[3] This is despite the fact that the Yalanji put forward a proposal for an agreement that met the state's interest in creating new national parks on lands subject to native title. It is despite the fact that the Queensland Premier committed himself to a protocol to bring the deal to a conclusion within a set timeframe. The deadline originally set by the Premier is now almost two years past and the bureaucrats are no closer to settling Yalanji than they were when the original Yalanji proposal obtained the in-principle support of the Premier.

The question hanging over the heads of many leaders and advocates of native title claimants at this conference is whether the hope of native title has been dashed. I suspect that the same question is harboured by those whose function it is to resist the recognition of native title. I am compelled to confront this question, but as an advocate for native title I must confess that it is difficult to discuss the question with the frankness that is needed. The question necessarily raises questions of critical strategic importance to those who are in favour of native title and whose function it is to achieve its recognition at law. How can questions of crucial legal and tactical importance to Indigenous people be discussed in the midst of the opponents of native title from the natural resources industries and governments? I have never been able to comprehend why this conference is open to parties that are opposed to native title, and I and the Cape York Land Council have voiced our objections to this for a number of years now. If this is the one opportunity advocates for native title have to take stock of the strategic political and legal situation facing Indigenous claims and to discuss potential solutions, then how is it that we invite those who are resolutely opposed to the legal rights of our clients to participate in these discussions? How naive can we be? Have we not, with nearly ten years' experience of these miserable processes, yet learned that the interests of *our* clients and the policy of *their* clients are at mortal odds — one against the other? It would be one thing if we devoted as much time, attention and resources to convening confidential strategic discussions involving the interests of Indigenous claimants — we could then afford the collegial dialogue with those who are contemptuous opponents of the rights of our people. But I know of no such other opportunities.

It is like we are playing a game of pretend. They pretend that they are not resolutely opposing native title. We pretend the same thing in return. What do we think we are running: an objective, dispassionate university seminar? Or are we running native title claims where the opponents to these claims are ruthless, determined and resolute? Despite these unsatisfactory circumstances, I am compelled to answer the question of what is left for native title after the High Court's decisions in *Miriuwung Gajerrong* and *Yorta Yorta* as follows. Native title is not a dead issue. It will continue to represent a crucial factor in land tenure and use in Australia for many decades to come. It will still need to be dealt with so far as the development of natural resource industries are concerned. It will continue to be an impediment to development where Indigenous groups have not given consent. However, Indigenous people will need to develop alternative strategies, because allowing native title to continue as a delegated industry involving lawyers and anthropologists, as has been the case over the past ten years, will get many of our clients nowhere.

Let me now go back and review where we have come from with native title.

THE HIGH COURT DECISION

There is no doubt in my mind that the High Court decision of 3 June 1992 was correct and truly represented an opportunity to settle the question of land justice for Indigenous people in the Australian nation. If the spirit, and I would argue *the law*, of *Mabo* had been faithfully implemented, then the High Court's decision would have fulfilled the hopes that many Australians held for settling this fundamental outstanding issue of land justice for Indigenous people.

There were at least two reasons why I thought that non-Indigenous Australians should have embraced *Mabo*. The first reason was that it was because native title and the *Mabo* decision was the product of their heritage — the English common law heritage of this country. How could they repudiate their own law? If their legal traditions delivered justice, why would they not claim it as theirs? The second reason was that native title could never result in anyone losing any legal rights they held in land or in respect of land. Where native title existed in its own right under the common law or where native title coexisted with other tenures, the native title could not result in the extinguishment or any derogation whatsoever of any rights granted by the Crown or by legislation. So why wouldn't non-Indigenous Australians embrace a title that could never dispossess them of their own accrued rights and titles?

We forget this second point too easily. In fact, it is probably not even a matter of forgetting because we have never planted this point in our own heads in the first place and we have never succeeded in getting Australians to understand this truth: the truth that native title is not about anyone else losing any legal rights that they have accumulated in the two hundred years since colonisation. We have never convinced anyone of the truth that native title is all about the balance, it is all about the remnants, it is all about what is left over — and no finding of native title can disturb the rights of any other parties other than the Crown.

And land rights have never been about dispossession of the colonisers and their descendants. Whether it be statutory land rights or common law land rights, these land rights have always been focused on remnant lands.

So why such bitter and expensive struggles over remnant lands? This is the question white Australians must ask themselves. And an ancillary question is whether white Australians feel that it is important that our nation settles the longstanding question of Indigenous land justice. Because history tells us — all over the planet — that land injustice is one of those tenacious wounds that never heal if no honest justice is done. If there is no just compromise, then land injustice will plague our nation long into the future.

What Eddie Mabo had achieved with the *Mabo* decision was that he had forged the opportunity for a just compromise. From the common law of Australia, the Murray Island plaintiffs had constructed the best possible framework for the Australian people to settle the grievance in relation to land. That broad framework encompassed three principles that underpinned the compromise: non-Indigenous people get to keep all of their legal rights and titles in relation to land, Indigenous people get recognition of any remnant rights and titles, and Crown-derived titles and native title coexist in certain situations where the Crown interest prevails over the native title interest in the event of any inconsistency. I have often expressed this as the whitefellas keep their land rights, the blackfellas get what is left over, and we share some categories of land where the Crown title prevails over the native title in the event of conflict.

Why is this form of compromise not reasonable? Why have white Australians and their governments resisted this compromise? Do we not feel anxious about losing the opportunity that is Eddie Mabo's legacy to us as Australians — white and black?

I would like to now briefly review the problems with the responses of the Commonwealth Parliament, Indigenous people and the courts to the opportunity that native title represented.

THE PROBLEMS WITH THE PARLIAMENT'S RESPONSE

The Commonwealth Parliament's response to the *Mabo* decision was the enactment of the NTA in 1993, which was then, of course, amended in 1998. The strengths of the parliament's response were the recognition of common law rights and the protection against wholesale extinguishment by hostile governments.

It was this second issue that was the greatest strength of the NTA. The prospect of state and territory governments enacting legislation to extinguish native title was the gravest threat against which Indigenous leaders fought during ructions leading up to the enactment of the NTA. After all, the then Australian Mining Industry Council's position was that native title had to be extinguished within mining leases, despite the fact that mining leases never extinguished any other form of underlying tenure. And, of course, the Western Australian Government had enacted its *Land Titles and Traditional Usages Act*, which attempted to extinguish native title across the whole of Western Australia. In the *Native Title Act* case Richard Court's provincial Act was struck down and the effectiveness of the NTA in protecting native title against extinguishments by hostile governments was affirmed.[4]

There were several fundamental problems with the parliament's response to *Mabo*.

The unfair allocation of certainty

This is probably the greatest failing of the native title system in Australia. Certainty has been unfairly allocated and the judiciary are completely blind to these facts. Native title legislation gives protection against hostile extinguishment to Indigenous people but it gives certainty of the existence and indefeasibility of title to non-Indigenous people. Wherever non-Indigenous titles were subject to any question as to their validity, and as to the scope of the rights to which they gave rise, the legislation provided certainty. All the certainty that was provided to native title was protection against extinguishment.

And certainty for non-Indigenous rights and interests — including the rights and interests of the Crown — was guaranteed up front: in the NTA. They did not have to go through any procedures or meet any tests or prove any legal rights before they obtained their certainty. Certainty kicked in on day one of the legislation. In contrast, whether Indigenous people held any native title and what those interests amounted to was left uncertain and had to be proved.

It was not only the vested rights of non-Indigenous people and the Crown that were afforded certainty. It was also a whole range of expected rights and interests that were made certain through the broad definition of 'past acts', especially, of course, with the 1998 amendments. The extinguishment of native title was made certain in the legislation, but the existence of native title was not. All that was guaranteed was protection from hostile extinguishment.

This whole unfair allocation of certainty is testament to the fact that Indigenous people — in 1993 and in 1998 — were preoccupied with the primary struggle to protect native title from extinguishment. Protection was what we got out of the certainty deal. Of course, our opponents on behalf of the Crown and on behalf of industry got a lot more out of the certainty deal than protection of their rights from extinguishment or defeasibility. They got certainty as to the definition of their rights and as to the impact that any native title would have on their rights.

The granting of party status to third-party interests whose rights and interests were already secured under the common law — or by the NTA

This point, too, is lost on the judiciary and in the public understanding of the native title claims process. As I have already explained, the native title claims process is not a true litigation in the sense that one party may win and the other party may lose. The non-Indigenous third parties can never lose any rights of interests that they hold. It is only the Indigenous parties that can ever lose a case. All that the non-Indigenous third parties have to lose in any litigation is an argument to the effect that there is no native title. But if they have legal rights and titles, the validity and utility of these rights can never be affected. And these rights and titles were first guaranteed at common law by the *Mabo* decision itself. We can take the *Mabo* case as authority for the law that rights and interests granted by the Crown or by legislation cannot be invalidated or derogated from by the existence of native title.

The only real uncertainty that existed was due to the effect of the *Racial Discrimination Act 1975* (Cth) (RDA), and the validation provisions of the NTA operated to cure any uncertainties caused by the RDA.

So, if all of the rights and interests of the third parties are guaranteed at law and can never be affected by a finding of native title, why are third parties allowed to become parties to native title claims? Why are they treated by governments and the courts as if they have rights and interests that are at stake, when they do not? Why are they funded by the Commonwealth Government to represent themselves in these claims? Experience has shown that if there is a third party that (a) has all of their rights and interests already guaranteed at law and therefore can never lose anything, and (b) has all of their costs paid for by the Attorney-General of the Commonwealth, then, of course, these third parties are not going to be amenable to negotiated settlement of claims and will resist recognition until the cows come home, or until the native title holders have surrendered most of their rights.

Procedures rather than substantive rights

This is, of course, another feature of the legislation: it is full of procedures rather than substantive rights for native title holders. I will deal with the transaction and opportunity costs, which the country pays for, in relation to this aspect of the legislative scheme.

The suspension of the Racial Discrimination Act and the breach of the International Convention

I will not expand at length on this problem with the legislation, but I will make two comments. Firstly, I wish to say that Geoff Clark, Les Malezer and others who brought this issue to the attention of the CERD committee (United Nations Committee on Elimination of Racial Discrimination) must be commended for their advocacy. Indeed, ATSIC's (Aboriginal and Torres Strait Islander Commission's) Native Title Unit, and particularly the work of Greg Marks, was crucial — and as a long-distance observer of this process, I can only say that the prosecution of this issue was done diligently and with great perseverance. They have highlighted the fact that Australia is in breach of the International Convention on the Elimination of All Forms of Racial Discrimination. This is an issue that the nation will never escape or be able to hide in the long term, even if it is difficult to raise as an issue of domestic importance in the present.

Secondly, it is my view that the RDA problem is not just a 1998 problem; it was a problem with the 1993 legislation, as well. I do not accept the political argument that was constructed at the time that the 1993 legislation amounted to a 'special measure' within the meaning of the Convention, whereby the beneficial provisions of the NTA somehow cured the suspension of the RDA in relation to its validation provisions. The fact is that suspension of the RDA was seen in 1993 as the only way that the validation provisions could be made absolutely certain. The 1998 amendments simply widened the provisions in the NTA which were not made subject to the RDA. My point is that the racial discrimination problem with native title legislation in Australia is a problem of the Labor Party as much as the Coalition — and the country will need to find a resolution for this issue. The country will have to find a way of validating titles without discrimination against Indigenous people by suspending the application of the RDA in relation to native title — but not in relation to any other titles. Otherwise we will remain, in constitutional terms, as we exist today, no different from Zimbabwe, in that we sanction racial discrimination in relation to how our Commonwealth laws deal with land title.

THE PROBLEMS WITH THE INDIGENOUS RESPONSE

Disputes and conflicting, overlapping claims: the inability to control greed and power struggles and the lack of strategic leadership by native title representative bodies

The way in which claims were organised, lodged and prosecuted by Indigenous groups and their advisors following the enactment of the 1993 legislation could not have been more harmful to Indigenous interests. We failed to control greed and the power struggles within and between claimants groups, not the least between conflicting parts of families.

The representative bodies largely failed to provide any strategic leadership to address the emerging problems — though this was, of course, very hard after 1993 when freelance lawyers roamed the countryside picking off clients and setting them off against rivals, including the representative bodies themselves. The 1998 amendments helped to put more rigour into the process but many of the claims that are registered were prepared with as much planning, strategy, forethought and consultation as went into the European dismemberment of colonial Africa.

The legacy of this madness and the problems that they represent for the future conduct of these claims still remains an outstanding responsibility for the representative bodies and the claimants. There is no use just hoping that litigation will provide resolution instead of subjecting all claims to proper research and intra-Indigenous consideration and mediation.

I was recently struck by some comments made by the late Professor Bill Stanner in a note on 'Aboriginal law and its possible recognition', where he concluded:

> The social situation of many Aborigines will change with rapidity over the next decade. Many will die wealthy, in possession of money or other assets for which their traditional law provides no disposal-procedure. There will be conflicts of interest between Aborigines which may be insoluble unless their own doctrine of what I have termed rights, duties, liabilities and immunities can be developed. The 'Aboriginal problem' thus goes beyond the 'retention of their traditional lifestyle': there is a problem of development as well as one of preservation.[5]

We have so far failed to develop our own doctrines to deal with our lands and resources as commercial property, which can be accumulated and developed. Greed and conflict will continue to plague our people as long as we fail to confront Professor Stanner's prescient advice.

The failure of Indigenous leaders and organisations to resist the development of a second-rate native title legal and consultancy industry

I will not go on at length about the problem being that the native title legal and consulting industry that sprung up in the wake of the NTA is, at best, second rate. It is a generalisation that does not do full justice to everyone; but it must be our predominant conclusion. My main point is not just that the quality of the professionals who have been involved on the Indigenous side has been poor — often they are not — but it is the failure of Indigenous leaders and organisations to control their actions and activities. Having protected native title through the legislative battles, the Indigenous leadership then delegated to the lawyers and the consultants the whole responsibility for prosecuting native title. And we allowed an unaccountable, undirected, often wasteful, industry to develop around native title claims — and failed to insist on strategic leadership. That we have ended up in a hole is, in considerable part, the consequence of poor strategic, intellectual and political organisation on our part.

The failure to develop a high-standard legal discourse on the common law meaning of native title

The Australian legal and intellectual discourse on the common law meaning of native title in my view is embarrassing compared with the Canadian discussion. Most of the discourse and publications since 1993 have centred on procedural issues arising from the legislative framework.

There has been comparatively little quality discussion of the common law. We have no equivalents to Kent McNeil and Brian Slattery of Canada. In fact, Kent McNeil's few commentaries on the Australian law represent the best that there is. And the Australian academic and intellectual discussion of native title has had no impact on the judiciary in the way that the Canadian commentators have had on the decisions of their Supreme Court.

Of course, the publications and commentaries produced by the one-time research division of the National Native Title Tribunal and the Centre for Aboriginal Economic Policy Research did not answer the need for a high-quality discourse on the meaning of native title at common law.

There are still today so many crucial conceptual issues that remain unresolved and unarticulated in native title. These issues are just left dangling — we hope that the courts will give meaning and clarity in the absence of any serious consideration from advocates for native title.

Poorly argued test cases

I particularly have a problem with the way in which the interpretation of section 223(1) of the NTA was approached in the test cases that went before the High Court, but I will expand on my complaints in the next section.

THE PROBLEMS WITH THE RESPONSE OF THE COURTS

Discriminatory conceptualisation of native title by misapplication of the common law

Fundamental to the ruling in *Mabo* was the High Court's refusal to allow the social and cultural organisation of the Indigenous peoples of Australia to preclude them from recognition of their land entitlement surviving the acquisition of sovereignty by the Crown. Indeed, the High Court explicitly rejected the decision of the Privy Council in *Re Southern Rhodesia* to the effect that there may be societies that are 'so low in the scale of social organisation' such that the common law could not recognise them as having rights and interests in land.[6] In this rejection of terra nullius on the basis of prejudicial assessments of social and cultural organisation, Justice Brennan made strong declarations on behalf of the common law of Australia when he said that the common law could no longer be, nor be seen to be, 'frozen in an age of racial discrimination'.[7]

This was an important rejection of discrimination concerning the law of native title.

The problem with the application of this principle of non-discrimination is that whilst it has been applied in respect of the question of *whether Aboriginal title survives sovereignty* — where social and cultural organisation is irrelevant to whether there be recognition by the common law — it has not been applied to *the form of Aboriginal title which survives sovereignty*.

On the question of form of title, native title has been devalued and discriminated against by reference to the different social and cultural organisation of Indigenous Australians. The very discrimination in *Re Southern Rhodesia* is maintained against Aboriginal people so that the content of their title is less than the content of non-Indigenous titles derived from the English legal tradition. This is done by reference to Indigenous laws and custom. You only get what you can prove your Indigenous laws and customs entitle you to — and it is the laws and customs that existed at the time of sovereignty that must be proved.

This is blatant racial discrimination of the very kind articulated in *Re Southern Rhodesia*. It is discriminatory for at least two reasons. Firstly, why should the Indigenous conception of ownership of land be any less comprehensive than that of landholders in the English legal tradition? It can only be through miscomprehension and all of the difficulties of the fact-finding process of the courts that courts can say that Indigenous people only owned the land in any sense less than possession. But it is this very miscomprehension and the difficulties of process that is resulting in native titles being determined to be less than ownership. And the courts are able to carry out this discrimination by saying that these minimal rights are what the traditional laws and customs of the people have disclosed as a matter of fact. But what people — of whatever social and cultural organisation — do not conceive of their occupation and possession of land as being anything less than what the holder of a fee simple would understand? As against the world, the conception of possession of the Englishman, the Trobriand Islanders, the nomadic peoples cited by Justice Brennan in the *Western Sahara* case and, indeed, the Indigenous peoples of Australia is a universal conception. This is what Justice Brennan meant when he said in his classic statement in *Mabo*, 'Land is susceptible of ownership, and there are no other owners'.[8]

The second reason why this approach to the content of native title as a lesser right than would be accorded to a fee simple holder of title is discriminatory is that it fails to apply the common law principle that it is occupation that gives rise to possession. It matters not what the nature of the Indigenous social and cultural organisation may be; it matters not what arcane and idiosyncratic laws and customs the Indigenous people may have governing their internal allocation of rights, interests and responsibilities amongst their members. It matters not whether it is an English lord slaughtering innocent fowls on his estate or whether it is an Australian Aborigine standing on one leg in the sunset on his father's ancient homelands — the title is the same. The common law is only concerned to presume possession in those who are in occupation. And the content of this possession is not determined by the nature of the occupation and certainly not by the laws and customs of the occupants. The form of the title is the title that occupation affords, which is possession.

But this is not how the Australian courts have approached native title. They have recast the prejudice in *Re Southern Rhodesia* so that prejudice against social and cultural organisation is used to justify Indigenous Australians being accorded a lesser form of ownership than would be accorded by the common law to someone who was in wrongful occupation, such as that of an adverse possessor.

Stripping native title of any economic meaning or benefit

The courts have reduced native title to what they conceive of as a social and cultural artefact, not a legal title to land that encompasses any economic meaning or benefit. And, of course, the whole mediation and negotiation process with governments and third parties leading to consent determinations is resulting in native titles being stripped of almost all economic or commercial meaning. The position taken by the courts in their discriminatory conceptualisation of native title stands in stark contrast to the decision of the Supreme Court of Canada in *Delgamuukw*, which affirms that communal native title involves the right to possession, of the surface and the subsurface.[9]

Failure to see and implement Mabo as a reconciliation of the Crown acquisition of the country with the pre-existing occupation of the Indigenous peoples

In Canada the Supreme Court has treated Aboriginal title as a special responsibility of the Court and the Chief Justice has repeatedly referred to it in terms of 'reconciliation'.

3. Where we've come from and where we're at

In *Delgamuukw* Chief Justice Lamer laid down what is a fundamental, overarching principle of Aboriginal title. His Honour said:

> In cases involving the determination of Aboriginal rights, appellate intervention is also warranted by the failure of a trial court to appreciate the evidentiary difficulties inherent in adjudicating aboriginal claims when, first, applying the rules of evidence and, second, interpreting the evidence before it. As I said in *Van der Peet*, ...
>
> In determining whether an aboriginal claimant has produced evidence sufficient to demonstrate that her activity is an aspect of a practice, custom or tradition integral to a distinctive aboriginal culture, a court should approach the rules of evidence, and interpret the evidence that exists, with a consciousness of the special nature of aboriginal claims, and of the evidentiary difficulties in proving a right which originates in times where there were no written records of the practices, customs and traditions engaged in. The courts must not undervalue the evidence presented by aboriginal claimants simply because that evidence does not conform precisely with the evidentiary standards that would be applied in, for example, a private law torts case.
>
> The justification for this special approach can be found in the nature of aboriginal rights themselves. I explained in *Van der Peet* that those rights are aimed at the reconciliation of the prior occupation of North America by distinctive aboriginal societies with the assertion of Crown sovereignty over Canadian territory. They attempt to achieve that reconciliation by 'their bridging of aboriginal and non-aboriginal cultures'. Accordingly, 'a court must take into account the perspective of the aboriginal people claiming the right...while at the same time taking into account the perspective of the common law' such that '[t]rue reconciliation will, equally, place weight on each'.[10]

This statement of fundamental principle, and, of course, its very important guidance for the proof of native title, puts to shame the Australian High Court's desultory comments in relation to proof in the *Yorta Yorta* case. This is what Chief Justice Gleeson and Justices Gummow and Hayne said in this case on the question of evidence:

> When the primary judge was hearing evidence in this matter the NTA provided that, in conducting proceedings under the Act, the Federal Court, first, was 'not bound by technicalities, legal forms or rules of evidence' and, secondly, 'must pursue the objective of providing a

mechanism of determination that is fair, just, economical, informal and prompt'. It may be that, under those provisions, a rather broader base could be built for drawing inferences about past practices than can be built since the 1998 *Amendment Act* came into operation…The kinds of evidentiary questions which may arise in this regard are well illustrated by *Milirrpum* but it is neither necessary nor appropriate to consider whether the answers given to the questions that arose in that case were right. Were they to arise again, in proceedings in the Federal Court, it would be necessary to consider them by reference to the *Evidence Act* 1995 (Cth).[11]

There is no sense that the High Court has any high policy or perspective in relation to the way it approaches native title as a reconciliation between Crown sovereignty and the original occupation of the land by the Indigenous peoples. This may have been understandable if their predecessors in *Mabo* had not stated that the historic denial of native title had left the country with what Justices Deane and Gaudron had called a 'legacy of unutterable shame'.[12] It is completely incomprehensible when you consider the preamble to the NTA upon which the High Court relies in its interpretation of native title. Parliament was unequivocal about the larger policy perspective on native title and its historical and contemporary significance — and the High Court is completely unmoved by any such largeness of spirit.

Misinterpretation of the NTA

I will not repeat here at length what I said in the Sir Ninian Stephen Lecture about the High Court's misinterpretation of the definition of native title in section 223(1) of the NTA.[13] The short judgment of Justice McHugh in *Yorta Yorta* tells the truth about what parliament intended the statutory definition to mean: that it was supposed to define native title according to the common law decision in *Mabo*.[14] In other words, the section 223(1) definition did not replace or in any way alter the common law meaning of native title, but was intended to be an accurate and faithful reflection of its meaning at common law. As Justice McHugh said, the majority adopted a 'narrower' interpretation of section 223(1) than parliament intended[15] — to the great detriment of the Yorta Yorta and to Indigenous Australians generally.

In effect, in the *Yorta Yorta* case, the High Court disavowed native title as a doctrine or body of law within the common law. This amounted to a gross dereliction of the Court's duty to approach native title law according to what a member of the Supreme Court of Canada, Justice McLachlin, had referred to in *R v Van der Peet* as 'the time-honoured methodology of the common law'[16] — instead, the High Court denied that there were 'common law requirements' and 'common law elements' for the establishment of native title.[17] The judgment of Chief Justice Gleeson and Justices Gummow and Hayne is, in this respect, the most transparently scholastic attempt to disregard this large body of case law on native title drawn from right across the common law world. As I said in the Sir Ninian Stephen Lecture, whilst native title is not a common law title (being a title recognised by the common law), there is a vast body of common law that deals with its recognition, proof, enforcement and extinguishment.[18] This body of law has developed over two centuries in decisions of the Privy Council, the United States Supreme Court, the Supreme Court of Canada and numerous other cases concerning West Africa, subcontinental Asia and the Pacific, not the least New Zealand. It is this body of common law which informed the original *Mabo* decision in 1992 and numerous overseas cases were cited by the High Court in that case.

What has happened in *Yorta Yorta* — and in the cases leading up to it — is that the High Court has decided to draw a line between the two centuries of common law preceding *Mabo* and the development of Australian native title law since the NTA. By resorting to the legislative definition of native title in section 223(1), the Court is intent upon treating the development of native title law as essentially an exercise in statutory interpretation. Rather than diligently grappling with what is a complex and unsettled body of law — and importantly, rather than explaining why overseas precedents should be distinguished from the Australian law on the subject — the High Court has conveniently confined their duty to one of interpreting the meaning of statutory clauses. They have conveniently set out for themselves a clean slate upon which they can rule on critical, unresolved conceptual issues in native title, simply on the basis of statutory interpretation. Two critical, unresolved conceptual issues — namely, the meaning of 'connection' and 'continuity' in native title law — cannot be analysed in isolation from the international jurisprudence on native title. Otherwise, all is bare assertion.

And, indeed, it is bare assertion which the High Court has served up to the Yorta Yorta who pleaded their case in the expectation of a fair hearing of their claim in accordance with the common law. The High Court has served up fundamental derogations of the rights of Indigenous people — largely on the basis of bare assertion.

The most startling evidence for this abandonment of the common law is a survey of the cases which are referenced in both *Miriuwung Gajerrong* and *Yorta Yorta*. Despite the fact that these cases occupy hundreds of pages of judgment, there is literally no reference to native title cases other than recent decisions of the Court dealing with statutory interpretation. Even the judgments in *Mabo* are not discussed. *Mabo* is only mentioned for contextual and historical purposes — not as precedent for many of the bald assumptions and assertions made by the Court.

In my commentaries in honour of Sir Ninian Stephen, I pointed out that the problem did not just lie in the majority judgment of the Chief Justice and Justices Gummow and Hayne. Justices Kirby and Gaudron were also responsible for this disaster. It was reported in the media that Justice Kirby had admonished counsel at the time of the appeal hearing of *Miriuwung Gajerrong* to 'stop foraging around the common law' and to instead understand that native title had been 'transmogrified' by the NTA.[19] Transmogrification, indeed — what we now have is a deformed and unjust Australian native title law, the foundation of which is a blatant misinterpretation of what was intended by the Commonwealth Parliament.

In sum, what we are left with is:
1. native title without any economic benefit;
2. unfair denial of land justice and the failure to use Eddie Mabo's legacy to settle the Indigenous land justice problem in our country;
3. lose–lose procedural framework that is marked by debilitating high transaction costs and debilitating high opportunity costs;
4. the prospect of long-term Australian under-performance in land and resource development; and
5. the problems with revisiting the allocation of rights and interests under the NTA and other legislation.

MOVING FROM A LOSE–LOSE FRAMEWORK TO A WIN–WIN FRAMEWORK

The opportunity and transaction costs of the NTA must be the subject of careful and urgent consideration. The administration of the legislation, the costs of preparing and prosecuting claims and following the procedures of the NTA — versus the returns in terms of title determinations and economic and social advantages for Indigenous people — do not add up and do not make sense. When the costs and lost opportunities are considered for all parties (including governments and industry parties), then the opportunity and transaction costs problems seem to be a universally shared problem: all sides, including Indigenous people, are paying high costs for small or no returns.

The situation is a lose–lose situation and strategic thinking is required to see how it is that win–win approaches to native title might work. The advantage for Indigenous interests in the current strategic context is that those interests that oppose or at least resist native title are also suffering from the high opportunity and transaction costs. Whilst Indigenous people may be getting limited and delayed returns from the native title systems, the other parties are also bearing significant burdens. These other parties also have an interest in reform and new strategies.

The current legislative scheme is flawed because it is the outcome of a (necessary and inescapable) win–lose struggle between Indigenous people and other interests (governments and industries). Whilst both sides have secured 'wins' against 'losses' by the other side, the total outcome is in reality a lose–lose situation for all parties.

Whenever change is considered, both sides think in terms of winning against losses by the other side. This is what the governments and industry did in the 1998 amendments to the 1993 legislation. Whilst they succeeded in derogating from the rights of Indigenous people in a discriminatory and unjust way, the totality of the outcome has not delivered a clear 'win' for governments and industry. The alternative state regimes have not delivered the kinds of solutions to the mining industry for which they were hoping.

The fact is that a win–lose approach to thinking about native title will not work for either the proponents or opponents of native title. Only win–win solutions are likely to lift parties out of their entrenched and defensive positions.

The difficulty is that win–win solutions are unlikely to emerge from any process sponsored by government. Indeed, governments, whilst purporting to be independent arbiters or brokers representing the interests of the whole community, including the Indigenous communities, are partisan in favour of their own interests and that of industry — ahead of Indigenous interests. When reform or any form of change is placed into the public policy/legislative reform process, the struggle immediately becomes one of parties seeking to advance at the expense of other parties. Each side enters into the debate seeking not only to preserve their own position, but to enhance that position at the expense of concessions or defeats by the other side. What emerges from this adversarial, tug of war public reform process is then usually some form of compromise that is cobbled together. Whilst compromise is inevitable and probably necessary, the problem is that rather than being a 'highest common denominator' outcome, the results from the adversarial public policy development process is the worst form of compromise: 'the lowest common denominator' outcome.

So the native title process — whilst producing meagre native title determinations for Indigenous people and producing some land-use outcomes for governments and developers — is really not optimal. It is nearly grid-locked by an adversarial framework that encourages parties to only see what is in their own interests, rather than seeing how mutual interests could be served.

At its essence, two of the most basic challenges facing the native title system are:
1. How can we have a system where it is in the interests of, or at least not seen to be at all contrary to the interests of, government, industry and the public interest for native title to be settled where it potentially exists?
2. How can we have a system where it is in the interests of Indigenous people for economic development to proceed efficiently and with the support of Indigenous people?

RULES OF ENGAGEMENT

The first phase of any serious exploration of reform must be to see if there are any solutions that will address the needs of all parties. Such an exploration would need to be premised on several principles:
- that parties are not required to surrender or to concede any property or procedural rights under the law;
- that, if there is a change in the allocation of rights under the law, rather than losing such rights, such rights should be 'converted' into rights that are of equivalent or greater value;
- that such 'conversions' or 'exchanges' in the allocation of property or procedural rights should be rationally attractive to the parties so that they choose to make the changes because they see it is in their own interests for the changes to be made.

In other words, the challenge is to find truly win–win solutions.

Native title legislation and the allocation of rights in property and procedure is vastly and particularly complicated — not the least because of the adversarial political process that followed the *Mabo* decision and the passage of the NTA — and they were not constructed with an eye to mutual interest and common ground. There are potentially other ways to achieve 'certainty' which are more workable and which encourage both sides to support outcomes for the other side. It is not the case that all options and possibilities have been explored and exhausted.

Let me now close with one final point. Contrary to the High Court's dismissal of the *Yorta Yorta* appeal, the Yorta Yorta people had proved their case. The trial judge, Justice Olney, made three crucial findings of fact that, in my view, mean that the Yorta Yorta proved their case.[20]

Firstly, Olney found that Indigenous people were in occupation of the claimed land at the time of sovereignty.[21] Secondly, Olney found that two of the ancestral figures were descended from those who occupied the land at the time of sovereignty.[22] Thirdly, Olney accepted that many of the contemporary Yorta Yorta claimants were descendants of these two ancestral figures.[23]

So the Yorta Yorta had proved that a native title burdened the radical title of the Crown at the time of sovereignty. Native title came into existence. They had proved that these occupants included two ancestors of the claimants. They had also their descent from these two elders.

They had proved their case. So how is it that Olney and the High Court could then presume to cast the Yorta Yorta into an identity wilderness — a *homo nullius*, people who didn't exist as a people anymore? This represents misapplication of the common law — and we cannot accept this.

4.
Native Title Conference, Wurundjeri Country, 2000

NATIVE TITLE IS PROPERTY*

GREG MCINTYRE

The decision of the High Court in *Mabo v Queensland [No. 1]* proceeded on the basis that the 'traditional rights and interests' asserted by the Meriam people were property which they were entitled to own, and they were entitled not be arbitrarily deprived of it.[1] The fact that native title is a form of property has a number of consequences for how it is to be regarded; as against other property interests and the manner in which the Sovereign, and agents of the Sovereign and others who hold interests granted by the Sovereign, are obliged to treat that title.

This paper argues that native title, as property in land and waters, includes property in the resources that are part of or are associated with the land and waters. As property, it necessarily connotes a capacity to control the land, the waters and those resources. This paper also argues that native title — of its nature as an interest in the land and waters and those resources — cannot be partially extinguished, although it may be that the capacity to exercise rights associated with the title may be curtailed by competing interests. Specifically, I take issue with the conclusions of the majority judges in the full Federal Court decision in *Western Australia v Ward* (*Ward* FC) in relation to the extinguishment of native title.[2]

4. Native title is property

WHAT IS PROPERTY?

Property is not a 'monolithic notion of standard content and invariable intensity'.[3] As the High Court said in *Yanner v Eaton*, 'property does not refer to a thing; it is a description of a legal relationship with a thing. It refers to a degree of power that is recognised in law as power permissibly exercised over the thing.'[4] Quoting from Gray, they state that:

> An extensive frame of reference is created by the notion that 'property' consists primarily in control over access. Much of our false thinking about property stems from the residual perception that 'property' is itself a thing or resource rather than a legally endorsed concentration of power over things and resources.[5]

Gray and Gray extrapolate to say that '"property" is not a thing, but rather the condition of being "proper" to a particular person' and land 'may be the subject of multiple, and wholly reconcilable, claims of property vested in a number of different persons'.[6]

Justice North in *Ward* FC adopts the analysis of Gray and Gray, that 'The idea of "property" oscillates between the behavioural, the conceptual and the obligational, between competing models of property as a fact, property as a right and property as a responsibility'.[7] At the factual level, property is control over access to territory. As an 'artificially defined jural right', 'property' is held as an abstract right 'which is itself a pre-packaged bundle of tightly defined entitlement' associated with a particular interest.[8] The third alternative view is that 'property' is an abstract bundle of isolable utilities and advantages, each capable of being characterised as a species of 'property'. The combination, mixing and balancing of those utilities is subjected to an overarching publicly defined responsibility through state intervention.

The view of Gray and Gray is that 'property' under modern day real property law most closely resembles the third of those alternatives, which brings them to the view that 'the deep structure of "property" is not absolute or oppositional in nature'.[9] Chief Justice Gleeson and Justices Gaudron, Kirby and Hayne in *Yanner* apply this analysis in concluding that 'native title rights and interests must be understood as what has been called "a perception of socially constituted fact" as well as "comprising various assortments of artificially defined jural right"'.[10]

What that means for understanding the nature of native title as property, in my view, is that native title, if it is to be any form of property (as a socially constituted fact), must contain elements of the capacity to control access to use of territory and resources. However, native title is not extinguished as a property interest because that capacity to control is not an absolute right. Native title and other property interests (as jural rights) will rarely be absolute in their capacity to control territory. If those property interests are not absolute in their capacity to control access to territory and resources, then that permits the coexistence of native title as a property interest with other property interests, each having some capacity to control access to use of territory and resources, concomitant with their defined jural rights.

WHAT IS NATIVE TITLE?

Native title has frequently been described:

> The content of native title, its nature and incidents, will vary from one case to another. It may comprise what are classified as personal or communal usufructuary rights involving access to the area of land in question to hunt for or gather food, or to perform traditional ceremonies. This may leave room for others to use the land either concurrently or from time to time. At the opposite extreme, the degree of attachment to the land may be such as to approximate that which would flow from a legal or equitable estate therein.[11]

However, I would argue there can be no 'native title' usufructuary interest unless it arises from a communal title based in possession, which is a native title because the possession is under traditional laws and customs of an Aboriginal people.[12] Yanner's interest was an example of a usufructuary interest arising out of a broader possessory community title.

NATIVE TITLE AS A POSSESSORY TITLE

Justice Toohey in *Mabo [No. 2]* said that '"Possession"…may be said to be a conclusion of law defining the nature and status of a particular relationship of control by a person over land'.[13] It is not necessary for native title claimants to bring evidence of an intent to control or possess or acts of control, possession or exclusion in order for the conclusion of law to be reached that a title includes the element of possession. The Meriam people were determined in *Mabo [No. 2]* to hold a possessory title in the absence of any direct evidence of expressions of intent or acts of control or exclusion as against persons who were not Meriam.[14]

4. Native title is property

NATIVE TITLE AS AN INTEREST IN LAND

Where an Indigenous community is in occupation of an area, its title arises from that occupation to define the community's title as against the Crown or third parties;[15] (a) regardless of the specific content of their traditional laws and customs;[16] and (b) regardless of changes made to rights and interests within the community by modifications of laws and customs;[17] and that title may be described as the 'external' content of native title. That title is a communal title, whether or not the traditions and customs of the community recognise public or general ownership.[18] Traditional laws and customs apply only 'internally' to determine the nature of the rights and interests of members of the community *inter se*.[19]

Where an Indigenous people are claiming a native title right to a particular use of an area only, it will be necessary to show that the right has been exercised in the context of a system of laws and customs, and those laws and customs will determine which individuals and sub-groups are entitled to exercise that right.[20] The role of traditional laws and customs does not depend on whether the native title arises in the context of occupation and possession or use and enjoyment.[21] Justices Beaumont and von Doussa, in *Ward* FC, in requiring proof of both rights and interests under traditional law *and* physical use and enjoyment of the land, imposed standards of proof of native title which are not in accord with *Mabo [No. 2]*: 'The primacy of the underlying right to the land is confirmed in the observation [in *Yanner*] that the regulation of the "artificially defined jural right" does not sever the connection with the land.'[22]

A title that has its basis in occupation of land is properly described as an interest in land. Neither the elements nor the nature of the title are limited to the activities which may be engaged in by the holder of such a title.[23] The activities are a form of exercise of the right to the land, and, as such, provide some evidence of the existence of that right. They do not describe its limits. The High Court in *Mabo [No. 2]* considered evidence of particular activities on the land and the manner of their execution in order to arrive at the decision 'that the Meriam people are entitled as against the whole world to possession, occupation, use and enjoyment of the island of Mer', subject to specified exceptions. Such evidence did not lead it to a conclusion as to the content of the title limited to the particular activities or the manner of their exercise. The Court did not find, for instance, that the Meriam people, by their title, based on the content of the evidence, had the right to build houses (using palm fronds or otherwise) or the right to garden for bananas, paw-paws and coconuts in accordance with the method described in the evidence.

What Justice Brennan in *Mabo [No. 2]* meant when he said, 'Native title has its origin and is given its content by the traditional laws acknowledged by and the traditional customs observed by the indigenous inhabitants of a territory. The nature and incidents of native title must be ascertained as a matter of fact by reference to those laws and customs',[24] is illustrated by the following statement:

> Of course in time the laws and customs of any people will change and the rights and interests of the members of the people among themselves will change too. But as long as the people remain as an identifiable community, the members of whom are identified by one another as members of that community living under its laws and customs, the communal native title survives to be enjoyed by its members according to the rights and interests to which they are respectively entitled under the traditionally based laws and customs as currently acknowledged and observed.[25]

It was that conceptualisation which allowed the High Court to make a declaration of 'the native communal title of the Meriam people',[26] even though Justice Moynihan 'found that there was apparently no concept of public or general community ownership among the people of Murray Island, all the land of Murray Island being regarded as belonging to individuals or groups'.[27] Thus it involves a fundamental misconception to conclude that one of the native title rights established on the evidence in *Ward* FC was the right to use and enjoy ochre.[28] The use and enjoyment of ochre, like the use of water found on the land or the taking of wildlife, is merely activity which can be undertaken upon land because one holds title.

At trial in *Ward v Western Australia* (1998) (*Ward* TJ), Justice Lee recognised that where, in that case, there was a 'significant connection of an indigenous society with land under its customs and culture',[29] native title comprises the right of occupation, and such a right or title is an interest in land. Justice Lee's conclusion is consistent with the dictum of Justices Deane and Gaudron in *Mabo [No. 2]* that common law native title 'may be a community title which is "practically equivalent to full ownership"...',[30] and does not depart from the view that native title is to be given its content by reference to the traditional laws and customs of the Indigenous inhabitants of the area.[31] The Indigenous traditional laws and customs give the title its identity as a native title protected by the common law, and confirm its communal and inalienable qualities, and the interests of the holders of that title *inter se*, but do not otherwise qualify the nature of the title as against the rest of the world.

Interpreted correctly, section (s) 223 of the NTA is indicative of the correct relationship to be understood between 'native title' and 'native title rights and interests', on the one hand, and traditional laws and customs, on the other. Traditional laws and customs connect Indigenous people to the land or waters (s 223(1)(b)) and provide the basis under which rights and interests are possessed (s 223(1)(a)). However, the rights and interests are not described by the traditional laws and customs, but are those which are recognised by the common law (s 223(1)(c)). If what is being asserted is a native title (as in this case), then, once the title is established, by the evidence showing that an Indigenous group is connected by its laws and customs to the area (in compliance with s 223(1)(b)) and the group's laws and customs vest in it rights and interest in land (in compliance with s 223(1)(a)), what the common law will recognise is an interest in the land, which is properly described as the right to possess, occupy, use and enjoy the area.

If, at a later time, an individual from the group wished to enforce a particular right based upon the title, as against other members of the group or the state, such as the right to take a particular resource from the land (as was the case in *Yanner*), then a determination may be made as to the existence of that right in that person.[32]

NATIVE TITLE AS A BUNDLE OF RIGHTS

Because native title has both a socially constituted factual base and a jural right base, it is not properly defined solely as a bundle of rights to engage in particular activities. Those activities comprise the manifestations of the exercise of a proprietorial right, which is underpinned by the factual base of a spiritual, cultural and social connection. Still less are title rights restricted to rights to engage in particular activities of which evidence has been given of prior similar activity upon the area by one or more members of the native title holding group.

Justices Beaumont and von Doussa in *Ward* FC were prepared to acknowledge the concept of rights being pendant or parasitic upon a title. However, while acknowledging such a concept in relation to their view of what constituted 'common law tenures' (by which they appear to mean a title derived from the British Crown), they were not prepared to acknowledge such a possibility in relation to native title. Their reason for not doing so was, in their words, because to do so would result in native title being 'elevated to something akin to a common law tenure'.[33] There is no cogent reason expressed by Justices Beaumont and von Doussa for not treating native title and a 'common law tenure' similarly in this respect. To accord each substantive equality does not mean that one is treating the two forms of title as indistinguishable.

Justices Beaumont and von Doussa deny native title its existence as an artificially defined jural right in relation to land for the purpose of recognising rights pendant upon title.[34] They rely on the view of the High Court in *Yanner* that native title has an 'artificial jural' quality, in addition to comprising a 'socially constituted fact'; an aspect of which is manifested in a spiritual, cultural and social connection with the land.[35] However, they are of the view that the limit to the artificiality of native title rights as jural rights is that they are recognised by the common law when they arise from traditional laws and customs under a different system from the common law. Beaumont and von Doussa appear to have failed to apply or have misunderstood the way in which Gray and Gray have defined 'property' as an 'artificial jural right', 'which is itself a pre-packaged bundle of tightly defined entitlement' associated with a particular interest.[36]

In my view, native title (based on traditional laws and customs) does not need to be an 'institution of the common law' or a 'common law tenure' in order to be regarded as a title to property, defined as property and recognised by the common law, as is any other title. Because it is newly recognised by the common law does not make it any less a title to 'property'. It is, therefore, just as capable as any other title of being regarded as 'an abstract form of title from which pendant rights are derived'.[37]

In this respect, Justices Beaumont and von Doussa are expressing in a slightly different way the views of Lord Sumner in *In re Southern Rhodesia* (which were rejected by the High Court in *Mabo [No. 2]*) that the rights and duties of aboriginal groups cannot be transmuted into 'rights of property as we know them'.[38]

The correct view is that of Justice North, dissenting, where he says:

> The incidents of native title depend upon the connection of aboriginal people with the land. The underlying connection is the foundation for the exercise of various rights. The land is not just the place to hunt. Rather the right to hunt follows as a result of the significance of the land as the centrepiece in aboriginal law and culture.[39]

GENERAL PRINCIPLES OF EXTINGUISHMENT

The general principles that apply when considering whether or not native title has been extinguished are now well established and they are:

a. the intention to extinguish native title must, either expressly or by necessary implication, be clear and plain;[40]
b. general provisions of a statute ought not to be construed as intended to bring about an extinguishment of native title if they are susceptible of some less burdensome construction;[41]
c. whether, by necessary implication, the act extinguishes native title depends on its language, character and the purpose it is designed to achieve;[42]
d. the phrase 'necessary implication' imports a high degree of certainty as to legislative intention;[43]
e. it ought to be assumed that the object of the statute was to achieve its desired result with as little disruption as possible and without affecting accrued rights and existing status any more than was necessary;[44] and
f. what is required is inconsistency between native title rights and rights created by legislation. If the two can coexist, no question of implicit extinguishment can arise.[45]

TESTS OF EXTINGUISHMENT

Justice Lee's analysis of the authorities in *Ward* TJ, with which Justice North (dissenting in appeal) agreed, suggested three ways in which legislative or executive acts might extinguish native title.[46]

1. Positive express act — native title may be extinguished by a positive express valid act, unqualified by any law which prevails over it or which authorises the act.[47]
2. Inconsistent act — native title may be extinguished by the doing of an act that is inconsistent with the continued right of Aboriginal people to enjoy native title, unqualified by any law which prevails over it or which authorises the act.[48]
3. Adverse dominion — native title may be extinguished by a grant which confers rights to use the land in a way inconsistent with the exercise of rights that attach to native title upon the exercise of those rights.[49]

Justice Lee pointed out that an equivalent to the 'adverse dominion' test was set out by Justice Brennan in *Mabo [No. 2]* in relation to public works and in *Wik* by Justices Gaudron and Gummow, who were referring to conditions on pastoral leases.[50]

In identifying the 'adverse dominion' test, Justice Lee was not rejecting the other two methods of extinguishment, to which he adverted, or the three categories of extinguishment isolated by Justice Brennan in *Wik*[51] and adopted by Justices Beaumont and von Doussa;[52] that is:

a. purposive act — a law or executive act which has the purpose of extinguishing native title, where the objectively assessed intention to do so is *clear and plain*;
b. inconsistent act — a law or executive act which creates rights in other parties inconsistent with a continued right to enjoy native title;
c. Crown acquisition — a law by which the Crown acquires a full beneficial interest:
   (i) by statute, or
   (ii) by appropriation together with use for a purpose inconsistent with continued enjoyment of native title.

Those three categories postulated by Justice Brennan in *Wik* are reflected in Justice Lee's categories, albeit slightly differently arranged and expressed. A 'positive express act' is essentially the same as a 'purposive act', the 'inconsistent act' tests are the same, and Justice Brennan's 'Crown acquisition' category is one example of the 'adverse dominion' principle.

It will be a rare circumstance when a law is validly in place which expressly positively adopts the purpose of extinguishing native title, not least because of the international admonitions against deprivation of property on a racial basis.[53]

The 'inconsistent act' test will be most applicable in relation to acts of extinguishment at the higher end of the scale; for example, in the case of a fee simple grant. It will, therefore, fall to the 'adverse dominion' test to provide the decisive criterion for determining instances which fall closest to the dividing line between extinguishment and non-extinguishment.[54]

In a case such as *Ward* TJ, therefore, it was not surprising that it was the adverse dominion test which was most often applied by Justice Lee. That is so because it was a case where the claim area was deliberately chosen so as to delete current tenures where the prospect of extinguishment was, at the time of the application, contentious. No current pastoral leases, for instance, were included, and current vacant Crown land was favoured. As it turned out, the tenure history which emerged introduced a wide variety of tenures into what was required to be considered. However, a substantial proportion of what the Court was required to consider comprised Crown reserved lands and various forms of statutory Crown leases, which, on the basis of the High Court's decision in *Wik,* would not satisfy the 'purposive/positive express act' test, or ordinarily be expected to satisfy the 'inconsistent act' test. It was, therefore, appropriate, where the other limbs of the test did not dictate extinguishment, to consider whether 'adverse dominion' could be established, as Justice Lee did.

Justice Lee's analysis of 'inconsistency' and 'coexistence', in my view, is the only practical way in which those concepts can be understood and inter-related. It has a practical application in relation to a statutory Crown lease coexisting with a native title, where each of the competing titles allows for the right to occupy the whole of the land and to engage in activities on the land which may from time to time be inconsistent with one another.

For instance, if an occasionally used ceremonial ground was also an area where it might be most convenient to drive cattle through from time to time, the two rights could not be exercised at the same time; however, they are not inconsistent with one another if carried out at different times. The suspension of the exercise of the native title right to occupy the ceremonial ground does not constitute a partial extinguishment of a native title which includes the right to occupy the area.

Temporary suspension of the capacity to *exercise* rights is not conceptually the same as the rights ceasing to exist for a period of time and then being revived. If Justice Lee had adopted only the 'inconsistent act' test, then it may well have been that even fewer acts would have been found by him to have extinguished native title.

SUSPENSION AND REVIVAL

Justices Beaumont and von Doussa in *Ward* FC said that 'The notion that native title can revive at the conclusion of the term of the lease is, in our view, inconsistent with the joint judgment in *Fejo*'.[55] However, the joint judgment in *Fejo* did not deal with leases, but with an unqualified grant of fee simple title, and, so, cannot be regarded as authority for that proposition.[56] On the other hand, in *Wik*, the majority members of this Court deliberately disavowed reaching any view on the issue of 'suspension of any native title rights during the currency of the grants' of pastoral leases under the Acts in question.[57]

Justices Toohey, Gaudron, Gummow and Kirby of the High Court in *Wik*[58] expressed views which disagreed with the view of Justice Brennan in *Mabo [No. 2]*;[59] that is, the Crown must have acquired a full beneficial interest in the land. The same principle underpinned the view of Justice

Brennan, in *Wik*,⁶⁰ that native title cannot be temporarily suspended by the grant of a lease. I adopt the submissions of the appellants in *Ward* FC in support of the argument that a temporary suspension of the capacity to exercise native title rights does not result in the extinguishment of native title.⁶¹

PARTIAL EXTINGUISHMENT

Justices Beaumont and von Doussa in *Ward* FC disagreed with Justice Lee's view that native title cannot be partially extinguished.⁶² They were content with the view that native title is a bundle of rights for the purpose of concluding that native title may be partially extinguished. They explained that only some of the bundle of rights may be extinguished by the creation of inconsistent rights and reached that conclusion on the basis of the dicta of Justice Brennan in *Mabo [No. 2]*, that 'Where the Crown has validly alienated land but granting an interest that is wholly or partially inconsistent with a continuing right to enjoy native title, native title is extinguished to the extent of the inconsistency',⁶³ and Justice Toohey in *Wik*, that 'If inconsistency is held to exist between the rights and interests conferred by native title and the rights conferred under statutory grants, those rights and interests must yield to that extent to the rights of the grantees'.⁶⁴

I would argue that the preferable analysis is that of Justice Lee and that 'partial inconsistency' is not synonymous with partial extinguishment, on the one hand, or extinguishment of one or more of the rights in a bundle which comprises the native title, on the other.⁶⁵

Reference in passing in *North Ganalanja*⁶⁶ and *Fejo* to native title as a bundle of rights does not reduce it to a 'mere bundle of rights' capable of being extinguished right by right.⁶⁷ The proper understanding is that native title, to the extent that it is a bundle of rights, is a collection of 'jural rights', which maintain integrity as a whole upon the 'socially constituted factual basis' of its existence as spiritual, cultural and social connection to land and waters.

In order to extinguish native title, the rights created by legislative or executive acts must be inconsistent with the continuing relationship of the Indigenous group to the land. Inconsistency at the level of a current incapacity to exercise rights contingent upon or incidental to that relationship does not extinguish the title; it merely limits the form of its exercise from time to time.⁶⁸

A native title based in occupation is an interest in land that cannot be partially extinguished, though it may be impaired in the form of regulation, suspension or curtailment, arising from legislative or executive acts granting rights to third parties to use Crown lands.[69] The impairment may have an impact upon the exercise of the 'artificially defined jural rights' comprising the 'property' which is described as native title without extinguishing the title.

Chief Justice Brennan, in his minority judgment in *Wik*, suggests in an obiter dictum that 'the Crown's exercise of its sovereign power to use unalienated land for its own purposes extinguishes, *partially* or wholly, native title interests in or over the land'.[70] Chief Justice Brennan does not further explain what he means by partial extinguishment and does not relate it to the extinguishment of one or more of a bundle of rights. The authorities he refers to for the proposition are the judgments of himself and Justices Deane and Gaudron in *Mabo [No. 2]*, which make no mention of 'partial extinguishment'.[71]

Also in *Mabo [No. 2]*, Justice Brennan states as a conclusion, without any preceding analysis in relation to any question of *partial* extinguishment, that:

> Where the Crown has validly alienated land by granting an interest that is wholly or partially inconsistent with a continuing right to enjoy native title, native title is extinguished to the extent of the inconsistency. Thus native title has been extinguished by grants of freehold or of leases but not necessarily by the grant of lesser interests.[72]

In the examples Justice Brennan gives to illustrate the stated principle, he refers only to the dichotomy of extinguishment versus no extinguishment and does not illustrate or explain any concept of partial extinguishment.

Justice Toohey in *Wik*, on behalf of the majority judges, restricts the decision in that case to the issue of whether there is necessary extinguishment of '*the* rights and interests conferred by native title'.[73] In other words, the majority judgments do not consider whether native title is or may be partially extinguished or whether any right from any 'bundle of rights' might be separately extinguished. None of the dicta of the other judges suggest anything to the contrary.

Likewise, *Fejo* is authority for the fact that extinguishment by a grant in fee simple is permanent, not temporary, but the judgments do not provide any analysis of any concept of partial extinguishment.[74] That is now an issue of law, which is under consideration by the High Court in *Western Australia v Ward* (2002) (*Ward* HC).[75]

When one considers the form of the declaration of the native title rights and interests in *Mabo [No. 2]*, that is, an entitlement 'as against the whole world to possession, occupation, use and enjoyment of the lands…', which is the same form of title which Justice Lee found to exist in *Ward* TJ, it is not an appropriate legal analysis, in my view, to separate any rights out from a bundle as a part of the title to be extinguished.

The majority of the Full Court in *Ward* FC, in the form of the determination which they reached, and in their reasons for decision, acknowledged that the native title may be such that:

> the indigenous community is entitled as against the whole world to possession, occupation, use and enjoyment of the land, [and] that entitlement may be similar in its enjoyment to the incidents which attach to a freehold title. Subject to the general laws of Australia which regulate or restrict the use and enjoyment of the land, insofar as those laws apply to the general community, the community will have the right to control access to the land, to make decisions as to its use and as to the use and enjoyment of its resources, subject to its own traditionally based laws and customs. The activities which members of the community may undertake are not frozen in time at sovereignty, and may include activities of the kind undertaken from time to time by other members of the Australian community who use and enjoy a freehold title.[76]

Where the majority judges diverge from Justice Lee and Justice North (dissenting) is that the majority judges' view is that (1) the *exclusive* nature of the native title right to possess, occupy and enjoy the land is 'destroyed' (a) upon the grant of any inconsistent rights to a third party in relation to the grantee,[77] (b) upon the imposition of restrictions in relation to the control, use and enjoyment of water,[78] and (c) by a general use of an area leased or reserved for watering cattle and/or as a pastoral lease and/or public uses;[79] and (2) the exclusivity of the right to make decisions about the possession, occupation, use and enjoyment of water is 'removed' by the imposition of by-laws under the *Rights in Water and Irrigation Act 1914* (WA).

However, Justices Beaumont and von Doussa found that native title is 'regulated' only in relation to third parties engaging in activities reserved from a grant[80] and regulations that stringently control activities which may be carried out in a national park do not prohibit those activities, and, thus, though they 'curtail' the enjoyment of rights, do not extinguish them.[81]

4. Native title is property

Justices Beaumont and von Doussa are in error, I would suggest, in treating the exclusivity element of the native title right to possess, occupy, use and enjoy an area as a separate right which is capable of being permanently incapable of future exercise by reason of the advent of another entitlement coexisting on the same area, however temporarily. The native title right is the right to possess, occupy, use and enjoy the area. The fact that another prevailing title may come to exist in relation to the same area will necessarily mean that the native title holder cannot exclude that prevailing title holder from exercising whatever rights are incidental to that title. It does not mean that the element of exclusivity of the native title is not good against others who may come upon the land, either during or after the period of the existence of the other title.

Further, it is the element of exclusivity of the native title, when juxtaposed with a coexisting title (for example, a pastoral lease) with its element of exclusivity of use of the area for the purpose which it has been granted, which dictates the requirement of 'coexistence on terms of reasonable user' which the majority judges identify as the practical consequence of coexistence.[82]

EXTINGUISHMENT AS A METAPHOR

Justice French in *Lardil and other Peoples v Queensland* makes the interesting comment in the course of his judgment that 'Extinguishment of native title by the legislative or executive or other action is a metaphor for limits upon the extent to which recognition will be accorded by the common law'.[83]

Justice French points out that 'where extinguishment of native title is said to have occurred, the common law will not recognise it notwithstanding the subsistence of rights and interests in land according to the traditional law and custom of the relevant indigenous group'.[84] As the High Court said in *Fejo*, 'The underlying existence of the traditional laws and customs is a necessary pre-requisite for native title but their existence is not a sufficient basis for recognising native title'.[85]

When one grasps this elusive nature of the application of this metaphor of 'extinguishment', one is drawn toward concurring with the view of Gray and Gray that 'Property talk is ultimately reducible to a dialogue about moral space, about the mutual frontier between vulnerability and autonomy, between social accommodation and immunity from predation'.[86]

Perhaps it is at that level of decision making that Justices Beaumont and von Doussa chose to draw a line in relation to the recognition of native title, to conclude that 'the common law applies to protect only the physical enjoyment of rights and interests that are of a kind that can be exercised on the land, and does not protect purely religious or spiritual relationships with land'.[87] They relied upon the dicta of the High Court in *Fejo* where it was said that a grant of fee simple 'simply does not permit of the enjoyment by anyone else of any right or interest in respect of the land' and '[t]he rights of native title are rights and interests that relate to the use of the land by the holders of the native title'.[88]

I would suggest that, if the relationship of Indigenous people with their traditional land is understood by the courts to be 'primarily a spiritual affair',[89] then it is difficult to reconcile that with the conclusion of Justices Beaumont and von Doussa.

EXCLUSIVITY AS A METAPHOR

'Exclusivity', in its metaphorical sense, is the right to exercise the powers of ownership or control of what makes up the property or title being asserted. In that sense, 'exclusivity' is part of the essence of any title. When the High Court declared in *Mabo [No. 2]* that 'the Meriam people are entitled as against the whole world to possession, occupation, use and enjoyment of the Lands of the Murray Islands',[90] it was declaring that an exclusive title existed in the Meriam people. It was a consequence of the existence of the title that it was an exclusive title. The declaration did not follow any inquiry into the extent of exclusivity of the occupation of the Meriam people as against the rest of the world.

'Exclusivity' or the 'right to exclude others' is not a separate element of any title to land. Title is not an absolute but a relative concept.[91] Whether one has the right to exclude another is determined by reference to who has the better title. It is not something that exists in the abstract. Whether or not the right to exclude exists depends on the competing interests at stake. It does not follow from the fact that the rights of a native title holder coexist with those of a pastoral lessee that the native title holder is unable to enforce the right to exclude against a stranger or third party.

The essential relationship of 'exclusivity' to title is exemplified by the fact that 'exclusive' titles may overlap. It is not uncommon, for example, for a mining lease, which grants 'exclusive rights for mining purposes', to be held over an area of land subject to a freehold title which is held for farming purposes.[92] Chief Justice Lamer in *Delgamuukw* suggested that 'exclusive use and occupation of the land' is a defining element of aboriginal title.[93] He also allowed that 'joint title could arise from shared exclusivity' and asserted that 'The meaning of shared exclusivity is well known to the common law'.[94]

As Justice Lee said in *Ward* TJ, 'Coexistence of competing interests in land, whether recognised at common law or derived from statute, is accommodated under common law and in Australian land law'.[95] It is not contrary to legal principle for two interests in land to coexist in respect of the one area of land and it is not a requirement of law in such circumstances that a concept of 'extinguishment' or 'partial extinguishment' be applied to defeat one of those interests, despite the fact that there may be some inconsistency between the incidents of the respective rights as exercised.

McNeil speaks of the occupation from which a native title would arise as being an 'exclusive occupation'.[96] However, he makes it clear that the 'exclusive occupancy' that he is referring to is that adverted to by Justice Toohey in *Mabo [No. 2]* where he says:

> This principle of exclusive occupancy is justified in so far as it precludes indiscriminate ranging over land but it is difficult to see the basis for the rule if it precludes title merely on the ground that more than one group utilizes the land. Either each smaller group could be said to have title, comprising the right to shared use of land in accordance with traditional use; or traditional title vests in the larger 'society' comprising all the rightful occupiers.[97]

Understood in that sense, any reference to the occupancy which provides the basis for the title does not require (a) that it exist as an absolute exclusive occupancy, or (b) that it be proved to exist as an occupancy which is exclusive. Evidence of mere occupancy, it is contended, is a sufficient basis for reaching a conclusion of a communal native title to the land, as against the Crown, and exclusivity (subject to other valid interests) will be presumed as an incident of a title based in occupancy.

In my view, exclusivity is an essential element of title, which is not required to be proved, and coexisting titles may all have elements of exclusivity, exercisable subject to prevailing interests.[98]

CONCLUSION

Property is best understood as the power to control something. Much ink has been spilt in attempting to conceptualise the limits of control which may exist between competitors for control of land and resources, particularly since the *Mabo [No. 2]* decision in Australia. Much of the difficulty for the common law courts in Australia has been in reconciling the accommodation which the *Mabo [No. 2]* case concluded must be made between property accorded pursuant to the English land tenure system and Australian statute law and the property now to be recognised by the common law which arises out of the laws and customs of a colonised Aboriginal peoples. If the native title of Aboriginal peoples is to be recognised as property, as the High Court in *Mabo [No. 2]* concluded it should be, then the common law must recognise that native title accords degrees of control of the things which comprise the essence of native title. That control, if it is to be effective, must sometimes include the capacity to exclude others from access to a place, but at least must always include an ability to control the behaviour of others sufficiently to preserve the essence of the rights and interests constituted by the relevant native title.

5.
Native Title Conference, Larrakia Country, 2006

A CURIOUS HISTORY OF THE *MABO* LITIGATION

JOHN BASTEN

My thanks to our hosts, the Larrakia People.

In his Mabo Lecture, Galarrwuy Yunupingu spoke in engaging terms of how Indigenous Australians understood their connection with their lands, seas, reefs and islands.[1] Let me tell you of my early perceptions of those matters. I still have a large picture book, prepared for primary school children, called *The Australia Book*, written by Eve Pownall and illustrated by Margaret Senior. It was published in 1952.[2] It noted the voyages of Spanish and Dutch explorers and the arrival of Captain James Cook in April 1770. It says that Cook had raised an English flag 'on an island off Cape York' and claimed for England 'the whole of the eastern part of the New Holland, which he called New South Wales'. The narrative continued: 'At first the English did not bother about the new country', but with the loss of the American colonies, the prisons in England were rapidly filling and there was a need for 'something… to be done about the convicts'. This, it was explained, led the English to remember 'the land that Cook had found. It was just what they needed.' 'Aborigines', whose prior occupation the book described, stood on the cliffs, shook their spears and called 'Warra warra!', which, it said, means 'go away'. That objection was treated as trivial: 'But the white men took no notice. This time they had come to stay.'

No doubt behind the blandness of the account, there lies an aura of threat. Nevertheless, if the claim of British sovereignty dispossessed Indigenous people of all beneficial interests in their own lands, this remarkable event went unnoticed in the history book. As a result, I, and presumably millions of other non-Indigenous Australians, grew up in ignorance of what must have constituted one of the most remarkable uncontested expropriations in world history, without a cent in compensation. (Of course, it had to be 'uncontested' because the expropriated owners were blissfully unaware that it had happened.)

In 1987, in *Walden v Hensler*, which involved the prosecution of an Indigenous man, Herbert Walden, for taking a protected brush turkey, Justice Brennan stated:

> It would not have been surprising if a question had been raised by the appellant as to whether and how it came about in law that Aboriginal people had their traditional entitlement to gather food from their own country taken away, but that question was not raised.[3]

That question was, of course, asked and answered in *Mabo v Queensland [No. 2]*.[4] The answer given by the High Court denied that a claim for sovereignty over a large territory effected a disposition of ownership of the land.

Mabo was, inevitably, a legally and socially unsettling judgment. That fact is not diminished by acceptance of the conclusion explained by Lisa Strelein that *Mabo* brought the common law in Australia into line with that of other former British colonies.[5] The judgment is, appropriately, a subject of historical study. It was addressed by Michael Connor in *The Invention of Terra Nullius*, with the subtitle 'Historical and legal fictions on the foundation of Australia'.[6] The subtitle may have raised less of an eyebrow than the primary title, with the focus on the Latin label 'terra nullius' and its description as an 'invention'. Much of Dr Connor's thesis is wrong-headed and its exposition contradictory, a matter to which I will return. If one learns a lesson from Dr Connor's book, it is to take care when moving beyond one's own discipline, training and research. I will therefore avoid too much by way of comment on the history, though the vitriol he expends on modern Australian historians, particularly Professor Henry Reynolds, suggests that balanced judgment may not be one of the author's claims to authority.

In a purely historical sense, I am happy to assume that terra nullius was not, as he explains, a phrase used by the British Government in 1770 or

5. A curious history of the *Mabo* litigation

1788. However, from a lawyer's point of view, that would be to accuse the majority judgments in *Mabo* of using a neologism, something less than a serious offence according to the canons of good judgment writing. Importantly, it falls a long way short of demonstrating a fatal flaw in judicial reasoning.

The term 'terra nullius' has three meanings, as I think Dr Connor accepts, although it does not help his case (based on supposed confusion) to set them out with any particularity. The meanings are:

a. a country which is not recognised in international law as being under the control of a sovereign power;
b. a land having no occupants or inhabitants; and
c. an area of territory which is inhabited, but the inhabitants of which do not have a system of laws recognisable under British law, or who do not recognise legal possession of land vested in individuals.

Dr Connor asserts that the phrase 'means a territory without sovereignty'.[7] That, he later observes, was a concept of international law and not part of the domestic common law of England. That meaning can be put to one side.

The second meaning (unoccupied land) may be one in ordinary parlance amongst those who use Latin tags but, if it is, it too can properly be put to one side. No one believed in 1788 (as I assume the picture on the dust cover of Dr Connor's book was intended to demonstrate) that Australia was a land without inhabitants. However, the real question that Dr Connor needed to address, and possibly needed some legal understanding in order to do so effectively, was the third meaning.

Before embarking on that issue, one needs to identify the principles applied by the common law in relation to Indigenous interests in land in settled colonies in order to determine whether Indigenous Australians had such interests. In other words, there are both legal and factual questions.

The legal question has several limbs. The first issue is whether the acquisition of sovereignty of itself instantly dispossessed all Indigenous Australians of land that they had previously owned, so that the Indigenous inhabitants immediately became potential trespassers, capable of exclusion from the whole landmass, subject to the continued occupation under licence from the Crown. This, as Justice Brennan noted, would 'make nonsense of the law'.[8] The next issue focuses on the kinds of interest that Indigenous people held in land. In the judgment of the Privy Council in *In re Southern Rhodesia*, Lord Sumner had stated that:

> The estimation of the rights of aboriginal tribes is always inherently difficult. Some tribes are so low in the scale of social organization that their usages and conceptions of rights and duties are not to be reconciled with the institutions or the legal ideas of civilized society.[9]

One way of describing that phenomenon was that the land in such colonies was owned by no one, because the Indigenous tribes had no relevant concept of interests in land of a kind capable of protection by the common law. As a factual issue, in relation to Australia, that issue was addressed in *Milirrpum v Nabalco Pty Ltd*, a decision of Justice Blackburn sitting as a single judge of the Northern Territory Supreme Court.[10] *Milirrpum* was the only case before *Mabo* in which an Australian court had ruled on a traditional land claim based on extensive evidence of the culture, structures, laws and customs of the traditional claimants. Although Justice Blackburn accepted that Indigenous people had a close relationship with land, based on fixed principles conforming to our concept of the rule of law, he dismissed the claim primarily on the basis that the nature of the interest was not one which the common law recognised; that was because the interest was both communal and inalienable. The basis of the belief that the common law would not protect such an interest might indeed be a fascinating topic for historical research, but it is not the subject of the present discussion. The High Court in *Mabo* rejected the proposition that the common law was so constrained. As noted by Justices Deane and Gaudron:

> In different ways and to varying degrees of intensity, [Indigenous people] used their homelands for all the purposes of their lives: social, ritual, economic. They identified with them in a way which transcended common law notions of property or possession.[11]

The history of British attitudes to the settlement of Australia may be seen to have reflected, somewhat inconsistently, on the one hand, the ideas expressed by Lord Sumner and, on the other, a recognition that settlement involved a deprivation of Indigenous rights in land.

I do not wish to belabour the point that the decision of the High Court in *Mabo* was less radical in legal terms than both its champions and its denigrators would have it. That point can be made good by a careful comparison of the reasoning of Justice Brennan, speaking for the majority, and Justice Dawson in dissent. The points of departure are readily identifiable and even more readily referable to different applications of established principles of legal reasoning. However, in a passage with which I would wish to agree, Justice Dawson stated:

> There may not be a great deal to be proud of in this history of events. But a dispassionate appraisal of what occurred is essential to the determination of the legal consequences, notwithstanding the degree of condemnation which is nowadays apt to accompany any account.[12]

Although the footnote to that statement is a reference to a judgment of Justice Murphy, it is equally apt as a reservation about the language used by Justices Deane and Gaudron, which their Honours themselves described as 'unusually emotive for a judgment in this Court'.[13] Indeed, Justice Brennan, whose judgments are often a delight to read, also adopted colourful language.

I would be inclined to put the use of the phrase 'terra nullius' into the category of emotive phrases which might well have been left out or better explained. Nevertheless, a critic must also adopt dispassionate appraisal of the reasoning and should ignore the emotive elements and analyse the underlying substance. If that course is taken, and references to 'terra nullius' are understood appropriately, the reasoning of the majority is easily supportable.

Justice Brennan sought to adapt the common law to what he identified as modern notions of justice and fundamental values of equality. He did not need to do this. The facts about Aboriginal and Islander culture were established in *Milirrpum* and by Justice Moynihan in *Mabo*. They rendered irrelevant the racist and denigratory views expressed in *In re Southern Rhodesia*. The ability of the common law to protect an allodial, communal and inalienable title was all that needed to be addressed. There is a danger with colourful or emotive language in judgments: it can suggest that the Court has stepped outside its proper role of dispassionate appraisal and has allowed emotion or prejudice to colour its judgment, either with respect to matters of fact or with respect to legal principles. What the judges may have been anxious to dispel was the impression that what was being recognised was belatedly and grudgingly conceded. Indeed, as Justice Dawson himself approached the matter, much depended ultimately not on recognition of pre-existing rights in land, but on questions of extinguishment. The reasoning of Justices Deane and Gaudron to the effect that expropriation by inconsistent grant was wrongful and did not extinguish native title had much to commend it. The majority view, identified in the judgment of Justice Brennan, was that, although native title must be accepted and discriminatory views of Indigenous society rejected, a Crown grant would validly extinguish native title, although it would be invalid if the land was subject to private rights acquired pursuant to an earlier Crown grant. The non-discrimination principle was not applied consistently in determining the scope and operation of the common law. As a result, the colourful language tended to satisfy no one and led to a charge of hypocrisy.

Similarly, whereas the existence of the power of the government to grant titles under Crown lands legislation was held not to extinguish native title, until exercised in respect of particular land, there is little explanation in the jurisprudence as to why a grant which has never been taken up and has later been relinquished should extinguish, rather than suspend, the pre-existing native title which depended for its recognition, as a factual matter, on evidence of continued use and enjoyment of the land under traditional law and custom. *Fejo v Northern Territory* established that as part of the common law principle, thus missing an opportunity to limit the extent to which a Crown grant extinguished native title in a manner which would not have occurred with respect to an earlier entitlement derived directly from the Crown.[14] Lisa Strelein says the flaw in the reasons lies in the language (again emotive) of the 'vulnerability' of native title and the failure to address with particularity the concept of inconsistency, so as to distinguish *necessary* from merely *preferred* consequences.

It is not necessary to suggest that *Fejo* was wrong, as a matter of application of the principles established in *Mabo*; rather, the point is that *Fejo* was an application of those principles, thus demonstrating the limited scope of the judgment in *Mabo*. Those limitations would have been better understood and the conservative nature of the judgment better appreciated had emotive language not been deployed.

Exaggerated language is the language of politics; thus, no doubt appealing to one audience but appalling another, the Prime Minister in 1997 announced his Ten Point Plan, which the Deputy Prime Minister promised would provide to his constituents 'bucket loads of extinguishment'.[15] It is then something of an irony to note that the resulting legislation was more protective of traditional rights than the High Court in *Fejo*, accepting in sections 47A and 47B of the *Native Title Act 1993* (Cth) the very principle that had been rejected as a matter of the common law.

To those who remain devoted, for political reasons, to the hypothesis that the Howard government has been largely responsible for undermining the judgment in *Mabo* and is responsible for funding (and therefore approves of) popular texts such as that produced by Dr Connor, it is necessary to offer a more nuanced picture. As Frank Brennan has pointed out, the *Native Title Amendment Act 1998* (Cth) involved an acceptance by the Howard government of the basic principles underlying not only *Mabo*, but the political outcome of that judgment, namely the *Native Title Act 1993* (Cth) (NTA).

More importantly, one can say from experience of the negotiations which continued between the National Indigenous Working Group (NIWG) and the government during 1997 and 1998 that there was a willingness to consult and address the significant practical difficulties that the recognition of native title entailed. Both the NIWG and the government operated, as is common in the political process, at a number of levels. I want to comment only on that level in which I had personal involvement, namely the identification of policy and the transmission of it into statutory language. Those discussions took place primarily with Phillipa Horner, then working in the Department of Prime Minister and Cabinet, and Robert Orr, now senior counsel in the Office of Parliamentary Counsel. The fact that those discussions continued over many months and probably involved weeks of face-to-face negotiations demonstrated a commitment of the government to a level of detailed consultation, which is, I suspect, rare in the history of legislative drafting in this country. I am not an apologist for the Native Title Amendment Act, but the point should be recognised that, to a significant extent, the amendments finally accepted by the government reflected some, though of course not all, of the legitimate Indigenous concerns.

Furthermore, to the extent that the NTA failed to deal with particular problems, all parties should be willing to bear some level of responsibility. One area of weakness is the failure of the NTA to deal in any significant fashion with the results of a successful native title claim.

To return to Dr Connor's thesis that terra nullius was a doctrine critical for the majority reasoning in *Mabo*, the answer is found in the statement of Justice Dawson: 'There is thus no need to resort to notions of terra nullius in relation to the Murray Islands. The law which applied on annexation was the law of Queensland…there is no issue about that in this case.'[16]

Once one accepts that proposition, and Dr Connor does not refute it — indeed, he quotes it at one point — a major part of his thesis collapses.

Let me finish by drawing together some lessons which I think may be derived from the comparison, which is apt at this conference, of the *Aboriginal Land Rights (Northern Territory) Act 1976* (Cth) (ALRA) and the NTA.

First, the ALRA did not give Indigenous communities rights to oil, gas or minerals, but it did give them a share of royalties. In that respect, the NTA denied the possibility of returning land with economic value to native title holders.

Secondly, the ALRA automatically returned reserves and set up an administrative tribunal to determine connection to other areas. The NTA took neither of these procedural steps.

Thirdly, the ALRA established Indigenous-controlled land councils, which have been extraordinarily effective in both pursuing claims and protecting Indigenous lands from ill-advised development or alienation, whilst providing Traditional Owners with administrative support. The administrative structures under the NTA almost entirely neglected these lessons. Escape from the cycle of poverty, indignity and frustration requires economic development and employment. Without these the effectiveness of education and health spending will be at best severely limited. Recovering traditional lands is a step in the process of recognising basic humanity and personal dignity. But if the land restored is limited to that for which others have, as yet, found no economic value, its return will not solve the basic problems.

The judgment of the High Court in *Mabo* was far less radical than was widely thought at the time, but it was not fundamentally flawed as new historians would have it. *Mabo* provided an opportunity for resolution of many afflictions facing Indigenous peoples. It was an opportunity which was embraced by the government of the day, but only in part. *Mabo* gave Indigenous people a place at the negotiating table, although, unfortunately, that was seen by too many as a threat rather than an opportunity.

The primary weaknesses in *Mabo* were twofold. First, it accepted the validity of extinguishment by inconsistent government grants of title to land, thus limiting successful claims to areas with which the Traditional Owners had been able to maintain their connection and which had not been the grant of anything more invasive than a pastoral lease or grazing licence. Secondly, the common law did not recognise native title in minerals or oil which had not been the subject of exploitation by Indigenous people. The combined effect of these two factors was to diminish almost to vanishing point the possibility that native title would restore to Indigenous peoples land having economic potential. To a significant extent, that goal must be sought through the fitful, but now solid, progress achieved by the Indigenous Land Corporation. The availability of funding to acquire and purchase valuable land for development has been successfully exploited by the Larrakia Development

5. A curious history of the *Mabo* litigation

Corporation, a story which will need to be replicated in other parts of the country.

These things grew out of the opportunity created by *Mabo*; this conference has grown out of the existence of the judgment in *Mabo*. There is reason to hope that with some level of mutual trust, which still needs to be developed, the progress which the government has asserted that it wishes to achieve will occur.

6.
Native Title Conference, Bindal Wulgurukaba Country, 2001

THE ROLE OF THE HIGH COURT AND THE RECOGNITION OF NATIVE TITLE
Address in honour of Ron Castan QC AM*

ROBERT FRENCH

THE SHOCK OF THE OLD

Recognition between people is the human experience of seeing each other anew. In a related sense it involves acknowledgment of our shared humanity and the dignity and rights of each individual. Recognition is also the metaphor that names the legal act which lies at the heart of the law of native title. The human experience and the legal act are not far apart. For Ron Castan, whose memory we honour by this address, they were inseparable. He put to the High Court of Australia that legal recognition of the relationship between Aboriginal and Islander peoples and their country was something the judges could and should do. His argument was informed by a powerful personal conviction, which I can no better express than in his own words:

> At the heart of the legal fiction of terra nullius lies an obnoxious racism, which involves treating aboriginal people as less than human. The ultimate denial of the inherent humanity of one's fellow human beings consists of saying that those persons, although manifestly physically present and alive, are not worthy of being treated as 'people' at all — they are no more than part of the flora and fauna of the land.[1]

6. The High Court and recognition of native title

Linked to this was his consciousness of the denial of the history of Australia's treatment of its Indigenous people and the failure to acknowledge that history — the 'Cult of Disremembering' or 'The Great Australian Silence' as Professor Stanner called it.[2] The answer to it, he said, was:

> to write more books, give more talks, fight more native title cases in the courts, tell more stories of the Stolen Generation, teach more courses in schools and universities and build more monuments and statues of indigenous freedom fighters so that the cult of disremembering can never take hold again.[3]

The Cult of Disremembering was dealt a great blow with the decision of the High Court in *Mabo* in which Ron Castan appeared for the plaintiffs. It was seen as a moment of discontinuity in our legal history, later described by Justice Gummow in the *Wik* case as a shift in Australia's constitutional foundation.[4] Castan did not see it that way. What the High Court had to deal with in *Mabo* was not a revolutionary doctrine but accorded with what had been accepted in other British colonies. Nor, in his view, did it represent a change by that Court, for the Court had never previously been asked to pronounce on the issue.[5] It is right to say that the decision involved not so much the discovery or the creation of a new principle but the doing of a new thing — the legal act we call, metaphorically, recognition. It is a legal *act* rather than a new principle because it takes its character from the human act of recognition. That is not just a passive seeing of something afresh. Its key element is an acknowledgment of truth and validity. It translates the old into the new. It conveys, within our history, the reconstruction of understanding — the shock of awareness — the new realisation of what we have passed over unseeing. It brings a knowledge of what has always been and, for many, a sense of the loss of what could have been. This is a powerful strand in the still unfolding history of native title in Australia.

That unfolding is a small part of a much larger history. It resides in the law and custom of Aboriginal and Islander people expressed in oral and artistic traditions, in the paintings, songs, dances and storylines which create and define their Australian landscapes and their places in them.

Galarrwuy Yunupingu wrote of these traditions in 1976 in his 'Letter from Black to White':

> The land is the art. I can paint, dance, create and sing as my ancestors did before me. My people recorded these things about our land this way, so that I and all others like me may do the same. I think of the

land as the history of my nation. It tells us how we came into being and what system we must now live...My land is my foundation... Without land I am nothing.⁶

The rules of the Federal Court provide for evidence in native title proceedings to be given 'by way of singing, dancing, story telling or in any other way...'⁷ Ten years ago such a rule of court would have been unimaginable. So the judicial system has been moved. And the first movement came from the High Court.

QUESTIONS POSED

The focus of this paper is on the way in which High Court decisions have created and developed the common law of native title. The decisions considered are not only the few made to this date about native title but others that have set the scene for its recognition and protection. What has been decided so far is incomplete. It leaves open many issues. They include the nature of what is called 'recognition' and its limitations and qualifications, some of which attract the misleading metaphor 'extinguishment'. The decisions made so far also point to the need to understand the limitations which the nature of the High Court and, indeed, all courts place upon what may be achieved through them. The act of legal recognition takes place in a virtual reality, the universe of legal discourse. It defines rights and assigns their relative priorities. The management of the relationships between those rights and the people who hold them is part of the human experience of recognition. It takes place in the real world between real people.

TERRA NULLIUS, RECOGNITION THRESHOLDS AND ODIOUS COMPARISONS

To understand the jurisprudence of native title it is necessary to refer to the cases that have been decided in the High Court and what they did. Before *Mabo* that jurisprudence was fairly straightforward and embodied in the judgment of Sir Richard Blackburn in the Supreme Court of the Northern Territory in 1971 in the Gove Land Rights case.⁸ He held, in accordance with his reading of nineteenth-century Privy Council authority,⁹ that Australia, at the time of colonisation, was settled or occupied rather than conquered or ceded. In *Cooper v Stuart*, Lord Watson had said:

> There is a great difference between the case of a Colony acquired by conquest or cession, in which there is an established system of law, and that of a Colony which consisted of a tract of territory practically unoccupied, without settled inhabitants or settled law, at the time when it was peacefully annexed to the British dominions. The Colony of New South Wales belongs to the latter class.[10]

This was consistent with the approach taken by the colonial courts of New South Wales. In 1833 Indigenous inhabitants were described as 'wandering tribes…living without certain habitation and without laws [who] were never in the situation of a conquered people'.[11] It was, moreover, received wisdom that the lands in the colony were the property of the Crown from first settlement.[12]

Justice Blackburn concluded from *Cooper v Stuart* that the doctrine of terra nullius applied and there was no common law doctrine of native title in Australia. In any event, he found there were no rights under traditional law and custom of the kind necessary to attract recognition at common law. A threshold of equivalence of traditional rights and interests in land with those of the common law had been set up as a condition of recognition by the Privy Council in *In re Southern Rhodesia*.[13] Lord Sumner spoke of Indigenous people whose place in the scale of social organisation was so low that their usages and conceptions of rights could not be reconciled with the institutions or ideas of civilised society. It was not open, on his approach, to impute to such people 'some shadow of the rights known to our law and then to transmute it into the substance of transferable rights of property as we know them'.[14] He did, however, contemplate recognition of Indigenous rights in land above a certain threshold of comparability with common law rights and used the word 'transmute' where the word 'recognise' might be used today. By way of contrast, in *Amodu Tijani* three years later, the Privy Council cautioned against the tendency to fit traditional title to land into conceptual categories appropriate only to systems which had grown up under English law.[15] Justice Blackburn found on the evidence before him a 'subtle and elaborate system highly adapted to the country in which the people led their lives', a system to which he was prepared to attach the appellation 'a government of laws, and not of men'.[16] Nevertheless, he would have applied the approach taken in *In re Southern Rhodesia* to conclude that, absent rights under traditional law and custom that could be described as rights of property, there could be no common law native title.

In the year that terra nullius was affirmed in Australia, and traditional law and custom found wanting of the attributes necessary for recognition, Ron Castan represented Indigenous New Guinean people in a land compensation case in the Supreme Court of Papua New Guinea which was then still an Australian territory. Neither its creation as a territory nor its previous status as a British protectorate had disturbed the customary title of its people which was recognised by Australian Land Ordinances. So the High Court could say, 'The law of the Territory of Papua and New Guinea affords clear recognition of native interests in land, whether those interests are communal and usufructuary or individual and proprietary'.[17]

It struck Castan as 'particularly strange that in that part of what was then Australia, this was accepted as a matter of course', whereas 'back on the mainland for some reason Indigenous people were treated totally differently'.[18] He reflected also upon the position of Indigenous people in New Guinea under German occupation in the nineteenth century, observing:

> the German colonial land law which I studied, and then argued in detail in a Supreme Court hearing in Lae before an Australian judge, was truly enlightened compared to the position in Mainland Australia. The first German settlers were not entitled to claim ownership of any land that was owned by indigenous natives according to their own customs. Having claimed sovereignty over the Territory, the only land that could be actually settled and owned by the German New Guinea Kompanie was land not owned by local native peoples according to their own customary laws.[19]

For Castan, as a Jew, this also raised what he called the 'strange irony' that the Germany which could show such an enlightened attitude to Indigenous people could deliberately seek to kill him and succeed in killing a small number of his own family and a very large number of his wife's family.[20]

STATUTORY LAND RIGHTS

Australia's national conscience was moved to some extent following the Gove Land Rights case. The Woodward Royal Commission was established, which in turn led to the enactment of the *Aboriginal Land Rights (Northern Territory) Act 1976* (Cth) (ALRA). Its recommendations proposed the establishment of a regime for the grant of statutory land rights underpinned by a process of inquiry and recommendation by an Aboriginal Lands Commissioner. The aims of the regime as formulated by Woodward were:

1. The doing of simple justice to a people who have been deprived of their land without their consent and without compensation.
2. The promotion of social harmony and stability within the wider Australian community by removing, so far as possible, the legitimate causes of complaint of an important minority group within that community.
3. The provision of land holdings as a first essential for people who are economically depressed and who have at present no real opportunity of achieving a normal Australian standard of living.
4. The preservation, where possible, of the spiritual link with his own land which gives each Aboriginal his sense of identity and which lies at the heart of his spiritual beliefs.
5. The maintenance and, perhaps, improvement of Australia's standing among the nations of the world by demonstrably fair treatment of an ethnic minority.[21]

Justice Toohey, the first Aboriginal Lands Commissioner appointed under the ALRA, described its object thus: 'Essentially the object of the *Act* is to give standing, within the Anglo-Australian legal system, to a system of traditional ownership that has so far failed to gain recognition by the courts.'[22]

The process of claim, inquiry and recommendation set out by the Act involved an administrative recognition by the Aboriginal Land Commissioner of traditional Aboriginal owners of the land under claim. Only unalienated Crown land could be claimed. The grants made under the Act were made after recommendation from the Commissioner. They were not made as of right, but in the exercise of the statutory power of a Commonwealth minister. The same general concept of administrative recognition, followed by a grant effected by legislation or a legislative process, informed land rights statutes passed subsequently in New South Wales, Queensland and South Australia.[23]

Statutory land rights for Aboriginal people did not pass unnoticed by the Australian public. As the historian CD Rowley pointed out in 1986, for nearly two centuries systems of land ownership and government land management had been developed 'free from any real understanding of or influence by the dispossessed Aboriginal owners'. He described reaction to such statutory rights thus: 'Self interest is a firm basis for beliefs and mores in us all, and one can at least understand the shocked disbelief turning to wrath as miners and pastoralists now hear what they claim as their legal rights questioned, or see them restricted.'[24]

In so saying, he foreshadowed that which was to come, but far more acutely, in the wake of the High Court's decision to recognise native title rights in *Mabo [No. 2]*. As Ron Castan would write in 1993:

> The notion that Aboriginal people have rights in this country is a difficult one for many in our community to grapple with. That Aboriginal people have the right to be consulted, to be up at the table when it comes to negotiating matters such as land is very difficult for those companies, or groups, or governments which have been accustomed to deciding that we need to use the land for a particular purpose, whether it be mining or pastoral or building new homes.[25]

TERRITORY LAND RIGHTS IN THE HIGH COURT

The ALRA had a litigious history involving contests between applicants and the Northern Territory Government and other parties in relation to a variety of issues, many focusing on the jurisdiction of the Commissioner and the legal limits on the class of land available for claim. In a sense this foreshadowed the extinguishment debates of the native title era. The attempts by the Northern Territory Government to extend town sites to take land out of the category of unalienated Crown land, available for claim, was a case in point. The High Court was involved in deciding many of these matters. There are no less than fourteen reported decisions of the Court touching matters connected with the administration of the Act. Ron Castan appeared as counsel in seven of them. The issues raised in the cases were various.

i. Whether land under a pastoral lease held by the Aboriginal Land Fund was thereby 'alienated' and unavailable for claim.[26]
ii. Whether the validity of regulations extending town areas to exclude land from claim could be considered by the Lands Commissioner.[27]
iii. Whether the Commissioner had failed to deal properly with evidence in relation to sites and their significance to the question of traditional Aboriginal ownership.[28]
iv. Whether the Commissioner had to have regard in making his recommendation to the effect of a grant on third parties.[29]
v. Whether Crown land unalienated at the time of application remained available for claim notwithstanding subsequent rezoning as a town.[30]

vi. Whether the grant by the Crown of a perpetual lease on land under claim to the Northern Territory Development Land Corporation after the inquiry had commenced was valid and/or took the land out of the claim.[31]
vii. Whether a claim could be made to part of traditional country when all relevant sacred sites were outside the claim area.[32]
viii. The obligation of the Minister to take into account the detrimental effect of a grant on applicants for mining leases in the claim area.[33]
ix. Whether legal professional privilege existed in relation to communications between the Northern Territory Government and its legal officers with respect to regulations extending the townships of Darwin and Katherine with a view to excluding areas around them from claim.[34]
x. Whether the assignee of an agreement under section 44(2) of the ALRA which permitted mining of uranium at the Ranger Project Area in Kakadu was authorised by the *Atomic Energy Act* to enter Aboriginal land the subject of a grant under the ALRA.[35]
xi. Unconscionable dealing by the Commonwealth and whether it owed a fiduciary duty to the traditional Aboriginal owners in relation to an agreement under the ALRA.[36]
xii. Whether Aboriginal claimants waived legal professional privilege in relation to source materials for a claim book by lodging the book with the Commissioner.[37]
xiii. Whether the Commissioner could recommend the grant of land on which a research station was conducted by the Northern Territory Government.[38]
xiv. Whether Cabinet notes could be required to be produced in proceedings set aside at agreement between the Northern Land Council and the Commonwealth under section 44(2) of the ALRA.[39]

The ALRA provided for the restoration of some areas of land to Aboriginal control and gave legislative recognition to Aboriginal rights and interests in that land.[40] Section 50, which described the function of the Commissioner, was not to be construed as though contained in 'a textbook on traditional land tenures in the feudal system'. Its context was the novel concepts and arrangements that entered into Australian law through the provision of statutory land rights.[41] Importantly, however, statutory land rights, while providing a legal framework within which Traditional Owners could exercise their rights under Indigenous law and custom, did not operate as a model of such rights. Having regard to the nature of traditional ownership described by Justice Brennan as 'primarily a spiritual affair rather than a bundle of rights', they could not.[42]

In these cases, the High Court was essentially involved in the construction of a Commonwealth statute in the context of what were largely judicial review applications. But it was a statute in which the concept of traditional land ownership was firmly embedded and recognised by the Court. The Court was also exposed to the very adversarial relationship between the Territory government and the statutory representatives of Traditional Owners. And in the context of an agreement made under section 44(2) of the Act, common law native title was raised before the Court in 1987. It arose in the long-running litigation between the Northern Land Council and the Commonwealth over their 1978 agreement about the mining of uranium in the Ranger Project Area. The Council sought rescission of the agreement. It alleged unconscionable conduct and breach of fiduciary duty by the Commonwealth in connection with the making of the agreement. The statement of claim was amended in October 1986 to include an allegation that the Traditional Owners had native title in the land preceding the vesting of the land in the Land Trust established under the ALRA. The existence of this antecedent native title was relied upon in support of the plea of a fiduciary relationship with the Crown. The Court rejected the existence of a fiduciary duty based upon the statute alone but went on to say:

> Whether the nature of the relationship at common law between an identified group of Aboriginal people and the unalienated Crown lands which they have used and occupied historically and still use and occupy is such as to found a fiduciary relationship or a trust of some kind is a question of fundamental importance which has not been argued on the present stated case.[43]

Members of what was to be the *Mabo* Court, involved in many of these decisions, were Justices Mason, Brennan, Deane and Dawson. Justice Mason covered the entire span of the cases to which reference has been made. Justice Toohey was directly involved as the first Aboriginal Land Commissioner, seeing and hearing evidence on country under claim, including evidence from Traditional Owners, anthropologists and other experts. When the first *Mabo* decision was made, seven of the land rights judgments listed above had been given. Another six had been given by the time *Mabo [No. 2]* was delivered.

It would be unwise to link the High Court's recognition of native title in 1992 too directly to its exposure to a decade of land rights litigation.

But the values informing the ALRA, as enunciated by Woodward, could not have been lost on the Court. There was a strong normative element in the *Mabo* judgment. It is not unreasonable to suppose that some of it may have been informed by the experience of that contentious statute. But there was another very strong and more explicit normative input which also had significant practical consequences for native title law. That was the *Racial Discrimination Act 1975* (Cth) (RDA), the vehicle by which Australia honoured its obligations under the International Convention for the Elimination of all Forms of Racial Discrimination.

THE *RACIAL DISCRIMINATION ACT 1975*, *MABO [NO. 1]* AND THE RACE POWER

Native title, once recognised, initially derived much of the protection which it enjoyed not from the act of recognition, but from the RDA. Section 9 of the RDA provides:

> (1) It is unlawful for a person to do any act involving a distinction, exclusion, restriction of preference based on race, colour, descent or national or ethnic origin which has the purpose or effect of nullifying or impairing the recognition, enjoyment or exercise, on an equal footing, of any human right or fundamental freedom in the political, economic, social, cultural or any other field of public life.
>
> ...
>
> (2) A reference in this section to a human right or fundamental freedom in the political, economic, social, cultural or any other field of public life includes any right of a kind referred to in Article 5 of the Convention.

Ron Castan played an important role in securing the constitutional validity of that section, and of the RDA generally, in the *Koowarta* case.[44] In 1974 the Aboriginal Land Fund Commission, a Commonwealth authority, entered into an agreement to take a transfer of a Crown lease of a pastoral property in Queensland. The Minister for Lands in Queensland refused consent to the transfer under the *Land Act 1962* (Qld). He did so in furtherance of a government policy which opposed the acquisition by Aboriginal people of large areas of land in the state. John Koowarta was a member of the Winychanam Group for whose use the Commission had contracted to buy the Crown lease. Koowarta commenced proceedings in the Supreme Court of Queensland against the then Premier Bjelke-Petersen and other members of the Queensland Government. He claimed damages under section 25 of the RDA. Queensland challenged the statement of claim on the grounds that the RDA was outside the legislative power of the Commonwealth and was invalid. John Koowarta was represented by Castan. As junior counsel appearing with him were Paul De Jersey, now Chief Justice of Queensland, and Tony Skoien, now a Judge of the District Court of Queensland. The Commonwealth intervened to support the validity of the Act. The Solicitor-General, the late Sir Maurice Byers QC, represented the Commonwealth; Ian Hanger from Queensland and myself from Western Australia were his junior counsel.

Two provisions of the Commonwealth Constitution were in issue. The primary provision debated was the power of the Commonwealth to make laws with respect to external affairs (section 51(xxix)). The second was the power of the Commonwealth to make laws for the people of any race for whom it is deemed necessary to make special laws (section 51(xxvi)). The latter provision had been amended by constitutional referendum in 1967 to remove the exclusion of Aboriginal people.

Four of the seven justices held that the provisions of sections 9 and 12 of the RDA were valid laws with respect to external affairs. This was globalisation at work through the nation's Constitution. For in this case the High Court upheld the validity of laws made by the Australian Parliament, which imported norms of conduct derived from international law and applied them to the way in which Australians were to deal with each other. The dissenters saw the growth of the external affairs power as generating new subjects of legislative hegemony for the Commonwealth and eroding the federal balance of powers established by the Constitution.[45] Sir Ninian Stephen, who formed part of the majority, encapsulated the High Court's acknowledgment of globalisation:

> The great post-war expansion of the areas properly the subject-matter of international agreement has…made it difficult indeed to identify subject-matters which are of their nature not of international but of only domestic concern… But this does no more than reflect the increasing awareness of the nations of the world that the state of society in other countries is very relevant to the state of their own society.[46]

The growth in the content of the external affairs power reflected 'the new global concern for human rights and the international acknowledgement of the need for universally recognized norms of conduct, particularly in relation to the suppression of racial discrimination'.[47] These universally recognised norms of conduct were also to play a role in the *Mabo* litigation, which went beyond defining the content of the external affairs power to informing the development of the common law itself.

The race power under section 51(xxvi) was also relied upon by those arguing for validity. However, it was held not to support the Act because the Act applied equally to all persons and was therefore not a special law for the people of any one race. In the course of their judgments, however, a number of the justices expressed the obiter view that the race power would support laws which discriminated against the people of a particular race, as well as laws discriminating in favour of a particular race.[48] Justice Mason, having found the act supported by the external affairs power, did not consider whether it was also supported by the race power and expressed no view as to the scope of that power. Justice Murphy considered the power could only be exercised for the benefit of the peoples of a particular race but did not elaborate.[49]

The race power was again considered by the High Court in the *Tasmanian Dam* case in 1983.[50] Ron Castan appeared for the Commonwealth with the Solicitor-General, Sir Maurice Byers QC. The case concerned a number of constitutional issues affecting the validity of Commonwealth legislation under which the Commonwealth sought to restrain Tasmania and its Hydro-Electric Commission from proceeding with the construction of a dam on the Gordon River. Certain parts of the *World Heritage Properties Conservation Act 1983* (Cth) provided protection for specified Aboriginal sites. Section 8 of the Act declared that it was necessary to enact the protective provisions as special laws for the people of the Aboriginal race. Four of the justices, Justices Mason, Murphy, Brennan and Deane, held that the provisions were within the legislative power under section 51(xxvi) of the Constitution. In a passage that again may be regarded as reflecting the conceptual scene setting for the later recognition of native title, Justice Mason said:

> the cultural heritage of a people is so much of a characteristic or property of the people to whom it belongs that it is inseparably connected with them, so that a legislative power with respect to the people of a race, which confers power to make laws to protect them, necessarily extends to the making of laws protecting their cultural heritage.[51]

There were now two justices, Justices Murphy and Brennan, prepared to say that the race power could only be exercised to benefit the people of the particular race to which its exercise was directed. Justice Brennan said:

> The approval of the proposed law for the amendment of par (xxvi) by deleting the words 'other than the aboriginal race' was an affirmation of the will of the Australian people that the odious policies of oppression and neglect of Aboriginal citizens were to be at an end, and that the primary object of the power is beneficial. The passing of the *Racial Discrimination Act* manifested the Parliament's intention that the power will hereafter be used only for the purpose of discriminatorily conferring benefits upon the people of a race for whom it is deemed necessary to make special laws.[52]

The RDA, having been held to be valid, at least so far as sections 9 and 12 were concerned, was to play a critical role in the progress of the *Mabo* litigation towards the recognition of native title for the Meriam people. That litigation commenced in 1982 with a writ and statement of claim filed in the High Court. Interlocutory steps were lengthy. On 26 February 1986, the Chief Justice of the High Court, Sir Harry Gibbs, remitted the matter for trial of all factual issues to the Supreme Court of Queensland. The trial began on 13 October 1986 but, the time set aside being patently inadequate, it was adjourned, part heard, on 17 November.[53]

In the meantime Queensland had passed the *Queensland Coast Islands Declaratory Act 1985*. The Act applied to islands in the Torres Strait that were part of the State of Queensland and included Mer. It declared that upon the islands becoming part of Queensland, they were vested in the Crown in right of Queensland 'freed from all other rights, interests and claims of any kind whatsoever'.[54] The State amended its defence and pleaded the Act against the *Mabo* claim. Its asserted effect was to extinguish the rights which Mabo and the other plaintiffs claimed in Mer and to deny any right of compensation in respect of that extinction.[55] The validity of the Act and the viability of Queensland's newly pleaded defence were challenged by the plaintiffs on a demurrer in the High Court, which was argued in March 1988. Ron Castan was counsel for the plaintiffs. In December 1988 a majority of the justices held that the Act was inconsistent with section 10 of the RDA. In substance that section provides that if a Commonwealth state or territory law discriminates between persons of different race, colour, national or ethnic origin, so that a person from one group enjoys a right to a lesser extent than a person from another, then, by force of the Commonwealth law, they shall enjoy the right to the same extent. In the joint judgment in what became known as *Mabo [No. 1]*, Justices Brennan, Toohey and Gaudron said:

6. The High Court and recognition of native title

> In practical terms, this means that if traditional native title was not extinguished before the *Racial Discrimination Act* came into force, a State law which seeks to extinguish it now will fail. It will fail because s 10(1) of the *Racial Discrimination Act* clothes the holders of traditional native title who are of the native ethnic group with the same immunity from legislative interference with their enjoyment of their human right to own and inherit property as it clothes other persons in the community. A State law which, by purporting to extinguish native title, would limit that immunity in the case of the native group cannot prevail over s 10(1) of the *Racial Discrimination Act* which restores the immunity to the extent enjoyed by the general community. The attempt by the 1985 Act to extinguish the traditional legal rights of the Miriam people therefore fails.[56]

The invalidation of the Queensland law raised the question whether other state or territory laws or executive acts, done after the RDA came into effect, might be invalid because of their discriminatory operation in relation to native title, if native title were able to be recognised. For the Commonwealth there was the further question whether its laws or executive acts might have operated to effect acquisitions of native title rights without just compensation and therefore contrary to the requirements of the Constitution. None of this would matter, of course, if native title were not able to be recognised at common law. And that question remained to be answered in *Mabo [No. 2]*. But it is not surprising that when native title was recognised in *Mabo [No. 2]*, it gave life to the general issue of the validity of past acts implied in *Mabo [No. 1]* and the need to ensure that future acts affecting native title did not offend against the RDA or the requirements of the Constitution. The question of compliance with the RDA had particular implications for state and territory governments in relation to land use management, and for the pastoral and mining industries and other users of land in areas in which native title claims might arise. So it was that Castan was able to say in 1993 that the RDA lay at the heart of the *Mabo* debate.[57] As he wrote:

> It is the *Racial Discrimination Act* which has so frightened and angered the politicians, the miners, the pastoralists, the journalists and some lawyers. For if indigenous people have rights to land, then those rights may only be taken away in a non-discriminatory way. Thus since 1975 the continuing dispossession of Aboriginal people may have been unlawful, unless the RDA is overridden or suspended.[58]

MABO [NO. 2] — THE ACT OF RECOGNITION

The decision of the High Court in *Mabo [No. 2]*,⁵⁹ in which Ron Castan again appeared for the plaintiffs, was the culmination of ten years of forensic effort. It was an act of legal recognition expressed in the declaration made on 3 June 1992 that 'the Meriam people are entitled as against the whole world to possession, occupation, use and enjoyment of the lands of the Murray Islands'.⁶⁰

The 'recognition' was, however, limited and qualified in its terms by reference to a parcel of land leased to the Trustees of the Australian Board of Missions and other parcels of land validly appropriated for use for administrative purposes which use was inconsistent with the continued enjoyment of the rights and privileges of the Meriam people under native title. The recognition was also qualified by the further declaration made:

> that the title of the Meriam People is subject to the power of the Parliament of Queensland and the power of the Governor in Council of Queensland to extinguish that title by valid exercise of their respective powers, provided any exercise of those powers is not inconsistent with the laws of the Commonwealth.⁶¹

The orders declared rights enforceable at law under the designation 'Possession, occupation, use and enjoyment…as against the whole world'. The rights so declared were, however, subject to extinguishment. The orders reflected the two metaphors of recognition and extinguishment, key elements in the High Court's jurisprudence of native title from the outset.

The essential principles underpinning the common law of native title in Australia, or what may be called the common law rules for the recognition of native title as set out in the *Mabo* decision, can be summarised thus:

1. The colonisation of Australia by England did not extinguish rights and interest in land held by Aboriginal and Torres Strait Islander people according to their own law and custom.⁶²
2. The native title of Aboriginal and Torres Strait Islander people under their law and custom will be recognised by the common law of Australia and can be protected under that law.⁶³
3. When the Crown acquired each of the Australian colonies, it acquired sovereignty over the land within them. In the exercise of that sovereignty, native title could be extinguished by laws or executive grants which indicated a plain and clear intention to do so — e.g. grants of freehold title.⁶⁴

4. To secure the recognition of native title today, it is necessary to show that the Aboriginal or Torres Strait Islander group said to hold the native title:
   (a) has a continuing connection with the land in question and has rights and interests in the land under Aboriginal or Torres Strait Islander traditional law and custom, as the case may be;[65]
   (b) the group continues to observe laws and customs which define its ownership of rights and interests in the land.[66]
5. Under common law, native title has the following characteristics:
   (a) it is communal in character although it may give rise to individual rights;[67]
   (b) it cannot be bought or sold;[68]
   (c) it may be transmitted from one group to another according to traditional law and custom;[69]
   (d) the traditional law and custom under which native title arises can change over time and in response to historical circumstances.[70]
6. Native title is subject to existing valid laws and rights created under such laws.[71]

These principles embody the rules of what is said to constitute legal 'recognition' of Indigenous relationships to land defined by traditional law and custom. They do not operate directly upon those relationships or the traditional laws and customs from which they are derived. And that is so even where common law native title is said to be extinguished. For such extinguishment is no more than a qualification of the common law rules of recognition. It says nothing about their subject matter.

Before considering further the notions of recognition and extinguishment, it is useful to bear in mind the normative setting of the legal act of recognition which the Court undertook. The decision was a manifestation of the continuing globalisation of Australian law. It was also reflective of perceived contemporary social or community values. This is made explicit in the judgment of Justice Brennan, with whom Chief Justice Mason and Justice McHugh agreed. Justice Brennan aligned what he called 'the expectations of the international community' with 'the contemporary values of the Australian people' and said:

> It is contrary both to international standards and to the fundamental values of our common law to entrench a discriminatory rule which, because of the supposed position on the scale of social organization of the indigenous inhabitants of a settled colony, denies them a right to occupy their traditional lands.[72]

Justices Deane, Gaudron and Toohey made no express reference to international norms of conduct. Justices Deane and Gaudron referred, however, to longstanding principles of 'natural law' embodied in the works of early international law jurists such as Wolff, Vattel, de Victoria and Grotius.[73] They also referred to authority applicable to a wide spectrum of British colonies including New Zealand and Canada. In so doing, they accepted as a correct general statement of the common law what the Privy Council said in *Adeyinka Oyekan v Musendika Adele*, that 'the courts will assume that the British Crown intends that the rights of property of the inhabitants are to be fully respected'.[74]

When they posed for themselves the normative question, 'Should the proposition supported by the Australian cases and past practice be accepted?', Justices Deane and Gaudron did not mince their words. They saw the terra nullius principle and the proposition that full legal and beneficial ownership of all the land in the Australian colonies was vested in the Crown at annexation as 'the legal basis for the dispossession of the Aboriginal peoples of most of their traditional lands'; they said:

> acts and events by which that dispossession in legal theory was carried into practical effect constitute the darkest aspect of the history of this nation. The nation as a whole must remain diminished unless and until there is an acknowledgment of, and retreat from, those past injustices.[75]

As Justice Gummow was to observe later in his judgment in the *Wik* case, the majority judges in *Mabo [No. 2]* moved to a new and particular view of past historical events upon which they declared the content of the common law. The gist of *Mabo [No. 2]* lay in the holding that the long-understood refusal in Australia to accommodate concepts of native title within the common law rested upon past assumptions of historical fact now shown to be false.[76] That shift of view was affected by powerful normative considerations.

What, then, is the nature of the recognition which the common law accords to Indigenous relationships to the land. As already observed, it does not affect those relationships. It is expressed in a declaration of rights comprehensible in common law terms. This does not mean a selection of closest analogues from the common law library. There is, however, a right or set of rights, whether expressed severally or holistically, that are ascertained in the common law universe when a determination is made. They answer to the designation 'common law native title'. They are *sui generis*, or unique, creatures of the common law. To the extent that the word 'title' suggests a land law analogue, it is, as Justice Toohey said, 'artificial and capable of misleading'.[77]

The character of common law native title as *sui generis* is mandated by the range of traditional Indigenous relationships to country that may be recognised. Justice Brennan was prepared to categorise what he called 'the interest possessed by a community that is in exclusive possession of land' as 'proprietary'.[78] This classification could be made even though the land was inalienable according to traditional law and custom. And it could be made even though individual members of the community might enjoy usufructuary rights that themselves are not proprietary in nature.[79] It is questionable, though, whether they can accommodate the full range of spiritual relationships with land, including the relationship maintained at a distance which was seen as capable of recognition by the Full Court of the Federal Court in *Western Australia v Ward*.[80]

Justices Deane and Gaudron unequivocally rejected the proposition that Indigenous relationships to land, able to be recognised by the common law, were confined to 'interests which were analogous to common law concepts of estates in land or proprietary rights'.[81] They rejected the narrow approach of the Privy Council in *In re Southern Rhodesia* in favour of the more flexible principles expressed in *Amodu Tijani* and *Adeyinka Oyekan*. It was inappropriate to force native title to conform to traditional common law concepts. It should be accepted as *sui generis*.[82]

Justice Toohey, speaking of common law native title, in my respectful opinion, stated the position most clearly when he said, 'In the case of the Meriam people (and the Aboriginal people of Australia generally), what is involved is "a special collective right vested in an Aboriginal group by virtue of its long residence and communal use of land or its resources"'.[83] Here his Honour was quoting from the report of the Australian Law Reform Commission on the Recognition of Aboriginal Customary Laws (1986). He added that 'in truth what the courts are asked to recognise are simply rights exercised by indigenous peoples in regard to land, sufficiently comprehensive and continuous so as to survive annexation'.[84]

What, then, is the 'recognition' of native title? To speak of recognition by the common law is in one sense to personify the common law and attribute to it a cognitive function. Avoiding personification and cognitive metaphors, recognition can be regarded as the outcome of the application of rules under which certain rights arising at common law are ascertained which vest in an Indigenous community by virtue of its relationship to land or waters.

When the fundamental propositions of the common law of native title enunciated in *Mabo* are understood as rules of recognition, a proper distinction can be drawn between the content of Indigenous law and custom and that of the common law. The common law does not operate directly upon the traditional laws and customs or the relationships with land to which they give rise. That is so even where native title is extinguished. For extinguishment is a barring or qualification of the common law rules of recognition. It has nothing to say about traditional law or custom or the relationship of Aboriginal people to their land.

The identification of Indigenous groups, their rules of definition and membership, their traditions and customs, their relationship to land and waters to which they relate may be described and interpreted in court proceedings by anthropologists and other experts. Those things constitute the subjects of the common law of native title. The common law establishes the rules — lawyer-made or, to be more precise, judge-made — which are the rules for recognition. Certain benefits attach to that recognition. They include common law protections for that which is recognised. Beyond the common law protections there are those conferred by statute such as the prohibition against discriminatory impairment conferred by the RDA, the right to negotiate and the entitlement to compensation for extinguishment or impairment conferred by the NTA. The rules of recognition are qualified and limited in their terms and by the provisions of the NTA. The common law native title which they yield is a poor reflection of the full cultural, historical and human reality from which it is derived. They are confined and reductionist although ambulatory in nature. They refract that holistic reality as through a prism into specified rights and interests. Nevertheless, they largely define the terms of the debate in which lawyers who participate in native title litigation, applicants and their expert witnesses must engage if recognition, for what it is worth, is to be invoked.

Justice Brennan used the term 'extinguish' as a label for the consequence of acts of the Crown wholly or partially inconsistent with the continuing right to enjoy native title. His Honour also used it in a quite different sense when he said:

> Native title to an area of land which a clan or group is entitled to enjoy under the laws and customs of an indigenous people is extinguished if the clan or group, by ceasing to acknowledge those laws, and (so far as practicable) observe those customs, loses its connexion with the land or on the death of the last of the members of the group or clan.[85]

The use of extinguishment in these two senses risks confusing two quite different concepts. One is that of extinguishment as a limit on common law recognition which does not, and cannot, of itself affect the relationship between the Indigenous group and its country. The other concerns the loss of that relationship which means there is no subject matter for recognition by the common law.

The idea of extinguishment as a limit on what the common law can do is affected by the nature of the metaphor that the word imports. It is too easy to think of common law extinguishment as something which annihilates the Indigenous relationship to country. But as Justice Toohey said in the *Wik* case, native title rights affected by inconsistent grants are 'unenforceable at law and, *in that sense,* extinguished'.[86] There is a risk, in using this metaphor, of conceptual confusion. Indeed, it may be an impediment to the development of a coherent theory of extinguishment which is best regarded as a mutable rule of recognition or non-recognition.

In *Fejo v Northern Territory of Australia*[87] the High Court held that native title is extinguished by a grant in fee simple and is not revived if the land reverts to the Crown. In explaining the common law underpinning for this proposition, their Honours said, 'The underlying existence of the traditional laws and customs is a *necessary* pre-requisite for native title but their existence is not a *sufficient* basis for recognising native title'.[88] In dealing with the issue of the revival of native title, it was said —

> The rights created by the exercise of sovereign power being inconsistent with native title, the rights and interests that together make up that native title were necessarily at an end. There can be no question, then, of those rights springing forth again when the land came to be held again by the Crown. Their recognition has been overtaken by the exercise of 'the power to create and to extinguish private rights and interests in land within the Sovereign's territory'.[89]

— putting the matter as one about recognition rather than any direct operation upon the traditional laws and customs of the people.

The NTA tries to give permanence to extinguishment by its definition of the word in section 237A which provides:

> The word 'extinguish', in relation to native title, means permanently extinguish the native title. To avoid any doubt, this means that after the extinguishment the native title rights and interests cannot revive, even if the act that caused the extinguishment ceases to have effect.

This definition only applies to extinguishment for which the Act provides. But extinguishment recognised by the common law is mutable; whether derived from common law or imposed by statute, it can be reversed by statute law. The NTA itself demonstrates the revocability of the concept in sections 47, 47A and 47B. Those sections provide that under certain circumstances prior extinguishment of native title is to be disregarded for all purposes under the Act. Those circumstances relate to pastoral leases held by native title claimants and to reserves and vacant Crown land covered by claimant applications.

In summary, *Mabo [No. 2]* established rules of recognition creating or ascertaining common law native title as *sui generis* rights and interests which could be enjoyed by Indigenous communities whose relationship to the land in question fell within those rules. The rules are qualified or limited by rules relating to extinguishment of common law native title.

I should acknowledge that Noel Pearson has written about rules of recognition, although he places native title in what he calls a 'recognition space' which belongs neither to the Indigenous or common law universes.[90] This analysis also carries with it the implication that extinguishment is no more than a limitation or qualification upon recognition. That view is supported in *Lardil v State of Queensland*.[91]

THE STATUTORY RESPONSE — THE NTA

The requirements in *Mabo [No. 2]* for the proof of traditional title and the complexity of the interaction of common law native title with Commonwealth, state and territory laws and grants made under such laws meant that the litigation of claims for common law native title would be time consuming and expensive. A process was needed to facilitate recognition by agreement where that was possible. In the meantime dealings with land were proceeding and there was a need to protect Indigenous communities pending the recognition of their title at common law and, when recognised or otherwise, to provide for compensation where the common law native title was found to be extinguished or impaired. The general question of validity raised by *Mabo [No. 1]* in respect of past acts of the states and territories had to be addressed, as did the possible invalidity of past Commonwealth acts for non-compliance with requirements of the Constitution that the acquisition of property be on just terms.

The NTA had, as its objectives, the establishment of a process for the recognition of native title, the protection of native title in respect of future acts and the validation of past acts. It established the National Native Title Tribunal to receive applications for determinations of common law native title, to accept and register them, to notify and identify parties, and to assist applicants and parties to reach negotiated outcomes. Provision was made for applications to be referred to the Federal Court for determination in the event that agreement was not achieved.

In respect of the protection of native title, governments proposing to pass laws or do executive acts affecting native title were required to observe a non-discrimination principle in relation to native title holders. Onshore dealings with land affecting native title holders were to be done in a way that would not discriminate between them and freeholders. Entitlements to compensation were created. Provision for compulsory negotiation and arbitration was made in respect of the grants of mining and mining exploration tenements and the acquisition by governments of native title rights and interests where the purpose of the acquisition was to confer rights or interests on a third party.

Legislative and executive past acts of the Commonwealth, which were invalid to an extent because of their impact on native title, were validated by the Act subject to compensation. The states and territories were permitted to pass laws to validate their own past acts. Validation so effected or authorised was linked to statutory extinguishment, partial extinguishment or temporary suppression of native title and to compensation rights according to the class of past act validated. Freehold grants and pastoral, residential and commercial leases so validated extinguished native title completely albeit the effect of the leases at common law was not addressed by the Act.

THE FIRST CHALLENGE — THE *NATIVE TITLE ACT* CASE

Immediately prior to the passage of the NTA, the Western Australian Parliament passed the *Land (Titles and Traditional Usage) Act 1993* (WA). The Act purported to extinguish native title and to replace it with statutory rights of traditional usage under a regime prescribed by that Act. Western Australia also commenced proceedings against the Commonwealth seeking a declaration that there was no part of Western Australia in which, or in relation to which, there were 'native title' or 'native title rights and interests' within the meaning of the NTA and that the Act, in so far as it had application in respect of such rights and interests, had no operation in, or in relation to, Western Australia. Alternatively, a declaration was sought that the Commonwealth Act was beyond the legislative powers of the Commonwealth and invalid.⁹² In the same year, Indigenous groups, the Wororra people and the Martu peoples, sued the State of Western Australia in the High Court seeking declarations that the state Act was invalid for inconsistency with the provisions of the RDA and/or the provisions of the NTA. Ron Castan appeared for the Martu peoples.⁹³

The Court held that the history of the establishment of the Colony of Western Australia did not reveal an intention on the part of the Crown to extinguish generally the native title existing over land within the proposed colonial boundaries. The presumption that the acquiring sovereign did not intend to extinguish native title was not rebutted. The holders of statutory rights under the state Act were found not to enjoy the same security in the enjoyment of those rights as would the holders of common law native title. The state Act was therefore inconsistent with section 10(1) of the RDA and was invalid to the extent of the inconsistency by operation of section 109 of the Constitution.

The NTA was held to be a valid law of the Commonwealth, supported by the race power conferred by section 51(xxvi) of the Constitution. It was a 'special' law for the purposes of the race power, as it conferred uniquely on Indigenous holders of native title a benefit protective of their native title. *Koowarta* and the *Tasmanian Dam* case were applied. The question whether such a law was 'necessary' in terms of section 51(xxvi) was a matter for parliament and there were no grounds on which the Court could review parliament's decision if it had the power to do so.

The Court rejected an argument that the NTA purported to control the exercise of legislative power by Western Australia or directly to render its laws invalid. It did not impermissibly discriminate against Western Australia or impair its ability to function as a state. The requirement imposed by the Act that the state should pay compensation if it exercised a power of compulsory acquisition imposed a burden on the exercise of state power but did so as an incident of the protection of native title. The race power was not impliedly limited so as to prevent the Commonwealth from protecting the holders of native title in that way. Section 12 of the NTA, a curious provision, which purported to give to the common law of native title the force of a Commonwealth statute, was held to be invalid.

Six of the justices, Chief Justice Mason and Justices Brennan, Deane, Toohey, Gaudron and McHugh, delivered a joint judgment. Justice Dawson wrote separate reasons but substantially agreed with the majority and agreed with the outcomes proposed which were by way of answers

6. The High Court and recognition of native title

to questions which had been reserved to the Full Court by Chief Justice Mason. The rule of recognition of traditional Aboriginal title and of extinguishment was encapsulated in the following passage in the joint judgment:

> Under the common law, as stated in *Mabo [No 2]*, Aboriginal people and Torres Strait Islanders who are living in a traditional society possess, subject to the conditions stated in that case, native title to land that has not been alienated or appropriated by the Crown. The content of native title is ascertained by reference to the laws and customs of the people who possess that title, but their enjoyment of the title is precarious under the common law: it is defeasible by legislation or by the exercise of the Crown's (or a statutory authority's) power to grant inconsistent interests in the land or to appropriate the land and use it inconsistently with enjoyment of the native title.[94]

It is to be noted that the rule thus expressed assumes the process of recognition to be one of ascertaining common law native title as a right already possessed by those who satisfy the conditions of recognition set out in *Mabo [No. 2]*.

The extinguishment principle was stated early in the joint judgment in the context of Western Australia's submission that native title in that state had been extinguished upon annexation. Their Honours said:

> After sovereignty is acquired, native title can be extinguished by a positive act which is expressed to achieve that purpose generally… provided the act is valid and its effect is not qualified by a law which prevails over it or over the law which authorises the act. Again, after sovereignty is acquired, native title to a particular parcel of land can be extinguished by the doing of an act that is inconsistent with the continued right of Aborigines to enjoy native title to that parcel — for example, a grant by the Crown of a parcel of land in fee simple — provided the act is valid and its effect is not qualified by a law which prevails over it or over the law which authorises the act.[95]

It is clear enough from this passage that extinguishment operates upon the common law native title rights which would otherwise exist. It identifies two modes of extinguishment. The first is a law or an act expressed to achieve that outcome. The second is by a law or act which is inconsistent with the enjoyment of common law native title.

Against this background, the Court characterised the NTA as removing the common law defeasibility of native title and securing Aboriginal people and Torres Strait Islanders in the enjoyment of their native title subject to prescribed exceptions which provided for it to be extinguished or impaired. The Act provided only three exceptions. The first was the occurrence of a past act which had been validated; the second, an agreement on the part of the native title holders; and the third, the doing of a permissible future act.[96] So the Act effectively limited the application of the extinguishment qualification upon common law recognition of native title to the circumstances for which it provided or which it authorised. The Court's characterisation of the Act was necessary to determine whether it was supported by the race power. It was seen as conferring its protection upon native title holders who, *ex hypothesi*, are members of a particular race. The observation of Justice Deane in the *Tasmanian Dam* case that the relationship between Aboriginal people and the lands which they occupy lies at the heart of traditional Aboriginal cultural and traditional Aboriginal life was cited as indicating the undoubted significance of security in the enjoyment of native title by its holders.

The judgment is important for its discussion of the race power which carries the unusual conditions that it must be 'deemed necessary' that 'special laws' be made for 'the people of any race'. The special quality of a law made pursuant to the race power was to be ascertained by reference to its differential operation upon the people of a particular race. The possibility that the power might be exercised to the disadvantage of a particular race was implicit in the observation of the joint judgment that '[a] special quality appears when the law confers a right or benefit or imposes an obligation or disadvantage especially on the people of a particular race'.[97]

The NTA was held to be 'special' in that it conferred uniquely on the Aboriginal and Torres Strait Islander holders of native title a benefit protective of their native title. Whether it was 'necessary' to enact the law was a matter for the parliament to decide and, having regard to *Mabo [No. 2]*, there were no grounds on which the Court could review the parliament's decision, even assuming it had power to do so.[98] So Western Australia's submission that the NTA generally did not answer the constitutional description of a law within section 51(xxvi) was rejected.

The Court also considered the relationship between the RDA and the NTA. It pointed out that the RDA 'protects native title holders against *discriminatory* extinction or impairment of native title'.[99] The NTA, on the other hand, 'protects [them] against *any* extinction or impairment of native title subject to the specific and detailed exceptions which the Act prescribes or permits'.[100]

FOCUS ON NEGOTIATION — THE *WAANYI* CASE

The validity of the NTA and the invalidity of the Western Australian Act having been established in the NTA case, it fell to the Court in the *Waanyi* decision to consider the operation of the registration and mediation provisions for which the Act provided.[101] In that case, as President of the National Native Title Tribunal, I had directed that an application by the Waanyi people over land in the area of the proposed Century Zinc mine in North Queensland not be registered on the basis of the extinguishing effect of prior pastoral leases granted in the area. An appeal to the Full Court was dismissed. The High Court held that the procedure adopted, which included receiving material and submissions from the state and affected mining companies, was wrong, that the claim was fairly arguable and that the application should have been accepted. Again, Ron Castan appeared for the appellants. The Court observed that it was 'inevitable that the recognition of native title by the common law and its protection by the [RDA] would generate novel legal problems relating to the title to land claimed by Aborigines in accordance with traditional laws and customs'.[102] The issues of fact raised by claims to native title 'were complex and, in the event of opposition, would be likely to take significant time and resources … to determine'.[103] The preservation of the status quo pending determination of claims 'would pose a particular problem, not only for the claimants and the Crown but also for those who might be seeking access to the land for mining or other non-traditional purposes'.[104] The preamble to the NTA indicated a legislative preference for resolving these problems by negotiation.[105] It was necessary to read the NTA with an understanding of the novel, legal and administrative problems involved in the statutory recognition of native title. The Court recognised that the 'remoteness of many Aboriginal communities and their lack of familiarity with the legal criteria for determination of native title [would pose] practical difficulties for many people who might be entitled to claim [it]'.[106] The task of tracing the tenure history of any parcel of land during the previous two hundred years was likely to be beyond the resources of many prospective claimants. On the other hand, there was a 'perceived commercial need for despatch in the settlement of claims for native title and in the administrative disposition of applications by miners and others seeking access to unalienated land'.[107] Native title claims required an examination of facts that fell broadly into two categories — the continuity of the connection of the claimants and their ancestors with the land in which native title was claimed and the 'tenure history' of that land so far as it appeared from Crown grant, Crown licence or Crown use.[108] The Court adverted to two factors in favour of the determination of native title by negotiation and agreement rather than by judicial determination. The first was the saving in time and resources. The second, and perhaps more important, was 'if the persons interested in the determination of those issues negotiate and reach an agreement, they are enabled thereby to establish an amicable relationship between future neighbouring occupiers'.[109]

The Court's construction of the procedural provisions of the NTA in the *Waanyi* case did not involve any reflection on the common law of native title beyond its indication that the extinguishing effect of pastoral leases was an open question.

The decision in *Waanyi* had important implications for the screening processes of the Tribunal and the facility with which applications for native title determinations could be made and registered and the right to negotiate attracted. Acceptance of claims was to be based on the papers submitted by the applicants unless there were some extraneous indication that the claim was frivolous or vexatious.

This decision, combined with a line of Federal Court decisions that registration of claims was to be effected immediately upon lodgement and prior to acceptance,[110] had the practical result that some claims were lodged without adequate preparation, without proper consultation within the relevant Indigenous community and in competition with, and overlapping, other claims. In some cases in the Goldfields area, there were up to twenty overlapping claims on the same area of land. Each attracted the right to negotiate in relation to the grant of mining tenements. In the event it was accepted by all parties that there was a necessity to change the system for acceptance and registration of native title determination applications.

In the same volume of the *Commonwealth Law Reports* in which the NTA case is reported was another decision of the High Court which had nothing to do with native title but which sounded the death knell for the statutory scheme under the NTA in so far as it provided for the Tribunal, following a negotiation process, to make consent determinations and register them in the Federal Court to take effect as judgments of the Court. A similar regime in relation to the Human Rights and Equal Opportunity Commission was struck down by the Court in *Brandy v Human Rights and Equal Opportunity Commission*.[111] The Tribunal altered its procedures to direct them to the reaching of an agreement for the making of a consent determination on the basis that no determination would be made by the Tribunal; thereafter the matter would be referred to the Federal Court under section 74 of the NTA on the basis that no consent determination was made by the Tribunal and the parties would then seek a consent order directly from the Federal Court. This left in place the process whereby applications were received by the Tribunal and the Tribunal process had to be exhausted before the proceedings could be referred to the Federal Court.

WIK — EXTINGUISHMENT AND THE TIME-HONOURED METHODOLOGY OF THE COMMON LAW

The next decision of the High Court in *Wik Peoples v Queensland*[112] was concerned primarily with the question of extinguishment in relation to pastoral leases.

The decision was upon preliminary questions of law in a native title determination application pending in the Federal Court. It was the only native title case in which Ron Castan did not appear. The principal question concerned the prior grant of pastoral leases over areas of the land the subject of the application for a native title determination. By a majority of four to three, the High Court held that the law did not confer exclusive possession of the areas to which the pastoral leases applied and that the grants of the leases did not necessarily extinguish all incidents of native title.

The Court's conclusion turned upon a detailed consideration of the terms of the grants of the lease and the statutes under which they were made. The Court did not resolve the question whether the leases did extinguish native title in the areas to which they applied. That could only be decided after considering the particular native title rights and interests asserted and established. If there were inconsistency between the native title rights and interests and those conferred by the grants of the leases then the native title rights and interests would yield to that extent to the rights of the grantees. The test for extinguishment was considered in this case. In the NTA case two kinds of extinguishing law or executive acts were identified. The first was that expressed to extinguish native title. The second was that which extinguished by reason of inconsistency. Wik was concerned with the case of an act conferring what were said to be rights inconsistent with the enjoyment of common law native title.[113]

Justice Kirby addressed the nature of the interaction between the Indigenous relationship to the land and the non-Indigenous law. He referred to the submission by the Thayorre people that native title was outside the common law, had its own sources and integrity, and could not be destroyed by a legal theory outside its own regime, although the Australian legal system would determine whether and when it would grant recognition and enforcement. But the title itself would continue to exist. This argument he rejected as 'suggested neither by legal authority applicable to this country nor by legal principle or polity':

> What is in issue is *title* in respect of the land. …As such, it is not a question about the intention or actions of the Aboriginal parties, any more than of the Crown or governmental officials. The question is not whether indigenous people have *in fact* been expelled from traditional lands but whether those making claim to such lands have the *legal right* to exclude them.[114]

If what the Thayorre people were contending was that their relationship to their country as defined by traditional law and custom was independent of recognition by the common law, then it is difficult to see why Justice Kirby rejected their proposition. In any event, as will be seen, their proposition was consistent with what was later said in *Fejo*, discussed below.

A second contention that an agreement between the State of Queensland and Comalco (which was given the effect of a statute by an agreement Act) and the grant of mining leases pursuant to that agreement were in breach of requirements of procedural fairness and in breach of trust or a fiduciary duty owed to the applicants was rejected. The agreement had the force of law under the relevant agreement Act and obliged the state to grant the mining leases in issue. The validity of the leases could not be impugned for want of procedural fairness or breach of fiduciary duty.

Justice Gummow emphasised that to extrapolate native title principles from the particular circumstances of the case to an 'assumed generality of Australian conditions and history' would be 'pregnant with the possibility of injustice to the many, varied and complex interests involved across Australia as a whole': the better guide was the method of the common law 'whereby principle is developed from the issues in one case to those which arise in the next'.[115] Consistently with this view, it was apparent from all the judgments that the question of extinguishment of native title by statutory grants and interests generally would be resolved on a case by case basis. It was of little consolation to those who were the grantees of pastoral leases that if native title rights and interests subsisted in the same land, they must yield to the rights and interests conferred by the statutory grant. They were concerned about facing an inchoate regime of coexisting rights. Miners seeking to conduct operations on land which was or had been the subject of a pastoral lease were now subject to the right to negotiate processes of the NTA. Governments were concerned about the validity of acts done on the assumption that pastoral leases had extinguished native title. From their perspective, the 'time honoured methodology of the common law' referred to by Justice Gummow was not going to deliver certainty of outcomes nor, on the High Court's record to that point, the outcomes they wanted. These concerns, combined with the agendas of some state governments in relation to their land management powers, forced substantial amendments to the Act.

THE 1998 AMENDMENTS TO THE NATIVE TITLE ACT

The *Wik* decision may be viewed, from a legal perspective, as a not very dramatic application of the *Mabo* principles embodying the proposition that just because a statutory grant is called a lease does not mean it has the incidents of a lease at common law. The practical impact of the decision for the pastoral and mining industries and for state governments, however, generated the political momentum which led to the 1998 amendments to the NTA.

Some amendments had been foreshadowed by reason of the decision in *Brandy*, referred to earlier. Indeed, a Bill to give effect to them was introduced into the parliament in 1995 but lapsed when parliament was prorogued for the federal election. Those amendments were then subsumed in much more extensive changes introduced by the Coalition Government. Issues which, as a result of the *Wik* decision, were pressed upon legislators included:

1. the validity of intermediate period acts done by governments on the assumption that pastoral leases extinguished native title;
2. the application of the right to negotiate in relation to grants of mining interests over land which were or had been the subject of pastoral leases;
3. the ability of pastoralists to undertake activities authorised by their leases without the requirement to comply with provisions of the NTA and their ability to undertake other activities which they had customarily undertaken without such authority;
4. the possibility of continuing uncertainty about the subsistence of native title in conjunction with a wide range of statutory interests in land.

The amendments provided for the validation of intermediate period acts. The system for recognition of native title was changed so that all applications were initiated as proceedings in the Federal Court with provision for mediation by the National Native Title Tribunal. A much more extensive and demanding registration test was introduced which had to be satisfied before the right to negotiate could be accessed by applicants in relation to the grant of mining tenements and certain other future acts. Provision was made for statutory extinguishment of native title in respect of certain classes of past acts, known as previous exclusive possession acts. Another class, known as previous non-exclusive possession acts, extinguished native title rights and interests to the extent of inconsistency between them. A wider range of future acts, being acts affecting native title, were able to be done validly without any obligations to negotiate with native title holders, although some procedural obligations were to be observed and compensation paid. Provision was also made for registrable Indigenous Land Use Agreements which would confer validity upon acts done under them.

The amendments were controversial. They were seen as withdrawing benefits conferred by the original NTA and, by extending the categories of statutory extinguishment, were seen as adverse to Indigenous interests. There was debate about whether, in the circumstances, the amendments were supportable by the race power. That is a debate upon which the High Court has not yet been called to rule, although its decision on the race power in another context is not encouraging.[116]

FEJO — EXTINGUISHMENT IS FOREVER

In December 1996 the Larrakia people lodged an application for a determination of native title covering land in the area of Darwin, Palmerston and Litchfield in the Northern Territory. The application was accepted in April 1997. Between March and November 1997 the Northern Territory granted Crown leases in respect of five parcels of Crown land the subject of the application. The land the subject of two of the leases had formed part of a tract of land granted to James Benham in 1882. It had subsequently been acquired for the purposes of a quarantine station in 1927 and was so proclaimed in 1935. The land was appointed to be a leprosarium in 1956. These appointments were revoked in 1980. The applicants sought declarations that native title existed in the area the subject of the Crown leases to the mining company and that the Northern Territory was obliged either to negotiate with the Larrakia people or compulsorily acquire their native title before it could grant a valid lease. The Territory sought summary dismissal of the proceedings and the Larrakia people sought interlocutory injunctions. The application was summarily dismissed at first instance on the basis that the grant to Benham had been effective to extinguish all native title rights and interests so that on the land being reacquired by the Crown no native title rights and interests could then be recognised by the common law. An appeal was taken to the Full Court of the Federal Court, but that aspect was removed to the High Court pursuant to the *Judiciary Act 1903* (Cth). Ron Castan appeared in that case also, this time intervening for the Yorta Yorta Aboriginal community.

The Court, now comprising Chief Justice Gleeson and Justices Gaudron, McHugh, Gummow, Hayne and Callinan, unanimously held that native title is extinguished by a grant in fee simple and not revived if the land is later again held by the Crown.[117] The Larrakia people in their argument relied upon the joint judgment in the *Waanyi* case with respect to the priority to be given to mediation procedures in relation to applications for determination of native title. This rule, it was argued, had been broken in the *Fejo* case by the primary judge deciding, before the exercise of the right to negotiate, that the claim to native title must fail.

The Court distinguished the *Waanyi* case on the basis, inter alia, that it had concerned the adoption of a procedure by the Tribunal that inverted the statutory regime. In the case before it, however, the Registrar had accepted the claim lodged on behalf of the Larrakia people. The Tribunal had dealt with it in the ordinary way, observing the statutory procedures. The Larrakia people chose to seek relief by way of interlocutory injunction. The relief sought from the Federal Court was relief of the character known under the general law and in accordance with long-established principle; they had to demonstrate a sufficiently arguable case to obtain that relief. They also sought final relief, including declarations of right that native title existed. The respondents sought summary dismissal, and to decide their motion the primary judge had to determine whether the claims made were plainly bad.

The Court did observe that ordinarily the fact that 'an applicant for injunction is a registered native title claimant will suggest, if not demonstrate, that there is a claimed native title that is arguable' — the Registrar being obliged to accept the application unless of opinion that it was frivolous or vexatious or that prima facie the claim could not be made out.[118] Nevertheless, the Registrar's administrative act of accepting an application would not 'put the question of title beyond debate on an application by a registered native title claimant for injunction or on an application to dismiss summarily an action instituted to obtain relief of that kind'.[119] Having concluded that the primary judge was not precluded, by the provisions of the NTA, from proceeding as he did, the Court turned to the substantive issue of the effect of the grant of a fee simple.

The appellants acknowledged it had been said more than once in previous decisions of the Court that native title was extinguished by a grant of an estate in fee simple. The Court referred to its observations in that respect in *Mabo [No. 2]*, in the *Native Title Act* case and in *Wik*. The references in those cases to extinguishment rather than suspension of native title rights were not to be understood as being some incautious or inaccurate use of language to describe the effect of a grant of freehold title. A grant in fee simple did not have only some temporary effect on native title rights or some effect conditioned upon the land not coming to be held by the Crown in the future. And in a significant passage, their Honours said:

> Native title has its origin in the traditional laws acknowledged and the customs observed by the indigenous people who possess the native title. Native title is neither an institution of the common law nor a form of common law tenure but it is recognised by the common law. There is, therefore, an intersection of traditional laws and customs with the common law. The underlying existence of the traditional laws and customs is a *necessary* prerequisite for native title but their existence is not a *sufficient* basis for recognising native title. And yet the argument that a grant in fee simple does not extinguish, but merely suspends, native title is an argument that seeks to convert the fact of continued connection with the land into a right to maintain that connection.[120]

The distinction between the existence of traditional law and custom and the question of its recognition at common law undermined the observation of Justice Kirby in *Wik* rejecting the submission of the Thayorre people that native title is independent of recognition, if, as seems likely, the reference to native title was to the relationship of Indigenous people to their country as defined by their traditional law and custom.

The extinguishing effect of freehold title is derived from the inconsistency of native title rights and interest with the rights of a holder of an estate in fee simple. For:

> Subject to whatever qualifications may be imposed by statute or the common law, or by reservation or grant, the holder of an estate in fee simple may use the land as he or she sees fit and may exclude any and everyone from access to the land.[121]

The non-revival of common law native title following a grant of freehold title flowed from the position that the rights created by the exercise of sovereign power being inconsistent with native title, the rights and interests that together made up that native title were necessarily at an end. There could be no question then, the Court said, of those rights springing forth again when the land came to be held again by the Crown: 'Their recognition has been overtaken by the exercise of "the power to create and to extinguish private rights and interests in land within the Sovereign's territory"'.[122]

If it be accepted, as is implicit in the Court's reasoning, that extinguishment relates only to common law native title and not to the subject matter of recognition, then it is not clear why revival is precluded. It may be that the non-revival principle is linked to the notion of recognition as the ascertainment of pre-existing common law native title rather than the creation of such title by the process of recognition.

YANNER — THE POSSIBILITY OF 'REAL' EXTINGUISHMENT

In the case of *Yanner v Eaton*,[123] the Court held that a native title right to hunt crocodiles was not extinguished by the *Fauna Conservation Act 1974* (Qld). Hunting activities were merely regulated by that Act. Hunting in the exercise of native title rights were thereby permitted by the overriding operation of section 211 of the NTA.

The Court revisited the topic of extinguishment. In the joint judgment of Chief Justice Gleeson and Justices Gaudron, Kirby and Hayne, native title rights and interests were referred to as 'a perception of socially constituted fact', as well as 'comprising various assortments of artificially defined jural right'.[124] Their Honours then went on to make an observation which seemed to imply that non-Indigenous law could sever the connection of Aboriginal people with their country:

> an important aspect of the socially constituted fact of native title rights and interests that is recognised by the common law is the spiritual, cultural and social connection with the land. Regulating particular aspects of the usufructuary relationship with traditional land does not sever the connection of the Aboriginal peoples concerned with the land (whether or not prohibiting the exercise of that relationship altogether might, or might to some extent).[125]

Indigenous people would find it hard to accept that a statute could ever sever their connection with the land. The words in parentheses might be thought to leave the question open.

Justice Gummow, in a separate judgment, spoke of the relationship between a community of Indigenous people and the land, defined by reference to that community's traditional law and customs as the 'bridgehead to the common law'.[126] Justice Callinan dissented on the basis that the fauna in question were vested in the Crown.

The joint judgment at least raised questions about how the justices perceived the nature of native title, particularly given their apparent acceptance of the possibility that the Indigenous relationship to land may be affected by a non-Indigenous law.

CONTINUING ISSUES

There are two important cases presently reserved for judgment by the High Court, namely *Ward* and *Yarmirr*. The first decision will raise issues of connection and the nature of extinguishment, as well as the question whether the common law can contemplate temporary suppression of native title, perhaps analogous to the operation of the non-extinguishment principle in the NTA. The practical question of the effect on common law native title of pastoral leases and mineral leases in Western Australia also falls for decision.[127] *Yarmirr* has raised the question of the existence and nature of common law native title in offshore waters and the operation of the NTA itself as extending the case law in that regard. It is to be hoped that these decisions may provide the opportunity for some refinement of the theoretical framework of common law native title.[128]

THE LIMITS ON WHAT THE COURT CAN DO

The High Court decisions that have been referred to in this paper set the scene for the recognition of the common law of native title and its protection against discriminatory action. They have also illuminated the operation of the NTA and secured its validity as an exercise of the race power of the Commonwealth. Major questions remain to be addressed about what is necessary to prove native title, the concept of partial extinguishment, and the existence and nature of common law native title in offshore waters. The contribution of the Court to the recognition of native title has plainly been fundamental, and Ron Castan, in whose honour this paper is given, has played an historic role in that course of judicial decision making. At the beginning of this paper, reference was made to the legal act of recognition as a metaphor derived from the

6. The High Court and recognition of native title

human experience of recognition. It is appropriate to conclude on that theme.

Although the role of the High Court, and the judicial system generally, has been of fundamental importance in the development of native title, there are inherent limits on what can be achieved by court decisions. A fundamental limitation was stated by Sir Gerard Brennan in *Patrick Stevedores Operations No. 2 Pty Ltd v Maritime Union of Australia*. His Honour said:

> The courts do not — indeed, they cannot — resolve disputes that involve issues wider than legal rights and obligations. They are confined to the ascertainment and declaration of legal rights and obligations and, when legal rights are in competition, the courts do no more than define which rights take priority over others.[129]

This statement sets out the core business of courts generally — making decisions about legal rights and obligations and, where necessary, their priorities inter se. The limitation on that business so defined is constitutional in its character — a rule by which courts are distinguished in their functions from executive governments and legislators. In a postscript to the judgment of Justice Toohey in *Wik Peoples v Queensland*, which postscript was authorised by the other majority justices, Gaudron, Gummow and Kirby, his Honour said, 'If inconsistency is held to exist between the rights and interests conferred by native title and the rights conferred under the statutory grants, those rights and interests must yield, to that extent, to the rights of the grantees'.[130]

In public debate much has been said about the coexistence principle enunciated in *Wik*. But when native title litigation proceeds to judgment and common law native title is recognised, the content of the judgment will be a determination that native title exists; that it is or is not exclusive; the identity of the holders; the native title rights and interests of importance; and the other interests to which it is subject. If native title is determined to exist in land the subject of a pastoral lease, it will be expressed to be subject to that lease.

There is no mechanism by which the Court can embody in its determination rules or directions for the management of the relationship between coexisting rights. Yet these are matters of fundamental concern to those involved in native title litigation. They go beyond pastoral leases to the whole array of tenures with which native title potentially coexists. The formulation of practical arrangements for the exercise of declared rights is not within the normal range of judicial functions. This suggests perhaps a closer integration between the courts' determinative role and consensual mechanisms for the resolution of management issues. In the case of consent determinations, it is not unusual that they are backed by ancillary agreements which deal with the management of coexistence. In the end, however, those agreements depend upon the people who have to coexist. That requires application of the human act of mutual recognition in the real world. This is a work that neither the High Court nor any of the courts can undertake. The significance of what they do, and of the work of Ron Castan and people like him, will depend on how a still incomplete legal theory of native title is put into practice on country.

7.
Native Title Conference, Yamatji Country, 2002

HYPOTHESISING SOCIAL NATIVE TITLE

DAVID RITTER

PROLOGUE

This paper was delivered at the 2002 annual Native Title Conference, which was held at Geraldton in Western Australia and subtitled 'Outcomes and Possibilities'. This is not a paper I would write now and does not represent my current thinking.[1] The version of the paper that appears here has been edited, but there has been no serious re-engagement with the central hypothesis and no reference to recent cases or analysis. Above all, this paper should be seen in context, as an expression of a particular political moment; a certain instant in the history of native title when one generation of land council advocates was scrabbling around for additional devices to add to the tool box for a legal and political struggle that was appearing increasingly problematic. The paper proved controversial at the time, prompting a yelling match between two audience members, one a senior Indigenous leader and the other a prominent public servant. Yet the argument contained in this paper is disarmingly mundane and to a large extent lexical. What the law recognises as 'native title', and where it can be recognised, falls short of the social reality experienced by Indigenous people living within traditional normative systems. The paper suggests that the remainder — which cannot be recognised at law, but might provide a basis for additional forms of political and administrative recognition — could be usefully described as 'social native title'. The intention was to give conceptual cohesion to a certain dimension of reality with some actual and potential political and administrative consequences, in the hope that public policy makers would feel more inclined to positively respond.

The early years of the native title system can be seen as a struggle over the depth and breadth of what would be recognised. What subsequently took place in the mid- to late nineties — the transition to 'agreement making' as the hegemonically accepted way of resolving native title matters — was not the product of slow awakening, but the consequence of a protracted and multidimensional legal and political tussle. Only once the principal avenues of appeal and amendment had been legally and politically exhausted, resulting in a set of rules that were broadly acceptable to Australian political economy, did agreement making become embedded as the way of dealing with native title issues. Much was lost on the journey. For those who entered the native title system early — as believers in the redemptive power of *Mabo*[2] or seekers of comprehensive regional agreements, thinking that a new city of social justice could be built on a foundation of doctrine, or that native title might open the road to economic independence or some recognition of sovereignty, or assorted other visions of the good society — the late nineties and the first years of the new millennium were a period of profound disappointment and frustration. For all of their ideological and instrumental incoherence (more visible with hindsight), the sense of right behind these ideals was deeply felt, and as the native title system became increasingly sclerotic and the gulf between vision and reality drew ever wider, those becoming isolated by the rising waters (whether because of their Indigenous identity or, more prosaically, their vocation as professionals working for Aboriginal groups) cast around for means of remaining afloat. The loose hypothesis of social native title was one such effort, proposed to try and pull something back, a vain attempt against the legal and political tide of the times and the settling internal logic of the system.

Taking place in the midst of this disordered moment, 'Outcomes and Possibilities' was itself a conference of discontents. Key speeches by Hal Wootten and Tony Lee were affecting highlights of the conference and stand in the memory as poignant indictments of a system that was regarded as having lost broader potential. Wootten's speech, delivered in a plenary session, captured the tone:

> While some outcomes can be praised, overall the process has been a failure by almost every criterion. It has been inordinately expensive, extremely slow, only fortuitously related to sensible land use, stressful and divisive for Aboriginal participants, unresponsive to Aboriginal needs and wishes, and arbitrary, haphazard and minimal in its delivery of benefit to Aboriginal people.[3]

A number of sessions were marked by exchanges of genuine acrimony between participants as the tensions identified by Wootten reached the point of simmering. Accidental events seemed to provide their own commentary on the state of play: at one of the conference dinners, styled as a 'seafood feast', the food ran out long before everyone had been served and a number of attendees later became stuck in a crowded lift, unable to move up or down. The farce seemed apt. Behind the scenes, the host representative body, the Yamatji Marlpa Land Council (as it is now styled), was in the midst of internal turmoil with increasingly open conflict between the executive director and the governing committee. For staff of the organisation, the conference was a tense few days of keeping up appearances, while the interstitial conflicts that are endemic to the representative body system were given a vivid private showcasing.[4] In the midst of the consternation, and putting to one side the matter of conceptual slightness, it is small wonder that the suggestion of social native title sank without trace.

THE 'DARK MATTER' OF NATIVE TITLE

Justice Robert French, the inaugural President of the National Native Title Tribunal (NNTT), began his tertiary education in science before, at the suggestion of one of his teachers, he shifted his academic allegiances to the law.[5] Notwithstanding the shift, Justice French retained an abiding interest in the sciences and his clear and precise rhetoric is punctuated by metaphors and analogies borrowed from that quarter. Indeed, native title in Australia can be interpreted as having been developed in a scientific way, consistent with a positivist view of the law. Numerous hypotheses of the law have been developed and then experimentally tested before the courts. Many surmised in the early confused years that an emerging corpus of test case results would provide clear and rational principles by which to understand the law of native title. The boundaries of science advance with time, not just through tests, but by drawing inferences that cannot actually be tested — deducing the existence of phenomena not because they can themselves be observed but in order to explain the apparent, but otherwise unaccounted for, behaviour of known objects. Even if not actually observed or observable, such phenomena can nonetheless be named.

The purpose of this paper is analogous to the scientific endeavours just described: to name a non-legal idea based on observable tendencies within existing legal and institutional structures. However, while this paper is written from the laboratory, it is written with a political agenda: that is, in support of increasing the exogenous legitimacy of Indigenous aspirations that extend beyond what the law of native title can recognise. In essence, what is argued is that, additional to the formal 'doctrine of native title' as recognised by the *Native Title Act 1993* (Cth) (NTA) and the judiciary (henceforth called herein 'jural native title'), there is the matter of 'social native title'. In part, the argument is that the recognition of jural native title itself leads to a logical inference of other political 'matter' of which the state is implicitly cognisant. Jural native title, as Mick Dodson and Lisa Strelein put it, demands 'an acknowledgement of the continuation of Aboriginal law and Indigenous society as a source of authority…recognised by virtue of their existence as distinct…'.[6] Here it is argued that the recognition of jural native title necessarily implies a non-jural concomitant that might be termed 'social native title'.

Social native title can be understood as a concept that embraces the human and citizenship rights and political aspirations of Indigenous people in relation to country that are outside of conventional jural native title, but emerge as expressions of Indigenous law and custom. This paper presents a hypothesis of social native title, describing both its origins and where it can be seen to have gained tacit recognition. Most obviously, social native title is not constrained by the same preconditions as jural native title, as it is unaffected by extinguishment. It inverts the High Court's formulation in *Ward* that 'looking to the use that has actually been made of land distracts attention from the central inquiry which is an inquiry about rights created in others or asserted by the executive, not the way in which they may have been exercised at any time'.[7] The touchstone of social native title is lived reality.

In summary, social native title:
- arises from the fact of normative Indigenous dominion over an area of land or waters;
- is likely to be recognised by neighbouring Indigenous polities, can be given recognition by the legislative and executive arms of the state, and arguably draws support from international law;

- is implied by the judicial recognition of jural native title;
- derives its content from both Indigenous law and custom and the outcome of political and administrative recognition;
- is not diminished by the demise of jural native title and may include elements that are incapable of being recognised under common or statutory law;
- is not subject to extinguishment, but may be destroyed by power-political realities and may — by the same token — revive.

It has been suggested that native title is a kind of recognition technique. This analysis suggests that the intersection of Indigenous customary law and Australian common and statutory law establishes a 'native title recognition space'. However, that 'recognition space' is circumscribed by the limitations of common and statutory law: of what the judicial arm of government can recognise. Such a delimitation of the recognition space to the province of what can be done by the courts within a narrow legislative and common law context amounts to a de facto delegation of executive decision-making power to the judiciary.[8] Social native title describes the 'non (jural) native title' outcomes that can evolve from the facts that (can) give rise to jural native title, but are themselves beyond the boundaries of what jural native title is capable of recognising. It also names the political doctrine that (implicitly) legitimates such outcomes. 'Social native title' is thus a social reality that may give rise to substantive political and administrative outcomes.

The jural native title process itself has given rise to statements of recognition of the foundations of social native title. The content of jural native title has its origins in the traditional laws and customs of Indigenous people, yet not all such customs and laws will be recognised and respected by Australian law.[9] As the majority of the High Court noted in *Ward*, 'recognition may cease where, as a matter of law, native title rights have been extinguished even though, but for that legal conclusion, on the facts native title would still exist'.[10] In a similar vein, Justice Kirby in *Fejo v Northern Territory* acknowledged the disjunction between law and fact in the doctrine of extinguishment, noting that the relevant principles are not 'based on the factual use of land'.[11] As long ago as 1994, the then President of the NNTT commented that the law of extinguishment 'must seem perverse to those who maintain their association with their country and upon whom indigenous tradition confers responsibility for that country'.[12] Clearly, the judiciary knows that there is something else there, arising from the facts of Indigenous society and polity which is beyond what the bench is capable of recognising.[13]

The existence of social native title is predicated on contemporary social dominion over a prescribed area of land or waters. That is, if one puts to one side issues of legal 'rights' and the application of the doctrine of extinguishment, there are places in Australia that in terms of (and these expressions are used here in a lay sense) use, occupation, enjoyment and dominion of land are controlled by Indigenous societies. The conventional image here may be of the desert, the tropical north or the hinterland scrub, but the same principles apply to relevant urban locations. As a matter of administrative reality, and jural native title to one side, where an Indigenous group has a cultural association with area, that group is likely to be accorded some respect (even if only by convention) within the processes of government, amounting to tacit executive recognition of the existence of social native title.

INTERNATIONAL HUMAN RIGHTS

The Australian jural native title process falls below international human rights standards.[14] International human rights principles recognise that Aboriginal people retain rights over their traditional land and waters, regardless of the actions of the sovereign power. International law, then, legitimises Indigenous political authority on its own terms, rather than requiring any act of legitimation by the sovereign colonial power. Indigenous peoples have internationally recognised human rights that include, prominently, the right to self-determination.[15] Thus the rubric of social native title is bolstered by the *grundnorms* of international law. International human rights principles look behind the petty domestic concerns of sovereign powers and conceive, instead, of inalienable rights of subject Indigenous peoples. International human rights principles, then, provide a convenient doctrinal foundation for, and legitimation of, social native title.

INDIGENOUS DECLARATIONS AND THEIR ENFORCEMENT

The clearest endogenous expression of social native title occurs when an Indigenous group asserts a political interest in an area on a normative cultural basis through, for example, a proclamation of internal sovereignty. It is open to Aboriginal people to utilise the power of declaration in relation to their traditional lands. Further, the power of such declaration is not contingent on the existence of native title or having escaped the random axe of extinguishment. Any Aboriginal group can say, 'we are here, this is our land, this is our political mandate and this is what we assert', before articulating its own declaration of principles. The power of such a declaration is that it is allodial: its source is the ongoing internal political sovereignty of the Aboriginal group in question, not anything recognised (or judicially recognisable) by the Crown. A number of Aboriginal groups within the Yamatji region have made such declarations, and the Badimia people's *Declaration of Principles for Engagement with Resource Developers* is attached to this paper as an example. It is a very clear statement of the ongoing internal sovereignty of the Badimia people and its legitimacy is not dependent on any non-Indigenous source of authority.

Obviously the strength of a declaration will depend upon both its persuasiveness and the capacity for it to be enforced. Declarations exert the greatest moral and political force when they are, themselves, grounded on, or consistent with, broader ideological rationales or declarations of universal human rights.[16] However, it is possible for a declaration to be empty when there is no power to enforce it. In order to enforce declarations, a group can resort to jural native title, to such legal redress as exists outside of native title — or use the native title process in imaginative ways not envisaged by its makers. That is, Indigenous groups can make political declarations, which they then use such legal and political power as is available (and which was definitely not designed for that purpose) within Australian society to enforce. The implementation of strategies of this nature requires lateral and counter-intuitive thinking, assisted by the provision of practical (and creatively cynical) advice. An Indigenous group might, for instance, use freedom of information, mining laws, environmental laws, planning laws, the targeting of investors, the corporate due diligence process and so on as ways of enforcing declarations of principle. Such machinations might be discounted as 'illegitimate', but this becomes harder if they are expressly legitimised by the principled declaration of the Indigenous group in question founded in the reality of social native title.

'NON-NATIVE TITLE OUTCOMES'

Almost from the outset of the native title process under the NTA, it was recognised that Indigenous groups would be seeking outcomes that went beyond what would or could be included within a jural determination of native title. Accordingly, the National Native Title Tribunal began, at an early stage, to encourage parties to consider options for resolution that did not result in an agreed determination of native title.[17] Indeed, one of the strengths of the native title process was always thought to be that parties could secure from the mediation process 'non legal outcomes' that would not be available were the matter decided only by a determination of the Federal Court. The agreed lexicon quickly became 'non-native title outcomes'. Such outcomes might not result from the native title claim per se, but were achieved as a result of the 'mutual satisfaction of interests' that was said to accompany the resolution of a claimant application for a determination of native title by consent. It might even be suggested that the High Court has shown some cognisance of 'non-native title outcomes', stating in the *North Ganalanja* case, for instance, that 'if the persons interested in the determination' of a native title claim 'negotiate and reach an agreement, they are enabled thereby to establish an amicable arrangement between future occupiers'.[18] Presumably the kind of 'amicable arrangements' envisaged could include non-native title outcomes.

A non-native title outcome is distinct from jural native title; but it is also only partly coincident with social native title. Non-native title outcomes can be as broad as the aspirations of Aboriginal people and need not be predicated on any ongoing tradition or normative society. Indeed, non-native title outcomes have often been regarded as the panacea for the frustrations of Indigenous people who, by force of historical circumstance, lack the kind of law and custom required under Australian law to found jural native title. Social native title is more limited: in order to exist, it still requires the same normative foundations as jural native title, but is not limited by the doctrine of extinguishment or the confines of what the courts can recognise: however, it does not extend to simply any outcome achieved by Indigenous people through creative use of native title processes. The distinction is significant. The expression 'non-native title outcome' seems suggestive of something that is not derived from the ongoing vitality of traditional law and custom and, in cases where social native title exists, is wholly inapt. The phrase disguises the political actuality, that so-called non-native title outcomes are often the clearest possible sign of the existence of social native title: a dead giveaway that, beyond the boundaries of jural native title, exist a range of matters that will be politically recognised because of the fact of an Indigenous society tied to a particular area of land. Though not always so, non-native title outcomes are often the proverbial smoking gun, smudged with the fingerprints of state recognition demonstrating tacit acceptance of the state of the existence of social native title.

SOCIAL NATIVE TITLE IN SPECIFIC CLAIM NEGOTIATIONS

The native title process has encouraged Indigenous people to come together in land-holding communities and to identify their aspirations. Common experience suggests that many of these aspirations are outside of jural native title. Hal Wootten, for instance, has remarked of his experiences of talking with Indigenous people, that:

> One message that stands out is that grog is ruining their communities — leading to violence, murder, sexual abuse, wrecked houses, no money for good food, and sleepless hungry children who can't compete at school, won't take any notice of their parents, grow up seeing no future and end up in gaol or take their own lives. Another message is that they want a more effective system of law and order in the communities. A third is that they want education and real jobs for their kids. These are things that will help them take back control of their lives and their communities. These are very concrete demands that fall within a context of community development.[19]

Such aspirations fall — with bleak clarity — well beyond the ambit of jural native title. The experience of Indigenous people may be that if such matters are raised in the context of native title claim negotiations, state agencies will attempt to de-legitimise them by ruling them out of order, pleading that such matters are the province of another agency or outside the functions of the native title representative body, or by baldly stating that such matters 'are not native title'. Social native title is an answer to such declamations; it is a rejoinder, indicating that the limitations of legal doctrine need not be the end of the matter. How the state engages with social native title is not a matter for the courts, but a function of the administrative and executive processes of government.

The relationship between the strength of jural native title and social native title needs considered analysis in the context of specific native title claim negotiations. In all likelihood, the power of an Aboriginal group in terms of social native title will, in some instances, depend on the extent to which they have jural native title leverage. The key point is that the relationship is never a simple one. Rather, the ability of a group to project influence on the basis of their social title is dependent on a confluence of non-legal factors: the government in power, market forces, land tenure, political unity, the mineral wealth of the area in question, the state of fluctuation of the common law and so on.

A RHETORICAL CONCLUSION: 'FEELING RIGHT ABOUT THE PLACE'

It would be wrong to just see the political doctrine of social native title as merely an emancipative tool for Indigenous people: it also recognises a transformative opportunity for government. Part of the power of the original *Mabo* decision lay in the reality that it gave some legal expression to what had come to be acknowledged as social truth: that Indigenous peoples owned their lands under traditional law and custom. However, the limits of jural native title mean that there continue to be societal facts that can only be given recognition outside of court processes through the province of social native title. This paper has argued that government processes already give some acknowledgment to social native title — providing a clue to recognising its existence — but much more can be done through formalising recognition. The alternative might be bleak. If Indigenous Australia does not accept its jural lot, does not stop at what the courts and the government say are the limits of the doctrine of native title, then what? Do Indigenous people simply go away? Do the enraged frustrations, denied aspirations and suppressed ambitions of Indigenous groups dissipate? It is unlikely. Paul Keating famously observed apropos of Indigenous affairs that we would 'never be any good, never feel at home until we set things right with them'.[20] 'Setting things right' will take more than just the application of the doctrine of 'jural native title'; it will take something more besides, which this paper has argued should logically include recognition of social native title.

APPENDIX

Badimia people's declaration of principles for engagement with resource developers

We, the authorised native title representatives of the Badimia People, hereby declare that the following forms the corpus of principle upon which we, as the Traditional Owners of our land since time immemorial, will negotiate with those who wish to exploit the mineral riches of our country for commercial gain.

Whereas:

A. 'Badimia' is the name of the people who are the Traditional Owners of a large area of the Midwest of Western Australia in the general vicinity of the town of Mt Magnet. Much of Badimia traditional country is encompassed within the Badimia native title claim WC96/98 that was lodged in 1996 by Badimia people wishing to assert their rights over their traditional country.

B. The basis of the Badimia claim has always been inclusive: that all Traditional Owners of the area subject to claim should be included within the native title claimant group.

C. We are represented by the Yamatji Land and Sea Council, which provides us with assistance under division 3 of part 11 of the Commonwealth *Native Title Act 1993* ('NTA'). The Badimia native title claimant group has appointed applicants under section 61(4) of the NTA. The Badimia native title claimant group and the applicants have been collectively appointed a Badimia Working Group to have day to day conduct of the Badimia native title claim under section 62A of the NTA.

D. Badimia country is highly prospective and has produced a number of mines and significant mineral wealth. Historically, we have not benefited from resource development on our traditional country. Rather, we have suffered economically, socially and culturally and our country has been ravaged as a result of the activities of the resources industry. Even since the advent of Aboriginal heritage and native title legislation, our experience with the resources industry has been mixed. Some companies treated us with great respect, while others continue to demonstrate an attitude of flagrant and arrogant disregard for our rights, interests and culture.

E. Just as resource developers have their own commercial and organisational imperatives, so the Badimia People have our own social, cultural and economic imperatives derived from our traditional laws and customs and contemporary social and economic circumstances.

It is hereby declared that:

I. All dealings on Badimia land should proceed on the basis that, regardless of the position at common law, Badimia people should be accorded the respect due to those with a unique proprietary interest in the Badimia area. Badimia people should be treated as the true owners of their own land.

II. All negotiations and dealings with resource companies are to take place in good faith and in a culturally sensitive and appropriate manner, paying due respect to our customs, laws and traditions.

III. We will seek to negotiate with each resource proponent in respect of each resource development on our country, regardless of whether a formal right to negotiate exists under the NTA or not. As the High Court of Australia has recognised, our feeling for our country and our law does not live or die with the formal legal extinguishment of native title. A prudent and culturally sensitive proponent will regard us as having a moral right to negotiate, regardless of the legal position.

IV. Unless specifically agreed otherwise, all negotiations and dealings with us are to be through our appointed representatives, the Badimia Working Group and the Yamatji Land and Sea Council.

V. Our places of cultural significance are to be protected. The custodianship and care of these places is our fundamental right and responsibility.

VI. We will not work with any anthropologist or archaeologist who is not acceptable to us.

VII. We will not deal or negotiate with any consultant or representative of a resource company who is disrespectful to us. We reserve the right to nominate specific individuals in this category.

VIII. In general terms we accept that exploration and prospecting activity can occur subject to appropriate level heritage clearance. Mining activity will require a comprehensive agreement. An intermediate form of agreement may deal with lesser mining activity. Miscellaneous activity such as infrastructure will be dealt with on its merits.

IX. We expect that each major resource development on our country will proceed, subject to our negotiated consent. It is expected that such agreements will include provisions in relation to compensation, heritage management, cross-cultural education, employment, training, implementation and monitoring, environmental rehabilitation, business opportunities, elimination of racial discrimination and symbolic recognition of our traditional ownership.

X. All dealings on Badimia land should be subject to the non-extinguishment principle under the NTA.

XI. In the course of dealing with matters on Badimia land, proponents will be expected to take measures to ensure that the Badimia group does not suffer from a disadvantage in terms of negotiating resources available to the group.

XII. The Badimia Working Group reserves its right to vary these Principles from time to time as it learns from experience and in response to traditional law and custom.

XIII. We state the Principles contained in this document without prejudice.

The Yamatji Land and Sea Council is at liberty to distribute this document at its discretion to resource companies proposing to conduct activities within the Badimia area.

Native Title Conference, Kaurna Country, 2004

SYMBOLISM AND FUNCTION
From native title to Indigenous self-government*

LISA STRELEIN

High Court Chief Justice Gleeson, when delivering the judgment in *Western Australia v Ward*, suggested that no one had been entirely successful in the case.[1] But what does this mean in relation to the recognition and protection of native title? For Indigenous claimants it has generally meant that their rights have been inadequately protected by the law, and for non-Indigenous interests it has meant that Indigenous peoples' rights are not as limited as they might have hoped. Neither the courts nor the legislature has done anything to build upon the recognition and protection of Indigenous rights under *Mabo v Queensland [No. 2]*.[2]

Certainly, the disappointment over decisions in *Ward* and *Yorta Yorta* must give pause for thought.[3] The limits of the legal concept of native title raise the question whether the development of the common law has left an empty vessel for most Indigenous peoples. In the years since the decision of the High Court in *Mabo,* there has been sharp criticism of the lack of outcomes from the native title process despite the substantial resources expended, not least by Indigenous communities themselves.

However, before we can assess the outcomes against the cost, we must first consider what we count among the outcomes of native title and how much we value them. It is important, when we try to understand the effort that has been put into the native title process, that we look at both the legal conclusions of native title as well as its place in the recognition of Indigenous self-government. The changes in the political and legal environment occasioned by the recognition of native title should also be considered amongst the outcomes of native title.

Despite being one of the most potent critics of the native title process, Noel Pearson has been adamant that native title is not a 'dead issue'.[4] Native title is important to Australia's legal and political structures because it is a measure of our ability to accommodate the rights of Indigenous peoples. The arms of the state cannot ignore the intensely symbolic nature of native title in their engagement with Indigenous peoples. For Indigenous peoples in Australia, it is not merely a form of title: it is a fundamental recognition of the distinct identity and special place of the first peoples. The rights of Indigenous peoples that (however inadequately) are reflected in native title are recognised by virtue of their existence as distinct peoples and as a constitutional entity, and not merely a cultural minority within an otherwise homogenous Australian polity.[5] As a concept, native title is an acknowledgment of the continuation of Indigenous society as a source of authority. For these reasons, the *Mabo* case is seen as a high watermark in the relationship between Indigenous peoples and the state.

In this paper I consider how the potential of native title may have been curtailed by the courts as a result of impossible standards of proof, intricate inquiries and problematic jurisprudence. Yet, the idea of native title, or what native title symbolises, may have formed the basis for greater recognition of the rights of Indigenous peoples to negotiate directly with government from a position of sovereign authority.

THE LIMITS OF NATIVE TITLE

In *Ward* and *Yorta Yorta* the High Court has confirmed their view that native title rights and interests must be construed as deriving from traditional law and custom. The common law recognises those rights and interests through the concept of native title. The Court held that native title is defined by the *Native Title Act 1993* (Cth) (NTA) in section 223(1), not by the common law. The Court interpreted the statutory definition as needing two inquiries.[6] The first is to determine whether the claimants have established that they hold rights and interests under traditional laws and customs. This requires the identification of laws and customs themselves and then the articulation of the rights and interest conferred by those laws. The second inquiry is into the connection of the group to the land or waters. This does not require proof of physical occupation or continued use, but a connection through law and custom. That is, the Court has said that it is not how Aboriginal peoples use or occupy the land, but what the laws and customs say about their connection.[7]

Nevertheless, there still appears to be a level of confusion in the reasoning of the courts as to whether they require claimants to demonstrate a system of law and custom that binds them as a society, through which internal ordering or rights and interests in land is determined; or whether the courts are setting themselves as arbiters of traditional law, by requiring a detailed articulation of the laws and customs relating to entitlement to the land claimed. The High Court, in particular, has demonstrated their inability to articulate Indigenous systems of law and custom. The majority in *Ward* clumsily excused themselves by lamenting the inherent difficulty of translating what they describe as the 'essentially spiritual' relationship with the land.[8] In *Ward*, the Court accepted that the 'right to speak for country' encapsulated a relationship to land that was as complete as any under common law, thus would be reflected in a right of exclusive possession.[9] Yet, the Court was quick to exploit the relationship of dependence and the irresistibility of sovereign power that had been established in the *Mabo* case in order to undermine Indigenous authority by readily imputing extinguishment of any native title right to make decisions with respect to access and use.

The Court in recent cases has displayed a disappointing readiness to find that the 'exclusive' character of native title was extinguished by almost any act, resulting in the loss of rights to control access or future development. The ever-expanding doctrine of extinguishment is recognised by the courts to operate in the common law sphere to withdraw recognition of rights that might otherwise continue under Indigenous law. In *Ward*, however, extinguishment and the impact of non-Indigenous interests was conflated with questions of proof so that the onus was shifted to Indigenous claimants to establish how their laws and customs could be explained in greater detail to build the concept of 'non-exclusive' native title from a bundle of distinct rights and interests.

Similarly, in *Yorta Yorta*, while the High Court recognised that native title protects rights and interests that emerge from a different body of law, the extent of recognition is determined by the colonising regime on its own terms. The Court requires proof that the society and the system of law and custom that gives rise to rights to land has remained intact. Yet, they deny any continuing authority in that society. By operation of legal fiction the system of legal authority is treated as a matter of fact but somehow not an exercise of sovereign jurisdiction.

The doctrine of native title has replaced terra nullius with a basis for dispossession no less reliant on a conception of Indigenous society as a relic of 'prior sovereignty'. The illogicality of such an impoverished judicial theory has led some commentators to reject, wholeheartedly, any role for traditional law and custom in the proof of native title, preferring an occupation-based analysis.[10] Noel Pearson's argument for an occupation-based doctrine of native title has a great deal of attraction for a legal theory that has become constrained by impossible internal contradictions, extraordinary levels of proof, and unmanageable inquiries into competing interests and tenure histories.

Whatever the doctrine of proof applied in the courts, and whatever the limits that are placed on the 'legal conclusion' of native title, the 'idea' of native title reflects a deeper recognition of Indigenous identity. This recognition has led to fundamental changes in the status of Indigenous peoples in negotiations with the state. While the courts may be in a position to isolate the functional doctrine of native title from the symbolic recognition of Indigenous authority on which it is based, the separation cannot be so easily drawn in negotiations between Indigenous peoples and the state.

AGREEMENTS UNDER THE NATIVE TITLE ACT

From the outset, the recognition of Indigenous peoples in the *Mabo* case invigorated agitation for negotiations with the state and gave a new-found legitimacy to Indigenous peoples' claims in the eyes of governments. In the original NTA section 21 was included to allow native title holders to enter into an agreement with a state, territory or Commonwealth government to surrender their title, or to authorise future developments. Subsection (4) contained a negative reference to the fact that this section did not prevent agreement being made on a regional or local basis. Hence, a number of large-scale agreements began to be negotiated. Movements for regional autonomy in Cape York and the Kimberley, for example, had a new framework within which to negotiate.[11]

As part of the 1998 amendments to the NTA, the Indigenous Land Use Agreement (ILUA) provisions sought to encapsulate the needs of smaller ventures for greater security for agreements entered into with Indigenous communities. Despite the aggressiveness of the government's amendment plan, most parties to the native title process accepted a more detailed legislative regime to support these kinds of agreements. The

8. Symbolism and function

ILUA provisions also recognised the desire on the part of commercial and Indigenous interests to be able to deal directly with each other in relation to particular projects, removing government parties from some negotiations. The resulting ILUA regime provides a strict framework within which these agreements can be developed and continue to operate with some level of certainty for the non-Indigenous parties.

South Australia state-wide ILUA

With their genesis in providing contractual security for small commercial interests, the ILUA provisions do not recognise any status for native title holding groups beyond one of many private users of land. Nevertheless, this has not stopped Indigenous peoples from pushing the limits of the ILUA process.

Native title claimants in South Australia, for example, have entered into direct negotiations with the South Australian Government and peak industry bodies under the ILUA process to negotiate a 'state wide comprehensive settlement' of native title issues, with a view toward progressive legislative, administrative, constitutional and procedural reforms.[12] The process has been a collaborative one, with government providing substantial resources and a dedicated team of negotiators and the Aboriginal Legal Rights Movement of South Australia, as the native title representative body, facilitating Indigenous peoples' direction of and engagement in the process. The process has also been supported by considerable research and procedural advice.[13]

For the claimants in South Australia, the idea of negotiating within the ILUA regime was initially met with some scepticism, particularly at the prospect of having to negotiate on the basis of extinguishment of native title. However, the negotiating strength and direct community empowerment that could be gained through working together at the state level was seen as an opportunity worth pursuing. The focus of efforts has been in the development of appropriate processes and capacities within the claimant groups to participate effectively in negotiations of this scale.[14]

The South Australian partners have invoked criticism over perceived lack of outcomes and for the amount of funding required to establish this kind of 'bottom-up' negotiating structure. The process of engagement and the building of Indigenous governance structures is clearly seen by the negotiating partners as an 'outcome' from native title.[15] Nevertheless, the ILUA regime operates within the constraints of native title, thus the subject matter of the resulting negotiations in South Australia are currently focused primarily on land use and resource exploitation. Understandably, claimants perceive the native title process as part of a broader political context.[16] As a result, however, the processes for engagement that have strengthened the decision-making structures of the native title claimants may well extend beyond the current process.

State-wide framework agreements and comprehensive processes

The emergence of state-wide framework agreements recognised that providing a mechanism for future act agreements does not remove the need for negotiations between Indigenous peoples and the state over outstanding issues, including historical loss, government service delivery and autonomy options. These agreements have taken a number of forms, and while they have been primarily directed to native title, some also seek to incorporate other issues. Even at this level, however, the limits of the framework agreements are clearly based on the constraints of the current national legal framework. The first such agreement was signed in Victoria in November 2000. The Victorian protocol committed the state government to negotiating native title outcomes in Victoria, recognising that litigation would pose difficult obstacles for native title claimants in Victoria, and to a further process of negotiation on a state-wide basis.[17]

Western Australian comprehensive agreements

In October 2001 the Western Australian Government signed a *Statement of Commitment* for 'a new and just relationship' with Indigenous peoples in that state to achieve, among other things:

- recognition of the continuing rights and responsibilities of Aboriginal peoples of Western Australia, including traditional ownership and connection to land and waters;
- legislative protection of Aboriginal rights; and
- regional and local approaches to address issues that impact on Aboriginal communities, families and individuals.

A 'partnership framework', which forms part of the statement, commits to reform formalised through 'agreements'.[18] The scope of this statement is clearly much broader than others of its kind and is unique in combining land and other issues across the broad spectrum of Indigenous peoples' relationship with the state.

Pursuant to the *Statement of Commitment*, the Western Australian Government established the Indigenous Affairs Advisory Committee to oversee its implementation and set priorities under the statement. This commitment was underpinned in the 2003–04 Budget papers, where the Western Australian Government committed to negotiating three comprehensive agreements under the *Statement of Commitment*: the first with the Tjurabalan community, who secured one of the first native title determinations in the state;[19] the second with the South West Aboriginal Land and Sea Council and the Noongar people; and a third with the Shire of Ngaanyatjarraku.[20] The other relevant major initiative concerned a proposal for negotiations over Martu local government, who were also the subject of a substantial positive determination of native title.

Tjurabalan scoping study and Martu local government

The Tjurabalan people of the East Kimberley and the Martu people of the Western Desert in the Pilbara region were chosen as the focus of two of the original priority projects under the *Statement of Commitment*, in anticipation of large-scale determinations of native title. For the Tjurabalan people, the native title matters, so far as recognition is concerned, are resolved by the positive determination of native title. The Federal Court determined that the native title holders had the right to possess, occupy, use and enjoy the land and waters of the Determination Area to the exclusion of all others.[21] That right includes the right to live on the land, to make decisions about use and enjoyment, and control access and use by others; the right to hunt and gather, to take water and other traditionally accessed resources for personal and communal needs; the right to maintain and protect sites of significance; and the right to be acknowledged as the traditional Aboriginal owners of the area. The rights and interests are also exercisable in accordance with traditional laws and customs. Implementation and future native title negotiations will remain a significant part of the community's ongoing engagement with the state and other interests.

The project was adopted by the Council of Australian Governments (COAG) whole-of-government process, which sought to coordinate government agencies in the provision of services to Indigenous communities in a number of trial sites. Tjurabalan was one of up to ten sites around the country that were the focus of this new approach between Commonwealth and state governments.[22] The scoping study formed the basis for an agreement and examined land use, as well as service delivery, infrastructure and local government options. The COAG trials, however, avoided confronting outstanding claims to land either by choosing sites where land needs have been met through native title or land rights, or by excluding land issues from the scope of the project.

Like the Tjurabalan determination before it, the Martu determination of native title recognises exclusive possession and the distribution of rights and interests over the land in accordance with the laws and customs of the Martu. While the determination of native title says nothing about municipal government, the determination prompted the state government to examine options for self-government for the community within the local government regime. The Shire of Ngaanyatjarraku is an example of the application of local government models to remote regions where populations are predominantly Indigenous. The recognition of Martu self-government is an important step that many native title claim groups envisage as among their ultimate aims.

Noongar Nation

The profile of Indigenous peoples in the south west region of Western Australia and the limited extent of the claimable lands are recognised as severely restricting the potential for legal processes to deliver significant native title outcomes. The process of determining the impact of extinguishing acts in the south west is significantly more complex even than the process engaged in by the High Court in the *Ward* decision.

Noongar people and the South West Aboriginal Land and Sea Council have initiated a single claim policy that resulted in a united, single claim covering all Noongar country. The cultural, social and political reality of Noongar people made this approach the most feasible basis for negotiating outcomes in the south west. The internal process of negotiating agreements for representation and decision making among the Noongar people also proved to be a vehicle for social relationship building out of processes that may otherwise have been a source of social atomisation.[23] The positive work done to achieve support for the single claim may also provide a strong base, with ongoing structural reinforcement, for the cohesive identity of the Noongar community.

This renewed self-confidence engaged the government, and it responded with a commitment to negotiate a comprehensive agreement.[24] While the proposed comprehensive agreement process for the Noongar Nation may result in a settlement of the native title claim, it is not likely to be solely focused on land use agreements and protocols, but also financial arrangements and autonomy structures for Noongar people.[25] The contrast for Noongars is that their fight for self-government and autonomy must occur outside existing land-based models of ownership and jurisdiction. This has forced a detailed assessment of all the tools currently available to them to achieve their goals. Native title, and the single claim, however, remain central.

USING EXISTING TOOLS

Native title has not replaced the myriad avenues for recognition of Indigenous involvement in land management and jurisdiction over Indigenous governmental functions. Developing a comprehensive approach toward self-government and regional autonomy within existing structures can achieve a significant amount. There are existing mechanisms for substantive native title determinations, procedural rights attaching to extant applications, heritage protection under state and federal legislation, Indigenous Land Corporation purchases, joint management of national parks, state land rights legislation, existing Indigenous service delivery, and grassroots organisations in health, legal assistance, schooling, regional authority options and, more recently, whole-of-government commitments to service delivery.

However, Noel Pearson commented some years ago on the need to understand such tools for what they can and cannot provide:

> We are in a political guerrilla war, in a colonial circumstance which is powerful and against which we infrequently prevail. People in situations like ours must make do with the tools which are on hand… They are limited tools and to optimise results we must use them wisely and skilfully.[26]

Indigenous peoples often make use of the tools available to them without necessarily accepting the legitimacy or authority of the various institutions. As such, Pearson has argued that both radical and moderate strategies must be implemented to secure results.[27] But the existing tools have severe limitations, some of which are practical, while others go much deeper, to the heart of the colonial relationship. These limitations prove even more of an obstacle when responses across levels of government and between departments are inconsistent. Recent initiatives in whole-of-government projects have begun to recognise the difficulties that Indigenous peoples face in confronting bureaucratic intransigence and the constraints of current structures.

TACKLING BIGGER ISSUES

The value of emerging comprehensive self-assessments by Indigenous peoples are that they are expressions of Indigenous sovereignty in action. However, incremental approaches do not require governments to commit to negotiation over broader issues on terms determined by Indigenous peoples. Using existing structures avoids the politically sensitive and potentially divisive public debates on the merits of a treaty and Indigenous self-government. But the outcomes from a piecemeal approach will remain incomplete and will be reliant on the existing statutory and bureaucratic arrangements. The outcomes will not be those that emerge from a reflective consideration of what it is that Indigenous peoples want to control. The question is whether there is truly an exercise of self-determination in this process. It means that the Australian state and the Australian people have still not come to terms with the fundamental rights of Indigenous peoples to self-determination and self-government where that is their expressed desire.

The decisions of the minority judges in *Ward* called for significant reform. Justice McHugh expressed concern that the native title system had been stacked against native title holders and called for an arbitral system that would determine claims based on their merits, and not bound by historical tenures and the common law superiority of non-native title rights.[28] Justice Callinan went a step further, calling for a 'true and unqualified' settlement of lands or money.[29] In articulating the immense detail required to compare the rights and interests conferred by successive tenures, the High Court in *Ward* appears to have made a strong argument for an alternative process based on negotiated settlement.

The reconciling of Crown sovereignty with Indigenous peoples' rights and status must acknowledge the diversity of Indigenous peoples and thereby accommodate the needs, demands and potential of each community. It must be recognised that the kinds of issues where an Indigenous people may want to take control will be shaped by their experience of colonisation. The vision of self-determination of the Noongar Nation may differ markedly from that of the Martu. However, the response from the state must be coordinated and comprehensive.

Where the legitimacy of Indigenous autonomy, authority and jurisdiction is accepted by governments at all levels, much greater attention can be paid to how this authority will operate in the different circumstances of Indigenous peoples. A national commitment to comprehensive settlement of Indigenous claims would be able to set a framework that allows broad-ranging and creative negotiations based on recognition of rights, and negotiated options and limitations, where Indigenous people can address issues not as a corporate interest but as a collective, self-governing and sovereign interest.

THE ROLE OF NATIVE TITLE: SYMBOLISM AND FUNCTION

While acknowledging the limitations of the courts, Indigenous peoples will continue to utilise the available tools to pursue their objectives. Governments must choose whether they will facilitate these initiatives or frustrate them. While the courts have made the first move to recognise Indigenous systems of authority, other institutions of the state must now take the further step of developing alternative processes for negotiation of Indigenous governance structures.

Jeremy Webber has argued that lawyers tend to think of rights in terms of the legal mechanisms that protect them (such as a written constitution or an Act of Parliament), but ignore their 'symbolic charge'.[30] However, Webber argued, it is impossible to escape the symbolism. Legal discourse is not insulated from popular discussion of issues of law and justice because that general discussion and the 'connotations, implications and points of resonance' impact upon interpretation and shape the evolution of law.[31]

The judges in *Mabo* were aware of the symbolic nature of their decision.[32] The significance of the *Mabo* decision is carried in 'legal' native title, which is its practical or functional outcome. Native title became the symbol for, and therefore the measure of, non-Indigenous relations with Indigenous peoples. Native title recognised not just an interest in land, but also the legitimacy of Indigenous peoples' claims to be lawmakers, and to be recognised as a legitimate source of rights and obligations.

The symbolic and functional aspects of native title can diverge and, indeed, operate in tension with one another. Nevertheless, the failure of governments to understand the connection between the recognition of native title and agreement making on a sovereign to sovereign scale can be a source of immense frustration for Indigenous peoples. Each of the comprehensive negotiations between native title claimants and the state that have been highlighted here has been shadowed by vehement opposition to particular claims in the courts. For South Australia, while promoting negotiations under the state-wide ILUA, the state was arguing that native title had been extinguished and that the Yunkuntjatjara people of De Rose Hill station were not native title holders of their traditional country.[33] For the Noongar Nation, negotiations over a framework agreement will take place against the backdrop of litigation of the Perth metropolitan claim. Agreements in relation to the Martu and Tjurabalan must deal with the fallout from *Ward*. The COAG trials more generally operate alongside the opposition to native title outcomes from the Commonwealth and state governments.

The state's opposition to native title in the courts is difficult to correlate with the rhetoric of framework agreements and whole-of-government commitments to improving the lives and opportunities of Indigenous peoples. These 'joined-up' approaches by governments appear to exclude the offices of native title within the government who remain dedicated to opposing the recognition of native title as a legal outcome. As Noel Pearson has expressed, it is like playing a game: 'They pretend they are not resolutely opposing native title. We pretend the same thing in return.'[34]

Both functionally and symbolically, native title will continue to play a central role in any political settlement because, for better or worse, it now provides the framework within which non-Indigenous people conceive of Indigenous rights and provides the bulwark against which Indigenous peoples can build their claims for greater recognition. Native title provides Indigenous peoples with one of the only processes in which the state is required to engage. For Indigenous peoples, too, native title is not merely a form of title. It is a fundamental recognition by the colonising state of the distinct identity and special place of Indigenous peoples as the first peoples.

Symbolism reflects, as well as defines, what is important to us as a society. By suggesting what is important, symbols influence people's sense of involvement in the society in which they live. Native title is such a symbol. At its foundation, native title reflects the relationship between Indigenous and non-Indigenous peoples in Australia. It matters what we do and what we achieve with native title.

9.
Native Title Conference, Gimuy Walubara Yidinji Country, 2007

SOCIETIES, COMMUNITIES AND NATIVE TITLE*

KINGSLEY PALMER[†]

In this paper I examine the use and meaning of the terms 'community' and 'society' in native title cases. I consider this use from an anthropological point of view but situate it within legal contexts relevant to native title law. I explore whether there is a difficulty for anthropologists in the way these terms may be used in the context of native title processes and, if this be the case, how such difficulty may be alleviated or circumvented.

There is a body of anthropological writing and thinking that has been critical of the interface between anthropology and native title law. In an earlier paper I reviewed some of this material and made mention of a number of articles that addressed ethical issues, the nature of anthropological evidence and practical issues related to participation in the legal process.[1] One aspect of this critique views the anthropology of native title as compromised by the demands of native title law, or perhaps subverted by it. I discussed the Yulara case as an example where anthropology had suffered as a result of the demands of the legal system through forcing anthropology into a 'highly constrained reductionist form'.[2] Paul Burke, in his PhD thesis, has examined this interaction between anthropologists, lawyers and judges.[3] He argues that his analysis of social process allows for a comprehensive explanation of relationships, removing tensions otherwise present between the dichotomising of law and anthropology. By considering materials taken from native title cases,

Burke demonstrates some of the issues that arise when anthropologists bring their understandings to bear upon native title (and legal) constructs.

Morton, in a short note concerning the Yulara judgment and Professor Sansom's commentary upon it,[4] sees law as in the business of imposing order; anthropology as generating conceptual contradictions and complexity.[5] Morton sees one consequence — 'intolerance of "unreason" evident in the regimentation of anthropologists' reports'.[6] He describes the native title process in such circumstances as one marked by 'a question of how much chaos a judge is willing to tolerate before deciding that a system is not in evidence'.[7]

These accounts together demonstrate the difficulties of anthropology's encounter with the law and the useful application of the anthropologist's expertise in native title matters. They invite further consideration of why these problems are so much in evidence.

In this paper I seek to explore the causes for these difficulties, rather than their manifestations or ramifications. My proposition is that the dissonance between anthropologists and the application of their science in native title inquiries develops from differences between the characteristics of the former and the demands of the latter. At the heart of this difference is the nature of the process whereby anthropologists seek to describe and understand social process (relationships, meanings) on the one hand and another that seeks evidence (statements, expert views) to support or deny that a particular criterion or requirement has been met. The former sees social process as lacking absoluteness, the latter requires it. The former stresses change and mutability, the latter stasis and immutability.

This distinction finds parallels in anthropological practice. The application of anthropology in native title inquiries and the gathering of data and comprehending them are two different undertakings. In native title cases an anthropologist is often asked to provide an expert view based on his or her knowledge, training and the discipline of anthropology. In this the anthropologist is asked to bring data to bear on a legal point of proof. This is not the same as undertaking an anthropological study ('doing anthropology'), which is variously a study of process or structure, change and meaning or a combination of one or more of these, and perhaps more besides. While the application of anthropology to the legal matter develops from the doing of anthropology, the two represent distinct fields of operation, with different parameters and theoretical underpinnings. In understanding this we can come to an appreciation of the reasons why there may appear to be disjunction between doing anthropology and the use of skills developed in that discipline to provide opinions to a Court that will have status as expert testimony.

At a practical level, too, there is dissonance. In providing an expert view, the anthropologist must, to be of assistance to the Court, accommodate the procedural and methodological differences that characterise the practices of the two disciplines. Providing an expert view is constrained by a range of rules and conventions that stem from the legal context, including the rules of evidence. In Sutton's view, this has led in one instance to the application of the 'lawyer's Occam's razor'.[8]

The juxtaposition of law and anthropology is nowhere as immediate as when respective practitioners are required to develop an understanding of words that have attracted a special privilege, status and consequential meanings in both discourses. One example is the use of the terms 'society' and 'community'. These are both legal terms (derived, in this case, from native title law but not statute) that are entrenched in jurisprudential thinking. They are also terms of anthropology. The words and the ways whereby they come to have different meanings provide a springboard for this paper. In this context I consider, below, how anthropologists must treat, in a native title process, terms that are words of law rather than of anthropology, while being an expert by virtue of being an anthropologist.

In this paper I look first at examples of how some legal thinking has defined or commented upon the terms 'society' or 'community'. In turn I then examine some of the anthropological thinking that develops from a consideration of these terms. Finally, I will look at how the two can be brought together, and examine the implications for doing so, potentially, for anthropologists.

LEGAL CRITERIA

The decision of the High Court with respect to the application made by members of the Yorta Yorta Aboriginal community provides a point of departure for a consideration of legal ideas about the centrality of a society to the concept of the perdurance of native title rights.[9] It also raised critical issues about the nature of the society, as required for native title law, at sovereignty, and a consideration of the relationship of the society at sovereignty to that of the claimants.

In the judgment of the High Court, the relationship between the continuity of laws and customs, and rights to land or water and the society is set down:

> To speak of rights and interests possessed under an identified body of laws and customs, is, therefore, to speak of rights and interests that are the creatures of the laws and customs of a particular society that exists as a group which acknowledges and observes those laws and customs. And if the society out of which the body of laws and customs arises ceases to exist as a group which acknowledges and observes those laws and customs, those laws and customs cease to have continued existence and vitality. Their content may be known but if there is no society which acknowledges and observes them, it ceases to be useful, even meaningful, to speak of them as a body of laws and customs acknowledged and observed, or productive of existing rights or interests, whether in relation to land or waters or otherwise.[10]

The identity of the pre-sovereignty claimant society is thus of fundamental importance to any consideration of the continuity of laws and customs, rights and interests. Strelein commented:

> The need to establish a coherent and continuous society defined by a pre-sovereignty normative system creates enormous ambiguity in the requirements of proof. The nature of the group has emerged as a fundamental threshold question for native title claimants. The High Court's deference to the views of the trial judge in *Yorta Yorta* demonstrated the vagaries of an assessment based to a significant degree on a judge's perceptions of the group...Native title claimants must rely on the ability of a non-Indigenous judiciary to conceptualise the contemporary expressions of Indigenous identity, culture and law as consistent with the idea of a pre-sovereignty normative system.[11]

In considering these matters, the judiciary is also likely to have regard to the evidence of experts. Since no first-hand evidence can be adduced as to the nature of the society at sovereignty, the court is likely to rely on experts to provide a view in this regard. In determining the nature of the contemporary society, the Court is also likely to need the assistance of an expert, since the concept is a product of law, not of Indigenous culture.

In another native title decision (largely in favour of the applicants), Justice Weinberg quoted one of his colleagues as helpful in defining a society. He also went back to *Yorta Yorta*:

> The concept of a 'society' in existence since sovereignty as the repository of traditional laws and customs in existence since that time derives from the reasoning in *Yorta Yorta*. The relevant ordinary meaning of society is 'a body of people forming a community or living under the same government' — Shorter Oxford English Dictionary. It

9. Societies, communities and native title

does not require arcane construction. It is not a word which appears in the NT Act. It is a conceptual tool for use in its application. It does not introduce, into the judgments required by the NT Act, technical, jurisprudential or social scientific criteria for the classification of groups or aggregations of people as 'societies'.[12]

His Honour asserted that for the application of native title law, the common English sense of the term 'community' is what is relevant. 'Arcane construction' (the likely province of an expert, perhaps?) is not only unnecessary but would involve application of criteria 'foreign' to native title law.

His Honour Justice Merkel was less critical of potential experts but made it clear as to what was required. Justice Merkel wrote, in relation to the *Rubibi* claim, that the applicants made claim for the recognition of native title as a community:

> As stated above, the Yawuru claim is a claim for communal native title rights and interests as it is claimed to be made on behalf of a community of people, namely the Yawuru community as defined in the application. The Yawuru claimants, relying on *Members of the Yorta Yorta Aboriginal Community v State of Victoria* [2002], claim that the Yawuru community is a body of persons united in and by its acknowledgment and observance of a body of traditional laws and customs. Those traditional laws and customs are said to constitute the normative system under which the rights and interests claimed are created.[13]

In other judgments I have read, the term 'society' is used freely, but to convey the sense that it comprises those who share cultural commonalities and adhere to the same system of laws and customs. For example:

> In 1838 there was an established Aboriginal society close to the western boundary of the claim area (Glenelg River). It was an organised society, the members of which built structures and adorned their environment with paintings including Wanjina paintings, made artefacts of wood, and used stone to crush and grind seeds and to shape into spearheads.[14]

In native title law, according to one authority, 'society' is chosen over 'community' because the former serves to emphasise 'this close relationship between the identification of the group and the identification of the laws and customs of that group'.[15] Presumably this differentiation is drawn from the ordinary English use of the terms, rather than from anthropology. Conversely, anthropologists might use the term 'society' for larger, complex groupings — I provide some general examples of this in the next section. The term 'community' is sometimes used for smaller groups characterised by closer social ties and interaction and the typical subject of anthropological inquiry.[16] The point is simple. Legal meanings and those of the social sciences show no automatic correlation.

In summary, there is a consistent legal view that a community has to be recognisable, because the laws and customs (the normative system) of its constituents unite members through joint or common observance. While it is not stated, it would be a reasonable assumption that those people who did not share these laws and customs but observed others would constitute a different society or community.

The legal concept of community, to date at least, is clear enough. Native title is a product of recognition of customary laws of a community or society of people. Land law is not going to be their only law, but will form a component of a set of laws which makes up a normative system that characterises the community or society.

ANTHROPOLOGICAL CRITERIA

Anthropological terminology

Social scientists in Australia have used the terms 'society' and 'community' without specialist sense to mean a set of people who can be grouped together because of shared cultural attributes. For example, the term has been used in the title of a few books and articles that treat Aboriginal topics. Ken Maddock had *A portrait of their society* as a subtitle to his 1974 book on *The Australian Aborigines*.[17] CD Rowley wrote a classic account of *The Destruction of Aboriginal Society* in 1980.[18] More recently, Ian Keen has used the term 'society' in the title of his book *Aboriginal Economy and Society*, as well as from time to time in the text without defining it.[19] It is not included in his glossary of terms. However, the meaning is to my mind evident from the context.[20]

The term 'society' as used in the examples cited above provides, then, a useful concept rather than a specific one. It has the facility to convey a meaning that implies a group of people who together have things in common. This might include cultural practices, language and beliefs. However, it does not provide for a very tight or exact definition of what might be meant and therein lies its usefulness, perhaps, for those who have chosen to use it. Should this use be not understood for the shorthand it probably is, the use obfuscates important distinctions in the way anthropology understands the nature of social groups.

Generally, a 'society' for an anthropologist is not a 'thing' but comprises sets of relationships.[21] Beattie counsels that thinking of 'society' as a thing, like a frog or a jellyfish, was 'more embarrassing than useful'.[22] It is essential to jettison any analogy with an organism in order to focus on the relationships that exist between people who thereby recognise commonalities.[23]

Michael Herzfeld, in what he describes as 'an overview of social and cultural anthropology', tells us that at the beginning of the twenty-first century, 'one thing is for sure: the attempt to abolish uncertainty has failed'.[24] He cited the 'most obvious victim' as being 'the idea of the bounded human group — the "society" or "culture" of the classic anthropological imagination'.[25] Earlier he cites Arturo Escobar, who wrote, 'societies are not the organic wholes with structures and laws that we thought them to be until recently but fluid entities stretched on all sides by migrations, border crossings and economic forces'.[26]

These views reflect a trend that typifies anthropology in its interest in understanding diachronic relationships and meaning, developed over time, through social process, rather than a science based on synchronic and structural classification. More recent anthropology has, according to Weiner, been 'dominated by social constructionism in its own "strong" voluntarist version — that, as agents, human beings make their own world consciously and deliberately'.[27] This manner of understanding social process as construction and agency through time is in marked contrast to the idea of a society as a relatively stable and discretely modelled entity.

Based on some of the legal views cited above ('repository of traditional laws and customs'), it would appear that in law a society is, indeed, a thing. In anthropology, it is made up of sets of relationships, changing through time, defying reification and certainty. Herein, then, lies a fundamental point of difference.

WHAT DO ABORIGINAL STUDIES TELL US?

In Australian Aboriginal studies terms like 'nation', 'community' and 'tribe' abounded, particularly in the early literature as early ethnographers sought to identify the building blocks (sets of relationships) that constituted Aboriginal society (or societies).[28] These early accounts are of importance in native title research, since establishing a view as to the continuity of a social formation (a society) must rely, to some extent, upon the accounts provided by early ethnographers. Those assisting or assessing an application for native title are likely to go to this early literature to see what was said about the society in question at or about the time of sovereignty.

With two exceptions (Meggitt and Hiatt), which are discussed by Sutton,[29] anthropologists writing post-1950 generally did not use the term 'community'. The term 'nation' was dismissed on the ground that its use implied a degree of political unity that was never apparent.[30]

Applications for recognition of native title have used a variety of different models of society as a means of establishing the parameters within which laws and customs were held in common.[31] Peter Sutton took the view that there were several kinds of Aboriginal groups that could be defined in relation to land.[32] He observed that a choice in how a claimant community was to be defined reflected the reality of 'different landed entities', which would yield 'a number of overlapping "territories" for the same population'.[33]

Sutton also noted that there were different sorts of Aboriginal 'community' — he identified two, one defined in relation to geography, another defined in terms of the relationships of its members.[34] Each was different and neither necessarily comprised members who were the same as members of a native title community — that is, a group who together shared rights in the same country. By this account, then, not all 'communities' will be relevant to a native title application. For the anthropologist there is choice in how the word will be applied. There is no absolute 'community'. The anthropologist needs to ensure that the sort of community chosen is relevant to the group understood to have customary rights to the application area.

The two-fold question in relation to any native title claim, then, is which sort of 'landed entity' is to be chosen and how broad a compass does its collective interest in land circumscribe?

It is not my intention here to review and categorise the types of society that have been presented in native title applications, even if this were practical. However, there are some sorts of societies that can be regarded as models that are relevant to this paper. For the most part they relate to models that might be applicable to larger rather than smaller-scale social formations. All would appear to me to be anthropologically defensible in terms of meeting the requirements of a society for the purpose of a native title application.

9. Societies, communities and native title

Cultural bloc

The concept of a 'cultural bloc' as an aggregation of constituent tribes or other groups has been the subject of a number of early studies, including Radcliffe-Brown, who was interested in expansions of 'social solidarity' beyond the range of the local group.[35] Similarly, Roth characterised larger aggregates in western Queensland as 'messmates', united by the use of mutually intelligible languages, 'bonds of comradeship' endogamy and cooperation in times of war.[36]

Sutton reviewed other accounts that provided evidence of aggregations or 'nations'.[37] In the context of a discussion of both Mathews and Howitt, Sutton states that the early accounts support the view that there were regional aggregations with substantial cultural commonalities.

> Certain extensive areas of south-eastern Australia, for example, were characterised by a widely reported classical complex in which were to be found matrilineal moieties, sections, matrilineal unlocalised social totems, single linguistic groups numbering several thousand (not just a few hundred people), a *bora* (sacred ceremony) type of initiation system, emphasis on site-bound increase rites, a prominent religious and social role for the medicine-men of high degree who were able to fly, a belief in an 'All-Father' figure located in the heavens, fragmentary evidence of primary recruitment to country through birth or, possibly, conception and, probably, a system of individualised life-time site or tract tenure resting on an underlying communal estate title system.[38]

Sutton also noted that some later writers attempted to identify regional aggregations in relation to drainage divisions.[39]

The 'cultural bloc' is sometimes associated with the Western Desert region. In 1959 RM Berndt published an account of local organisation for some Australian desert regions, suggesting that the term 'tribe' was 'not entirely applicable'.[40] Instead, he suggested that the use of a common language, with dialect variations, resulted in 'a common awareness of belonging to a cultural and linguistic unit, over and above the smaller units signified by these [dialect] names'.[41] Berndt identified such a group as a 'culture bloc'.[42] Berndt suggests that within the culture bloc was a 'wider unit' 'formed seasonally by members of a number of hordes coming together for the purpose of performing certain sacred rituals'.[43] These wider units would have changed composition over time and the degree of interaction would have been variable. There would not necessarily have been a consistency of horde membership of a 'wider group'.[44] He concludes that:

> One might expect to find a number of these [wider groups] throughout the Western Desert, with some of their members interchangeable from time to time…Each one of these might be termed a society, with the main criteria being, (a) sustained interaction between its members; (b) the possession of broadly common aims; (c) effective and consistent communication between them. It is suggested, therefore, on the basis of material presented here, that it is more rewarding to speak of Western Desert societies, rather than ambiguously of tribes.[45]

For Berndt the Western Desert cultural bloc was made up of a number of societies — it was not a single 'society' in the sense that he used the term. The characteristics he ascribed to a society do not clearly equate to the characteristics of a society of native title law. The societies were both labile and ephemeral, so lacked corporate attributes and were social rather than land-holding groups. 'Broadly common aims' is the closest we get to any idea that the members of such a society might share laws and customs — although their social interaction might imply that they do.

In a later paper the same writer was to apply this concept to a non-arid region, which he called the 'northeastern Arnhem Land bloc'.[46] This identity was marked by a 'local recognition of a broadly common culture', an acceptance of dialect variation constituting a common language and acknowledgment of 'mythic' relationships — that is, relationships that existed between constituent groups or individuals that developed from spiritual ties between themselves, the land and each other.[47]

Berndt's comments on tribes and societies provide a useful introduction to what is, to my mind, a more problematic concept and one that Berndt found unhelpful, at least for Western Desert societies.

Tribes

The term 'tribe' retains some popular currency, in part as a result of Tindale's 1974 map and, to a lesser extent, because of subsequent reincarnations by Horton (1994) and others.[48] There has been an assumption, common in lay thinking, that a set of language speakers may form a discrete community with an internal political structure that merited the appellation of 'tribe'.[49] Thus the name of a spoken language becomes a 'tribal' name. A corollary of this is a view that the 'tribe' was the maximal territorial unit, whose members together held a defined area of land in common. There was also an assumption in much early Australian anthropological literature that this model was generally applicable.[50]

Anthropologists in Australia have not always been in agreement as to how best to characterise Indigenous societies in terms that can be shown to have empirical validity. This is a consequence of the fact that the social units that comprise Aboriginal groupings are not easily or simply identified. It is likely that within what was a hunting and gathering society there were several ways by which people identified, according to activity (economic, ritual or regional), as well as by reference to kin relationships. This multiplicity of referents presents a problem if a single unambiguous identity is sought. Moreover, some aggregations are likely to have been labile and so would have changed composition over time, providing an obstacle to the identification of enduring social formations.

The assumptions and preconceptions about Aboriginal political organisation are particularly common in the early Australian literature. They developed from conjecture that a 'native' society would take the form of a named 'tribe' with little or no understanding of the variety of social formations and the multitude of names applied by Aboriginal people themselves to social and regional groupings. For many early writers a 'tribe' was explicitly or implicitly understood to comprise a community of people, with a classifying name, whose members spoke the same language and adhered to a system of government that included a chief or leader. In early (and, indeed, in some later) ethnographies, the use of a name to identify the 'tribe' was then a convenience born of a preconception which obfuscated a more complex reality. In any event, unless the term 'tribe' was being used in a narrowly defined sense, the field data did not support the existence of 'tribes' in the popularly understood sense of the term, as later writers were to show.

As far back as 1938, Davidson, who also provided an early example of a 'tribal map', stated that the largest political unit in Aboriginal local organisation was what he termed the 'horde'.[51] He understood that:

> Larger groupings are recognised and named by the natives on the bases of dialect and cultural similarities and geographical contiguity. These larger units, which furnish a more practical basis for ethnological considerations, can be spoken of as tribes in spite of the fact that there is no semblance of centralized political authority nor any sense of political confederation.[52]

For Davidson, then, the use of the term 'tribe' was a convenience, the term used to identify groups whose members recognised 'dialect and cultural similarities', furnishing a practical basis for 'ethnological considerations'.

Later writers pointed out the difficulties and errors of 'tribal' models. For example, Ian Keen wrote:

> Many early ethnographers assumed that Aborigines were divided into relatively large and discrete 'tribes', each of which shared a common language, culture, and territory. This model survived through the first two-thirds of the twentieth century, adhered to, with variations, by Radcliffe-Brown, Elkin, Tindale and Birdsell…the tribal model had begun to unravel more than a decade before Tindale published his book and maps of Aboriginal tribes in 1974.[53]

As mentioned above, RM Berndt had questioned the applicability of the term to Western Desert societies in 1959.[54] Rumsey provides a helpful critique of the use of the term 'tribe' and exposes some of the assumptions related to its unquestioned use, particularly with respect to the relationship to both a single language and territory.[55]

Tindale's characterisation of 'tribes' and 'boundaries' was examined in detail by Monaghan in a thesis presented in 2003. Monaghan sought to understand the extent to which Tindale's representations were, in fact, the result of his theoretical preoccupations and his ideas of linguistic and racial purity. While the focus of his study was on areas identified as 'Pitjantjatjara', his arguments are relevant to this review.

> This thesis argues that, in producing his tribal representations, Tindale effectively reduced a diversity of indigenous practices to ordered categories more reflective of Western and colonial concepts than indigenous views. Tindale did not consider linguistic criteria in any depth, his informants were few, and the tribal boundaries appear to a large extent to be arbitrary. In addition, Tindale's linguistic work was heavily biased towards the category 'Pitjantjatjara' and was informed by notions of racial and (to a certain extent) linguistic purity. Moreover, because these (among other) preoccupations played a direct role in shaping the historical linguistic record, they must be considered when interpreting the historical records rather than simply accepting them at face value, as lawyers, anthropologists and linguists have done in the past.[56]

Keen noted that the early ethnographer Howitt wrote of 'mixed' language group areas and that some marriages took place between people of different language varieties, making their children, presumably, in his view, of mixed language identity.[57] More recently, researchers (in Queensland) have demonstrated that the relationship between language, social identity and community is complex.[58] People tend to be multilingual (or to speak several dialects of the same language), people sometimes marry those from other language or dialect groups, and this language, while important, could not be seen alone as a diacritic of group membership. The formation of an identity also involved references to a locality or a relative appellation, like 'northerner' or coastal dweller.[59]

While accepting that much of the early literature casts Aboriginal social life and culture in terms of discrete 'tribes', Keen concluded, 'several critiques have cast doubt on the validity of a cellular model of Aboriginal society'.[60] With respect to the named 'tribal' groups that were the subject of his analyses, he warned, 'it should not be assumed that these names refer to societies or localised "social systems", especially given the degree of heterogeneity of both ecologies and cultural forms documented for some regions'.[61]

I agree with Alan Rumsey that the misconception regarding tribes is still current.[62] 'Tribes' are well represented in NNTT research reports that reproduce maps produced by linguists (and others) — of which there would appear to be many — showing 'tribal' territories drawn onto maps by means of boundary lines. This would appear to confirm my view that 'tribes' are regarded by at least some of those involved in native title research as a valid unit in defining customary native title groups. This stems from the lingering popular misconceptions about 'tribes' in Aboriginal Australia.

Since the 'tribe' was not a political entity, it could not have a bounded territory. The territorial regime was, as Davidson pointed out, a matter for what he called the 'horde' or local group. Boundaries were a product of the assertion of rights by members of these groups. Where several groups recognised linguistic commonalities, it seems reasonable that boundaries might also be conceptualised in language-group terms, especially in a regional context. In some cases it is evident that language was imputed into country by reference to both place names and myth, further enhancing the association of language and country. However, it is not the case that this is only by reference to one language.[63] From my own experience, this process was not universal and was (and is) more strongly marked in some areas than others.

Defining what might constitute a 'society' or a 'community' in terms of the account of 'tribes' will need to accommodate these difficulties and avoid these obstacles. This is not to say that a 'tribal' model is not sometimes helpful. However, designation of a 'tribal group' cannot, of itself, assume commonalities of law, language and culture. Conversely, a society could comprise more than one 'tribe', since laws and customs transcend the territorial boundaries of country groups and commonly traverse a number of different language groups.[64]

Language groups

If 'tribes' are problematic for anthropologists, a characteristic of groups of people that have been labelled a 'tribe' might provide for a more profitable line of inquiry. Language is a useful tool in defining a society for the purposes of native title. In so far as a language-speaking group corresponds to the old fashioned notion of a 'tribe', there are likely to be ethnographic references resting on assumptions of 'tribal' unity to support the representation of the society as a relatively unified body of people.

Language variation, however, is an issue that has to be addressed in such cases. Pertinent questions include whether dialect variations are a means of asserting difference, and what is the Aboriginal understanding of similarity and difference in this regard. Analyses effected by linguists can be misleading in cases where languages are shown to be technically similar, and so classed together, while social and political difference between speakers marks substantial difference. Conversely, there are instances where languages that are technically classed as being quite different are regarded by multilingual speakers as being much the same. Linguist Bill McGregor made relevant comment on the nature of linguistic classifications in this regard. Writing of the Kimberley, he distinguished between technical classification and how speakers understand languages spoken by others to relate to that which they themselves speak: 'It should be noted that speakers may classify languages quite differently from linguists, and may perceive similarities on the basis of cultural affiliations over and above formal resemblances of either typological or the genetic type, which are the basis of linguists' classifications.'[65]

Linguists and others have also made a distinction between language-speaking groups and language-owning groups.[66] The distinction between an ability to speak a language and being regarded as an owner of the language was first made over twenty-five years ago by Peter Sutton.[67] In short, the former are characterised by members who speak the language in question; the latter by those who consider they are associated with a language name, but who do not themselves necessarily speak the language. It is, however, something that they consider they own and thus is a cornerstone of their common identity. This distinction is obviously of importance for many areas of Australia where a traditional language is no longer spoken.

9. Societies, communities and native title

Cultural cohesion

A fourth model for a society is one characterised by close kinship, ritual and economic links, perhaps in relation to a unifying geographic feature, like a river or drainage system. Such an arrangement would not preclude the use of different languages, as multilingualism would be a necessary feature of the population's skills set where the society was comprised of speakers of more than one language. One such example was *Griffiths v Northern Territory of Australia* in the Timber Creek area. In his judgment, Justice Weinberg accepted that five discrete country groups, representing two different language-speaking groups, constituted the society whose members together held native title in the application area.[68]

Likewise, Justice Sundberg found that a number of groups together made up a community bound together through observance of a number of laws and customs. These were clearly enunciated in evidence.

> The body of evidence...shows that the claimants regard themselves as part of a community inhabiting the Ngarinyin, Worrorra and Wunambal region. Throughout the evidence there is an emphasis on shared customs and traditions that transcend any particular dambun or language area. Central to this sharing is the belief in Wanjina; that Wanjina impressed themselves on the landscape, principally in painting sites. Wanalirri, though in Ngarinyin country, is regarded throughout the claim area as the source of the laws and customs laid down by Wanjina. This belief extends beyond the borders of the claim area into the claim region. The Wunggurr tradition also extends across the claim area and beyond, as do other practices and customs: moieties, the marriage rules, wurnan, wudu, rambarr, traditional burial, dambun and kinship rules. The evidence collected earlier is inconsistent with any description of the group or groups that hold the native title rights other than those who are members of the Wanjina-Wunggurr community.[69]

The Wanjina–Wunggurr community is substantially larger than the Timber Creek society, although the principle of recruitment would appear to have much in common. The commonalties, which the groups were held to exhibit by the judges in question, relate to the same sort of cultural beliefs, practices and norms as were outlined for regional aggregations by Sutton (see above) and is perhaps a contraction of the regional aggregation model, which I also noted at the same reference above.

Definitional progress

These models may provide a basis for developing an idea of a community or society. It is possible that no single one will match the ethnography, and the final construct be an amalgam of parts of more than one.

Overall and however the models are used, 'society' comes to have a specific meaning for an anthropologist considering the preparation of an expert view that will be helpful to those involved in adjudicating a legal recognition of native title. In this context a 'society' is a group (or body) of people who recognise themselves and are recognised by others to share commonalities developed and expressed through actual or potential social relationships. In this they identify themselves as having more in common with their fellows than they do with others who may be differentiated as 'strangers'. Cultural commonality is underpinned by the observance of common laws and customs. Other factors may also play a part, but not invariably. For example, members of a society may use the same language (or dialects of the same language), or be multilingual, utilising a suite of languages with varying degrees of proficiency. Members may also feel themselves to be united by social bonds and recognise kinship links by reference to classificatory, as well as consanguineal, reckonings.

A commonplace and perhaps obvious comment follows from this, but one which is in my experience sometimes not fully appreciated. It is not necessary for a member of a society to know all other members of that society or to expect to interact with all others. Neither is it necessary for all members of a society to live in perpetual peace and harmony, since the sharing of laws and customs does not mandate concord.

THE APPLICATION OF MODELS

Native title law requires recognition of a defensible society or community — one that is anthropologically viable in terms of both contemporary practice and past ethnographies. Thus the proper society for an application must be founded upon a reasonably argued expert view that such a body of persons were united through observance of common laws and customs in the past.

I have set out above some of the choices for a 'society' that have anthropological credibility. These have the potential, given the right supporting data and evidence, to have relevance to a consideration of native title. However, finding a fit between what might be a native title society or community, however understood, for the purposes of the NTA and a society or community defined by reference to the available ethnography presents a challenge for anthropology. There are three reasons for this.

First, for anthropologists unqualified terms like 'community' or 'society' invoke a number of different and sometimes conflicting referents. This is true generally in relation to the discourse of the profession, which counsels strict definitional use of the words. It is also true in relation to Aboriginal studies, in particular, where many different terms have been used, without consistency, for different types of social formation — real or imagined. As Sutton has pointed out, this may afford some flexibility and choice over the type of social formation identified as apposite in the context of a native title application. On the other hand, the form of the society used to characterise the claimant community needs to be robust and defensible, clearly defined and substantiated by the field data. In short, anthropologists need to do a proper job in their application and definition.

Second, demonstration of continuity of a society necessarily relies upon ethnographic reconstruction. While the early ethnographic accounts for some areas of Australia are many, quality and reliability are both questionable.[70] This is a consequence of assumptions made by observers about 'tribal' organisation and other groupings, their often inconsistent use of terminology and the manner in which their data were collected — mostly at arm's length and second or third hand.

Given substantial difficulties in developing reasonable reconstructions of social formations, expert views about correlations between a contemporary community of native title holders and that likely to have been in evidence at the time of first sustained European settlement will be qualified. Moreover, they will, at least potentially, be subject to criticism on the ground that the contemporary society has little or no correspondence with that developed from the early ethnography. Again, the anthropologist needs to be aware of this potential difficulty and ensure that it is addressed in his or her account.

The third issue relates to scale. As a general rule, the smaller a society, the more likely will be the uniformity of observance of law and custom. Conversely, the larger the society, the greater the likelihood of internal variation. In the case of a clearly bounded society, discontinuity is identified as a boundary. Such is the case, for example, with the so-called 'circumcision line' that Tindale drew on his maps.[71] The line purports to show a discontinuity of a cultural practice (a law) within geographic space. On one side of the line people practised circumcision, on the other they did not.

Such a boundary is necessarily a cadastral and cartographic construct. It has the intention of demonstrating the incidence of cultural practice in geographic space, at least in general terms. At the boundary of two distinct societies there would be a defined representation of difference. However, social space is not always so clearly bounded.[72]

In an arrangement where aggregations of groups recognise commonalities between themselves and their near neighbours, bounded cultural space as a recognition of cultural correlation is going to be a function of relative proximity. In such a case, distinctive commonalities would diminish gradually across space. At opposite ends of a spectrum would be those who understood one another to be observers of different laws and customs, while those at various intervals in between might appreciate more or less difference, a greater or lesser degree of correlation.

The question, then, is this: at what point, for the purposes of a native title application, is cultural dissonance tantamount to disunity and the admission of two or more different societies? Again these issues must be addressed in any expert anthropological view, although, as I explore below, issues of cultural process sit with some difficulty with many aspects of the native title legal process.

ANTHROPOLOGY AND LAW: DISJUNCTION OR SNUG FIT?

An essential task for the Court — or for the state if it is considering the acceptability of an application for a potential consent determination — relates to a necessity that certain criteria have been met. These are, like any matter of proof, a question of examining whether requirements set down in statute and encased by judgment can be understood to have been attained. In this activity, evidence is judged (by the Court or by another set of persons) either to have satisfied those conditions or not. While native title law can accommodate the notion that things have not stood still in relation to the form and structure of a society over time, the essentially synchronic process of adjudication remains fundamental to the enterprise.

I noted above, in my discussion about the extent of a society, that forming a view of commonalities can provide a challenge for anthropologists. This is because an anthropological account often understands societies to be moving, vibrant entities, which do not remain the same from one moment to the next. Moreover, seeing societies as discrete entities is not a part of our contemporary discourse or a reflection of the manner whereby our science understands such things to be.

There is then a difficulty between a mode of thinking that sees a society as a thing and a snap-shot in time, and a society seen as sets of relationships which are likely to be in a constant state of flux and to change in some ways most of the time.

The ideas I have explored in this paper about community and society have one thing in common. They are all descriptive of structures. That is to say, they represent a view of a social formation during a single slice in time. While what I have called 'cultural cohesion' exhibits some propensity toward a diachronic analysis, it is still essentially a description of a society at a point in time. This fact is what makes them helpful in the context of the consideration of applications for the recognition of native title.

The sorts of social formations that I have set out above that could correspond to a 'society' for the purpose of an application for the recognition of native title are what could be termed 'models'. A model is (amongst other things) a small-scale replica founded after reality. It is also, by virtue of its replicated but small-scale construction, both an ideal and a representation of that reality presented at a particular moment in time. For an anthropologist, models are useful heuristic devices. But in the sense that I use the term here, models cannot easily accommodate social process: the ebb and flow of relationships; the fluctuations in identity in response to political motion; the rise of one man and the demise of another; and the essential uncertainties these vacillations generate. These are the sorts of things that provide the basis for an understanding of social process over time. The use of models, a legitimate instrument for the preparation of an expert view for an anthropologist, provides, then, for a means of mediation between a requirement of the legal process and the tools available to the anthropologist. It permits the anthropologist to provide expert views in a manner that will be comprehensible to the requirements of a legal process. Because models are founded after the ethnographic reality (and will be tested in Court to see if, indeed, they are so), they are the product of the anthropological endeavour. In this way there is a clear differentiation, but no necessary disjunction, between doing anthropology (understanding social process and meaning) and being an expert witness (furnishing a synchronic model based on that research).

What the Court requires is an understanding and a view that relates to the particular constructs and technical requirements of the law — in this case, the Native Title Act. The focus of an expert view needs to be a clear understanding of that requirement. The anthropologists' view then relates to the field of endeavour which is set and defined by the legislation and the legal process. The apparent difficulties that develop in this regard relate to anthropological and legal fundamentals. Social process is never discrete, final or absolute. In contrast, forensic determination is the absolute product of relating completed evidence to defined claim. In this paper I have argued that it is beneficial for anthropologists to pay heed to these facts and differences and so to recognise the process with which they are engaged. In the adoption of models, it is possible to follow the anthropological discipline while developing methodological discriminations that mediate between the fundamentals of social inquiry and the legal requirements for expert opinion and evidence.

10.
Native Title Conference, Lhere Artepe Country, 2003

SELF-DETERMINATION AND INDIGENOUS NATIONS IN THE UNITED STATES
International human right, federal policy and Indigenous nationhood

CHRISTINE ZUNI CRUZ

My paper will focus on self-determination.[1] Self-determination is a term that is used widely in the United States in respect to Indigenous affairs. In the time I have, I want to spend most of it discussing self-determination from the internal Indigenous perspective. Self-determination is being discussed in respect to Indigenous peoples at the international level, and it has long been used in respect to federal policy at the national level in the United States, since the 1970s. It is important to connect my discussion to both the international and national discussions because they impact one another.

At the international level, self-determination is a human right enshrined in both covenants of human rights, which state, 'All peoples have the right to self-determination'.[2] It has historical underpinnings, which begin with its application to nation states at the American and French revolutions.[3] Self-determination was first applied to 'peoples' after World War I.[4] Its application broadened after World War II when decolonisation of 'peoples subjugated by colonial or alien, i.e. European powers' occurred,[5] but the decolonisation movement stopped decisively short of including Indigenous peoples.⁶ Though it included 'peoples subjugated by colonial or alien, i.e. European powers', it emphasised that 'boundaries inherited from the colonial period were inviolate'.⁷ Under this approach, Indigenous peoples were 'impliedly barred from asserting self-determination' because colonisation by settler populations was not included in the movement to decolonise.⁸ Thus, the inclusion by the Working Group of Indigenous Populations of self-determination in the Declaration on the Rights of Indigenous Peoples represents a major assertion.⁹ Article 3 stated, 'Indigenous peoples have the right to self-determination. By virtue of that right they freely determine their political status and freely pursue their economic, social and cultural development.'¹⁰ The Working Group on the Draft Declaration constituted from within the membership of the Commission on Human Rights began considering the Draft Declaration in 1995.¹¹ Once the Commission on Human Rights finalised the text, the Draft Declaration was submitted to the United Nations General Assembly for final adoption and proclamation.¹² Although the Declaration is not legally binding, it will have considerable moral force.

The United States has asserted opposition to the provision on several grounds. The United States has made all the following arguments:
- international law does not recognise collective rights;
- Indigenous peoples are not 'peoples';
- right of self-determination applies only in colonial context, which does not include the situation of Indigenous peoples.¹³

The relationship of the United States to the Indigenous peoples within the nation has been described as a guardian–ward relationship, with Indigenous peoples having the status of 'domestic dependent nations'.¹⁴ That is US federal Indian law in a nutshell. Tribes are possessed of inherent sovereignty — that is, powers they have never been divested of¹⁵ — so it is that Tribes in the US have their own internal governments, with jurisdiction over their lands, yet are subject to the plenary power of US Congress.¹⁶ They are quasi-sovereign, and are possessed of self-determination, as Congress carved it in 1975 to include the ability of Tribes to administer or contract federal programs and hence control federal dollars.¹⁷

When I speak of self-determination and nation building in respect to Indian nations in the United States, it is in the context of this guardian–ward, domestic dependent nation relationship between the federal government and Indigenous peoples. It is further informed by the position the United States takes in respect to self-determination at the international level. This is self-determination from the outside in.

With this very abbreviated look at self-determination in relation to Indigenous peoples in the United States at the international and national levels, I turn now to discuss self-determination, and nation building within Indigenous nations. In doing so, I seek to shift the paradigm, from looking at self-determination as granted from without, to an inside view of self-determination from an Indigenous point of view — from within. I shift the discussion of Indigenous peoples as object and subject to Indigenous peoples as central, as voiced, and as self-possessed.

TRIBAL EXISTENCE AS SACRED

What is the Indigenous viewpoint of their right to self-determination? What is the Indigenous vision in nation building?

Autochthonous legal tradition

I begin by considering the legal tradition of Indigenous peoples. When first contact occurred, colonists ascribed little value to Indigenous ways. Indigenous peoples were viewed as uncivilised, unlearned, with everything to gain from the civilising influence of the colonist.[18] So unfamiliar was their legal tradition that by convenience and ignorance it was declared non-existent. All aspects of the way of the people were attacked: religion was outlawed, language, political organisation, dispute resolution, social and familial structure were devalued. Many Indigenous peoples did not survive, but those of us who did were able to retain and protect aspects of this legal tradition.

I have been studying traditional law closely now for over a decade. Recently, I came across a book that has been very helpful to me in this work. It was written by H Patrick Glenn, a comparative law professor from the United States.[19] I appreciate two things about his work. First, it recognises the distinct existence of a 'legal tradition' of Indigenous peoples as among seven of the most important and complex legal traditions of the world, including Talmudic, civil law, Islamic, common law, Hindu and Asian legal traditions. Second, it provides a broad understanding of chthonic or Indigenous law in terms of its institutions, and substantive law and its founding concepts and methods. Most importantly, it comports with the general conclusions I have drawn from my study of the traditional law of Indigenous peoples.

Glenn refers to Indigenous law as chthonic law, because it is the law of chthonic peoples — peoples 'who live ecological lives by being chthonic, that is, by living in or in close harmony with the earth'.[20] He then describes chthonic law 'by criteria internal to itself, as opposed to imposed criteria',[21] an extremely important methodology when approaching Indigenous subjects.

Chthonic legal tradition emerges from experience, through orality (spoken word) and memory.[22] 'It is the oldest of traditions'; 'all other traditions have emerged in contrast to chthonic tradition'.[23] Its most distinctive characteristic is its orality (oral tradition).[24] Human speech and memory preserve it.[25] 'Unreliable and vulnerable', one might say, except that tradition has 'preserved that which it says to preserve for hundreds of thousands of years'.[26] It is not concerned with 'voluminous detail';[27] 'it rejects formality in the expression of law'.[28] Transmission is through 'oral education, in daily life'; it is 'a matter of daily practice, for all ages'.[29] It is communal, conducive to consensus.[30] When 'dissent emerged…new traditions were generated or created'.[31] It 'does not lend itself to complex institutions'; though there were institutions, 'the most common' being 'councils of elders', sometimes referred to as 'gerontocracy'.[32] Within the chthonic legal tradition, 'greater authority' comes from 'assimilation of tradition over a longer period of time',[33] thus elders are important to the society. Dispute resolution is 'informal', process is 'neither confusing nor alienating'.[34] (This is why we struggled with the elders on the Pueblo of Isleta Appellate Court with rules of procedure, which can be both confusing and alienating).[35] The goal is 'reconciliation rather than adjudication'.[36] (The elders always give people an opportunity, even at the last stage of appeal, to go away and settle, and instruct parties not to blame the Court if they do not like the decision, because they have only themselves to blame for not settling.)[37] 'There is…nothing…analogous to [substantive law]…only shared information on the way to live.'[38] Land and personal or movable property was not accumulated for wealth; land was occupied.[39] 'The chthonic use of land consisted of communal or collective enjoyment with no formal concept of property' — although ownership was tied up with use and occupation[40] and the concept of territory is real. Land 'could be used for hunting, farming, for limited forms of excavation…and other uses'.[41] There is no right to alienation of land recognised.[42] 'Chthonic law is…interwoven with all beliefs of chthonic peoples',[43] 'you cannot understand it without understanding other things'.[44] 'Law has its place' and it does not control everything else.[45] There are no rights in chthonic law.[46] 'The natural world is sacred' with as much respect being accorded as to yourself.[47] Chthonic tradition and chthonic law are adhered to 'because you believe the world...depends on it'.[48] It supports a 'non-linear concept of time' and thus, 'a tradition of inter-generational equity', including 'ancestors and successors'.[49] The core of tradition is 'the sacred character of the world'.[50] '[T]radition cannot simply tell its members what it has always told them; it has to show why other ways are not better ways.'[51] 'The tradition had to continue to convince, or the people would lose their identity.'[52] 'Since the expansion of western and Islamic tradition, all chthonic peoples have recently seen their total information base expand, incorporating western or Islamic ideas or both.'[53] The great question is 'the extent to which the "new" information will have an impact' on the tradition or 'displace the core information or belief in the tradition'.[54]

It is through this legal tradition that we, as Indigenous peoples, know that we have the right to self-determination. It is the chthonic legal tradition that gives us our identity as peoples separate and distinct from other peoples in the world. It is critical to us. Yet, it is, in part, why we experience/have experienced the attacks we have endured on so many levels. The suppression of our religion,[55] our language,[56] the removal from and destruction and taking of our traditional lands,[57] the imposition of political organisation,[58] the physical removal of our children,[59] Western education,[60] all these impact and continue to impact our legal tradition, our identity, and it is this that I address when I speak of self-determination from the inside out. Assimilation has been a goal of United States federal policy toward its Indigenous population.[61] If we do not begin to see how our legal tradition is of utmost importance in our internal self-determination, we risk assimilating ourselves in the belief we are exercising self-determination.

It is interesting to me that the chthonic legal tradition is now being used as the measure of recognition of land rights and use of land in Australia[62] and Canada;[63] though legal tradition in the past tense is identified,[64] especially since chthonic legal tradition is alive. It exists.[65] In the United States, our adherence to chthonic legal tradition is being used to limit our jurisdiction over our territories and the people within those territories.[66] It is used in the negative sense,[67] in respect to the unacceptability of traditional law being applied to non-Indians and even to other Indians not of a particular Tribe[68] and there is great concern about what this does to the rights they enjoy as American citizens.[69] In some sense there is a degree of recognition of the very real difference between the chthonic legal tradition that survives in Indigenous communities in the United

States and the common law tradition of the country. However, the real problem is that there is not a serious understanding of the chthonic legal tradition. United States Supreme Court Justices write of traditional law as if unknowable rules will be applied to unsuspecting non-Indians in some unjust manner within our tribal court forums as justification for asserting that tribal court jurisdiction does not extend to the non-Indians who live, work and enter our borders. In *Duro v Reina*, Justice Kennedy spoke of 'unspoken practices and norms' in reference to legal method.[70] I am still trying to figure out what this refers to within a chthonic legal tradition, which is characterised by orality.[71] In *Nevada v Hicks*, Justice Souter laments the unwritten nature of traditional law and the difficulty of sorting out the 'complex' mix of law for 'outsiders'.[72] To me, the characterisation of traditional law as problematic because it is oral and unwritten represents an attack on the continued existence of our legal tradition because the underlying message is that we will gain more power and authority if we assimilate, if our law and our government and justice systems are just like the United States' system.[73] In my opinion, it is a great deception. It is also a continuation of the message that our legal tradition is inferior, when in fact it is a legitimate legal tradition; different, yes, less than — absolutely not.

So, this is my starting point for looking at self-determination from within. It is our chthonic legal tradition — our journey narratives, our origin stories — that provide the legal basis for our legitimate claim to self-determination. And once you begin with the chthonic legal tradition, everything else that has to do with self-determination, i.e. nation building, flows from it.

COUNTERVAILING FORCES

Assimilative forces

In 1934 the US Government enacted major legislation aimed at 'assisting' Tribes with their governance structures[74] which were badly affected by the allotment period in which millions of acres of land were taken from Indian reservations,[75] and by the removal of children to boarding schools,[76] and other policies of the government aimed at assimilating Indian people into the white population. As a result of the *Indian Reorganization Act*, non-traditional governance structures replaced traditional governance, many of which had broken down.[77] This displacement was accomplished for most Tribes through the adoption of Tribal constitutions.[78] These constitutions introduced such concepts as individual rights, elections, voting and majority rule, and the concept of three branches of government — executive, judicial and legislative, interestingly, without the separation of powers[79] and checks and balance principles ingrained in the United States Constitution. They introduced ideas and structures unknown in the chthonic legal tradition. Today, as some Indigenous legal scholars look critically at Tribal governance systems, this shift from Indigenous concepts of political and social organisation is seen as a starting point for more severe political crises Tribes are experiencing today.[80] It is no surprise that Indigenous peoples who continue to operate within a chthonic legal tradition would encounter problems in trying to operate under governmental systems which are not related to the way they organise the rest of their lives.[81] So as nation building is discussed in the United States at present, there has been a movement to rewrite constitutions to reflect the chthonic legal tradition of Indigenous nations. Unfortunately, an ever present concern is how much difference will be tolerated by the federal government, as well as recognising that a degree of assimilation to Western ideas is evident in the very starting point — the re-drafting of a constitution.

In 1968 Congress enacted legislation known as the *Indian Civil Rights Act*, which made certain Bill of Rights protections applicable to Tribal governments.[82] This Act reinforced the concept of 'individual rights' as paramount within tribal governments. I say reinforced, because many Tribes already possessed constitutions, which although not mirror images of the United States' constitution, contained Bill of Rights protections.[83] Thus chthonic legal traditions, which do not recognise individual rights, were faced with a prime directive to recognise and enforce individual rights. Chthonic legal tradition in the United States has thus been operating under at least two major acts, which have imposed non-chthonic legal traditions on peoples whose identity and existence is tied to their chthonic legal tradition.

My main point here is that Indigenous peoples faced with maintaining chthonic legal tradition within a nation state structure that imposes non-chthonic legal norms upon them must take special care that their chthonic legal tradition is preserved. As Tribes in the United States are contemplating 'nation building', it is imperative that we understand the importance of the chthonic legal tradition to our very existence as we reconsider our governance systems and how we are responding to the imposition of non-chthonic legal norms on our governments. I believe one of the most important steps is to consider what every act toward nation building we engage in does to our chthonic legal tradition, as well as thinking about nation building as reinforcing our chthonic legal tradition.

Education (Western versus Indigenous knowledge and approaches)

Education is a necessity in the struggle for self-determination and nation building. However, it is important to recognise Western education as a two-edged sword. Western education is essential to prepare us to engage the outside system, to protect our interests in that system and to keep abreast and, hopefully, ahead. On the other hand, Western education and all that it represents, in terms of values, approaches and ideas, can be counter to maintaining a chthonic legal tradition within our nations. Here I will use two examples from the legal field. The Navajo Nation Supreme Court Justice Robert Yazzie, in an address to Indigenous law students, asked them to be careful that the tools they acquired in law school were not used to destroy the home that they returned to.[84] He told them that some of their Western education was not going to be useful within Indigenous communities, and, in some instances, that it could be destructive.[85] A 1978 study was published on the impact on Indian Tribes of the first generation of Indian lawyers.[86]

> Medcalf concluded that, despite their best intentions, lawyers working on behalf of Indian people failed in their stated mission of strengthening native communities and had contributed to the breakdown of native culture by imposing upon the Indians the full panoply of Anglo-American values, particularly the emphasis on individual rights.[87]

There is Western knowledge and there is Indigenous knowledge. Indigenous knowledge and approaches are key in the struggle for self-determination. Western formal education must be informed by Indigenous knowledge within Indigenous communities.

> Medcalf acknowledge[d] that the Tribal lawyers she studied were, in one sense, successful because they were able to assert Tribal rights to obtain political and economic power for their native clients. She concludes, however, that American-trained lawyers ultimately fail because they do not provide their native clients with a meaningful choice between retaining a distinct Tribal existence and adopting a lifestyle indistinguishable from American society.[88]

SELF-SUFFICIENCY

Self-sufficiency is a critical aspect of self-determination. Economic development has always created great debate within Indigenous communities. Exploitation of natural resources, leasing, commercial enterprises and development have all been controversial throughout the years. This is not a surprise with an understanding of the chthonic legal tradition. Most recently, the development of gaming by Indigenous Nations throughout the United States has raised many issues. On the positive side, gaming has shown the benefits to Indigenous Nations of the advantages of successful economic ventures where tribal gaming facilities have met success. It has brought economic self-sufficiency and political power. On the other hand, success has resulted in political crises in some communities. In some of the analyses that have been written concerning these crises, it appears a connection is made between the breakdown of traditional methods of resolving intra-tribal disputes and the non-traditional method pursued to resolve the crises.[89]

Indian preference

Self-sufficiency applies also to Indigenous organisations, governance and other institutions. Indigenous peoples must be in charge of their own institutions. One of the greatest criticisms of the Bureau of Indian Affairs (BIA), the federal department responsible for Indian affairs from the 1830s to the present, has been its paternalism. In the 1970s the BIA was a bastion of top-level non-Indian bureaucrats. The 1934 *Indian Reorganization Act* had an interesting provision providing that preference should be given to Indian people by the agency in appointment to vacancies.[90] The provision lay dormant in respect to promotions until the 1970s when it was used by the BIA,[91] under pressure in respect to its paternalism and overwhelming high employment of non-Indians at the management level in the department responsible for overseeing the majority of federal programs for Indigenous peoples. The BIA began implementing the Indian preference provision in giving preference to Indians for promotion over non-Indians.[92] The policy was challenged and upheld by the United States Supreme Court in *Morton v Mancari*.[93] As a result of this Indian preference provision, the BIA today employs a majority of Indian people to administer its programs affecting Native peoples.[94] The implementation of Indian preference was tied to the self-government policy that was being promoted by the federal government.[95] The idea that Native peoples must be involved in the federal administrative body responsible for the development and administration of federal policy was an outgrowth of the federal self-determination policy. It is correct. Self-determination requires that Indigenous peoples must be in control of their own destinies. This principle applies at all levels — Indigenous, national and international.

EXISTENCE WITHIN THE NATION STATE

I want to conclude with two views of the operation of racism, discrimination and prejudice and speak to the barriers to self-determination they erect. I divide them into macro-aggressions and micro-aggressions, and begin with macro-aggressions. I had the opportunity this summer to hear Bartholemé Clavero, an academician from Seville, Spain, deliver a paper at the University of Arizona in Tucson, Arizona. It is his paper I use to describe the macro-aggression of racism, discrimination and prejudice in the United States.[96] Clavero makes the point that early on, and even currently, for some Indigenous populations, whether within nation states or subsets of nation states, Indigenous majorities have effectively been made Indigenous minorities through the constitutions creating the states, in particular those of Mexico and the United States.[97] He asks how it is that 'all current American states are Euro, either Latin or Anglo, but not Indigenous, regardless of the presence of Indigenous peoples as majority' within their own territory or in relation to the state as a whole.[98] He then shows how, through the construction of constitutions, the Indigenous are placed under the legislature and provisions of the constitution to create political subordination for Indigenous peoples. Clavero points out how, because of the historical inabilities of nation states to fully recognise self-determination of Indigenous peoples, the concept of self-determination as a human right is an important construction.[99] National governments on their own cannot easily be expected to overcome the historical layers of prejudice and discrimination that have given rise to such principles as wardship and domestic dependency. A restructuring of the relationship within nations to Indigenous peoples may, indeed, be possible, but the roots for constructions of federal Indian law principles run deep and may not be easily uprooted. The concept of citizenship, individuals participating equally with others, yet under status of wards, as exists in the United States for Indigenous peoples, runs counter both to the

Indigenous legal tradition and to self-determination and are imbedded with prejudice, discrimination and racism toward Indigenous peoples.

RACISM, DISCRIMINATION AND PREJUDICE — MICRO-AGGRESSIONS

Now I turn to micro-aggressions towards Indigenous peoples encountered in everyday life in the societies we are a part of. The existence of racism, discrimination and prejudice, whether it is based on colour, economics or status, has very real impacts on Indigenous populations.[100] They translate into alcoholism, suicide and exclusion from society. To the extent our people are lost to us through alcohol and drugs, death and imprisonment, we have lost their contributions to our societies, to our struggles. As a mother of two male children, I am acutely aware of the fact that in the United States the brunt of racism is borne by our young men of colour. It is for this reason that we must embrace struggles against racism, discrimination and prejudice as a part of the struggle for self-determination. Our liberation from these injustices is bound up with our struggle for self-determination. It is not just the macro-aggressions that hurt our people, it is the day to day micro-aggressions that take a major toll on the personhood of our people and cannot be tolerated.

I conclude by reiterating my major point. Our Indigenous legal tradition is central to our claim for self-determination. Our chthonic legal tradition is central to our identity. More of our attention should be focused on this legal tradition and its relationship to all that is proposed, imposed, contemplated, envisioned and ultimately accepted by Indigenous peoples. Everything should be reconcilable to our legal tradition. If it is not, we must rethink what it is we are doing. The struggle is ours and we will prevail. We can use all the help we can get. There is a saying for all those who would help: 'If you have come here to help me, you are wasting your time. But if you have come to help me because your liberation is tied up with mine, then let us work together.'[101] Let me leave you with the thoughts of an Indigenous person from the Sonoran Desert, a Tohono O'odham elder: 'If the education of our Indigenous peoples had been allowed to develop within the same framework as the American education system has been allowed to develop, our contribution to the world would be so much greater than what it is now.'[102]

11.
Native Title Conference, Larrakia Country, 2007

LEGAL PERSONALITY AND NATIVE TITLE CORPORATIONS
The problem of perpetual succession

MARCIA LANGTON AND ANGUS FRITH

The ideal of perpetual succession, which the law constructs for native title corporations, may be unrealised in a variety of circumstances. Successful native title applicants are required by law to establish a native title corporation. Such body corporates are not unique in those jurisdictions where customary land interests are dealt with under various legal, treaty and constitutional regimes, and they have parallels in Aboriginal descent groups under tradition and custom. However, there are several problems — inherent and practical — that may deprive the native title holders of full enjoyment of their hard-won rights and legal acknowledgment. In this paper the guarantee of perpetual succession that the legal personality of the native title corporation offers is discussed with reference to these inherent and practical problems arising from the native title recognition process. There are some long-term implications for the sustainability of the original nature of these corporations as they enter the market place; for instance, by entering into commercial agreements.[1]

THE NEED FOR NATIVE TITLE CORPORATIONS

Native title claimants who are successful either in obtaining a legal determination of native title or a negotiated settlement of their claims for land justice usually acquire a legal personality by establishing a corporation so that they can protect and manage their rights and interests. In the case of a determination of native title, the *Native Title Act 1993* (Cth) (NTA) provides that a Prescribed Body Corporate (PBC) must be established in order to provide a legal personality to the native title holding group.[2]

The NTA requires that, at the same time that a determination of native title is made, the Court must also decide whether the native title is to be held on trust for the native title holders or whether it is to be managed by an agent on their behalf, and, in either case, by which Prescribed Body Corporate.[3] Fingleton explains the nature of this entity: 'The term "prescribed" here means as laid down in the regulations', as a legally recognisable corporation as distinct from its membership:

> A 'body corporate' is the legal expression used for an artificial 'person' (as opposed to a natural person) created by law...the law regards the body corporate as having its own existence, and rights and duties, which are separate from the existence, rights and duties of the individual persons who make up the body from time to time.[4]

Fingleton notes further that 'There are parallels in Aboriginal and Islander societies, where language groups, sections, clans and lineages can be recognised as having a particular existence — and even rights and duties — distinct from those of the individual members which make them up';[5] thus Fingleton observed that 'there is nothing new in the bodies corporate approach'. In other countries, customary groups with traditional ownership have also adopted the device of giving management functions to bodies corporate and Fingleton provides a number of examples: some Pacific Islands states and New Zealand, and in Australia, in South Australia, the 'body corporate' approach was adopted for the return of land to its Traditional Owners in the case of Pitjantjatjara and Maralinga lands.[6]

The need for a body corporate is explained partly by 'legal reasons' — there is a 'need for a legal entity with its own separate existence' — and also by 'practical reasons' to enable dealings with the members by third parties and by 'a desire to protect the interests of the individual members of the native title-holding group'.[7] In the native title context the legal and practical reasons are clearly articulated by Mantziaris and Martin. They explain:

> The NTA establishes a framework for the holding and management of native title. It requires the use of corporations that stand in a relationship of 'trust' or 'agency' to the members of the native title group. The trust

or agency relationship is statutory in character. Delegated legislation made under the NTA specifies the characteristics and functions of native title corporations and lays down procedures to be followed by the corporation in decisions relating to native title matters. The corporate trustee and agency device allows non-native title interests dealing with the group to channel their transactions through a single legal person with perpetual succession. This is intended to avoid the problem of fixing obligations on the ever-fluctuating membership of a group of natural persons lacking legal personality.[8]

Conversely, the group, acting as a whole, can deal with non-native title interests through the legal personality of the PBC to take a wide range of steps, such as applying for credits and subsidies, entering into contracts with outsiders, collecting fees and enforcing rules.

In the case of a negotiated settlement not involving a native title determination, such as an Indigenous Land Use Agreement (ILUA), a variety of options is available. Most usually, the native title group (the group representing the Indigenous party to the negotiated settlement) can establish a corporation as their agent or as trustee to represent their interests in the outcome of the negotiated agreement in a manner similar to that where a native title outcome is involved. Alternatively, there may be no legal personality established, or the native title group may establish a trust that serves the role of a legal personality. Another option is for the group to delegate dealings with non-native title parties to a representative body, such as an Aboriginal land council or native title representative body (NTRB).[9] In most of these cases, similar concerns regarding the operation and sustainability of the corporation or trust arise as in respect of PBCs.

Kent McNeil has drawn attention to one of the important *sui generis* aspects of Aboriginal title that distinguish it from common law real property interests: it is *communal*. The PBC is a statutory device that provides legal personality for the collective of native title holders that is familiar to the common law. This is necessary because, as McNeil explains in relation to the normal common law property position, a group of individuals cannot, as an entity in its own right, hold title because it lacks legal personality. Citing Justice Lamer in *Delgamuukw*, McNeil explains:

> Aboriginal title cannot be held by individual aboriginal persons; it is a collective right to land held by all members of an aboriginal nation. Decisions with respect to that land are also made by that community. This is an extremely important passage in his judgment, as it provides

a foundation for a right of self-government...it also reveals how the law of Aboriginal title appears to diverge from the usual common law position on legal personality. As a general rule, in Anglo-Canadian law title to property must be vested in an individual person or persons, who can be either natural persons (human beings) or artificial persons (corporations). If a group of people owns property, title must be vested in all the members of the group *as individuals*. The group cannot, as an entity in its own right, hold title because it lacks legal personality. It is for this reason that the common law does not permit unincorporated associations as such to hold title to property. By holding that Aboriginal title is 'a collective right to land held by all members of an aboriginal nation', Chief Justice Lamer cannot have meant that the members hold as individuals, as there would then be no significant distinction between this aspect of Aboriginal title and landholding by members of unincorporated associations, and so Aboriginal title would not be *sui generis* in this respect. Instead, he must have intended to accord a form of legal personality to Aboriginal nations. If so, they have unique status in Anglo-Canadian law which probably enhances their claim to a right of self-government, but does not affect the proprietary nature of their Aboriginal title.[10]

Under common law, if a group of people owns property, say, as part of a partnership, title must be vested in all the members of the group as individuals in the form of a joint or co-tenancy. It is for this reason that the common law does not permit unincorporated associations to hold title to property. Incorporation has developed to provide an independent legal personality that has a high level of independence from its members. It can own property on its own, and importantly is invested with perpetual succession, which removes the need to transfer title from all members of the group to all the members of the newly constituted group on the death of any and all members of the group. A corporate entity was not required at law to hold common law native title. However, incorporation and perpetual succession align with the unique attributes of native title identified by McNeil. The prescribed form of the native title corporation means that specific legislation and regulations can allow particular functions and obligations to be bestowed on all native title holders consistently. Another advantage of the corporation is that it provides a single point through which third parties can engage with communal native title holders, who can thereby deal with their communal interests in land in a market economy.

PRACTICAL PROBLEMS FOR NATIVE TITLE CORPORATIONS

Despite the statutory structure governing the establishment and operation of native title corporations, and some of the practical advantages of the corporate model, several practical and systemic problems arise for them and their associated native title groups.

Until federal government policy changed in 2007, most PBCs did not have a secure funding base and there is no guarantee of government funding for their operation.[11] Unless they had negotiated financial benefits from mining or other developments on land held (or claimed) as native title, PBCs and other native title corporations were unlikely to be able to obtain income to ensure their ongoing operation. A minority of native title corporations had guaranteed funding for their operations; most of these were not PBCs. In these cases, the funding resulted from the remuneration provisions in agreements made with project proponents from the mining (including exploration) and agriculture sectors. In 2006 an inter-departmental Steering Committee report, *Structures and Processes of Prescribed Bodies Corporate*, observed that 'PBCs need to operate effectively so that native title holders can utilise their native title rights to enable them to derive significant economic and other benefits and to discharge their land management obligations'.[12]

Following the report on the *Operation of Native Title Representative Bodies* by the Parliamentary Joint Committee on Native Title and Torres Strait Islander Land Account in March 2006, the federal government accepted its recommendations and decided that PBCs would be eligible to apply for government funding to cover their administrative costs. Hence, procedures for funding were published as a set of guidelines.

Whether for lack of funding, lack of third-party engagement, or lack of capacity or interest from the native title group, many PBCs and other native title corporations lack robust governance arrangements. One possible cause of this situation is the PBC not being able to obtain the assistance of the relevant NTRB or land council because the PBC has refused to seek such assistance, or due to poor personal relationships, or independent funding decisions by other bodies or a NTRB's administrative burden preventing efficient dealings with PBCs. Other reasons for PBCs not having robust governance arrangements might include a lack of management skills in the corporation and being unable to obtain them externally; and there being no or an inadequate match between the structures and decision-making processes of the corporation and the group whose interest it is required to represent.

11. Legal personality and native title corporations

In any of these situations, the consequences for the PBC or native title corporation as a legal personality in itself are dire. Simple practical matters, such as banking, legal advice, meetings, keeping of records, accounting and auditing, are put at risk. Further, the capacity of the corporation to function in the best interest of its members is limited and thus the vulnerability of the native title corporation representing these groups is increased.

A wide range of agreements now exists between Indigenous peoples and public and private sector institutions in Australia.[13] Such agreements include those initiated on the basis of native title claims or determinations, together with resource, cultural heritage and local development initiatives. The native title corporations involved in these agreements have the same vulnerabilities as PBCs and native title claim groups that are founded on the recognition of native title based on the traditional laws and customs of the relevant group.

PERPETUAL SUCCESSION

In addition to these practical problems for native title corporations, there are potential difficulties for native title groups arising from the potential for disjunction between the statutory guarantee of perpetual succession for a corporation and the potential for changes in the traditional law and custom that govern the composition and purposes of the relevant native title group, which means that it is no longer identical to the group that established the corporation.

The courts have recognised the potential for that law and custom to change so that the nature of the recognised native title rights and interests develops with time.[14] It might be that the law and custom will change such that native title can no longer be recognised because it is no longer traditional.[15] Further, changing law and custom, which changes the composition and structure of the native title group, might mean that the corporation is no longer able to properly represent that group.

This vulnerability is accentuated by the manner in which the corporation is expected to provide a fixed point through which third parties can deal with the native title group, and the need to perform and reconcile legal duties to the membership arising under corporations law and the NTA, and cultural duties to the native title group.

In essence, these vulnerabilities arise from the need to reconcile or accommodate two systems of law (Indigenous law and custom and Australian statute and common law) in one locus: the native title

175

corporation. Thus, the legal space in which native title is recognised is an example of legal pluralism in practice. Mohr observes that 'Indigenous beliefs and practices challenge the claims to universality of Western conceptions of law and space deriving from Roman law and spatial practices'; in contradistinction to these Western conceptions of law, it is increasingly evident that 'a plurality of laws may apply in particular places'.[16] Noting that 'Law has had a traditional reference to land, conceived as territory, in the notion of a jurisdiction, where the law of the land applies equally to all individuals', Mohr proposes, rather, that space, law and identity constitute each other in complex forms. This interpretation is familiar in Canada, where 'bijuralism' is the accepted norm (involving both the British and the French legal traditions). Legal pluralism is also well documented in several jurisdictions on the African continent and in Asia.

The challenges of bijuralism in the structure and operation of native title corporations is in the evidence of maintaining their essentially bijural nature in circumstances that limit their functions to managing native title and providing a filter for outsiders wanting to deal with the native title group. A more pointed formulation of this question is how perpetual succession of the native title group under their laws and customs can be assured in these circumstances.

The integration of the operation of a native title corporation and law and custom will require the corporation to develop a public persona, based on the social and cultural nature of the identity of the native title group, which is recognised by others in their corporate environment and under the law and custom. It might be necessary for corporate governance arrangements to be adapted to support the bijural nature of the native title corporation. Consideration should be given to identifying other arrangements that could support the bijural functions of the corporation.

ESTABLISHING THE PBC

Each of the native title holding groups articulated through its PBC has been constructed through a process of individual statements, other ethnography, historical and anthropological work, legal submissions, and, sometimes, arguments and evidence put by opposing parties such as the state and other Indigenous groups, and finally by the judge's consideration. This lengthy process imports into the construction of a PBC not just customary principles of law and custom, but all the requirements of the NTA and judicial pronouncements on it, and the idiosyncrasies and conflicting aims of all the participants in the process of identifying and recognising the legitimate native title holders under traditional law and custom. In any event, the determination of native title and of the associated PBC only amounts to a snapshot of that law and custom at the time of the determination.

More than sixty PBCs have been established since the commencement of the NTA in 1994. The areas subject to these determinations of native title and associated PBCs show an extraordinary spatial diversity: ranging from small islands, such as Saibai Island in Torres Strait;[17] surviving interstitial areas of unallocated Crown land, such as the Bar-Barrum determination area in Mutchilba, Queensland;[18] to vast areas of land in the Western Desert, where 42,228 square kilometres of land extending west from the Western Australia and Northern Territory border are held in trust by the Tjamu Tjamu Corporation.[19]

The labels used to identify the groups and their PBCs vary. They include ethnicity, including language labels; geographical location, including both Indigenous and non-Indigenous locative labels; subgroup identity, such as clan names; and mixed identifiers based on both ethnicity and locality. Most of them use an Indigenous name (including those in combination with a locative term), while two use a locative term alone.[20] Several use locative terms in combination with their ethnic identity markers.[21] Some use a place name,[22] some the name ascribed to a system of law and custom,[23] and some a language name.[24]

The high variability in identity labels used by native title groups in establishing both their claims and their legal personalities may present problems in the longer term. This variability reflects differing approaches to identifying the law and custom on which group identity and structure is based. The question is whether such labels will survive the test of time and prove effective ongoing identity markers for highly labile groups. A more fundamental question is whether the underlying law and custom that gave rise to the determination of the native title group, the PBC and the identity marker of the PBC's name will remain substantially the same such that it still supports those constructions.

NATIVE TITLE CORPORATIONS AND BIJURALISM

Native title corporations have been established following the making of ILUAs or other negotiated agreements; for example, the Gelganyem Trust established by the Miriuwung Gajerrong and Kija native title holders recognised in the Argyle Diamond Mine agreement.[25] The groups that such corporations represent, the areas in respect of which they operate and their jurisdiction are determined by the terms of the relevant agreement. They are often able to design superior governance arrangements because of financial and other support provided through the agreement. For example, in the Miriuwung Gajerrong case, the native title group has been able to maintain unity of purpose and operation between their trust entity and their market entity by having the same persons as members of the respective boards of governance.

With more freedom to design and fund multiple corporations to accommodate transactional activity, native title groups can separate their (non-market) trust functions from their (market-based) transactional functions by creating separate but complementary entities. Hopefully, in this way, they will be better able to maintain the bijural nature of their legal personality and thereby their native title traditions.

CORPORATIONS AND PERPETUAL SUCCESSION

The match between the perpetual succession of the native title group and that of their corporation could also be affected by the confidential status of much of the evidentiary basis for the existence of the law and custom that forms the basis for the existence of the native title group itself. In the case of native title corporations established following negotiated settlements with mining companies (including ILUAs), the ethnographic reports that provide the evidence for the existence of communities of native title and the relevant laws and customs are confidential.

This confidentiality might become an issue for the temporal stability of these groups. In order to best integrate the future operation of the native title corporation with the law and custom on which it was based, it will be necessary for future members of the native title corporation to have regard to the founding documents of the corporations. They will potentially have to rely on anthropological reports that are difficult to access and understand. Members of these descent groups look to these representations of their past for their effective identity and constitution.

Third parties, such as state governments and development proponents, which do not necessarily have the expertise to understand the complexities of anthropologists' reports describing the native title traditions of such groups, will conduct their affairs with the group as if the native title corporations were mere market entities that operate outside this bijural context. Market pressure on native title corporations to behave as, and to become, purely market entities may lead to a divergence between the *sui generis* or unique native title traditions and the legal personality of a native title group. Thus, their bijural nature may become less significant as their transactional utility develops.

It should be noted that it is sometimes the case that there is only an agreement of convenience among the members of the native title group to the anthropologists' interpretation of their tradition, especially in cases involving disputes, overlapping claims, and communities of native title involving groups with disparate traditions and histories. This means that, even at the moment of formation of the corporation, when the snapshot of the group's law and custom is taken, the description of the law and custom under which the native title group is formulated may not reflect their reality.

These considerations mean that the members of the native title corporation will conduct their affairs, sometimes in accordance with the version of their laws and customs described in connection or anthropologists' reports, and sometimes diverging from them. Further, over time, the group will inevitably change, as will the content of their laws and customs.

BIJURALISM AND PERPETUAL SUCCESSION

Failure to include all apical ancestors in the original judgment, determination or legal submissions can mean that a native title corporation from the outset does not represent all the people it should under traditional law and custom. An example where a decision on the inclusion of apical ancestors was made for procedural reasons was the Federal Court decision in *Sampi*, where it was observed that:

> As to the addition of the three Mayala apical ancestors which is also proposed, I do not consider that that amendment should be allowed. Reference to those ancestors might well have affected the conduct of the case…In any event, having regard to the conclusions I have reached about the relevant community of native title holders, I do not see any way in which the addition of those Jawi/Mayala ancestors could affect the outcome of the application.[26]

Genealogies are a relatively low pixel snapshot of the social reality of a native title group. Despite the best efforts of anthropologists, genealogies are sometimes disputed, and apparent agreement among a native title group to a particular genealogical representation may be illusory. This is especially the case where ancestors have not been recognised or have been omitted in error.

Litigated native title outcomes, in particular, may distort the judicial description of the native title holding group, the PBC and its membership, and its relationship with the native title holders, especially where the description of the group has been contested and is the result of a judge's decision.[27] His Honour Justice French has expressed concern that the membership class of a prescribed body corporate be textually aligned precisely with the definition of the native title holders in the relevant native title determination.[28] The issue has arisen, for instance, in *Ngalpil v Western Australia*, in which Justice Carr was required to consider whether the Tjurabalan Native Title Land Aboriginal Corporation (the Corporation) was a duly nominated prescribed body corporate and whether the requirements of the *Native Title (Prescribed Bodies Corporate) Regulations 1999* (PBC Regulations) had been satisfied.[29]

Although disputes about membership will not affect the status of the legal personality, the utilitarian functions of the native title corporation will be affected by any such disputes and, over time, the content of native title which the entity exists to preserve may become disputed, thus weakening the fiduciary or trust duties of the corporation.

High mortality rates among Indigenous communities, including the death of claimants before determinations are made, could lead to failures of transmission from older to younger generations putting succession under traditional law and custom at risk. For example, in *Sampi*, it was observed that:

> The application was lodged by Paul Sampi and a number of other named applicants, seven of whom have since died…and…I will allow the amendments to the principal application…Affidavits were provided by six of the twelve named applicants in this regard…Of the remaining six named applicants four have died and two were suffering from dementia and lacked the necessary capacity to swear an affidavit.[30]

Other changes in cultural observation that may also impact on native title corporations include language loss, loss of ceremonial traditions, the loss of other traditions, such as naming of persons and places, and other impacts on cultural heritage and patrimony.

To some extent, the claims registration process has developed in such a way as to address, probably by default, some of the problems that limit prospect for perpetual succession of traditional law and custom. It provides another external consideration of the native title claim group description, but through the sieve of the statutory requirements governing the application of the registration test.[31] However, the registration process, by itself, is not a sufficient guarantee of the robustness of the legal personality that might result from a subsequent determination.

THE CHALLENGE OF ACCULTURATION

Where a native title group seeks the recognition or confirmation of its native title, it is necessary for it to address the traditional nature of its law and custom. In order to be traditional, the law and custom must be substantially similar to that subsisting at the acquisition of sovereignty by the British. The central purpose of the native title corporation or PBC is to maintain the identity of a native title group while providing a mechanism for the group to engage in market transactions. This purpose is challenged by the impact of the corporation's market (and even non-market) functions: how can the bijural nature of the legal personality be maintained while its utilitarian purpose is to engage in the market?

One of the most significant vulnerabilities of PBCs is the accommodation of perpetual succession implicit in traditional laws and customs that lead to recognition of native title with the perpetual succession conferred by the creation of a corporate legal personality to represent the native title holders.

Perpetual succession by way of a native title corporation may be in jeopardy, or may become an empty promise of arid black letter law, if, over time, as a result of rapid acculturation to the dominant Australian society, the relevant Indigenous customary law is not robust enough to sustain the transmission of the traditional principles that determined the membership of the original native title holding group. The 'social licence to operate' that non-native title parties have sought to secure by negotiating agreements with the Indigenous parties may diminish or cease if the customary descent and related principles that give legitimacy to the native title group under Indigenous law cease to operate within the lifespan of the agreement.

The effects of a failure of perpetual succession might include a transition in the constitution of the native title group from a group based on membership principles founded in Indigenous law to non-traditional principles such as local residence. The recognition of Indigenous heritage and associated law and custom may become less relevant than the agreement provisions for employment, education, training and business development.

Indeed, the successful implementation of provisions dealing with these issues may hasten the demise of the customary basis of the native title group and accelerate its incorporation into, and commitment to, a social organisation and lifestyle based on free market principles, such as labour market freedom rather than kinship, and income-generating personal attributes, such as individualist wealth generation, rather than collective sharing of material assets.

The implications of such changes for ILUAs involving mining operations where the life of the mine is expected to be a number of decades, or where the relevant state government is a party, are not clear. Moreover, in the case of future litigation resulting from challenges to the agreements, or the determinations of native title on which they are based, the courts may find it difficult to confirm that the contemporary native title group membership continues to observe the traditions and customs that give rise to the native title recognised by the original native title determination.

The challenge for the community of native title corporations is to obtain a reliable understanding of existing PBCs and native title corporations, their nature and functions, their capacities and vulnerabilities, their governance structures, and the types and extent of their dealings with native title. It will also be necessary to examine their financial security and other infrastructure. All this must be done while native title corporations are operating in the real bijural world, in order to find solutions to the present vulnerabilities of native title corporations with regard to their bijural nature, cultural challenges and practical problems.

12.
Native Title Conference, Noongar Country, 2008

NATIVE TITLE, AGREEMENTS AND THE FUTURE OF KIMBERLEY ABORIGINAL PEOPLE

WAYNE BERGMANN

I want to begin by acknowledging the Traditional Owners of this land, the Noongar people.

In the Kimberley, Aboriginal people have been very lucky because first contact with colonisation has been very recent. A large number of our people are either first contact people or their parents were first contact people that met with *katijya* (non-Aboriginal people) for the first time. This fact makes the basis of proving native title a little easier. I don't like to saying 'winning' in relation to native title because I don't think it's a win; it's more about proving native title, acknowledging what's already there; the traditional ownership of the land. This paper will explore some of the challenges and achievements that we have worked on in the Kimberley.

THE KIMBERLY LAND COUNCIL

The Kimberley Land Council (KLC) is a grassroots organisation that has been around for thirty years. But the spirit in which the organisation operates, in which Kimberley Aboriginal people operate, can be traced back to before the KLC even started. Back in the early to mid-1970s, there were many disputes resulting from Aboriginal people being kicked off cattle stations. The infamous Noonkanbah dispute was about AMEX, an American exploration company, wanting to drill for oil on sacred ground. That was the catalyst that harnessed the spirit of Kimberley Aboriginal people to come together and protect some of the most sacred things to us — our cultural values and cultural sites. These events led to the establishment of the KLC. We have a long and proud history in advocating for the rights of Kimberley Aboriginal people.

The kangaroo or Malu on the KLC's logo has a strong and deep cultural meaning. Some Aboriginal groups in the north Kimberley call it Wunan. It symbolises ceremonial cycles that connect everyone together. Not only are we a native title representative body (NTRB) in a statutory sense but our grassroots structure is a symbol of our strong cultural responsibility to each other and why we're sticking together. The lesson that we have learned when making development agreements on native title land is that you can achieve far more by standing together as one and far less if you stand alone. So the success of one group is celebrated as a success for all Kimberley Aboriginal people.

I think now is a really important time for native title and Aboriginal affairs and the role it is having in shaping our futures. If there is anything in the last seven years that I have learnt at the KLC, it is that we can make a difference and create our own futures. I have noticed a shift, with government and industry showing a greater willingness to find solutions and make agreements that we can live with; in a sense, this is the planets aligning for us to create our own futures. We have had a resources boom which has increased the demand for labour, and with that has come a high demand for companies to cooperate with, recognise and engage with Aboriginal people.

It has also been reported that the federal government wants to improve the *Native Title Act 1993* (Cth) (NTA). I have had politicians say to me they want to improve some aspects of the NTA, but they stop short of advocating for actual changes to it. I think we have already begun a process of change and many of the issues the federal government has raised about native title we are changing. We are initiating this change ourselves and we have struggled. But we are of the attitude that we need to do these things for ourselves because we can't afford to wait for governments to do it for us. This is about our future.

We heard in the official opening by the Noongar elders that it's about the future of our kids, the future of our families and the future of our identity. We have to get on with the job ourselves. But representative bodies do not have the resources to complete the tasks that are expected of them. There's a huge opportunity here that will be lost because the government and industry sectors do not understand. The loss will be that, without functional and resourced representative bodies, companies won't and can't engage with Aboriginal people in a manner that is timely and able to deliver certainty for all our futures.

Some activities that the KLC has been undertaking focus on looking at long-term benefits for the entire Kimberley region. All our agreements with industry have money for the present and money for the future. A lot of our people advocate for what we call 'no finger money', meaning no personal payments to individuals. At the end of the day, all our decisions come from the instruction and leadership of our native title groups and they want to use the benefits in a good way. A lot of senior people are saying that any funds we get under agreements must be used in a good way.

The work of the KLC is not just about land and native title. We are not just a representative body; we are an Aboriginal corporation doing a whole range of things. Native title is just one part of it. We do a lot of land management activities, although it's not our formal statutory responsibility. More than fifty percent of the Kimberley has native title determinations currently in our representative body area. Some of these determinations have been hard won through Court determinations, while some have been consent determinations with the state.

We have had a bit of a mixed bag of outcomes. In the initial days, the line was drawn in the sand. No one was prepared to recognise Kimberley Aboriginal people's evidence as evidence of the fact that we have strong connection to our Country. When I started at the KLC we had five matters in litigation compared to other land councils that had one or two. This had put incredible pressure on us. The government wouldn't increase our funding to deal with that. Even the Federal Court said KLC's funding concerns weren't their problem. We also had an expectation from another ten native title groups to move their native title matters forward quickly. So I had to convince the KLC Board of a strategy to only do a few native title claims at a time. Our priority then became to focus on the matters in Court. We worked out a strategy that if we were successful in one claim, it would provide a basis for resolving other bordering claims.

The biggest struggle we have at the moment is in working with the Commonwealth, the Attorney-General's Department and Commonwealth solicitors. There is also a big difference of opinion between what the state has been prepared to accept as prima facie evidence of traditional ownership, and what the Commonwealth solicitors are prepared to accept. How can one part of government accept that native title exists while another section plays a game of what I call 'nitpicking' as to the requirements needed to pass the threshold to accept native title exists? I believe this needs to be standardised. It is not the state or Commonwealth governments' role to act as a court of determination.

NATIVE TITLE AND AGREEMENT MAKING

The success of all our agreement negotiations has been underpinned by our native title success. Native title determinations have provided a foundation for the way we make agreements. We have noticed that if there is a native title determination on an area, companies wanting to develop in that area deal with you differently. They deal with you in a respectful way compared to when there is no native title determination in that area. Although native title provides you with a seat at the table, there's no guarantee of success. I work very closely on a lot of these agreements with Ciaran O'Faircheallaigh, our retained consultant on Aboriginal resource agreements, and he often speaks about how everyone has been talking about the economy, the real economy; take the example of when you want to sell your house and your right to say 'yes' or 'no'. If your house is worth a million dollars and someone offers you a hundred thousand dollars, you are going to say 'no'. But in native title, when it comes to determine what is fair and equitable, Aboriginal people don't have the right to say 'no'. There is a process in place, but the pendulum has swung too far to industries' side. The balance needs to be put back into recognising the rights and interests that Aboriginal people have through the native title system in relation to agreements.

I have learnt that success requires a sustained effort from Traditional Owners and the Kimberley Land Council from start to finish. The entire agreement process is tough and requires strong communication with Traditional Owners about what is going on. Often people don't realise that negotiations start well before you even sit down at the table with a company. There's a lot of preparation work that happens behind the scenes.

Our biggest project at the moment, which has received a lot of media attention, has been the potential development of Browse Gas, off the Kimberley coast. Browse Gas is found about 460 kilometres north west of Broome, and many companies are looking at how to bring that onshore to develop it. Shell has announced they are considering a floating LNG (liquefied natural gas) plant. From my understanding, the capacity of a floating LNG is not big enough to process the extent of the gas fields out there.

In the past, Traditional Owners have had regional engagement with Woodside, but they said 'no' to Woodside during that consultation process. Traditional Owners have changed their position since then and are engaging with them and Kimberley Aboriginal people to find an appropriate location in the Kimberley for an LNG development, subject to meeting some of our conditions. Our cultural leaders have set up a process to pull all the coastal native title groups together; this includes thirteen native title groups from the West Australian–Northern Territory border all the way south to Bidyadanga community, south of Broome in Karajarri Country. KLC has created an Aboriginal taskforce of sixty representatives from all those coastal groups. We have flown a total of 3000 kilometres to give people information about it, to tell them why we need to stick together and why we all need to agree to support a single hub location, on the basis that we can all share in the benefits of it. We have been negotiating real outcomes with and for Kimberley Aboriginal organisations and Kimberley Traditional Owners.

We're also becoming smarter in the way we negotiate agreements and we have learnt from those we have made in the past. Look at the Argyle Diamond Mine (ADM), for example. Although at the time Argyle was talked about as being a world-class agreement with Aboriginal participation, we are recognising that the people engaged in the ADM operations can have an effect on other Aboriginal communities — for example, people that live in Broome are being impacted by the ADM, by simple measures, such as increasing the population. This kind of impact needs to be taken into account.

The native title process doesn't allow for you to take into account the real social impacts that happen as a result of development. We hosted a Kimberley Futures Forum, for which an open invitation was sent to most Kimberley Aboriginal service delivery organisations, to work out how to deal with the social impacts that occur because of development. As development happens and the population increases, the demand for housing increases, the pressure on services increases, there are bigger queues in hospitals, more children enrol at our schools and the price of housing goes up — where does this leave our people that are already in a disadvantaged position?

Some people are talking about tourism. But there has been no planned strategy for the impacts of tourism. As much as people talk about tourism being a low environmental impact, I don't see our people as being major participants in businesses that are associated with tourism. Some of our people, who have run tourism businesses, don't have the capital to get into it in a big way. Today, you need bigger boats; everything is done on a bigger scale. People can travel around the Kimberley coast on a cruise, at perhaps $2000 to $4000 per head. It's a very small niche market of people who can afford to do that and there are immense cultural and environmental impacts that need to be taken into consideration.

That is why we want to ascertain our role and lead the decision about gas development along the Kimberley coast as a way to determine and provide for our future. We think it's the single biggest project in Australia's history. I'm advised that the gas reserves off the Kimberley coast are worth at least $200 billion. That is a huge resource, and if Aboriginal people can be part of that development in a real, meaningful way, we would be able to address our own needs. That has to be the way of the future. We can't be relying on governments to deal with our own issues. We need to do things for ourselves.

Miriuwung Gajerrong

The KLC established and managed negotiations between the Traditional Owners, the Miriuwung Gajerrong people, and the State of Western Australia about developing Ord Stage Two project, which involves agricultural development near Kununurra. This agreement includes acknowledgment for past wrongs.

When Ord Stage One happened in the 1960s there was no engagement with Traditional Owners and it had major impacts on the Traditional Owners' lives and traditional country that was flooded. Traditional Owners have talked about their experience of being thrown on the back of trucks to escape rising water levels as parts of their traditional country were being flooded to make way for Lake Argyle. People still talk about it as if it happened yesterday. They say that was the way things were done in those days, but the social impacts it had on Aboriginal people have never been addressed.

Through our process in negotiating Ord Stage Two, we were allowed to heal some of those past wrongs and people are now moving on. The Ord Stage Two Agreement delivers community development initiatives, provides for services, freehold land compensation, equity in the project, funding to operate the Miriuwung Gajerrong people's governance structures and its corporation.

Some people refer to the Ord Stage Two process as a 'Rolls-Royce process'. I do not think it was a Rolls-Royce process. It was what needed to happen in order to bring peoples' capacity in line with a certain position so Traditional Owners could move forward. There are still challenges happening, but it's a really positive story about engagement with government, and a robust engagement at times. It was a meeting of minds and people have enjoyed and respected that engagement, and have been able to move on.

The ADM agreement

The Miriuwung Gajerrong claim group involving the Miriuwung and Kija people has developed an agreement with Argyle Diamond Mines about future expansion, despite the fact Traditional Owners had no right to negotiate under the NTA. Past agreements were made without engagement from Traditional Owners but the company, and industry generally, are starting to change their views.

The need to work with and consult Aboriginal people has become much stronger now. We have to do the right thing. We can't have a world-class mine, where people live in poverty all around it. An international mine certainly can't be the way of the future if it is surrounded by Aboriginal people with high suicide rates, poor education and poor health outcomes. That's what happened and it needed to be addressed. The agreement process for the ADM expansion took more than three years and probably cost the KLC $2 million. But it delivered substantial benefits for Traditional Owners that are being felt today, as well as investments to provide for the future. That agreement was the start of a principle we strongly believe in today — that all Kimberley Aboriginal people share in the benefits of setting precedents from agreements made on another group's land.

Today, despite what the law says, we are determined to make our own decisions, such as the principle 'no means no'. That means to us that a company won't destroy a cultural site unless we agree to it. Argyle was founded on the basis of a disturbance or the destruction of a cultural site. For the company to be able to re-engage with Traditional Owners who were dissatisfied, they had to let go of the early way, on which the mine was founded. That was a really important step. Argyle agreed to this 'no means no' principle, that they will not destroy another site unless Traditional Owners agreed to it. A lot of people say, 'Oh, how can you sell sites?' But, it's not about selling sites, it's about peoples' ownership of their cultural property and having a process to understand how that's best managed. When you break it down, and deal with Aboriginal groups this way, people find a solution. If they can't find a solution, then it's not to be disturbed.

Koolan Island

Dambimangari people negotiated an agreement over the re-opening of Koolan Island (an iron ore mine north of Derby). The agreement includes equity for the native title group, and a substantial royalty based on the more the company makes, the more the Traditional Owners make. It has strong environmental provisions and a 'no means no' principle. Environmental assurances were important. People were really worried that if a ship came into the area and ran aground, spilled oil and destroyed trochus shell breeding areas and damaged reefs, that Traditional Owners would be subject to retribution or tribal punishment from other coastal groups. So they wanted to ensure they were being responsible to the rest of the coastal groups. We negotiated with the company to ensure there were extra insurance provisions so if there was environmental damage that went beyond the native title group's area, the outside native title group had some recourse to an insurance fund to fix up any damage.

This is not an obligation between the Department of Environment and the company; this is a contractual right between the native title parties and the company. Traditional Owners have insisted that they didn't want to rely on the State Department of Environment to protect their environmental values.

Tjurabalan

The Tjurabalan mob made a deal over the opening of a new gold mine on the West Australian side of the Northern Territory border, out past Balgo. The deal provides equity in the company, employment and training opportunities for Tjurabalan people, and royalties that increase as the project becomes more successful. We have been able to understand the company and its internal workings and tailor-make our economic modelling based on what the company can afford. Obviously you can't say, 'pay me a billion dollars today' when you're only making a thousand dollars; the company just can't do it. So we have been able to negotiate provisions to take into account the start-up operations and capital costs and when their capital starts being serviced by the income of the mine, and there's a fair balance between that and the return provided to Traditional Owners.

Under these agreements, senior executives of the company are required to go on a two- or three-day bush trip for cultural awareness. A big issue has been getting companies' senior management to understand the perspective of Traditional Owners. So part of the conditions of these agreements has been for senior management to go out bush with Traditional Owners' senior people.

Kija

In the east Kimberley the Kija mob made a deal with Kimberley Nickel Mines. Kimberley Nickel Mines was an existing lease where no right to negotiate existed. Part of the changing corporate culture is that companies are growing a social conscience and so feel they have an obligation to make sure they do the right thing. We were able to negotiate a significant benefits deal for Kija people, including equity in the company and payments dating back to the start of the operation. Traditional Owners have been able to set up a massive fund for the future, for the way they use money and how to build a capital base to ensure there is money for now and money for the future.

KEYS TO NEGOTIATION

Some keys to negotiation have been:
- Identify and implement an effective and focused outcome-based approach. You must understand the other side. You are going to have hard knocks and you must recognise those times but essentially it's about planning for the future. You are creating a partnership for the future with these companies. So even though you have hard knocks, you have got to manage these things because at the end of the day, the success of implementing these agreements is based on the relationship you have with these companies. So it's a kind of balancing act.
- Being innovative to close the deal. A lot of focus is on the negotiation, with sometimes little focus on what it takes to close the deal. Sometimes there is a hesitation when it comes to equipping yourself with the best leadership group, to ensure you have the right advice around you to work out when the deal should be closed. But having people to provide quality, expert advice is very important because you need to understand the company you're dealing with, what it wants and needs. It's all about building positive precedents through negotiation. At the KLC, we do all of this under the one umbrella, because we are one organisation that is built up from many different areas of expertise. We

have been able to use our expertise to brief other groups on what is happening in the Kimberley, what agreements have happened in other places in Australia, and what has happened overseas. These negotiations are a first for us, so we really need to understand what the benchmarks are now and what they have been in the past.
- Chief Executive Officers. I can't overstate the importance of building relationships between the CEOs of land councils and the CEOs or Chairs on the Boards of companies. These relationships are fundamental because different companies have different internal structures and leadership roles, so knowing a company and its structure and how you fit into that is imperative. The role of a CEO at a land council in negotiations is to provide a consistent approach because the internal structures of land councils are complex. Outside consultants that are brought in are focused on the short-term project at hand, while chairmen and CEOs are focused on the bigger picture and the future. This is why engagement at senior levels is so important in focusing on our vision. All of this leads to improved negotiations because when a company has the authority to make binding agreements at the table, the negotiation process and outcomes associated with that happen a lot quicker, while also fostering long-term relationships.

I believe there are four phases to negotiations.

1. Initiating contact and creating a framework. A lot of negotiations happen before any formal processes begin.
2. Building a knowledge base so you understand what people want. If an agreement doesn't have in it what you want and what is important to you, it's worthless. You can't bring in the shining stars of negotiations to negotiate in detail if they don't understand what people want.
3. Conducting the negotiations. There needs to be recognition here that there will be tough times and there will be good times.
4. Closing the deal and implementing action. A lot of people forget about what has happened, and what needs to happen the day after the deal is signed. Traditional Owners are involved in an intense engagement process during negotiations and then all of a sudden it disappears. We have a thorough planning process in place to make sure the vision doesn't disappear after the deal is signed.

After all these agreements are in place, the cost of retaining and resourcing people to continue to participate must be considered. Consideration must also be given to the ways we are going to initiate contact, create a framework and establish a clear decision-making authority. This all happens within the Traditional Owner group. It is vital, in doing this, that you understand the mining company or whoever it is that you are dealing with.

Developing funding arrangements is important. You cannot have good engagement without the appropriate resources and skills needed to engage. And these things cost money. Developing and executing a memorandum of understanding with the company is an alternative in this regard. This involves some kind of funding agreement or framework agreement that sets out procedures and provides the basis for negotiation.

The negotiating team

Designing and selecting a negotiation team is an essential step. This might sound a bit strange, but if you don't think about your negotiation team and match it to the team on the other side, you can come across some big problems. In order to do this, a team meeting and workshop needs to be held with Traditional Owners. This is going to be the first experience a lot of Traditional Owners, certainly those living in the Kimberley, are going to have with negotiating an agreement. This is about building the skills and capacity of people.

Building the knowledge base

Establishing a history of the key players helps to set the picture. As an example, Traditional Owners had a long history with Argyle Diamonds. Twenty years before the recent negotiated agreement, there had been a huge dispute about the initial establishment of the mine. Similarly, the negotiations for Ord Stage Two brought back all the pain Traditional Owners had carried with them for twenty years when they were removed from their land without consent. There was even the pain associated with the name Weber Plains (part of the Ord irrigation area). Weber Plains was named after some early settlers, who, according to Traditional Owners' oral histories, killed their grandparents. These memories come from early massacre stories. People feel offended by having the name Weber Plains on a sign. Traditional Owners have been asking the shire to change the name and those discussions have been ongoing. Some of these types of things are very important for Traditional Owners and therefore become key issues in negotiations.

Other actions to consider in these early stages of preparing for negotiations include:
- Establishing Traditional Owner principles. This involves asking Traditional Owners 'what's important to you?' and then understanding

why it is important. There's a lot of detail involved in establishing these principles.
- Building an understanding of the company you are working with. Who is the decision maker? Does the company have a published policy about engaging with Aboriginal people?
- Training and capacity building of Traditional Owners. Skilling people in the do's and don'ts of negotiations and so you have a more successful interface.

Conducting negotiations

Building and maintaining relationships with a company is very important. Negotiations can include a lot of robust positioning but what happens when you get a hard knock when dealing with key issues? You need to establish a set of basic rules to conduct negotiations. You've got to work out what to do if you hit a brick wall. How do you approach the Chairman of the Board, the Chairman of the Land Council and the CEO of the Land Council? The door has to always be open as a way to finding solutions.

Conduct ongoing reviews. It is important to keep reviewing what's going on right from the start, because things can change on a daily basis. When you conduct negotiations, you need to constantly monitor the process. Where we have come from, where we are now, how does this relate to the company's principles and those of the Traditional Owners? Are there outcomes in the agreements that are important to Traditional Owners? We have to continuously question these things. Periodic, strategic reviews, including providing alternatives to negotiation, is crucial. At the end of the day, if you can't do a deal, you are going to end up in front of the National Native Title Tribunal, where history shows that one hundred percent of those companies that go before the tribunal and expedite the procedure get their leases granted. So what are the alternatives?

Implementation

It is important to look to the future and how to implement the agreement, manage the income and benefits. If no thought is given to the ways benefits will be looked after prior to signing the deal, then Traditional Owners will have a lot to decide when it comes to setting up management procedures or disbursement procedures for looking after benefits.

When we close the deal we develop a desktop plan or a task sheet to finalise all the issues in the agreement. What are our obligations? What are the company's obligations? How are they going to be managed?

When reviewing the final draft agreement, it is essential that it is explicit and clear. In a lot of cases that I have seen in Canada, disputes are still happening between the state and Traditional Owners ten years after treaty agreements have been signed. Lots of the disputes are about how the state interprets the principles in the agreement, and if the bare minimum is being done to satisfy those principles. We make it a lot clearer in our agreements and clearly specify 'this is your obligation — do you agree to it, or don't you?'

Traditional Owner authorisation of the agreement must be understood by all. It is imperative that Traditional Owners are clear on what their rights and obligations are. Traditional Owners will sign an agreement, thinking it's great but then when a company goes out and does something, they often say, 'hey, we didn't know about that', and I say, 'It was in the agreement'. If a land council has to explain to Traditional Owners something about the agreement, after it has been signed, then it has failed in doing its job. A lot of work needs to happen to ensure Traditional Owners understand all aspects of the agreement, and this requires us to break everything down to make sure people understand what their obligations are. And if the company does things that they're not allowed to do under the agreement, it is important that Traditional Owners, on the ground, will hold the company accountable for it.

All of this needs to be done to ensure implementation. The logistics of implementation should not be underestimated. In some of the agreements we have done, it might cost $100,000 to $200,000 a year in administration — operating an office and its ongoing costs and salaries. From experience we have found that, generally, it costs a lot more than that to run an office and provide adequate support to ensure the process under the agreement happens properly.

BUILDING ON PRECEDENTS

In building on regional precedents, I think one of our successes has been that all Kimberley people share in the benefits of an agreement — whether it is on their Country or not. We haven't kept these agreements secret amongst ourselves. Instead, we have built up our corporate knowledge on negotiating agreements and continue to raise the bar and set precedents so we can continue to measure our success and improve on that.

Our success in negotiations can be seen in the extensive use of the 'no means no' provision across the region, in equity, financial compensation for past mining impacts, ongoing Traditional Owner involvement in projects including rehabilitation, post-mine phases, obtaining assets at the end of the project and the companies' hand-over of assets. Companies don't necessarily accept these things, so obviously it's a negotiation. A lot of these issues are fundamentally a commercial issue for the company.

CREATING A LEGACY

Compensation has been the key in creating opportunities for Aboriginal groups to create outcomes for themselves, and in addition to financial outcomes and land management concerns, these have included training programs and the building of outstations. How do we measure the community benefit from agreements? How do Traditional Owner groups benefit? The benefit is seen by Aboriginal people as 'this is our chance to build our future, our legacy for our kids'. The agreement must deliver on this promise.

I think land councils and Traditional Owners have been working together for a long time to empower Aboriginal people to make decisions for, and create outcomes for, themselves. But land councils need more support in order to improve on the job they are doing. I think we'll get more bang for the buck if there is greater recognition of what land councils are doing on the ground. Resourcing and effective legislative changes can improve our ability to do these things.

In terms of agreements we establish long-term benefit accounts for all Traditional Owners to ensure there are opportunities available now and into the future. I estimate in about fifteen years' time, Kimberly Aboriginal people will have between $100 and $200 million under management, under agreements and for long-term benefits depending on the outcome of the gas deal and other agreements. These are significant dollars for Aboriginal people.

The KLC has set up a benefits trust, in which the ANZ Bank is providing some management. We have also used other companies, like Plan B Trustees, for managing benefits for Traditional Owners, because we are not experts in financial management. We create benefit-sharing models for immediate Traditional Owners and the wider Traditional Owner group. But benefits continue well beyond the life of the project. If mines aren't sustainable they will operate for between ten and twenty years.

And when they stop, the income they provide to Traditional Owners stops. So we have built a benefit stream to ensure that even after the mining stops, Traditional Owners will still have an income to be able to create more opportunities and benefits that are important to them.

All the work that we do is aimed at leaving behind a positive legacy. Traditional Owners have bought dialysis machines, have paid for education programs, and have paid for school bags and tuition fees. People are fundamentally doing the right thing because we are all worried about the future of our kids and so we are trying to create opportunities for them. A lot of the agreements that have been made with Kimberley people have been pursued in a responsible manner so we can leave positive legacies and create a positive capacity for opportunity within our mobs. Most companies want to contribute to that so we can all leave behind positive outcomes for the future.

These agreements are only recent. Although mining has been happening in other parts of Western Australia for a lot longer, it's mostly new to us. I believe that there has been a huge transition in the way development companies negotiate with and engage with Traditional Owners. Successful negotiation must be well planned and implemented. We must understand the needs of all players because, at the end of the day, the relationship you have with a company is like a marriage, and you sign up to it for the life of the project. But that is not to say that you don't have your ups and downs in the process. There is now a greater recognition and respect for Traditional Owners and their rights. All the agreements now acknowledge us. Kimberley Aboriginal people want companies to acknowledge that we are the Traditional Owners of Country and the right people to speak to. We have always had an issue about how that's been expressed.

Agreements can deliver benefits for an entire community. And agreements are just one part of creating a vision. We see that vision as Aboriginal engagement, empowerment, advancement and legacy setting for the future.

This is a brief exploration of what the KLC has been working on, and overall I think we have been really successful. We are really proud of what we have achieved because underlying our success is a strong cultural connection that intertwines us all. We want to share our story because it shows that if we stand together and unite as one Kimberley mob, we can achieve more. We want this attitude to spread across the country because if we stand together as one mob across Western Australia, and even Australia, we will achieve more consistent native title outcomes.

13.
Native Title Conference, Noongar Country, 2008

ACHIEVING REAL OUTCOMES FROM NATIVE TITLE CLAIMS
Meeting the challenges head on

GRAEME NEATE

Sixteen years after the historic High Court judgment in *Mabo v Queensland [No. 2]*[1] and more than fourteen years after the *Native Title Act 1993* (Cth) (NTA) commenced, there is growing criticism of aspects of the native title system from some of its key participants and closest observers. Two ministers of the new Australian Government and the Aboriginal and Torres Strait Islander Social Justice Commissioner have identified what they see as deficiencies of the system, as well as the opportunities it offers.

In a comprehensive speech about native title on 29 February 2008, Attorney-General Robert McClelland said that he had come to realise that 'native title is highly technical'[2] and that, for various reasons, native title has become 'strangled in litigation and arguments over technical provisions of a complex Act'.[3] Yet he noted that 'native title negotiations can present a real opportunity to facilitate the reconciliation process',[4] and stated his belief that 'native title has a crucial role in forging…new', 'positive and enduring relationships' between Indigenous and non-Indigenous Australians.[5] He stressed that 'native title is but one way of recognising Indigenous peoples' ongoing relationship with the land'[6] and 'should not be seen as an end in itself'.⁷ Beyond that, one of the Australian Government's objectives for the native title system is 'making native title an effective mechanism for providing economic development opportunities for Indigenous people'.⁸ The knowledge and positive experience of native title that now exists provides the opportunity to improve outcomes.⁹

Also in 2008, the Minister for Families, Housing, Community Services and Indigenous Affairs, the Honourable Jenny Macklin MP, said that the 'recognition of native title and the establishment of new institutional arrangements have brought huge gains but substantial challenges remain'.¹⁰ Among the three areas that 'demand new approaches', the Minister nominated the processes to resolve outstanding native title claims, which she described as 'overly complex and exceedingly slow'.¹¹ Like the Attorney-General, she put native title in a broader context, and stated that native title is 'a right which must be used…as a tool to bring about positive change' for social, cultural and economic purposes.¹² In a subsequent speech, the Minister referred to the 'important role' native title plays in the relationship between the resources sector and Indigenous interests.¹³

In the *Native Title Report 2007*, tabled in the Australian Parliament in March 2008, Aboriginal and Torres Strait Islander Social Justice Commissioner Tom Calma said that the native title system 'has been successfully used in many parts of the country'¹⁴ and acknowledged a range of benefits and achievements. But it also suggested that the system is 'not delivering full recognition and protection of native title'¹⁵ and the NTA 'tends to humiliate the people it should serve'.¹⁶ In the Commissioner's assessment, the native title system is too complex, legalistic and bureaucratic, and 'it hinders rather than helps Indigenous Australians towards their full realisation of rights'.¹⁷ Adopting an expression used by Justice Merkel in the *Rubibi* case,¹⁸ Tom Calma described the native title system as being in 'gridlock'.¹⁹

Read in context, the statements of these three leaders give mixed assessments of the system. Quite properly, they acknowledge the positive outcomes achieved to date, but they express understandable frustration at the lengthy periods taken to obtain determinations of native title and concerns at the prospect of decades of activity to resolve the current and future claims.

This paper focuses on native title claims and provides a frank stocktake of key outcomes achieved to date; an assessment of the obstacles to resolving claims; and an analysis of the steps which could and should be taken by *all* participants to speed up their resolution.

It draws on recent ministerial statements that illustrate a commitment to approaches previously urged by others (including Aboriginal people, governments, judges and the National Native Title Tribunal (NNTT)) to find practical ways to improve the rate and content of outcomes from the native title system.

CURRENT SITUATION: A STOCKTAKE

In this section I will examine the current situation in relation to determinations that native title does or does not exist and Indigenous land use agreements negotiated over areas where native title has been recognised or where it might exist. I will also consider the number of unresolved claims in the system and the time it is likely to take to resolve those claims and other claims that will probably be made in the next few years.

Determinations of native title

In the more than fourteen years between the commencement of the NTA on 1 January 1994 and 31 March 2008:
- 1771 native title applications were made (1465 claimant, 33 compensation, 273 non-claimant);
- 1214 (69%) of the applications were resolved (952 claimant, 23 compensation, 239 non-claimant).

There have been 107 Federal Court decisions relating to determinations of native title affecting 135 applications.[20] Of these determinations:
- seventy-three are determinations that native title exists over the whole or part of the application area;
- thirty-four are determinations that native title does not exist (most of them in New South Wales).

Determinations cover some 828,650 square kilometres (or 11%) of the land mass of Australia.[21] The chart at Figure 1 shows the cumulative number of determinations made since 1994, with a steady rise in the number of determinations in recent years, particularly following landmark decisions of the High Court up to 2002. The legal ground rules having been established, there is a framework for negotiating outcomes rather than going to a Court hearing.

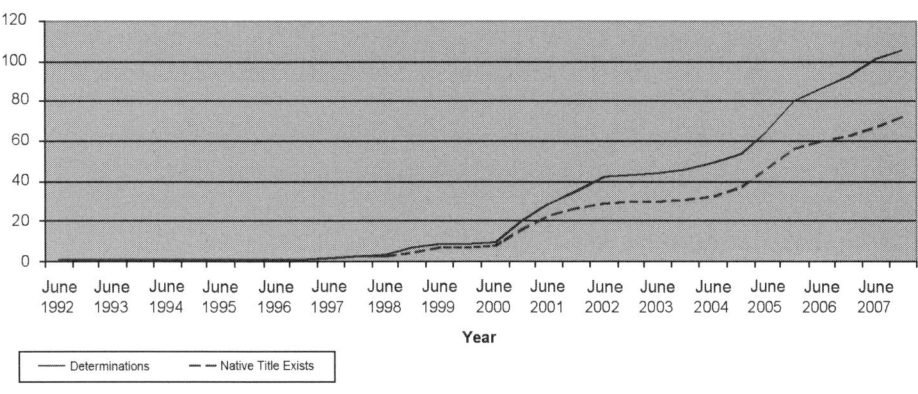

Figure 1: Cumulative determinations of native title to 4 December 2007

Indigenous land use agreements

The NTA provides for Indigenous Land Use Agreements (ILUAs), which are specific forms of agreements that can be negotiated, registered and given particular legal effect by the Act. ILUAs can be negotiated over areas where native title has been shown to exist or might exist. They can be used in conjunction with determinations of native title, or 'standalone' agreements negotiated before, and independently of, any determination of native title. ILUAs have been used to cover a range of land uses including the creation and management of national parks, community living areas, mineral exploration and mining, petroleum activity, marina development, defence facilities, pipelines, and the use of and access to pastoral leases. At 31 March 2008 there were 323 registered ILUAs. Most of the ILUAs are in Queensland (53%) and the Northern Territory (26%). Registered ILUAs cover some 913,000 square kilometres (or 12%) of the land mass of Australia. The potential growth in the number of ILUAs is significant. For example, on 14 May 2008 alone, twenty-four ILUAs were signed in relation to pastoral leases in the Gawler Ranges of South Australia.[22]

Current claims

As at 31 May 2008, there were 554 applications in the system, 511 of them claimant applications. Most of the claimant applications are in the Northern Territory (34%), Queensland (29%) and Western Australia (23%). Most of the non-claimant applications (91%) are in New South Wales.[23]

Although 283 (or 51%) of the current applications have been referred by the Federal Court to the NNTT for mediation and are described as being 'in mediation', many of them are not being substantively mediated. Indeed, it may be that only half of those applications could be described as 'active' because mediation is occurring, or because the NNTT is involved in developing research reports or is undertaking geospatial analysis to assist the parties.[24] Various factors delay or impede the active mediation of claims. I will identify the main obstacles and suggest means of overcoming them later in this paper.

LONG-TERM FORECAST

Historical trends

There were relatively few determinations of native title in the early years of the operation of the NTA, illustrated above in Figure 1. This trend can be explained by an examination of the history of the NTA, including amendments to it and judgments about it.

Many claims were made under the original NTA when the law on native title was unclear and the process allowed multiple overlapping claims (often by members of the same family or group), all of which attracted procedural rights. It took years for various 'test' cases to work their way through the appeals processes so that significant legal issues could be resolved. There was some reluctance to settle claims while the law was new, uncertain and politically controversial. As a result, in the first six years of the NTA's operation there were only eight determinations of native title, and after ten years there were forty-six determinations.

There was little, if any, involvement of the Federal Court in relation to most claims until the NTA was substantially amended from 30 September 1998 (including removing constitutionally invalid provisions in relation to the NNTT). All the claims at that date became proceedings in the Court and most were subject to the new registration test which, for some years, became the focus of the attention and resources of the claim groups, their representatives, state and territory governments, and the Native Title Registrar, and which led to a substantial reduction in the number of claims in the system. With the resolution of these issues there has been a steady rise in the number of determinations in recent years.

However, the claims that have been resolved to date have been relatively straightforward in terms of tenure and connection issues. Most of the areas involved have been in the northern and more remote parts of Australia, where Aboriginal or Torres Strait Islander communities have maintained a physical and traditional connection with the land and there have been few, if any, dealings in land which have extinguished native title rights and interests. In contrast, many of the remaining claims are in more densely settled areas where native title has been extinguished (in part or in whole) and it will be more difficult to prosecute both legally — in demonstrating the continuity of traditional laws and customs and the native title rights under them — and practically — in resolving the impact of extinguishing acts and tenures.

Projected period to resolve claim

The NNTT estimates that, on current trends, it will take about thirty years to resolve the current claims and those that are likely to be lodged in the next few years. An analysis of the 135 applications that had been determined as at 31 March 2008 shows that:
- for the sixty-two determined by *consent,* the average time for achieving a determination was sixty-seven months (five years and seven months);
- for the forty-nine *litigated* determinations, the average time for achieving a determination was eighty-four months (seven years);
- for the twenty-four determined *unopposed,* the average time for achieving a determination was twelve months.

Those averages are likely to increase rather than decrease in the immediate future. Of the 513 current claimant applications as at 31 March 2008:
- 119 (or 23%) were lodged in or since 2003, i.e. in the past five years;
- 282 (or 55%) were lodged between 1998 and 2002, i.e. in the past six to ten years;
- 112 (or 22%) were lodged earlier, i.e. have been in the system for between eleven and fourteen years.

The graph at Figure 2 shows the projected rate of resolution of claimant applications to the number of applications lodged. At the current rate of claim lodgement and claim resolution (averaged between 2000 and 2007), those claims will not be finalised (e.g. by determination, withdrawal, amalgamation or dismissal) until 2035.

An improved average rate of resolving individual claims would result in a significant reduction in the overall period for all finalising of current and expected claims. Equally, substantial delays in resolving individual claims or an increase in the rate of new claims would extend the overall period to finalisation well beyond 2035.

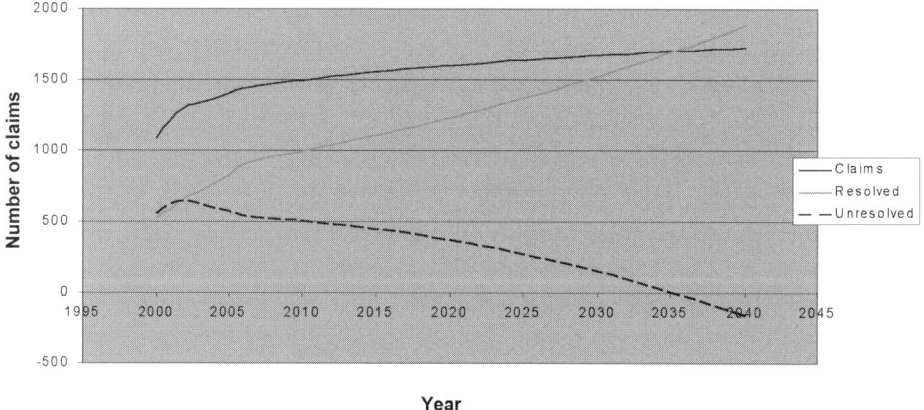

The graph was prepared on the basis that the number of claims lodged will continue to increase at the average of the past seven years (3.6% cumulative) and the number of claims resolved will continue to increase at the average of the past seven years (2.15% cumulative).

Figure 2: Estimated resolution of claimant applications

Comparison with land claims in the Northern Territory

While the projected timeframe for resolution may seem alarming, it is worth comparing the land claim scheme under the *Aboriginal Land Rights (Northern Territory) Act 1976* (Cth), which has been in operation since Australia Day 1977. Although not directly comparable, the land claim process is arguably more simple and straightforward than the process for resolving native title claims in at least the following respects:

- there is a statutory definition of 'traditional Aboriginal owners'[25] which does not require people to prove that they have substantially uninterrupted continuity of traditional connection to land back to the date on which the Crown first asserted sovereignty;
- the categories of land subject to claim are clearly delineated and have few, if any, tenures;
- there are usually fewer parties than in native title proceedings;
- there is an administrative inquiry about traditional ownership and related issues, which does not require the agreement of the parties before an outcome is reached;
- land councils are established and funded to do this work under the legislation; and
- there is extensive knowledge and experience of the process and what the law requires.

Despite those factors, it has still taken more than thirty years to resolve most of the traditional land claims, and many claims have yet to be finalised, either by negotiation or following a hearing and report of an

Aboriginal Land Commissioner. The Commissioner's annual report for the year ended 30 June 2007 listed 249 claims made between 1977 and 1997.[26] The Commissioner expressed frustration at the current position whereby, after thirty years, one claim 'remains unresolved and other claims have remained dormant for periods in excess of 20 years'.[27]

SOME OF THE OBSTACLES TO BE OVERCOME

Four critical tasks

The NNTT's analysis of the current applications indicates that the critical tasks that need to be carried out to ensure the steady progress of applications to resolution are:
- timetabling and working on tenure analysis (to identify areas where native title has been extinguished);
- timetabling and managing the preparation and assessment of connection material;
- resolving overlapping claims; and
- reducing the number of parties and clarifying their interests in relation to an application.

Each of these tasks is discussed later in this paper. At this stage it is appropriate to make broad observations about some of them.

The implications of extinguishing tenure

It has been clear for many years, both from the provisions of the NTA and judgments of the High Court and Federal Court, that native title will *not* be recognised over large areas of Australia where, as a matter of law, native title has been extinguished completely by certain dealings as specified in the NTA and in some High Court judgments. In other areas (such as those subject to 'non-exclusive' pastoral leases), any native title right to exclusive possession has been extinguished, with the remaining 'bundle' of native title rights and interests being recognised and exercised alongside the rights and interests of other landholders but subject to those other rights. Nevertheless, where there have been no prior dealings with the land, or where those dealings must be disregarded, and other conditions are satisfied, there may be a determination that native title rights and interests confer possession, occupation, use and enjoyment of that land on native title holders to the exclusion of all others.

There are some areas where, by reference to current tenures (assuming the dealings are not to be disregarded under a provision of the Act[28]), native title will *not* be found to exist, irrespective of whether Aboriginal people have retained strong traditional links to those areas. Those areas cover much of eastern and southern Australia. Over much of the rest of the land mass of Australia, current tenures (mostly forms of pastoral lease) have partially extinguished any native title rights and interests that might otherwise exist.

The challenge in relation to any claimant application (or cluster of claims) is to identify with certainty those areas where native title (or some native title rights and interests) might exist because either there have been no extinguishing tenures or the tenures have a limited effect on native title, or any extinguishment by specified acts must be disregarded.[29]

Establishing traditional connection to land or waters

It has been clear for many years (at the latest since the High Court's 2002 judgment in the *Yorta Yorta* case) that it will be difficult for many claimant groups to prove that they have native title rights and interests in relation to particular areas of land or waters. They have to satisfy the criteria in the definition of 'native title' in subsection 223(1) of the Act as those criteria have been interpreted by the High Court.

In the reasons for judgment on the appeal in relation to the Noongar claim to the Perth metropolitan area, a Full Court of the Federal Court stated, among other things, that:

- the existence, character and extent of native title rights and interests depend upon the traditional laws and customs of the community in question;[30]
- the acknowledgment and observance of the traditional laws and customs must have continued 'substantially uninterrupted' from the time when the Crown asserted sovereignty, and the connection must have been 'substantially maintained' since that time,[31] whether by physical presence on the country or otherwise;[32] and
- the connection inquiry can have 'a particular topographic focus within the claim area' so that there may need to be evidence that connection has been substantially maintained to a particular part of the claim area since sovereignty.[33]

If claimants want a determination of native title they need to convince other parties or the Federal Court of their traditional connection to the claimed area. Even if agreement is reached between the parties, judges will require some information about the native title claim group and its connection to the area before the Court will be satisfied that it is appropriate to make orders *in rem* in, or consistently with, the orders agreed by the parties.

Most respondent parties, including governments, will not engage in substantive mediation with claimants unless and until they have received satisfactory connection material. The collation and presentation of that material, whatever its form(s), is a multidisciplinary process. It can be lengthy and expensive, all the more so because of a shortage of people who are suitably qualified, experienced and available to do the work. An audit by the NNTT of current claims in 2007 showed that:

- connection reports had been prepared and provided in just under 20% of the claims;
- connection was not necessary for an outcome in another 6% of the claims; and
- connection material had not been prepared (and in most cases was not scheduled for preparation) in relation to the remaining 75% of the claims.

Disputed overlapping claims

Many claimant applications overlap other applications (in part or in whole) and many of the overlaps illustrate disagreement between neighbouring Indigenous groups about the extent of their traditional country. As at 31 March 2008, 49.6% of the land mass of Australia was either covered by determinations or single claimant applications, 10.7% was covered by two or more claimant applications and the remainder (39.7%) was not covered by any claimant applications. As at 31 December 2007, of the 521 active claimant applications, 55% of claims had no overlaps and the other 45% of claims comprised 17% with one overlap, 13% with two overlaps, 4% with three overlaps, 5% with four overlaps and 6% with five or more overlaps.

Although some groups acknowledge that others have traditional rights and interests over the same area (and that has been recognised in some determinations of native title to date [34]), the existence of disputed overlaps is a threshold issue that needs to be resolved. Some longstanding disputes between groups are revived or exacerbated by the native title process and can result in long delays in progressing any of the claims. They can lead to trials in Court. Governments and some other respondent parties will not participate in substantive mediation unless and until the overlaps are resolved (e.g. by a native title representative body exercising its dispute resolution functions, the NNTT mediating between neighbouring groups, or the Federal Court delivering judgment about who are the correct people for each area).

Integrated nature of the native title system

It is essential to bear in mind that the native title system is an integrated whole, with the major participants being:
- native title representative bodies (NTRBs) or native title service providers;
- native title parties (most of whom are represented by or via NTRBs);
- state and territory governments (as first respondents to native title applications);
- the Commonwealth Minister (currently the Attorney-General);
- other respondent parties;
- the Federal Court;
- the NNTT;
- the Commonwealth funding agencies — the Attorney-General's Department (which, among other things, administers respondent party funding) and the Department of Families, Housing, Community Services and Indigenous Affairs.

The performance of the *system* depends on the performance of the participants, most of whom are funded by the Commonwealth. The performance of each *participant* is contingent to a greater or lesser extent on the performance of other participants. Each participant only has capacity to perform their functions and exercise their powers if they have, or have access to, appropriate levels of funding, professional employees or consultants, and the skills and knowledge required to engage in a positive and productive way with others. Consequently, neither the Court nor the NNTT can perform their functions adequately, or produce appropriate outcomes, if the parties or their representatives lack the capacity to engage effectively and in a timely way with each other and with the Court or NNTT.

Despite the challenges, the native title system is not in a state of gridlock. The traffic is not always moving as it should. Each party is in a driver's seat and should cooperate with others so that they are moving in the same direction, toward the timely resolution of claims. Not every party will end up at the same destination. Some claimants will end up with determinations that native title exists. Others will not. Some will settle for an alternative arrangement and may withdraw their claim. Whatever their destinations, all participants in the native title system must work to find ways to reach outcomes in a timely and more efficient manner for the hundreds of current native title applications and those that are to come. Effective responses to the challenges require innovation, leadership and commitment to achieving results across the native title system.

MEETING THE CHALLENGES: CLAIMANTS

Deciding what the native title claimants want to achieve from their claimant application

There is a fundamental, threshold question which each native title claim group must answer: what do we want to obtain from the native title proceedings that have been commenced by our claimant application? The answer may be different for different groups, and some groups who lodged claims for one purpose may have changed their minds. The reason for asking the question and why different answers might be given can be summarised briefly.

Most claims have been in the system for many years. As noted earlier, approximately 22% were lodged before the substantial amendments were made to the Act in 1998, and a further 55% were lodged before the High Court's landmark judgments in the *Ward*[35] and *Yorta Yorta*[36] cases.[37] In other words, more than three-quarters of current claims were lodged before claimant groups could have understood, or been advised comprehensively about, such matters as the high evidentiary standard necessary to prove that they have native title, the limited content (from the standpoint of traditional laws and customs) of the native title rights and interests that the law will recognise, the vulnerability of native title and the nature and extent of extinguishment from the grants of past and present land tenures that has resulted in any prospect of recognition of their native title rights being removed, or in such recognition being confined to very limited native title rights and interests.

For many groups, the most they could obtain is a determination that is limited to a small proportion of their traditional country (perhaps a few parcels of land separated by significant distances) and only a few non-exclusive native title rights and interests. To obtain even that limited result the claimants will need to do (or have done on their behalf) a substantial amount of specialised research (potentially involving such professionals as anthropologists, historians, linguists and lawyers). Others (usually the relevant state or territory government) will need to be satisfied that the results of the claimants' efforts will be sufficient for them to agree to a consent determination of native title. And then, finally, all parties will have to wait while the relevant state or territory government investigates current and historical tenures, and all parties agree on the effect of those tenures on native title rights and interests that would otherwise be recognised. In short, for many groups the cost in time, money, specialist personnel and personal involvement that is necessary to obtain such a determination will be inversely proportional to the benefits to the group of obtaining it.

This stark picture might not have been clear when many of the claims were made. It still might not be clear to many groups, irrespective of how recently or long ago their claims were made or amended. Someone needs to explain to them in plain terms what is or is not potentially achievable, and what the alternatives to a determination of native title might be.

On the basis of relevant information (such as a map of the claim area showing the extent of extinguishing tenures) and advice, groups need to decide what they hope (and can reasonably expect) to achieve from the native title proceedings that they have commenced. The aspiration might include:

- recognition of the community or group as the traditional owners of an area of land or waters;
- the right to have a say in what happens on their traditional land or waters;
- protection of areas of particular cultural significance to the group;
- developing an economic base on which the community or group can build for itself and future generations.

Many see native title as the key to achieving these aspirations.

Social, psychological and cultural benefits of recognition

Although the native title claim process can be protracted, arduous and sometimes disruptive to Indigenous communities, one should not underestimate the social and psychological benefits for a group of Aboriginal people or Torres Strait Islanders of being recognised as the people for a particular area by the Australian legal system and, through those formal processes, by the rest of Australia. The process of negotiating native title agreements can result in the creation or strengthening of relationships that can be as valuable as the agreements reached. For some groups who have received native title recognition, the social and psychological benefits to them are profound, irrespective of any economic benefits.

As a result of the native title process in parts of Australia, some Indigenous groups have renewed relationships with each other and have strengthened their cultural ties to areas of traditional land. Most of the areas covered by determinations that native title exists and/or by ILUAs are in areas that are classified as remote or very remote. Accordingly, one benefit from those outcomes is the capacity for those Indigenous groups to remain on their traditional lands if they choose to do so. Such an outcome can be characterised as contributing to culturally (and, in some instances, economically) sustainable communities in those parts of Australia.

Procedural rights and economic benefits

Although native title is not 'title' in the ordinary real property commercial sense, and may not be an economically valuable commodity, significant economic benefits (as well as heritage protection and other outcomes) are being secured by groups as a by-product of the native title process. Where native title exists, or people have a registered native title claim, the relevant group of Aboriginal people or Torres Strait Islanders acquires various procedural rights under the NTA, including the right to negotiate with those who want to mine on the land. One benefit from these procedural rights can be the capacity to negotiate not only financial compensation for impact on native title, but also training, employment and business opportunities in relation to enterprises on particular areas of land, engagement in cultural heritage programs, and employment in national parks and other conservation areas.

Many of the negotiations under the procedural provisions of the NTA and some other legislation take place irrespective of whether the group has proved or can prove that it has native title. Indeed, many agreements (including ILUAs) are made long before native title is shown to exist and, potentially at least, with groups who could not prove that they have native title. Business can proceed without the delay of waiting for claims to be resolved, Indigenous groups can benefit from the agreements, and relationships can be created.

Approximately one-quarter of current claimant applications were lodged in response to future act notices. Most of these were in the Northern Territory and Queensland. Although the timing of the application may have been prompted by the publication of future act notices, it should not be assumed that such claim groups do not want a determination that native title exists. It is not clear how many of those applications will proceed to mediation and determination. However, once a claim is lodged, whatever the instigating reason, native title claim groups are expected to pursue the determination of native title sought by their application. Procedures introduced by amendments to the NTA in 2007 allow for the dismissal of claims which have not progressed after the future act has been done. To date, no claims have been dismissed on this basis.[38] But the courts have made it clear that such claims will not be allowed to sit dormant in the system.

Options for achieving a group's aspirations

Some of the aspirations of a native title claim group might only be realised if there is a determination that native title exists. Other aspirations may be realised without the need to obtain a determination of native title. However their aspirations might be realised, it is important for native title claim groups whose claims are still in the early stages of negotiation (even though they may have been lodged many years ago) to obtain sound advice and make strategic decisions about how to proceed.

Some groups may decide to proceed towards a determination that native title exists, with or without ancillary agreements (such as ILUAs). Some groups might seek to use the options available under section 86F of the NTA and invite the NNTT to assist them to negotiate outcomes other than a determination of native title in return for withdrawing their claim (and possibly surrendering any native title that they have to the Crown). Other groups might simply withdraw their claims permanently or with a view to reformulating them to better accord with legal requirements and to enhance their prospects of a negotiated outcome.

The options that native title claim groups might consider seriously could be influenced by the attitude of, and approach taken by, the main respondents (particularly governments) to connection requirements and options for alternative settlements. Having made a native title claim which, in part at least, is an assertion of group identity and rights, native title claim groups are unlikely to withdraw or vary their claims significantly unless meaningful offers are made that meet their reasonable aspirations for themselves and their descendants.

The cumulative effect of such informed decisions in relation to hundreds of current claimant applications could be significant to the rate of progress of the claims that are pursued and the cost of delivering just and enduring outcomes for the parties.

Preserving evidence to support a native title determination

If native title claim groups wish to proceed with their applications for a determination of native title (or at least retain the option of proceeding to a determination of native title), experience has shown (and the statistical projections indicate) that it will be many years before most claims are resolved. Consequently, it is likely that some of the most knowledgeable and authoritative members of the groups will not be able to participate actively in the proceedings (particularly if the claim goes to a hearing in the Federal Court) or may pass away before the claims are resolved.

There has been much concern from claimants, judges and politicians that some people are dying before their claims are resolved. Sad as that situation is, even with considerable goodwill on all sides, most claims will not be resolved in the immediate future. Native title claim groups need to consider whether the evidence of old or vulnerable members of the group should be preserved and, if so, how that should occur. The options include:

- recording witness statements in documents and, if appropriate, producing them in the course of a mediation conference subject to restrictions on their disclosure;[39]
- a native title application inquiry by the NNTT;[40] and
- preservation of evidence as part of a hearing by the Federal Court in advance of the general hearing (if any) of the claim.

Resolving disputed overlapping claims

As noted earlier, some parties will not wish to be actively involved in mediation until the threshold issue of overlapping and disputed claimant applications is resolved. Although willing to negotiate about native title issues, they do not want to decide between competing groups. In their view, that is a matter for the disputing groups (or the Federal Court) to decide before they will engage in substantive mediation.

There are risks for disputing claim groups that they will not secure sufficient resources to advance their claims to substantive mediation or their claims will not be given priority in the regional planning of the NTRB with the state or territory, the NNTT and others. At minimum, the areas of their claims that are not overlapped might not progress until the overlaps are resolved or removed. There is also a risk that there may be an application to have the claims struck out or that the Court may make programming orders for the hearing of the claims on the basis that there is no prospect of a mediated outcome within a reasonable period.

However, there are options for those groups to consider for dealing with the overlaps, including:
- sorting out the issue between themselves, perhaps in accordance with traditional decision-making processes;
- asking the NNTT for mapping and possibly research assistance to inform discussions between the disputing groups;
- getting the relevant NTRB to exercise its dispute resolution function to promote agreement, or to mediate, between its constituents,[41] possibly with the assistance of the NNTT[42] (as happened at Spear Creek in South Australia);
- if the claims have been referred to the NNTT for mediation,[43] having the NNTT mediate between the groups;
- asking the NNTT to conduct a native title application inquiry,[44] or a review of materials to see whether a native title claim group holds native title rights and interests in relation to the overlap area,[45] to assist in the mediation of the dispute; and/or
- asking the NNTT to refer the issue to the Court for determination.[46]

Given the extent of disputed overlapping claims, it is important that steps be taken as early as practicable (preferably before claims are lodged) to resolve them.

Resource issues for claimants

Historically, the debate about the adequacy of resourcing native title claim groups has focused on the amount of public funding provided to NTRBs and the ways in which NTRBs have applied those moneys to assisting in the resolution of claims and to the performance of their other statutory functions. The debate has proceeded on the basis that Indigenous groups lack the resources to prepare and prosecute claims in the way and to the standard required by the law, and it is appropriate, as a matter of public policy and social justice, to assist groups in that endeavour.

Consequently, groups who are represented by NTRBs have relied on those NTRBs to provide the relevant assistance.[47] If the NTRB lacks resources to assist some claimants, or if the priority given to their claim is such that the resources will not be provided for some years, then the claimants (and the other parties and institutions, such as the NNTT and the Court) have to wait. Native title claim groups who are not represented by NTRBs have to seek assistance elsewhere, often from professionals acting pro bono.

There are indications that, in the future, such dependence on publicly funded resources will not necessarily be the determining factor for programming and prioritising the resolution of some claims. At a 2007 directions hearing for claimant applications in the Greater Mount Isa region of north-west Queensland, the Federal Court reviewed the priority list of claimant applications prepared by the NNTT in consultation with the NTRB and the state government. The region is rich in minerals and some claim groups have entered into ILUAs with mining companies. Some claims that are low in the priority list for the preparation of connection material and substantive mediation are in areas of high level future act activity. Justice Dowsett made orders in relation to one claimant application that the applicant file and serve a work plan outlining the resources available within the claims group, both individually and collectively, including any money from ILUAs.[48]

His Honour has made similar orders in a number of other matters, including requirements that the applicants prepare a work plan including 'a timeframe for the disposal of the matter both on the basis of available resources and unlimited resources'.[49]

It remains to be seen what responses will be provided to the Court and whether subsequent orders in relation to the programming of those applications will be influenced by the capacity and willingness of a native title claim group (or members of it) to provide significant funding to advance their claim.

MEETING THE CHALLENGES: CLAIMANTS' REPRESENTATIVES

Establishing claimants' traditional connection to land or waters

One of the most complex aspects of native title proceedings is ascertaining whether a claim group has native title rights and interests in relation to the land or waters claimed. The NTA defines 'native title' to mean the communal, group or individual rights and interests of Aboriginal peoples or Torres Strait Islanders in relation to land or waters where:
- the rights and interests are possessed under the traditional laws acknowledged, and the traditional customs observed, by those people; and
- the people, by those laws and customs, have a connection with the land or waters; and
- the rights and interests are recognised by the common law of Australia.[50]

That definition has been the subject of considerable judicial analysis. In essence, the claimants (who bear the onus of proof) have to show that they have native title rights and interests in relation to the area under a system of traditional laws and customs which has its roots in a society that preceded the date on which the Crown asserted sovereignty (between 1788 and 1879 depending on where in Australia the claim is made) and which has maintained a substantially continuous connection with the area under those traditional laws and customs.

One of the statutory purposes of mediation is to assist parties to reach agreement on whether native title exists and, if it does exist, who holds the native title and the nature, extent and manner of exercise of the native title rights and interests in relation to the area claimed.[51] Research to establish whether a group has native title can involve historical, anthropological, linguistic and genealogical materials, as well as oral histories from the group and neighbouring groups. Written compilations and analyses of that material are often referred to as 'connection reports'.

However, the shortage of competent researchers (particularly anthropologists) available to prepare connection reports or assess them (e.g. to advise governments) and the lack of interdisciplinary collaboration in preparing connection materials (including insufficient involvement of lawyers to ensure that reports are fit for the purpose for which they are prepared), together with the limited resources generally to prepare and assess such material, lead to delays in researching and producing reports, or the preparation of some reports that do not address the rigorous requirements of state government connection guidelines (giving rise to requests for revision or supplementation). In addition, the practice of restricting access to connection reports limits the opportunities to educate other researchers and to share understandings about how connection material was assessed.

Such practical obstacles to resolving connection could be reduced or overcome by, among other things, arranging collaboration between external researchers, NTRBs and governments to scope the research that is necessary for each claim before that research is undertaken (e.g. by identifying matters that are not contentious and do not need detailed research and clarifying the information required in light of intended or possible outcomes) and to settle the form in which the material should be presented (including the best ways to incorporate more direct evidence from claimants).[52]

Prioritising claims and regional planning

Experience shows that claims progress best when there is a coordinated approach to their preparation and presentation. Given that there are limited resources to assist native title claim groups, it is necessary to develop a program for resolving claims. Working out regional priorities for claims in the area of an NTRB is a constant challenge; one which is sometimes assisted by conducting a regional research project to identify the strength of existing claims, the basis for resolving disputed overlaps and the lodgement of new claims.

Regional planning cannot be conducted in isolation from other key participants in the system, particularly where the claimant applications have been referred to the NNTT for mediation. Although each native title application is unique, there are many common factors affecting the potential resolution of claims in each NTRB's area. For example, each state or territory is a respondent to every claim in the region, and some parties or their representatives are involved in numerous claims. The Federal Court and the NNTT have roles in case management. The NNTT works with each NTRB to develop regional programs and provides regional mediation progress reports to the Court. In performing their functions, the Court and the NNTT recognise that limits on financial and human resources and a range of other factors affect the progress of individual claims or clusters of claims.

Resources issues for NTRBs

For some years there have been concerns about the perceived inadequacy of the human and financial resources available to NTRBs. NTRBs have important powers and functions under the NTA. For many Indigenous groups their local NTRB is the principal source of advice and representation on native title matters. The NTRB may represent people in mediations concerning claimant applications, and may be involved in future act negotiations (e.g. in relation to the grant of mining interests) and the negotiation of ILUAs.

The NNTT has consistently maintained that properly functioning NTRBs are not just important to the people they represent. The NNTT and parties to various native title proceedings and negotiations also benefit from them providing an efficient and effective service. Not surprisingly, the Minerals Council of Australia has been one of the bodies calling for more resources to be provided to NTRBs. In March 2006 the Parliamentary Joint Committee on Native Title and the Aboriginal and Torres Strait Islander Land Account reported on the operation of NTRBs. The Committee made recommendations in relation to such matters as the development of key performance indicators to assess the relative effectiveness of NTRBs in meeting their statutory obligations, and the funding and staffing of NTRBs.

Many native title claimants and their representatives experience difficulty in juggling mediation with complying with Court orders, responding to future act notices (particularly those asserting the expedited procedure), negotiating ILUAs, engaging in bilateral negotiations, dealing with related issues (e.g. cultural heritage) and dealing with the myriad of issues/problems that constantly arise within claim groups.

The resourcing of NTRBs is clearly on the Australian Government's agenda. In his 29 February 2008 speech on native title, Attorney-General McClelland said that NTRBs 'must have the resources they need to properly assist native title parties pursue timely and mutually beneficial native title outcomes'.[53] Minister Macklin said that there is 'not enough funding' for NTRBs to 'get the job done' and noted that they are 'calling for adequate resources for claim preparation and dispute resolution'.[54] She foreshadowed a reform package that 'will need to include proposals for strengthening the resourcing and statutory basis' of the existing NTRBs, including their role in resolving disputes within and between claimant groups.[55] In a speech to the Minerals Week Conference, the Minister for Resources and Energy, the Honourable Martin Ferguson, referred to 'long-standing industry concerns regarding the level of funding received' by NTRBs.[56]

MEETING THE CHALLENGES: GOVERNMENTS

The process by which native title applications are resolved by agreement requires the active and positive involvement of governments (particularly state and territory governments). Many of the options for settlement are exclusively in the control of governments.

Deciding what governments want to achieve in relation to claimant applications

Earlier in this paper, I contended that each native title claim group must decide what they want to obtain from the native title proceedings that they have commenced. In a similar vein, governments need to decide what they want to achieve in relation to native title claims. Although it is common for governments to say they want to negotiate rather than litigate, the question is what they want to negotiate about. Do they want to start by testing each claim to ascertain whether it might support a determination of native title or are they willing to consider, from an early stage in the process, a broader range of options from which to fashion a settlement of each claim? Do they consider claims to be primarily legal proceedings in relation to which they are the first respondent, or do they want to use native title claim proceedings as an opportunity to deal with a range of related issues?

Commonwealth, state and territory ministers responsible for native title have started to consider these issues. Following their inaugural meeting in September 2005, the ministers met in Canberra in 2006. They discussed, among other things, how native title can meet broader Indigenous policy objectives. The ministers noted the positive contribution that agreement making and the use of native title-related outcomes can make to fulfil the broader aspirations of native title claimants. In particular, the ministers noted that native title processes are being, and can be, utilised to identify measures that contribute to economic development for Indigenous Australians, opportunities for capacity building and other support for Indigenous communities, and assistance to secure long-term and lasting benefits for Indigenous communities from the land.

More recently, Commonwealth Attorney-General McClelland stated that all participants 'from governments down can do much better… in resolving native title claims…in creatively and innovatively using negotiations as a vehicle to achieve practical outcomes'.[57] He has suggested that there is 'room for all parties to take a step back, and adopt a more flexible and willing approach to negotiations'.[58] He has called on all governments to work together 'through cooperative federalism' to 'find a new approach to resolving native title claims' so that 'an enormous amount can be achieved'.[59]

Reforming means of assessing connection

One area of possible reform is the process for assessing connection. There is an ongoing debate about the best way to deal with connection issues, including debate about the role of state and territory governments and the role of the NNTT in this process.

The relevant state or territory government is the first respondent to each claimant application. It has a role on behalf of the whole community in the negotiations. It has (or has access to) suitably qualified people to assess whether the claim group can establish the native title rights and interests asserted. Some governments have published guidelines about the content and form of the connection material that they require in order to be satisfied that native title exists. Others (including the Commonwealth) do not have published guidelines. There are different processes for reporting on and assessing connection materials. Some governments require proof of connection as a pre-condition to entering into substantive negotiations with a claim group. As at June 2007 there were approximately seventy-eight connection reports, in a range of forms, awaiting assessment around Australia. Most were the product of a two- to three-year research process and most will enter an assessment process that can take up to three years.

It is appropriate for the relevant governments to assess the strength of a claim. Other (though not necessarily all) respondent parties will follow, or be assisted by, a government's assessment when deciding their approach to the resolution of the claim. It has been contended, however, that the current practice has largely relocated the evidentiary process from the Court to the relevant state or territory. Indeed, Justice North has questioned 'how far a State party is required to investigate in order to satisfy itself of a credible basis for an application'.[60] He wrote that '[o]ne reason for the often inordinate time taken to resolve some of these cases is the overly demanding nature of the investigation conducted by State parties'.[61] In his view, 'something significantly less than the material necessary to justify a judicial determination is sufficient to satisfy a State party of a credible basis for an application. The NTA contemplates a more flexible process than is often undertaken in some cases.'[62]

Although that view may not be universally held, it illustrates the issue about the role and requirements of governments in dealing with connection issues. In some parts of the country, connection issues are dealt with bilaterally between the applicants and the relevant government, with little if any involvement by the NNTT or other parties (each of whom must consent to any determination that native title exists, and some of whom will want to be satisfied independently that connection has been established).

In July 2007 the NNTT and the Australian Institute of Aboriginal and Torres Strait Islander Studies (AIATSIS) convened a native title workshop about the processes used by parties for dealing with connection issues. It involved forty practitioners engaged by NTRBs, state and territory governments, and others with significant experience in native title. A survey of participants before the workshop indicated that most believe that problems encountered in resolving connection issues are systemic in nature. In other words, there is no one way to solve the problem and several approaches must be undertaken to effect change. Various suggestions for improving the current system were made in the context

13. Achieving real outcomes from native title claims

of the stated preference of governments to reach mediated (rather than litigated) outcomes. Chief among these are:
- improving regional and operational planning (including claims prioritisation) between state and territory governments and NTRBs;
- mitigating the adversarial nature of the relationships between parties; and
- clarifying the needs and expectations of all parties in relation to connection material as early as possible (e.g. at a plenary conference convened by the NNTT).

Other suggestions for improving practice included:
- providing simpler, cheaper access to government records and/or using limited discovery orders for easier access to relevant information;
- revising government guidelines to ensure that they are flexible, clear (e.g. with checklists) and consistently applied;
- incorporating the preparation and assessment of connection material as part of the mediation framework and not a precursor to it; and
- mediating connection and other issues in parallel rather than sequentially.

Some of the suggestions made at the workshop would require a significant shift in the policies of governments, including:
- state and territory governments removing their requirement for comprehensive proof of connection *before* entering into negotiations;
- developing a national framework and standards for the assessment of connection.

There are indications of support for some of these suggestions. In February 2008, Commonwealth Attorney-General McClelland suggested that, rather than start by considering connection with its attendant problems,[63] there might be benefits in starting with a consideration of tenure and having a connection process run in parallel with discussions about a range of outcomes, native and non-native title.[64]

Settlements involving or comprising components other than determinations of native title

As noted earlier, it is now clear that native title has been extinguished, in whole or in part, over substantial areas of Australia — consequently, in large parts of eastern and southern Australia there are few parcels of land where native title might be recognised at law. In many areas where native title can be shown to exist, the recognised native title rights and interests will be limited to those few of the 'bundle of rights' that can exist alongside the rights of others in relation to the land. Moreover, many groups will find it difficult, if not impossible, to demonstrate that the relationship with their traditional country meets the standard of proof required for a determination that native title exists.

Consequently, Indigenous groups and their representatives, government, other parties and the NNTT have been forced to consider how best to proceed in this more clearly delineated legal context. Sometimes it may be possible for a claimant application to be settled through a mixture of native title and non-native title outcomes, or even by non-native title outcomes alone.

The NTA provides that some or all of the parties to a claimant proceeding may negotiate with a view to agreeing to action that will result in the application being withdrawn or amended; the parties to the proceeding being varied; and/or any other thing being done in relation to the application.[65]

The agreement may involve matters other than native title.[66] The possible outcomes are not limited to native title rights and interests, but need only relate to the resolution of the claim or some aspect of it. They could include social justice components. The parties may request assistance from the NNTT in negotiating the agreement.[67]

In his paper to the Negotiating Native Title Forum in 2008, Attorney-General Robert McClelland illustrated this approach when he said:

> [N]ative title is but one way or recognising Indigenous peoples' connection to land. Where Indigenous people have lost their native title by removal or through the passage of time, we should be able to find a way to recognise their relationship with the land. In summary, we need to move away from technical legal arguments about the existence of native title.[68]

Later in the speech, he said:

> Importantly, being unable to meet the required standard for a determination of native title at a particular point in history does not mean those Indigenous people do not have strong relationships with the land and with each other. But it does mean that claimants need to consider what other results they may be willing to achieve from a claim. And Governments need to consider how they might achieve those aspirations…Much can be achieved if parties are up front about what they really want and open-minded about finding creative solutions.[69]

Options that might be included in an alternative settlement include:
1. Recognition of traditional land, without native title rights, for example:
   - recognition under state or territory legislation or by other means of statutory protection;
   - recognition of traditional boundaries and traditional owner entities on state land title systems;
   - signage in appropriate locations and publications;
   - place naming rights and provision of 'welcome to country' on official occasions.
2. Grants of land or interests in land or water, for example:
   - grants of Crown land or land purchased by government/s, and possible leaseback of some land (e.g. national parks) to governments;
   - access to public land for cultural purposes (such as seasonal camping) or for business enterprise development (such as education, tourism);
   - the creation of special reserves for use by traditional owners;
   - the lease of government land to traditional owners;
   - revenue sharing, such as from land tax (e.g. *Aboriginal Land Rights Act 1983* (NSW)), or mining royalties (e.g. *Aboriginal Land Rights (Northern Territory) Act 1976* (Cth)), or land sales (e.g. in a subdivision of Karratha, Western Australia, under the Burrup Agreement) or by other means (e.g. tenement rental) to provide ongoing support.
3. Roles in managing what happens on land, for example:
   - joint management or co-management of conservation areas (e.g. national parks) or Crown reserves;
   - membership of boards advising on land management (e.g. Landcare, natural resource programs);
   - involvement in and increased resources for the protection of cultural heritage;
   - participation in relevant town planning and other aspects of cultural heritage protection.
4. Employment and economic opportunities, for example:
   - in areas related to public land management (e.g. tourism, fishing, conservation);
   - public–private agreements related to skills development and joint ventures in land and resource management (farming, mining);
   - enterprise development grants and support systems (e.g. commercial fisheries quota allocation);
   - equity participation in commercial enterprises on traditional land.

5. Financial payments or grants to the group, for example:
   - for capital works on the land (e.g. for commercial or cultural development);
   - to administer the land (such as funding of a traditional owner group);
   - enterprise development.

There are various examples of settlement 'packages' negotiated in different parts of Australia, although, in considering the precedential value of these packages, it should be stressed that the state and territory land management and cultural heritage systems are not uniform and the contents and implementation of state and territory native title policies are also not uniform. Each settlement package is a product of local circumstances (e.g. remote area or not, mining or farming, existing business imperatives) and state/territory priorities. Importantly, some packages were the result of imperatives other than native title (e.g. industrial access to land). Accordingly, the examples should be seen not so much as templates but as illustrations of what can be achieved when parties negotiate creatively and in good faith.

State and territory governments who are the first respondents to all native title claims have a pivotal role in the resolution of claimant applications. Most of the options for alternative settlements are primarily or exclusively within the power of governments to provide. Minimal effort has been made to explore public–private solutions for resolving native title claims where a native title determination is improbable.

In the current legal context, and in light of the general trend towards mediation rather than litigation, there needs to be a more robust approach to alternative settlements within the range of possible outcomes. State and territory governments, which have the power to provide alternative forms of settlement, need to be more creative in relation to outcomes where proof of native title is more problematic (e.g. in the south-west and south-east of Australia). The reasons why parties (particularly governments) might negotiate alternative settlements include the prospect that such settlements will deliver a degree of social justice to dispossessed Indigenous groups and provide the means of giving native title claim groups (particularly those with registered claimant applications) an incentive to withdraw their claimant applications.

Although a claimant application seeks a determination of native title, the negotiations are a means of dealing with all issues, rather than focusing narrowly and exclusively on whether a determination of native title can be justified. In some cases, a comprehensive land settlement might be negotiated.

In his February 2008 speech, the Commonwealth Attorney-General referred to 'the benefits that can be achieved if all parties take a flexible creative approach and seek to resolve a range of issues within the context of native title negotiations'. He said he would like to see 'more outcomes like these being achieved where native title rights are a basis for building sustainable long-term outcomes for communities'.[70]

Such an approach by governments could extend beyond a claim-by-claim approach to settlement options and involve consideration of regional or state/territory schemes to involve Indigenous people, whether or not they can prove that they have native title to their traditional land and waters. That approach would be consistent with the statement in the Preamble to the NTA that:

> Governments should, where appropriate, facilitate negotiation on a regional basis between the parties concerned in relation to:
> (a) claims to land, or aspirations in relation to land, by Aboriginal peoples and Torres Strait Islanders; and
> (b) proposals for the use of such land for economic purposes.

As noted earlier, ministers responsible for native title have started to consider these issues, including how native title can meet broader Indigenous policy objectives. Most recently, the Commonwealth Attorney-General said that one of the Australian Government's objectives for the native title system is 'making native title an effective mechanism for providing economic development opportunities for Indigenous people'.[71] Native title is not to be 'seen as an end in itself'.[72] Rather, the native title system should deliver 'real outcomes in a timely and efficient way' and provide Indigenous people with 'an important avenue of economic development'.[73]

Threshold issues for governments to consider in deciding options for settlement and when to offer those options

Alternative settlements can be negotiated through agreements:
- as part of a consent determination of native title;
- in exchange for the withdrawal, where appropriate, of claimant applications; or
- as part of a wider social justice package involving Indigenous people where it is commonly recognised that the native title has been extinguished over much or all of those peoples' traditional countries.

Each state and territory government has different requirements before it will consider a settlement 'package'. Some governments have published guidelines on what they require in order to be satisfied that native title claim groups have native title. Others have not. Some governments have published policies in relation to settlement 'packages'.

The assumption underpinning alternative settlement approaches adopted by some states is that these settlements can be offered to native title claimants when they cannot meet the state's connection threshold for a consent determination of native title, or might pursue non-native title outcomes. Accordingly, the level of evidence required for an alternative settlement is less than that required for obtaining a consent determination that native title exists.

The precise nature of this threshold has not generally been spelt out by state governments in any explicit detail. Although guidelines exist in several states explaining the information the government requires before it will consent to a determination of native title, to date only Victoria has detailed its evidentiary requirements for an alternative settlement. An issue for state governments is whether they should develop clear and publicly transparent written guidelines outlining their evidentiary threshold requirements for alternative settlements. Furthermore, governments should carefully consider and decide the precise content of any threshold.

Approaches to deciding when governments will negotiate alternative settlements vary across states. For example, the policy of the New South Wales Government is to resolve native title applications through ILUAs, particularly in circumstances where credible evidence of native title cannot be established. South Australia has the South Australian Native Title Resolution strategy, whereby the settlement of claims is achieved through a combination of ILUAs and either a consent determination of native title or the withdrawal, where appropriate, of each native title claim (a connection threshold is applied by the South Australian Government only to those claims wishing to pursue a native title determination). The Government of Western Australia, by contrast, obliges claimants to produce a connection report as a prerequisite for entering into any mediation, meaning that considerable time and resources are often expended before alternative settlements are considered.

When alternative settlements are negotiated there can be further (and sometimes substantial) delays because of the time taken for the necessary steps to deliver an option (e.g. change the status of a parcel of land, or survey and create a title to a parcel of land). In some instances a government has to develop a policy to deal with an issue that arises in a particular case (e.g. how to involve native title claimants in the management of a national park).

Governments usually want some degree of certainty that an alternative settlement of one claimant application will not be affected by subsequent claimant applications by the same or another group. This may involve more than the withdrawal of the original claimant application and could be settled in the terms of an ILUA. Sometimes, governments have required a determination that native title does not exist, as part of the settlement package.

Adopting targets for settling claims

Given the pivotal role of state and territory governments in the resolution of claims, it may assist all participants in the process if governments set targets for settling claims. Although, bearing in mind the factors noted earlier, it is difficult to predict when claims will be resolved, some governments have provided estimates. For example, the South Australian Native Title Resolution Program 2007–2008 confirms the objective 'to resolve 75% of all native title claims by 2014'.[74] The 2006–07 annual report of the Queensland Department of Natural Resources and Water stated that in that period the government planned to conclude seven native title determinations and continue negotiations of ILUAs or land dealings (and that it actually progressed seven claims, obtained one consent determination and signed fifteen ILUAs).[75]

Before each financial year the NNTT estimates a range of outputs and at the end of the year reports on the extent to which these estimates were or were not met. It is not easy to set and meet realistic targets, but surely it is not unreasonable to ask key participants to set targets toward which parties and institutions can work?

Those of you who heard or read Prime Minister Rudd's speech in parliament on the apology to Australia's Indigenous people will recall that he described Australians as 'a very practical lot' for whom 'great symbolism' must be 'accompanied by an even greater substance'.[76] He spoke of a 'partnership for the future…to close the gap between Indigenous and non-Indigenous Australians on life expectancy, educational achievement and employment opportunities' and said that the partnership will set 'concrete targets for the future', and identified targets to be met within nominated periods.[77]

In words equally applicable to native title, he said that we need 'real measures of policy success or policy failure' and 'sufficient flexibility not to insist on a one-size-fits-all approach…but instead allowing flexible, tailored, local approaches to achieve commonly agreed national objectives'.[78] When speaking about those other complex issues, he suggested that, unless the Australian Parliament 'set[s] a destination for this nation, we have no clear point to guide our policy, our programs and our purpose; we have no centralised organising principle'.[79] Such leadership from governments on native title would greatly assist in refining regional approaches to resolving native title claims and the allocation of resources to reach those targets.

The roles of the Commonwealth

Most of the preceding discussion relates primarily to state and territory governments. The Australian Government has three broad roles in the native title system.
- It administers the NTA and can initiate amendments to it.
- It provides funding to many of the major participants in the native title system (and potentially to the states and territories in relation to various liabilities, costs and expenses).[80]
- It is a party to some proceedings and is entitled to intervene in a proceeding in a matter arising under the NTA.[81]

There is no clear articulation of the new government's role as a party, but in his February 2008 speech the Commonwealth Attorney-General was critical of those who would 'bury native title in unnecessary complexity',[82] and he urged a change of attitude on the part of all participants, including the 'purists intoxicated by their expertise in a technical and complicated system'.[83] In his view, 'we need to move away from technical legal arguments about the existence of native title'.[84]

In urging all parties to 'take a step back, and adopt a more flexible and willing approach to negotiations'[85] and to adopt an 'interest-based approach to claims',[86] he suggested that after fifteen years of experience of the native title system, parties should be able to accept that 'an outcome does not have to be legally perfect to work in a practical sense'.[87] Speaking specifically about what the Australian Government might do, he said that he is keen to work with Minister Macklin to explore how land ownership and management opportunities through the Indigenous Land Corporation can be more readily accessed as part of a negotiated outcome where Indigenous people are unable to meet the required standard for a determination of native title.[88] Further, he said, it may be possible to negotiate where government can assist in developing comprehensive business plans.[89] He would also be consulting with his ministerial colleagues about principles the government will follow when undertaking future act negotiations.[90]

He also set out the Australian Government's objectives for the native title system as:
- wherever possible, resolving land use and ownership issues through negotiation, because negotiation produces broader and better outcomes than litigation;
- facilitating negotiation of more, and better, Indigenous Land Use Agreements and ensuring that traditional owners and their representatives are adequately resourced for this;
- making native title an effective mechanism for providing economic development opportunities for Indigenous people;
- avoiding unduly narrow and legalistic approaches to native title processes that can result in further dispossession of Aboriginal and Torres Strait Islander people.[91]

In recent years, the Commonwealth has taken a robust (though not always successful) role as intervener in litigation to argue points of law,[92] and it remains to be seen whether (and, if so, to what extent and on what issues) the Commonwealth as a party will take a more flexible, creative and innovative approach to the resolution of claims.

Resources issues for government

State and territory governments are the first respondents to native title proceedings. Some have expert staff, and engage consultants for native title work. However, some governments lack the resources or tenure recording systems to undertake detailed tenure research or assess connection reports in a timely manner, or to substantively mediate numerous claims concurrently.

The Commonwealth funds many of the participants in the native title system including NTRBs, some respondent parties, the Federal Court and the NNTT. For the system to work, the Commonwealth must ensure that sufficient resources are provided to the system and that those resources are distributed appropriately between the participants.

MEETING THE CHALLENGES: OTHER RESPONDENTS

As with claimants and governments, other respondent parties need to answer basic questions. For example:

- why they are and should remain as parties to particular proceedings?
- what role they will play in the proceedings?
- on what basis they will withdraw from the proceedings or settle the claim (e.g. by agreeing to a consent determination of native title).

It may be that a party's legal interests are so protected that they would not be adversely affected by a determination of native title. In those circumstances, the party may need only participate in order to ensure that their interest is accurately recorded in a determination of native title[93] and that agreement is reached (e.g. by way of an ILUA) about the exercise of the various rights and interests over relevant areas of land or waters.

A related issue is whether most respondent parties need to be satisfied about connection. One behavioural change that could lead to a faster rate of resolution of claims would be for respondent parties to limit their involvement in the claims resolution process to their interests, and not assert an independent role in the connection process, or at least limit the matters about which they need to be satisfied (e.g. to whether they are dealing with the right people in making land use and access arrangements).

Reducing the number of respondent parties to a proceeding

As a general rule, before there can be a consent determination of native title, every party to the proceeding must agree to it.[94] In some cases (particularly where there are scores, if not hundreds, of respondent parties) it can be difficult to obtain the consent of all parties and the requisite documentation of that agreement. For logistical as well as substantive reasons, it is important to ensure that only those people with a relevant interest become, or remain, parties to the proceeding. Given the many years that often elapse between the notification of a claimant application and its resolution, it is possible that some parties will not retain relevant interests in the claimed area. This may be, for example, because they have sold their interest or because the claim area is reduced in such a way that their interests are no longer affected. If people who should not be parties retain that status, a consent determination might be delayed or even denied.

The NTA was amended in 2007 to limit the range of persons who may become a party to claimant application proceedings and empower the NNTT to refer to the Federal Court the question of whether a party should cease to be a party to a proceeding. Although much of the previous scheme concerning parties remains, section 84 of the NTA has been 'tightened up' to make it more difficult to 'automatically' become a party to proceedings. Some persons who previously could become parties by giving notice to the Court will now only become parties if they have an 'interest, in relation to land or waters' that may be affected by a determination in the proceedings.[95] Further, the Court may now join a person as a party if not only the person's interests may be affected by a determination but also that 'it is in the interests of justice' that the person be so joined.[96]

If the NNTT member presiding at a mediation conference considers that a party does not have a relevant interest in the proceeding, the member may refer to the Federal Court the question of whether a party should cease to be a party to the proceeding.[97]

The NNTT might, for example, refer such a question to the Federal Court where a claimant application has been amended to remove certain areas or categories of land from the claim area and, as a consequence, some parties' interests are no longer affected by the claim. Analysis of current tenures in the claim area or the tenure history of the area might also disclose that some parties do not have interests that could be affected. Such analysis can be, and often is, conducted by the NNTT's geospatial specialist staff under the Act.[98] It should be noted that this is not the only process available for the removal of a party. The Federal Court may at any time order that a person, other than the applicant, cease to be a party to the proceedings.[99] The Court has issued self-executing orders in relation to parties who appear not to have relevant interests in the area claimed and who do not provide (by a specified date) a statement as to why they should remain a party.[100] One way of achieving that result is for the NNTT to include in a mediation progress report to the Court a statement about the apparent lack of relevant interest by one or more of the parties.

Resources issues for respondents

New *Guidelines on the Provision of Financial Assistance by the Attorney-General under s 183 of the Native Title Act 1993* came into force on 1 January 2007 and replaced guidelines that had operated since 30 November 1998. The aim of revising the guidelines was to encourage the resolution of native title matters through agreement making, rather than litigation, wherever possible. The guidelines relate to financial assistance that the Attorney-General may make to respondent parties in relation to native title inquiries, mediations or proceedings, or persons entering into an ILUA or an agreement about rights under subsection 44B(1) of the Act (rights of access for traditional activities), who are not members of the native title claim group concerned.[101]

The guidelines have been revised and strengthened to incorporate a number of features designed to encourage agreement making in preference to litigation, including:
- authorising assistance in stages of six to twelve months, or shorter timeframes, to facilitate improved and more transparent planning by funded parties focused on achieving outcomes;[102]
- varying or terminating assistance if a grant recipient fails to act reasonably by not endeavouring to reach a reasonable agreement with a claimant;[103]
- limiting the circumstances in which financial assistance for Court proceedings is provided;[104]
- strengthening reporting requirements imposed on grant recipients to include strategies to resolve issues in dispute;[105] and
- assisting in the drafting and development of an agreement or ILUA through access to agreements and ILUAs funded under the scheme, in which the Commonwealth retains a licence to use, adapt and exploit.[106]

The guidelines require reports to the Attorney-General's Department, generally at the end of each grant period.[107]

MEETING THE CHALLENGES: ALL PARTIES

At some point (and possibly a number of points) in the native title claim process, each party needs to consider what they will accept as an outcome rather than have the matter heard and decided by the Federal Court. In other words, what outcome would they rather fashion for themselves than submit to a Court-imposed outcome? There are two important components to this:
- what will each party put on the table as an offer to, or request of, the other party or parties?
- what each party will accept in order to settle.

Native title claim groups that want to explore alternative settlements (including or instead of a determination that native title exists) should be specific about what they want to achieve and how they want to achieve it. They should not wait to see what others might offer. For example, are the claimants seeking a role in the management of specific areas, title to other areas, assistance with capital works, or financial assistance for ongoing management of their interests or other specific outcomes?

Governments need to consider what they are willing to offer to native title claim groups to encourage settlement and what they will require in return; e.g. a lower standard of evidence from the claimants, the withdrawal of a claim, the surrender of native title (if any) or a determination that native title does not exist.

Whatever is being negotiated, there will be a time when each party needs to compromise. For many years, judges of the Federal Court have been pointing out the need for parties to compromise in relation to native title proceedings. Let me give you three examples of statements made by judges in quite different circumstances. In the course of delivering a consent determination that native title exists over part of the area covered by the *Wik* claim, Justice Drummond said that he accepted, 'at least for the moment, that an agreed resolution' of the balance of the Wik peoples' claim was preferable to 'a Court-imposed result' because such an outcome was 'more likely to provide a more useful framework than a court decision limited to specific issues'.[108] But he urged the parties to 'engage in the process of compromising, by giving up part of what each considers to be their full legal rights, that is essential if there is to be an agreed rather than a Court-imposed result'.[109] He cautioned:

> It is worthy of note that litigation rarely results in the complete vindication of the position of any one party. Much more commonly the Court, after having the opportunity to hear and consider all the evidence from all the parties, comes to the conclusion that there is at least some merit in the arguments put forward by each party. Few litigants win 100 per cent of their cases. I do not expect native title litigation to be any different in this respect.[110]

A Full Court of the Federal Court delivering judgment in the final stages of the Miriuwung Gajerrong litigation stated:

> It is generally true, in relation to any type of litigation, that the best outcome is one resolved between the parties, rather than one imposed by the court. This is particularly true of native title litigation.
>
> Orders resolving native title litigation are usually extremely complex. They usually deal in detail with the entitlements of people who will have an ongoing relationship with each other. Because of these factors, it is preferable that the affected people discuss, and attempt to reach agreement about, those entitlements…
>
> Agreements on resolution of a claim always require readiness to compromise. That is often difficult to achieve.[111]

Near the end of his final judgment in the *Rubibi* case, where he found that native title existed over land in the Broome district, Justice Merkel stated that parties to native title disputes should see the resolution of native title claims as 'a means to an end, rather than an end in itself'; 'Obtaining a final determination of native title, where that is achievable, can be a stepping stone to securing' a range of outcomes but it 'cannot, of itself, secure them'.[112] Those observations were intended to:

> [P]rompt parties to other native title disputes to increase their endeavours to reach compromises. Those endeavours will necessarily involve give and take on the part of all parties. Native title litigation, like other litigation, need not be conducted on an 'all or nothing' basis.[113]

He referred to the risk to Indigenous communities of failure in a native title claim, a risk that 'is far from hypothetical', and which 'can have devastating consequences for the claimant community'; but if claimant communities and state parties can achieve a mediated outcome, 'they can ensure that a broad spectrum of mutual benefits can follow the resolution of native title claims'.[114] He continued, '[I]f compromises are able to be achieved, the cause of reconciliation between Australia's past and present will be greatly advanced and the economic, social and educational benefits available to all Australians may be better able to be accessed by members of claimant communities'.[115]

Other judges have expressed the view that courts are unsuitable forums for native title issues to be resolved.[116] In any case, it is up to the parties to work out the on-the-ground practicalities of any determination that native title exists.[117]

Interest-based approach

The Attorney-General stated, 'By sitting down at the start and discussing what interests they have and what outcomes they are seeking, parties may be more readily able to identify opportunities for the timely and satisfactory resolution of the claim'.[118] He continued:

> Much can be achieved if parties are up front about what they really want and open-minded about finding creative solutions[119]…Through parties focussing on their interest in claims, and how these might be met in practice, it should be possible for parties to negotiate more timely and satisfactory outcomes.[120]

The Commonwealth Attorney-General's encouragement to parties to adopt an interest-based approach is entirely consistent with the NNTT's longstanding approach to native title mediation. From its inception, the NNTT has attempted to conduct interest-based mediation. The NNTT's internal guide to mediation, for example, states that the NNTT 'conducts multi-party, cross-cultural mediation in relation to areas of land or waters, and seeks to use a primarily interest-based model in a rights-based context'.[121]

Although the NNTT seeks to use a primarily interest-based model, native title mediation takes place in a rights-based context. Mediation occurs within a legal framework whereby parties may seek a judicial determination of their respective rights and interests at law. Because such native title outcomes are limited by what the law allows, negotiations are not at large so far as those outcomes are concerned.[122]

Five years before the Attorney-General put this view, a Full Federal Court stated, 'Not all agreements include a determination of native title, but nonetheless they may involve recognition of the historic association of the claimants with the relevant land'.[123] As discussed above, the outcomes could include statements of formal recognition of traditional ownership of lands in which native title had been or might have been extinguished, consultation or joint management agreements in relation to the use of traditional lands, and the grants of interests in those lands under state or territory land rights legislation or other legislation.[124] Therefore, while the mediation of native title applications is focused on matters specified in subsection 86A(1) of the NTA, the parties may negotiate about those and other matters. It is possible that if non-native title outcomes can be negotiated, at least some of applications will be withdrawn, or will be resolved by a determination that native title does not exist. That will dispose of the proceeding so far as the Federal Court is concerned, but will also lead to a mediated outcome that gives a measure of substantive satisfaction to the parties.

Agreements even where there is some legal uncertainty

For some years after the NTA commenced, there was uncertainty about important legal matters. After a series of test cases had run their course to the High Court, the law was much clearer, and more native title determinations were made, many of them by consent of the parties.

Legal certainty may be desirable, but it has not always been necessary for the settlement of claims. In 2001, before the *Ward* judgment of the

High Court, parties to a claim in Western Australia secured a consent determination from the Federal Court. In his reasons for decision, Justice Carr noted that parties to the application had incorporated into their agreement clauses which provided a mechanism to enable a variation to be made to the determination if the High Court were to overturn or set aside the Federal Court's decision in the *Ward* matter. His Honour had examined these clauses and was satisfied that they were an entirely appropriate way of reserving the rights of the parties pending the High Court's decision.[125] In similar circumstances in relation to another Western Australian claim, Justice French said that he was satisfied that it is appropriate that there should be scope for a variation of the form of the determination in light of the High Court's judgment, which was yet to be delivered.[126]

In February 2008 the Commonwealth Attorney-General urged parties to continue to take such an approach. He said:

> As in all areas of the law, there are, and will continue to be, outstanding questions in native title. However, fifteen years of experience with the native title system should enable parties to accept that an outcome does not have to be legally perfect to work in a practical sense. In particular, it is clear that in this area, there will sometimes not be clear cut legal answers or the court's decision will not be entirely predictable. So unless participants want to risk an all or nothing legal throw of the dice, there must be a will on both sides to devise workable solutions.[127]

Conduct of parties and their representatives in mediation

The native title scheme expressly favours resolution of claims by agreement. But the NTA and the structures created by it cannot compel agreement.[128] It is the parties who will determine whether, what and when any outcomes are agreed in relation to native title claimant applications. What they are willing to put on the table in their negotiations, as well as how they behave towards each other, are critical to the outcomes.

One of the reforms that has attracted considerable interest and comment is the requirement to act in 'good faith' in mediation. The scheme, in essence, requires that each party and each party's representative 'must act in good faith' in relation to the conduct of the mediation. If the presiding member of the NNTT considers that a party or a party's representative 'did not act or is not acting in good faith' in relation to the conduct of a mediation, the presiding member may report that failure to the person or body specified, or to the Federal Court. The protection of 'without prejudice privilege' provided in relation to words spoken or acts done at a mediation conference does not apply to those reports to the Federal Court or a legal professional body. If the presiding member considers that a Commonwealth, state or territory government party or that party's representative 'did not act or is not acting in good faith' in relation to the conduct of a mediation, the annual report of the NNTT may include details of that failure.

The obligation to act in good faith should provide an incentive to improve behaviour and to focus the attention of the parties and their representatives on the seriousness of the mediation process and the need to approach mediation in a professional manner and with a spirit of goodwill.

Parties might be assisted to meet the obligation by the *Mediation Guidelines: Guidelines for the behaviour of parties and their representatives in mediation in the National Native Title Tribunal* (Mediation Guidelines) issued in 2007. The preface to the Mediation Guidelines states that they 'set out principles of best practice in standards of behaviour which parties to mediation' in the NNTT and their representatives 'should seek to uphold'.[129] The *NNTT Procedural Direction No. 2 of 2007* sets out procedures to be followed by NNTT members when considering whether parties or their representatives have satisfied the good faith obligations.[130]

Partial determinations

In some cases it might be in the interests of parties to negotiate a consent determination over part of a claimed area. The NTA has been amended to make it easier to obtain such a consent determination. Subject to it being within power and appropriate, the Court may make a determination of native title in relation to the area in the terms sought by the persons specified in section 87A. This means that a consent determination may be made without the consent of a party to the proceedings where that party does not hold a specified type of interest in the determination area and who is not otherwise listed. That includes parties with lesser interests in the determination area and those parties who have an interest in the area covered by the application but outside the determination area.[131]

When a consent determination is made under this scheme, the application will be deemed to be amended to reduce the area covered by the application to what is left.[132] The registration test will not be applied to these 'amended applications', and if the application is registered, the entry in the Register of Native Title Claims must be amended to reflect the change in the area covered by the application.[133]

MEETING THE CHALLENGES: THE NATIONAL NATIVE TITLE TRIBUNAL
The 2007 amendments to the Native Title Act — an overview

The NTA was substantially amended in 2007. The reforms were designed to effect improvements in the system, in particular emphasising the primacy of mediation as a means of resolving claims and improving the behaviour of system participants. The amendments also gave the NNTT increased powers and responsibilities.

Among the many changes made, those which affect the resolution of claims include amendments that:
- ensure that only the NNTT mediates native title claims that the Federal Court has referred to it for mediation;
- empower the NNTT to conduct a review 'on the papers' of whether a native title claim group holds native title rights and interests in relation to the application area;
- empower the NNTT to hold an inquiry in relation to a matter relevant to a determination of native title;
- limit the range of persons who may become a party to claimant application proceedings;
- empower the NNTT to refer to the Federal Court the question of whether a party should cease to be a party to a proceeding;
- make it easier to have consent determinations over part of an area covered by a claimant application;
- empower the NNTT to direct a party to attend a mediation conference or to produce a document for the purposes of a mediation conference;
- focus on the regional management of claimant applications by empowering the NNTT to prepare and provide the Federal Court with reports on the progress of all mediations conducted by the NNTT in relation to regions (regional mediation progress reports) and work plans setting out the priority given to each mediation conducted by the NNTT in an area (regional work plans);
- give the NNTT the right to appear before the Federal Court at a hearing in relation to a matter that is with the NNTT for mediation;
- ensure that claimant applications which previously failed the registration test are re-tested and, if they fail the merit conditions, may be dismissed;

13. Achieving real outcomes from native title claims

- encourage the claimant applications made in response to future act notices to be progressed and, if not, provide for them to be dismissed once the future act has occurred.

The legislative changes reorient aspects of the relationship between the Court and the NNTT, and confer additional and expanded functions on the NNTT.

The Court and the NNTT have worked together and I have issued procedural directions aimed at achieving greater consistency of practice within the NNTT. It is still too early to indicate whether these legislative and related reforms will achieve the improvements in efficiency and effectiveness that were envisaged. Nonetheless, early indications are that in some areas parties are engaging in a more productive fashion in mediation with the consequent possibility of claims being better progressed.

Significant as they are, the powers and functions alone will not expedite the resolution of native title claims by consent. Any improvement to the processes and practices of the NNTT and the Court will have a negligible effect on the resolution of native title claims by agreement if the parties to the proceedings are unwilling or unable to participate productively or in a timely manner.

Regional management of claims

Experience has shown that the most effective and efficient way of managing hundreds of native title applications through the native title system is to adopt a state-wide or regional approach. Although each native title application is unique, there are many common factors affecting the potential resolution of each claim in a state or region. For example, each NTRB has numerous claims in its area, each state or territory is a respondent to every claim in its jurisdiction, many claims overlap one or more other claims, and some parties or their representatives are involved in numerous claims. The Federal Court and the NNTT recognise that limits on financial and human resources and a range of other factors affect the progress of individual claims or clusters of claims.

In an effort to align the resources of key parties with regional priorities, the NNTT secured the agreement of the Department of Families, Community Services and Indigenous Affairs (now the Department of Families, Housing, Community Services and Indigenous Affairs (FaHCSIA)) and the Attorney-General's Department to their involvement in critical regional planning meetings. The rationale for this initiative is that as the funding agencies, respectively, for NTRBs and certain respondent parties, these departments should be aware of significant developments at the regional level and assist relevant parties to plan activities in a more informed fashion. That, in turn, will inform the regional reports and work plans provided to the Court by the NNTT.

Since April 2007 the NNTT has also adopted a new National Case Flow Management Scheme. The NNTT has reviewed every current application and has allocated applications to one of three lists:
- a *substantive list* of matters that are likely to be resolved within the next two years;
- a *regional list* (managed by a regional member) of matters that require considerable preparation with regard to key features such as connection, tenure and resolution of overlaps before they can move to the substantive list; and
- the *Registrar's list* of matters that require registration testing or notification or have not been referred to the NNTT for mediation.

The NNTT is also taking a more directive approach to convening and conducting mediation conferences, and reporting about them to the Court. That approach is supported by amendments to the NTA that, for example, give the presiding NNTT member power to direct a party to attend a mediation conference[134] or produce documents.[135] It remains to be seen in what circumstances and how often such powers are used. They could be used to give effect to regional work plans that have been endorsed by the Federal Court at a regional directions hearing or case management conference. The general timetable having been set by the Court, the NNTT could ensure that the timetable is met by directing that specified parties attend mediation conferences or produce specified documents. That would build on a coordinated approach between the Court, the NNTT and the parties.[136]

Dealing with critical tasks in relation to individual claimant applications

The NNTT's analysis of the current applications indicates that the critical tasks that need to be carried out to ensure the steady progress of applications to resolution are:
- timetabling and managing the preparation and assessment of connection material;
- timetabling and working on tenure analysis (to identify areas where native title has been extinguished);

- resolving overlapping claims;
- reducing the number of parties and clarifying their interests in relation to an application.

Already NNTT members are responsible for programming and supervising the completion of the critical tasks, either by the parties themselves or by the parties with the assistance of the NNTT. The progress of activities in relation to these tasks will increasingly become the subject of regular regional reports to the Federal Court.

Among the procedural directions (referred to below) is Procedural Direction No. 9 of 2007, 'Specific actions to be taken by the Registrar, members and employees of the National Native Title Tribunal in relation to native title applications'. It sets out the procedure to be followed by members and employees of the NNTT:

- when developing programs and taking certain strategic actions in relation to claimant applications; and
- when monitoring and reporting on significant delays in achieving milestones in relation to the mediation by the NNTT of claimant applications.

The objective of Procedural Direction No. 9 and other initiatives taken by the NNTT in relation to its role in the claims resolution process is to narrow the issues between the parties and reduce the numbers of parties so that participants can focus on the main issues before them and work towards appropriate substantive outcomes with the optimum use of resources. Those resources could include, on occasion, the resources of the NNTT, for example in the preparation of research reports and geospatial products.

Assessing connection material — inquiry and review functions

The 2007 amendments to the Act enhanced the NNTT's existing role in the mediation of connection by enabling the NNTT, in certain circumstances, to carry out a review of whether there are native title rights and interests, or hold an inquiry in relation to a matter or issue relevant to a determination of native title. The President of the NNTT is empowered, on the recommendation of the NNTT member presiding over the mediation, to refer for review by another member (or presidential consultant) the issue of whether the native title claim group holds native title rights and interests in relation to land or waters within the application area.[137] The presiding member can only make the recommendation if he or she considers that the review would assist the parties to reach agreement in relation to matters listed in subsection 86A(1) of the NTA.[138]

Parties who give documents or information to the review can participate in the process.[139] According to the Explanatory Memorandum, '[i]t will be essential to have at least one participating party to a review, although it may only be necessary to have one such participating party'.[140] Participation is purely voluntary. Reviews are meant to be done 'on the papers'. There is no facility for holding hearings, and if these are required, an inquiry would be preferable.

Unless the parties agree otherwise, any word spoken or act done in the course of the review will be subject to without prejudice privilege.[141] The member conducting the review can prohibit disclosure of information given, statements made, or the contents of any document produced in the course of the review.[142] Mediation may continue during the conduct of the review[143] and the member undertaking the review may give progress reports to the presiding member if the reviewer considers that providing the report would assist in progressing the mediation.[144] The written report of the review *must* be made available to the presiding member and the participating parties.[145] A copy *may* also be given to the Court and the other parties to the proceeding[146] (that is, such provision is discretionary).[147]

The President of the NNTT (on his or her initiative, at the request of a party, or at the request of the Chief Justice of the Federal Court) may also direct the holding of an inquiry by the NNTT in relation to a matter or an issue relevant to the determination of native title under section 225 of the NTA. The direction can only be made if the applicant agrees to participate and the President is satisfied that the resolution of the matter or issue concerned would be likely to lead to:

- an agreement on findings of fact;
- the resolution or amendment of the application; or
- something else being done in relation to the application.[148]

Before the President directs the holding of an inquiry, at least seven days' written notice that the NNTT intends to hold an inquiry must be given to the applicant, the Chief Justice of the Federal Court, the Commonwealth and relevant state or territory ministers, the NTRB (or a person or body performing the functions of an NTRB) and any other person who is a party to the proceeding.[149]

Participation in an inquiry is voluntary. Unlike other inquiries conducted by the NNTT, there is no capacity to subpoena witnesses or documents.[150] The parties to an inquiry are the applicant, the relevant state or territory minister and the Commonwealth minister (if they advise in writing that they wish to be a party) and, with leave of the NNTT, 'any other person' who notifies the NNTT in writing that they wish to become a party.[151]

As these inquiries are intended to assist in the mediation of applications, hearings are generally to be held in private. The NNTT may direct instead that they be held in public. The customary and cultural concerns of Aboriginal peoples and Torres Strait Islanders must be given due regard in making such a direction.[152]

Mediation may continue while an inquiry is underway if the presiding member considers that it is appropriate.[153] An inquiry must cease if the relevant part of the proceeding ceases to be in mediation with the NNTT.[154] It may also cease if the President so directs on the basis that a party to the inquiry no longer wishes to participate.[155] The latter is discretionary and whether or not a direction is made will depend upon a variety of factors including the importance of the party to the inquiry and the stage the inquiry has reached.

The report of an inquiry must state findings of fact and may make recommendations, but these are not binding on the parties to the inquiry.[156] A copy of the report must be given to the Federal Court and each of the parties to the inquiry.[157] The Court must consider whether to receive into evidence the transcript of evidence of an inquiry and may adopt any recommendation, findings of fact, decision or determination of the NNTT in relation to the inquiry.[158]

Providing tenure analysis

Although some claimant applications specify the parcels of land claimed, many claimant applications cover all the land within a described boundary other than those categories of land where native title has been extinguished. Such descriptions are sufficient to satisfy the registration requirements of the NTA,[159] but it will not always be apparent which areas are claimed. Indeed, it is sometimes the case that neither the claimants and their representatives nor respondent parties know precisely which areas are the subjects of negotiation. On occasion it becomes clear during the mediation process that, having regard to current tenures and previous dealings in relation to the land, native title might only survive over small areas. Such a revelation can change the focus, tone and potential outcomes of the mediation.

To assist parties to gain a clear appreciation of the maximum possible extent of native title within a claim area, Procedural Direction No. 9 of

2007 directs NNTT members and the Native Title Registrar to ensure that, in respect of specified categories of claimant applications:
- tenure mapping (showing the *current* tenure or tenures in relation to land in a claim area) is prepared and is made available to the parties;[160]
- a 'preliminary tenure analysis' is prepared in relation to each claim area; that is, an analysis involving an ascertainment of the *current* tenure of a claim area to ascertain whether native title rights and interests may have been extinguished in whole or in part, or are not affected, in relation to land and waters within the outer boundary of the claim area.[161]

These steps are to be taken for strategic, as well as claim management, purposes. For example, the early preparation of a map of current tenures across a claim area and a preliminary tenure analysis should assist parties to identify the areas where native title has been extinguished (in whole or in part)[162] and over which areas native title may be recognisable (in whole or in part). This process will not be definitive, particularly as tenure histories may disclose previous dealings that had the effect of extinguishing native title rights and interests, but they will give a snapshot of the potential scope of any determination in relation to the claim area. In some parts of the country, it may be immediately apparent that very small areas of land may be susceptible to a determination of native title. Such a picture may encourage parties to look to a range of options for a negotiated outcome.

The preparation of maps and a preliminary tenure analysis may also assist in:
- resolving overlapping claims, particularly where there is little or any land in the overlap area where native title might survive; or
- identifying that some parties have interests that would not be affected by a determination of native title and providing the basis for those parties to be encouraged to withdraw from the proceedings early on.

Resolving disputed overlapping claims

As noted earlier in this paper, many claimant applications overlap other applications (in part or in whole) and many of the overlaps illustrate disagreement between neighbouring Indigenous groups about the extent of their traditional country. Moreover, some parties will not wish to be actively involved in mediation until any overlapping and disputed claimant applications are resolved.

NNTT Procedural Direction No. 9 of 2007 provides that where a claimant application on the regional list or the substantive list is overlapped by the whole or a part of the claim area of another claimant application, the relevant NNTT member must develop with the relevant parties a program for attempting to resolve the overlap.[163] Such a program could be prepared in light of, or include, a range of interdisciplinary products and procedures, many of which the NNTT can provide, including tenure analysis, research or outcomes from related reviews and inquiries.[164]

Reducing the number of parties and clarifying parties' interests

NNTT Procedural Direction No. 9 of 2007 requires the relevant NNTT member to consider whether any party to the proceeding lacks a relevant interest in relation to the land or waters in the claim area. If the member considers that a party does not have a relevant interest in the proceeding, the member should invite the party to withdraw as a party to the proceedings, and if the party does not withdraw, the member may consider referring the matter to the Court or reporting the matter to the Court.[165]

Providing factual reporting, analysis and options to the Court

In recent years the Court has come to expect the NNTT to provide more detailed reporting about the progress of mediation, franker analysis of the prospects of mediated outcomes and the impediments to such outcomes, and options to be considered by the Court (including draft orders to be made by the Court).

The 2007 amendments to the NTA have expanded the nature and means of communicating with the Court. The NNTT needs to ensure that such communications are accurate and considered, and that it is not merely conveying to the Court what some parties want it to say, particularly if the NNTT is not satisfied that those communications would be accurate or the NNTT is not convinced that a party will or could do what they say within a nominated period.

The NTA now provides that, at the request of the Court[166] or on the initiative of the NNTT,[167] the NNTT may provide to the Court a report on the progress of all mediations conducted by the NNTT in relation to areas within a state, territory or other region in Australia (a 'regional mediation progress report') and/or a regional work plan.[168] In each case the purpose of the document is to assist the Court in progressing proceedings in a state, territory or other region.

The preparation and provision of such documents builds on practice developed in some regions in Australia before the 2007 amendments to the NTA. The practice has the potential to substantially improve how claimant applications are prioritised and progressed in regions. It confirms the role of the NNTT in working with the NTRB and parties in a region to prioritise work on claims and optimise the allocation of scarce resources. Such planning takes the focus off the progress of individual claims and onto the relationship between claims in a region, allowing longer-term prioritisation and planning to be more transparent for all the participants.

Although some aspects of the practice have yet to be settled in some regions, there seems to be a general acceptance by the Court and parties of the utility of such documents. However, because they provide a clear picture of what is happening (or not happening) in a region, some concerns have been expressed about the extent to which the parties and others can or ought to have access to such comprehensive documents.

Resources issues

On occasion, critics have complained that the NNTT is over-resourced relative to some other participants in the native title system, particularly NTRBs. It is a matter of public record that, in recent years by prudent management of its resources, the NNTT has not spent all of its annual appropriation.[169] The focus for other participants should not be on whether the NNTT is relatively well resourced but on how those resources can be used to ensure that progress is made across the system. Resources of other participants should not be wasted by unnecessary duplication of activities that appropriately can be undertaken by the NNTT. As noted above, a range of parties can be assisted by research reports, geospatial products (such as maps, aerial photography, three-dimensional imaging), preliminary tenure analysis and enhanced research tools that combine data from literature searches and geospatial products prepared and paid for by the NNTT.

MEETING THE CHALLENGES: FEDERAL COURT

Viewing native title claims in a broader context than conventional litigation

Native title determination applications are particular forms of proceeding that are commenced in the Federal Court that seek specific relief, in the form of a determination of native title. For the Federal Court, each application is a proceeding that needs to be managed towards resolution by determination or dismissal, strike-out or discontinuance. The Court brings to the case management of each application its experience and practices in relation to other litigation, adapted to take into account some of the unusual features of native title litigation.

For the reasons outlined earlier in this paper, many parties (not just native title claim groups) see the proceedings as an opportunity to negotiate outcomes that may, but need not, include a determination of native title. The NTA clearly contemplates that possibility, and provides for the Court to adjourn proceedings to allow for negotiations that might result in an application being withdrawn or amended, the parties to a proceeding being varied or some other thing being done in relation to the application, and an agreement may involve matters other than native title.[170]

That specific provision aside, it is often the case that the progress of claims is delayed because the resources of the claim group and their representatives are directed to what (from their perspective at least) are more tangible, immediate and beneficial outcomes than a bare determination of native title (e.g. the negotiation of ILUAs or various future act agreements). For registered claim groups, the procedural rights which they have while their claim remains registered are as extensive as those they might secure from a determination that native title exists. Indeed, it is possible that, even if their claim ultimately results in a determination that native title exists, the native title rights and interests recognised will be fewer and narrower in scope than those on the Register of Native Title Claims. Hence their right to negotiate as native title holders will (in a legal sense, at least) be reduced compared with the rights they have with a registered claim.[171] The incentive to pursue a determination as a matter of priority is diminished accordingly.

On one view, such other negotiations cannot proceed with contractual certainty until there is a determination of native title in relation to the relevant area of land. Only when the Court has made an order *in rem* declaring who has native title and what the native title rights and interests are can another party negotiate with confidence an ILUA or future act agreement. In an ideal world, all native title claims would be resolved quickly, and the 'right people/right country' issues would be determined. Disputed overlaps would be no more, and miners, governments, infrastructure providers and others could negotiate with confidence that they were dealing with the proper people. Company boards and financiers could breathe more easily. But that is not the present situation for much of Australia, and such outcomes are unlikely for some years. Yet it is clear that major private and public corporations are willing to negotiate large deals on the basis that a registered claim or (better still) a registered ILUA gives them sufficient legal security to proceed with their enterprises long before, and independently of, any determination of native title. The disjunction between how some judges view native title claims and how at least some parties (not just the claim group) view them may expand rather than contract in the years ahead.

Recent statements by Australian Government ministers illustrate the point. Three themes from the 29 February 2008 speech of the Commonwealth Attorney-General seem relevant.

- First, he said that native title is 'highly technical' but should not be buried in 'unnecessary complexity', and 'we need to move away from technical legal arguments about the existence of native title'. Indeed, one of the Australian Government's four objectives for the native title system is 'avoiding unduly narrow and legalistic approaches to native title processes that can result in the further dispossession of Aboriginal and Torres Strait Islander people'.[172]
- Second, he said that we must no longer expect our courts to resolve issues that should be dealt with by negotiation rather than litigation.[173]
- Third, he said that another of the Australian Government's objectives for the native title system is, 'where-ever possible, resolving land use and ownership issues through negotiation, because negotiation produces broader and better outcomes than litigation'.[174]

Minister Macklin described the processes in place to resolve outstanding native title claims as 'overly complex and exceedingly slow'; in her view the legal and anthropological processes 'defy comprehension'.[175]

How the policy objectives that are explicit or implicit in those statements will be reached in practice remains to be seen, though examples of possible processes may be found in the state resolution process in South Australia and the alternative negotiating scheme proposed in Victoria.

For the purpose of this part of the paper, the issue to be considered is whether such approaches to resolving native title claims will affect case management practices of the Court or whether case management by the Court will affect the degree of flexibility (and amount of time) available to parties to negotiate settlement packages.

Whether or not individual judges think of claimant applications in this broader context and administer their lists accordingly, parties need to recognise that the Court is case managing native title proceedings that have been filed in Court. Consequently, whatever motivated the commencement, amendment or continuation of the claimant application, and whatever negotiations are taking place other than in relation to a possible determination of native title, parties must adapt their behaviour so that the proceedings remain in mediation and are not dismissed or listed for hearing before the Court.

13. Achieving real outcomes from native title claims

Assuming that the applications are not voluntarily withdrawn (e.g. because native title claim groups, particularly those with registered claims, want to retain some leverage with other parties), the challenge for them will be to demonstrate to the Court that real progress is being made toward a negotiated outcome of the claim. Where appropriate, they may apply for an adjournment of the proceedings under subsection 86F(3) of the Act to allow time for the negotiations.

Parties should not assume that alternative or even related agreement making will be accepted by the Court as legitimate reason for delaying the resolution of the claim. One judge has recently referred to a 'problem with the Act' which seems to encourage delay and encourage ILUAs, some of which were posing quite serious problems, e.g. by encouraging people not to do anything about their substantive claims.[176]

The challenge for judges of the Court will be to manage claims in their lists in a way that optimises the prospects of settlement while preserving the proper role of the Court in case management.

Dealing with delay

Judges have long bemoaned the delay in resolving native title claims and the length of time many claims have been in the Court's list, apparently with no prospect of immediate resolution or even progress.

These expressions of concern are not new, nor are they confined to judges of the Federal Court. Their significance is what consequences flow from them in terms of actions which judges take or orders they will make where they consider that cases have been in the system too long and have not progressed satisfactorily in the eyes of the Court.

Justice Dowsett recently indicated that he found it quite unsatisfactory that so many applications in a region had been 'marking time' for the past six months simply because there were no more funds available for them. Applications filed in 2001 or earlier should be at least at a stage where they would be proceeding to a hearing in the event that final negotiations might be unsuccessful. The Court should not allow native title litigation to 'go to sleep', and he was considering trying again to set trial dates.[177]

In another regional directions hearing, his Honour said that, in the absence of pleadings, he would consider ordering applicants to deliver statements of claim and setting orders for trial as a means of putting some real pressure on parties to narrow the issues and be sensible about their approach to negotiations.[178]

There are longstanding provisions in the NTA that enable the Court to order, at any time in a proceeding, that mediation by the NNTT is to cease in relation to the whole or a part of a proceeding if certain conditions are satisfied,[179] or even strike out a claimant application.[180] These provisions are rarely used, and parties (including state or territory governments) have been reluctant to invoke them. It may be that judges will increasingly act on their own motion to attempt to force matters to finality.

Taking a regional approach to case management

As noted earlier, experience has shown that the most effective and efficient way of managing hundreds of native title applications through the native title system is to adopt a state-wide or regional approach. The regional focus on claim management and resolution is highlighted in a Notice to Practitioners and Litigants (Native Title) on the 'Conduct of native title proceedings in the Federal Court of Australia' issued by the Chief Justice of the Federal Court in June 2007. The notice sets out 'revised arrangements for the conduct of native title cases, which will be managed regionally but within a national framework, by designated Native Title List Judges'.[181]

Native Title List Judges have been nominated for each state or territory to 'co-ordinate native title work and harmonise practice and procedure in accordance with this notice'.[182]

Much of the success of regional planning, and the progress of individual claimant applications, will depend on a coordinated approach between the Court and the NNTT. Such an approach should involve:
- clear communication between the Court and NNTT;
- the Court making orders consistent with those proposed by the NNTT to provide greater imperative to mediation;
- the reinforcement through the Court of timeframes for mediation.

To facilitate communication and coordination, the NNTT has been given the right to appear before the Court at a hearing in relation to a matter while that matter is with the NNTT for mediation for the purpose of assisting the Court in relation to a proceeding.[183]

Providing template determinations following test case decisions

As more determinations of native title are made over different categories of land, it should be possible to use such determinations as templates for agreements in relation to other claims where the facts and law are similar.

In the Northern Territory, the Federal Court has developed a strategy of grouping claims with similar key features and identifying a lead matter to be litigated.[184] Parties anticipate that, once the relevant legal principle is authoritatively determined, it should be possible to settle other claims in that group. Such groupings include sea claims, town claims and pastoral lease claims.

Judgment in the lead pastoral lease case (dealing with the claim to Newcastle Waters and linked claims) was delivered in 2007.[185] No appeal was lodged. The Federal Court is working with key participants to pursue a program for the negotiation and resolution of other claims which raise the same legal issues and have similar facts to the Newcastle Waters case.

Taking into account resources issues

Although the Federal Court recognises that limits on financial and human resources and a range of other factors affect the progress of individual claims or clusters of claims,[186] the Court is anxious to ensure that steps are being actively taken to advance the resolution of claims, whether in mediation or trial.[187] Lack of resources may not be sufficient for the Court to treat the claim as, in effect, in abeyance. Judges may request reports showing that some steps, however small, have been taken between each directions hearing in relation to each application in a state, territory or region.

CONCLUSION

After more than fifteen years since the High Court's historic *Mabo v Queensland [No. 2]* judgment, the native title system has provided a range of positive outcomes for many Indigenous Australians. The judgments delivered and the agreements reached have created a platform for future developments. But many have come at significant financial and emotional costs. The native title scheme expressly favours resolution of claimant applications (and other native title issues) by agreement. The process by which native title applications are resolved by agreement requires the active and positive involvement of applicants and governments. It also requires other respondent parties to have an incentive to consider and, where appropriate, negotiate options for settlement rather than proceed as if native title claims are necessarily headed for trial.

The NNTT and other participants face significant challenges in the current operating environment. There are finite resources available within the native title system. At the rate that native title applications have been resolved to date, it will take about thirty years to resolve outstanding applications, and many older Indigenous Australians will not see their claims finalised. In the meantime, clients and stakeholders can become frustrated at delays and the high cost of participating in the native title system. However, the negotiating positions of parties, especially government parties, remain pivotal to the timely achievement of quality outcomes. And even where a determination results, native title determinations often deliver few direct benefits to Indigenous Australians, and most determinations, in isolation, fall short of claimants' aspirations.

These challenges are not new. But despite them, the native title system is not in a state of gridlock. The traffic is not always moving as it should. Each party is in a driver's seat and should cooperate with others so that they are moving in the same direction, toward the timely resolution of claims. Not every party will end up at the same destination. Some claimants will end up with determinations that native title exists. Others will not. Some will settle for an alternative arrangement and may withdraw their claim.

All participants must work to find ways to reach outcomes in a timely and more efficient manner for the hundreds of current native title applications and those that are to come. The history of long and expensive litigation informs the need for a more rigorous agreement-making regime.

If we are to achieve this vision, all parties need to take an interest-based approach to the negotiations. Native title claim groups need to make informed and early decisions about the option they want to pursue and the basis on which they will settle (e.g. a determination of native title and/or some other form of agreed outcome). Negotiations need to be conducted with tenure and connection materials informing the process, rather than the provision of connection reports being a precondition to negotiations. Governments must actively and creatively explore options for settlement, including alternatives to native title outcomes. And other respondent parties need to decide whether, and to what extent, they need to be involved in the process, and then withdraw or participate only to the extent necessary to protect their interests (e.g. by negotiating ILUAs). The challenges are many. Effective responses to them require innovation, leadership and commitment to achieving results across the native title system. The NNTT stands ready, willing and able to help you achieve just and enduring outcomes.

14.
Native Title Conference, Wurundjeri Country, 2009

WHO'S DRIVING THE AGENDA?

TOM CALMA

I begin by paying my respects to the Wurundjeri people of the Kulin Nation, the Traditional Owners of the land where we meet, and I pay my respects to your elders, to your ancestors and to those who have come before us.

I would also like to acknowledge the many Traditional Owners gathered for this conference, and pay my respects to your elders, past and present. I admire your courage in fighting for the recognition of your rights as the Traditional Owners of this country.

It is a pleasure to be here today, Mabo Day, the anniversary of the historic decision of the High Court, which recognised the truth of this land's history, that it was cared for, occupied, and identified as lands belonging to its Indigenous peoples.[1]

This is my fifth and final native title conference as the Aboriginal and Torres Strait Islander Social Justice Commissioner. These conferences are a vital opportunity for us to get together and talk about something which is so critical to our existence as peoples — and which Eddie Mabo and his legacy stands for — our rights to country.

To AIATSIS, congratulations on ten years of successful conferences and, through them, ten years of important dialogue. To Native Title Services Victoria, thank you for having us back for this conference. It is an opportunity to return to where we started ten years ago, to reflect on just how far we have come and where we want to go next.

It is a pleasure to speak at this conference. Not only do I get the privilege of kicking off the proceedings, but I also get to speak to the most important people in the native title system. To you who have been through, or are going through, the complexity of a native title claim; and to you who dedicate your working, and in many instances your personal, lives to representing Aboriginal and Torres Strait Islander people who are trying to protect their rights through native title.

I have said it before at this same forum; I am both personally and professionally committed to native title. Personally, I am involved in a native title claim over the township of Batchelor in the Northern Territory and my Iwaidja countrymen were, and still are, involved in the *Yarmirr* sea rights claim.[2] I understand the processes, triumphs and frustrations of native title. I have seen the impact on my communities and my family, who work tirelessly for recognition of our traditional rights.

Professionally, native title is a central focus of my role as the Aboriginal and Torres Strait Islander Social Justice Commissioner. My position was created in 1993 to ensure ongoing monitoring of the human rights of Indigenous Australians. Some of you might not know that under section 209 of the *Native Title Act 1993* (Cth) (NTA) I must report every year to the Attorney-General on how native title impacts on our human rights.

I fulfil these roles through writing an annual Social Justice Report and Native Title Report, which are tabled in parliament each year.

Through these personal and professional experiences of native title, I have seen governments and ministers come and go, I've seen land claims settled and the native title system twist and turn. I've seen many parliamentary debates where ministers talk about our future and what is right for us. And I have witnessed Indigenous peoples and communities divide under a native title law which is defined by Western understandings of land ownership and Western priorities for land.

That has got to change. We cannot continue on this path if we are to achieve a sustainable and just system. And right now the landscape is changing in a way that opens up a few new opportunities for us to influence and drive the policy agenda. If we can take advantage of these opportunities, then native title, and the myriad of related policies, could be improved.

What new opportunities am I talking about? Over the past twelve months or so, a number of important changes have occurred. Among other things, at the international level we have seen this government signal its support for the United Nations Declaration on the Rights of Indigenous Peoples. At the domestic level, we are in the process of establishing a new national Indigenous representative body. And of particular interest to this audience, the government has signalled its openness to reconsidering some of the fundamentals of native title law.

So we are on a different path to when I first came to the native title conference as the Social Justice Commissioner in 2005. But who will decide what comes from these new developments?

My paper is called 'Who's driving the agenda?' I want to take this time, at the beginning of this gathering, and on this seventeen-year anniversary of the *Mabo* decision, to talk about who should be driving the agenda; an agenda which will impact each of our lives and the lives of our families and communities across Australia for generations to come.

When I ask that simple question — 'who is driving the Indigenous policy agenda?' — it should have a simple answer — Aboriginal and Torres Strait Islander people. As people who hold native title or who work for native title bodies who represent Aboriginal and Torres Strait Islander people, you are under extreme resource constraints. You have statutory obligations and timeframes to meet. Because of these constraints you need to think carefully about what opportunities and alternatives for change we want to create, or seize, as the landscape shifts.

But you, as a group of people, are in a very good position to participate and provide input into the new and emerging discussions on a range of policies. Why? For starters, you've either had your native title rights recognised or are working toward having the native title rights of Traditional Owners recognised.

Although the native title system is far from perfect, our rights to our country are at the core of our physical and mental wellbeing. And because of this, the protection of our native title and other land and water rights is essential to other aspects of our lives, like health. This crucial link is something that policy makers are just starting to grasp, but we know it intimately, and we must continually remind government, and all non-Indigenous Australians, of the connection between land and water and our wellbeing.

Rights to land and water are also a significant way Indigenous communities can leverage economic outcomes. For example, the biggest policy challenge the country now faces is climate change and carbon trading. These policies, and the impacts and opportunities they create, will depend on who has rights in the land, including native title.

Whether the impact of climate change on native title is positive — for example, whether native title is the basis for a potentially lucrative right to the carbon — or whether the impact is negative — for example, whether some native title is extinguished by changes to the climate — will be a matter of science and the government's policy response.

The government is considering if and how carbon rights will be granted to native title holders for the purpose of the reforestation scheme. It is a complicated policy on which the government will be consulting in a few months' time. And you, as native title holders, claimants and their representatives, will know better than anyone else how this policy will impact on native title holders.

You're also in a privileged position to drive the policy agenda because native title is one area where there are established bodies, which work across the whole of Australia, in one system.

Other policy areas, including land rights regimes, differ markedly across the states, many don't have an umbrella organisation like the National Native Title Council, and the vast majority doesn't have one unifying piece of legislation.

When you put all of these factors together, you are in a very good position to significantly influence the government's agenda and create positive change which will last for generations.

And your leadership and voice is essential in order to achieve this.

INTERNATIONAL — THE DECLARATION ON THE RIGHTS OF INDIGENOUS PEOPLE

In New York, at the United Nations Permanent Forum on Indigenous Issues, the Australian Government recognised that '[c]ritical to Australia meeting its human rights obligations and closing the gap is the degree to which Aboriginal and Torres Strait Islander peoples can set the agenda, and affect policy and service delivery'.[3]

Internationally, we have a relatively new, and admittedly largely untested, system for the protection of Indigenous peoples' rights that is quite comprehensive. The document that underpins it all, the Declaration on the Rights of Indigenous Peoples, recognises human rights that are inherent to us as the Indigenous peoples of this country. It is an aspirational document that sets out ambitions for a new partnership and relationship between Indigenous peoples and the nation states in which they live. For example, it affirms that Indigenous peoples make a unique contribution to the diversity and richness of civilisations and cultures, and promotes cultural diversity and understanding.

14. Who's driving the agenda?

Importantly for everyone here today, it includes a number of explicit references to rights related to our lands and waters. It refers to our rights to maintain traditional connections to land; for ownership of our lands; to redress and compensation for lands that have been taken; to conservation and protection of the environment; to protection of traditional knowledge; and access to processes for development on our land.

The Australian Government gave its formal support to the Declaration in April 2009. This commitment added significantly to the foundations for a new partnership between the federal government, Aboriginal and Torres Strait Islander peoples and the wider community.

INTERNATIONAL FORUMS

There is already a growing momentum around the Declaration at the international level. It will be the main basis for discussion at international human rights forums which are focused on Indigenous peoples, such as the United Nations Permanent Forum on Indigenous Issues, the Special Rapporteur on the situation of human rights and fundamental freedoms of Indigenous people, and the Expert Mechanism on the Rights of Indigenous Peoples.

The Permanent Forum on Indigenous Issues is a United Nations forum dedicated to considering the human rights of Indigenous peoples the world over. Formally, the Forum comprises sixteen independent experts, functioning in their personal capacity. One member is our very own Mick Dodson, who will serve until 2010.

Together, the members form a high-level advisory body that deals with Indigenous issues related to economic and social development, culture, environment, education, health and human rights. It will use the Declaration on the Rights of Indigenous Peoples as the framework through which it interprets its mandate, and accordingly the framework through which just about every United Nations agency and member countries will be held to account.

Another development at the international level was the appointment of Professor James Anaya as the new Special Rapporteur on the situation of human rights and fundamental freedoms of Indigenous people. He has a specific role in monitoring compliance with the Declaration on the Rights of Indigenous Peoples. His mandate includes considering individual communications, or complaints, as well as making country visits, including Australia.

After a country visit, the Special Rapporteur will provide a report to the Human Rights Council, the main human rights body of the United Nations, on his assessment of the main issues affecting Indigenous peoples' rights; and the member government will be expected to respond.

The new Expert Mechanism on the Rights of Indigenous Peoples commenced work in 2008. It will provide expertise on the rights of Indigenous peoples to the Human Rights Council. Because the Expert Mechanism has only been recently established, it is still developing its work program. But again, the Declaration on the Rights of Indigenous Peoples will be a focal point.

So, as you can see, there is a growing and extensive international system that will explicitly address the protection of Indigenous peoples' rights. These forums are supported by other human rights treaty bodies — which already interpret the binding legal obligations of governments under various treaties. For example, the United Nations Human Rights Council will continue to consider how rights, like the right to culture, apply specifically to Indigenous peoples. It will also continue to question and raise concerns about an individual country's policies and behaviour.

In April 2009 a United Nations committee gave its concluding observations on Australia's report under a treaty called the International Covenant on Civil and Political Rights. It raised concerns about the high cost, complexity and the application of the rules of evidence to native title claims. It recommended that the Australian Government 'continue its efforts to improve the operation of the Native Title system, in consultation with Aboriginal and Torres Strait Islander Peoples'.[4]

In May 2009 another United Nations Committee on Economic, Social and Cultural Rights said a similar thing, recommending that the Australian Government increase its efforts to improve native title and remove obstacles to the realisation of our rights to our land.[5]

THE APPLICATION OF INTERNATIONAL LAW IN AUSTRALIA

But what does this all mean for us here in Australia? The current government has made a renewed commitment to engaging with the United Nations. This commitment has opened up a powerful way for you to use the international human rights framework in your work, and in your fight to secure the rights of our communities. But for this to be effective, it is critical that we work to create a better understanding of our human rights.

Currently in our communities, people have a limited understanding of their rights. But this understanding goes to the capacity within communities to deal with serious violations of rights such as violence and abuse. Put in a positive way, better understanding and exercising of rights is something that can empower communities and contribute to better outcomes for those communities. So community education about human rights and the Declaration on the Rights of Indigenous Peoples is critical.

Even so, there are already good examples of people using the Declaration on the Rights of Indigenous Peoples to support better policies which will ultimately strengthen and empower communities. When the decision to reduce the resources for homelands in the Northern Territory was made, Jon Altman from the Australian National University referred to the Declaration, saying that the federal government has an obligation to support, rather than damn, the outstations. He referred to the Declaration, which provides that Indigenous peoples have a right to live on ancestral lands, even if it is more costly.[6]

When the government announced the compulsory acquisition of town camps in Alice Springs, the Indigenous Peoples' Organisations of Australia called on the government to comply with its international obligations to respect the rights of the Indigenous peoples of Australia by ensuring that the representatives of the Aboriginal people in the region of Alice Springs are able to make an informed decision about housing and services for the occupants.

And, finally, after negotiations were undertaken by the Kimberley Land Council for the location of the gas hub with Woodside and the Western Australian Government under the right to negotiate provisions in the *Native Title Act 1993* (Cth) (NTA), the land council held the other parties to the standard in the Declaration: that Indigenous peoples have the right to give free, prior and informed consent before their lands are used. This is a higher standard than required currently by the NTA.

As you can see, the impact of the Declaration will depend on the circumstances. But ultimately its value will lie in building a consistent pattern of usage over time. With constant and regular references to our rights, the government and other parties will not be able to avoid them.

NEW INTERNATIONAL HUMAN RIGHTS NETWORK

Although it has the potential to be a powerful tool, the international human rights framework hasn't always been easy to use or access. But

I hope this won't always be the case. In an attempt to improve this, my office, Oxfam and the Diplomacy Training Program at the University of New South Wales have partnered to create the Indigenous Human Rights Network of Australia (IHRNA).

Over the next three years we will establish a network of Indigenous people to advocate for Indigenous rights. So you will soon have a one-stop shop where you can keep up to date on these forums, and the opportunities that emerge through it. Many of you know that some of our brothers and sisters attend expert meetings and workshops around the world relating to extractive industries, biodiversity, water rights etcetera. Outcomes of these meetings will also be placed on the IHRNA website.

NEW NATIONAL INDIGENOUS REPRESENTATIVE BODY

As international forums are slowly becoming more influential in Australia, new home-grown opportunities are opening up, too. We all know that since ATSIC's demise there has been limited engagement with Indigenous peoples in policy-making processes by the federal government. That will soon change.

The federal government has committed to supporting the establishment of a new national Indigenous representative body. It has acknowledged that the system for administering Indigenous affairs that was created in the ashes of ATSIC is simply not working.

Much of the failure of service delivery to Indigenous people and communities, and the lack of sustainable outcomes, is a direct result of the failure to engage appropriately with Indigenous people and of the failure to develop priorities and programs in full participation with Indigenous communities. And this, ultimately, is what the discussion about a new national Indigenous representative body is about.

It is about our place at the table in making the decisions that impact on our communities and on our children. It is about creating a genuine partnership. With shared ambition, mutual respect and joint responsibility.

In 2008 the Australian Government asked me to convene an independent steering committee to develop a preferred model for the body. In March 2009 the steering committee convened a national workshop in Adelaide to identify the key elements. Consensus was reached at this workshop on a range of issues including gender equality throughout the organisation's structure but further consultation and discussion is needed to address four outstanding issues. Firstly, we're asking how the body can best represent Aboriginal and Torres Strait Islander peoples in a way that includes local and regional issues. Secondly, we also need to resolve the structure of the new body and determine whether members should be elected, whether they should be nominated to the national body through self-nomination or by regional or state/territory level organisations, or whether it should be a combination of both. Thirdly, we need to probe what the body's relationship with the federal government and the parliament should be and how it should be constituted. For example, should it be a statutory authority, a company limited by guarantee or a non-government organisation? And lastly, Aboriginal and Torres Strait Islander peoples have maintained throughout the consultations to date that the body should be sustainable and able to operate independent of government funding over time, so the question of funding and sustainability is another critical issue to be resolved.

This is probably our last chance to get this right, for a very long time at least. We have to get this right. We must ensure the new body provides a strong, independent and credible voice on issues that matter to Indigenous people now and into the future.

NATIVE TITLE LAW AND POLICY

Even once the new representative body is set up, you — as native title holders, claimants and those who work in native title — are in a privileged position that enables you to lead and engage in the policy agenda and the discussions that are taking place.

And at the moment, the possibilities are endless. Nearly every state and territory has been reviewing laws which relate to native title and Indigenous land rights. For example, the New South Wales Government is consulting on how to best recognise traditional fishing rights. The Queensland Government is amending the *Aboriginal Land Rights Act 1991* and the *Torres Strait Islander Land Rights Act 1991*. In South Australia, the government is reviewing the *Aboriginal Lands Trust Act 1966* and the *Aboriginal Heritage Act 1988*. The Northern Territory has already seen a review of how homelands will be resourced.

And across the country the federal government and federal parliamentary committees are consulting on climate change, environmental protection and biodiversity, heritage, Indigenous enterprise, the Indigenous Economic Development Strategy, and native title and broader land settlements. All of these laws will impact on native title and our rights to land and waters.

Regarding amendments to the native title system itself, it is fair to say that there is a lot wrong with the existing system. We all know that native title today has not lived up to the promise of Eddie Mabo's case that native title would result in some kind of justice and recognition of our cultures. But now, thanks to the involvement and commitment of many people over the years, not least Eddie Mabo and his co-claimants in the case, we are gaining traction.

While parliament was considering the Native Title Amendment Bill 2009, which gives management of mediation to the Federal Court, many Members of Parliament recognised the serious limits of the current native title system and mentioned the need for further and more significant reform.

During that debate, not one Member of Parliament said that the native title system was working. No one denied that further change was necessary. No one talked about native title threatening non-Indigenous lands.

Quite the opposite. Parliamentarians acknowledged what you here know all too well — that native title can create conflict in communities. It doesn't result in just outcomes. It has caused pain. It is not what it was held out to be.

Mark Dreyfus, a Labor Party member from Victoria, said that he is confident the Labor party will consider further amendments, and that:

> Sixteen years after the enactment of the *Native Title Act*, it has to be said that our nation has not realised the high hopes of that time. We must continue to strive towards the aim of recognition of native title, which is a beginning of reconciliation, not the end result.[7]

Rob Oakeshott, an independent from the north coast of New South Wales, said '[w]hilst the native title system that has been built up certainly provides access to the law, it is questionable, as of today, whether it is a process that is just in delivering the reconciliation outcomes that I would hope everyone in this chamber is looking for'.[8]

Mark Butler, a Labor Party member from South Australia, said:

> Sadly, I am sure that nobody in this House could argue that we do not still have a long way to go to fulfil the intention included within the preamble to the legislation...The delay that we have seen in the resolution of native title claims and the litigation that flows from those claims has resulted in millions of dollars being wasted, opportunities for reconciliation and development squandered, and the flourishing of distrust and disillusionment with the process by all parties involved, Indigenous communities and others with interests in the land...[9]

He went on to say that '[they] accept there is still more to do' and that '[t]his bill is part of an ongoing process of reform'.[10]

Daryl Melham, a Labor Party member from New South Wales, said:

> There is no doubt that it was legislation that was evolving in an area that was largely unsettled and unknown. But the principles were: protecting native title and providing this alternative system…It was always recognised that the legislation would need to be amended, that it would not be the final resolution of the matter because there would be court cases and there would be evolution and we would learn from experience…[11]

Barry Haase, a Liberal Party member from Western Australia, said:

> I simply reiterate that the act of 1993 made great changes in Australia, and the aspiration was to improve the lot of Indigenous people. It has not done that. Irrefutably, it has not achieved what it set out to achieve…[the Bill] has focused our attention on the subject once again, and that cannot be a bad thing. But this is an ongoing problem that needs a real solution.[12]

In conclusion, the Attorney-General said that 'it is also clear…that the system is in need of reform' and that he has 'an open mind to further legislative change that may facilitate resolution of native title claims'.[13]

Recognising that significant changes must be made, Rob Oakeshott introduced amendments that would shift the burden of proof to the state governments. He said:

> It should be up to the State, with its 220 year history of advantage, power and resources, to disprove a connection to the land rather than the current model that asks Indigenous groups, with a 220 year history of disadvantage, removal and dislocation. It is a small but significant shift in the burden of proof as it acknowledges a difficult and fractured 220 year history and replaces it with a legal framework that is a step closer to walking together and working together in the future.[14]

Unfortunately, his amendment didn't get through, but I am encouraged by the comments of other Members of Parliament, including those of the Attorney-General, who has committed to considering further change. And momentum for that change, and particularly a change to the burden of proof, is building.

The Law Council of Australia, which represents 56,000 legal practitioners across Australia, and various judges, including the highest judge in the country, Chief Justice French, and Victoria's native title judge, Justice North, all support it.

However, the Attorney-General has said that the 'government will not rush into such changes without first consulting stakeholders'; he recognised that '[i]t is very important that there be genuine community support for measures that are after all designed to or intended to promote the welfare of Indigenous owners and their descendants. Without such consultation history shows that changes can be controversial and counterproductive.'[15]

Although we must be careful not to make it look like shifting the burden of proof will remedy all the malfunction of native title, it appears that through the debate on this significant reform, a rare opportunity to improve the native title system may be opening up.

So we must take up the call of the Attorney-General to tell the federal government exactly what we think is needed to improve native title. We must not allow this opportunity to pass, and we must not give the government the opportunity to say that they weren't told these things by the most important stakeholders in the system — you and I.

In this process we will need to engage with government to work out important amendments that will actually improve the system in a real and tangible way. How do we want the compensation provisions changed? What about extinguishment, compulsory acquisition, connection reports, party status, strengthening procedural rights, commercial rights? The list goes on.

Some of it will include repeating ourselves and going over what feels like old ground, but we may finally be approaching a time when an honest discussion may finally be had, and our talk will be heard and addressed.

As the Member of Parliament Daryl Melham recognised:

> I think [the recent debate in Parliament] shows that in this area we are maturing, hopefully, which will be to the benefit of not just Indigenous people but our nation. For too long, a lot of this debate has been as a result of ignorance and prejudice, which has sidelined proper policy.[16]

It has been positive to hear parliamentarians speak some of the truths about the native title system: now we must hold them to it.

OTHER WAYS TO HOLD GOVERNMENT ACCOUNTABLE

So, finally, I want to turn briefly to a few other mechanisms which you can use to influence the policy agenda and hold government to its words.

Firstly, through my office: my role as Aboriginal and Torres Strait Islander Social Justice Commissioner is one of five commissioners who make up the Australian Human Rights Commission. As I mentioned before, one of my main roles is to monitor the enjoyment and exercise of human rights for Indigenous Australians, including human rights as they relate to native title. I am required to produce annual social justice and native title reports, which are tabled in the Federal Parliament and sent out to state and territory governments. Through these reports I advocate and lobby on behalf of Indigenous people to represent aspirations and issues of regional and national relevance. However, these reports are not just about identifying the issues. They must also be about promoting the participation of Indigenous people and their communities in the development of solutions.

In order for my office to advocate credible strategies, the advice and recommendations provided in the reports must be evidence based. This is where I rely on individuals, community, the leadership and representative organisations to provide feedback through surveys, requests for information and suggestions for case studies.

For example, in last year's Native Title Report, I did two case studies on how climate change and water policy are affecting two separate collectives of Indigenous communities. I looked at how climate change and water management and policy is affecting the Indigenous nations of the Murray Darling Basin and I also examined the possible impacts of climate change on Torres Strait Islanders. These case studies were only possible with the support, dedication and participation of people from those regions.

Information provided by you is the most valuable way I can illustrate to government where the policy gaps are, and how they can go about filling those gaps. Without you, and from my staff's desks in Sydney, the reports would be of very little use to anyone. So I encourage you to use my office to get clear and accurate messages to governments through my reports.

One thing that has helped me to present those messages in a way that supports some of what native title bodies have been saying is through an active relationship with the National Native Title Council.

I would like to congratulate you on establishing the Council. It has established itself as a driving force in lobbying government and industry to progress the development aspirations of Indigenous people on their lands and for their communities.

Through providing a united front to government, through effective consultation and engagement with all stakeholders, the Council will be a significant driver of policy and is another means through which you can set the agenda.

Today I asked who is driving that agenda. And I am pretty sure we all want the same response. The challenge we continue to face is how we can best position ourselves to drive and own the policies which affect us as Indigenous peoples and owners of this country.

I understand that a lot of the time government does not make things easy. You are under-resourced, information isn't always easily accessible and government generally gives ridiculously short timeframes to respond in. When you do respond, they often don't acknowledge your input.

But despite the constraints you are under, there are new and powerful opportunities opening up. There is a developing international human rights framework, a new Indigenous representative body is being established and the discussion on significantly changing native title is ramping up.

And you are some of the best people to be able to grasp these new opportunities. It is you who know native title; you know its power, its weaknesses and its integral role in our communities. And you know too well that governments come and go, but the legacy of the law and the policies they make remain, impacting our communities for generations.

By engaging strategically, you, as either Traditional Owners or people who work for Traditional Owners, can respond to communities' rights and aspirations creatively and constructively. You can drive the agenda in a way that ensures policies complement each other and provide our communities with the power to create the futures they want.

Finally, in closing I want to say thank you.

My term as the Aboriginal and Torres Strait Islander Social Justice Commissioner comes to an end this year. After that, you will have a new Commissioner, who, I am sure, will be equally dedicated to native title and to advocating for the realisation of the human rights of Aboriginal and Torres Strait Islanders people as I am.

Thank you for having me at the past five native title conferences. Thank you for inviting me into your communities and homes and for sharing your stories, your ideas, your heartbreaks, your plans, your jokes and your concerns with me.

I will continue to use all of the wisdom and knowledge I have gained through this time to help build stronger, healthier and happier communities whose rights are respected and recognised by the broader Australian community.

Enjoy the conference, and keep the legacy of our great advocates like Eddie Mabo in your hearts while you come up with your own plans for how we can take back control of our agenda.

Please remember, from self-respect comes dignity, and from dignity comes hope.

15.
Native Title Conference, Wurundjeri Country, 2009

MABO LECTURE
A long journey to climb the mountain

LES MALEZER

I have come today to praise Eddie Koiki Mabo, the man, and to continue his fight for dignity and respect.

Let me begin by acknowledging the Aboriginal people and Torres Strait Islander people who are not only the rightful owners of this continent, but who are the spiritual and inherent guardians of the living landscape. We will always be the heart and soul of Australia. I pay my respects to the local people who hold the law to this region and to their ancestors and to their descendents to come.

I acknowledge Bobby MacLeod, who has recently passed on, as a sign of respect to all our fallen heroes who have died without receiving the justice and dignity we demand as the first peoples of Australia and to all who have placed our existence as unified peoples ahead of individual gain and personal gratification.

I grieve for our many people who are divided from us, by politics and power, and who lie homeless or inebriated or in prisons, juvenile centres, foster homes, rehabilitation centres and mental institutions around the country. As long as they exist separated from us, from our families, from our communities and from our society, we may never really be a peoples, a peoples exercising the right of self-determination. My paper today is also dedicated to these people in the hope that we may be reunited in our struggle to survive into the future.

I formally express my appreciation to the Government of Australia for its recent announcement of support, unqualified support, for the United Nations Declaration on the Rights of Indigenous Peoples. I acknowledge the joint statement by representatives of Aboriginal and Torres Strait Islander peoples and the Australian Government that was recently presented, for the first time ever, at the United Nations.[1] In that statement we spoke of our joint determination to forge a new era of relations grounded in good faith and mutual respect. We also said we seek to demonstrate that trust and partnership are essential if we are to fully protect the rights of Indigenous peoples and we agreed that we each have a part to play in ensuring Aboriginal and Torres Strait Islander peoples' rights are fully protected. I hope those words will come to mean something in the days ahead.

Next year at the United Nations we intend to make a follow-up statement, a joint statement agreed by government and by our peoples, to announce progress made in implementing the rights of the Aboriginal and Torres Strait Islander peoples of Australia.

MABO, THE MAN

I want to now address Mabo, the man. First let me say, I knew Koiki Mabo and he knew me. We respected each other. We shared our common ideas and found common strength in our struggles for justice. We had both grown up under the Queensland racism and the repressive Bjelke-Petersen government.

Today Koiki Mabo is a hero, and the name 'Mabo' is well known in Australia and around the world. But in the early 1980s, when he commenced his legal actions, a ten-year battle for his inherent rights, he was not known to many people outside of his local communities in Townsville and Mer Island. His true greatness was not fully appreciated when it should have been.

Although his assertion to have lawful rights to his land was ultimately vindicated, he was humiliated in embarrassing ways in the process. He was humiliated before the courts — and here I am referring to the Queensland Supreme Court decision that found he did not have connection to his land — and he was humiliated by governments — that is, the government policy to oppose the inherent Aboriginal and Torres Strait Islander title to land. This is a policy that exists amongst the governments in Australia to this day, to this very minute.

15. A long journey to climb the mountain

Koiki Mabo died without hearing the final decision of the High Court. He did not die as a hero. Like every other Aboriginal or Torres Strait Islander that died before him and since 1788, he died as an alien in his own country. So to Koiki Mabo I say thank you. Thank you for being determined when others around you stood back. Thank you for not standing down, thank you for not compromising, thank you for not saying, 'how can I exploit this situation to my personal advantage'.

Perhaps I should say, '*Esso, esso, mina big esso*'.

I am a Gubbi Gubbi/Butchulla man from the region of south-east Queensland. (I detest the name 'Queen's Land'. It is a name I have learned that was personally created and chosen by Queen Victoria for her newest and latest colony formed 150 years ago, on 6 June 1859.)

When I was still technically a youth, in 1977, I helped form the Foundation for Aboriginal and Islander Research Action (FAIRA). FAIRA was not formed out of a need to have a legal service, health service, housing service or childcare agency; we were established for one clear purpose, to fight for Aboriginal and Torres Strait Islander rights.

The founding members especially included people from the remote reserves at that time; people who were sick and tired of being managed by the white government; people who refused to accept that we were inferior, and people who rejected the idea that our choices were that we must conform to Australian society or be locked away on reserves.

I am today Chairperson of FAIRA, as I was in 1977, and over the past thirty-two years, like Koiki Mabo, I have been rebelling against established Australian law and the idea that the Australian governments and their laws should control our future.

Like Haudenosaunee Chief Deskaheh, who approached the League of Nations in 1923, and like Martin Luther King, who was troubled by the continued segregation and racism after the abolition of slavery in the United States, I believe I have been on a long journey to 'climb the mountain' and 'see the other side'.

I believed I climbed my mountain in 2007. On 13 September 2007 I stood at the podium at the United Nations to address the General Assembly immediately after the adoption of the United Nations Declaration on the Rights of Indigenous Peoples. I pronounced that the Declaration belonged not only to the state members of the United Nations, but it belonged to the Indigenous peoples of the world.

The Declaration is delivered to those who are united against institutionalised racism and against segregated political power structures and who have fought without weakening for a true and meaningful human rights standard. In my speech I said:

> Today's adoption of the Declaration occurs because the United Nations and the Indigenous peoples have found the common will to achieve this outcome. The Declaration does not represent solely the viewpoint of the United Nations, nor does it represent solely the viewpoint of the Indigenous peoples. It is a Declaration which combines our views and interests and which sets the framework for the future. It is a tool for peace and justice, based upon mutual recognition and mutual respect.[2]

I believe that I, and FAIRA, have now accomplished our task at the international level to provide the framework for justice at home. International human rights law is no longer silent or vague on the Indigenous peoples of the world and our rights. It is now time for Australia to complete the process that began with *Mabo* in 1992.[3] This is the challenge now upon us.

MABO AND NATIVE TITLE

We are well aware of the significance of the *Mabo* decision of the High Court and many of the elements regarding native title law.

We know that the root of native title (and the systems now in operation) is the recognition in Australian law of a common law title held by Aboriginal and Torres Strait Islander people, and that this recognition only emerged recently, two hundred years after the British Crown claimed sovereignty over Australia. It also emerged as a decision of the High Court after the Government of Australia failed to introduce national land rights legislation in 1985.

We know also the government's decision to legislate to address native title was founded upon the wider need to identify where native title existed in Australia, and to establish procedures to ensure development in Australia could occur while respecting the rights of Aboriginal and Torres Strait Islander people, whatever they might turn out to be.

We know the resulting *Native Title Act 1993* (Cth) (NTA) carried a number of specific measures, such as:
a. establishing native title representative bodies;
b. redress for native title already impaired;
c. means for development where native title might exist; and
d. a tribunal to adjudicate native title claims.

The 1993 legislation had at least two fundamentally discriminatory aspects. The first of these was the presumption, made first by the High Court, that Crown sovereignty has the power to extinguish native title, and the second was that the onus of proof rested upon the Aboriginal and Torres Strait Islander people to claim and prove that they had customary connection over their territories.

The 1998 amendments to the NTA brought many more discriminatory provisions into Australian law, resulting ultimately in the failure of the NTA to work for the benefit of the Aboriginal and Torres Strait Islander people.

In 1999 the Committee on Elimination of Racial Discrimination (CERD) established that the native title laws were racially discriminatory and in breach of the International Convention on the Elimination of All Forms of Racial Discrimination.[4] CERD has made four such findings since, and consistently called upon the Australian Government to enter into negotiations with the Aboriginal and Torres Strait Islander people for an acceptable arrangement. No doubt CERD will make the same recommendations again when it next considers the periodic report from Australia.

LAND RIGHTS

In 1983 the Hawke government promised the Aboriginal and Torres Strait Islander people national land rights legislation. The return of an Australian Labor Party government after eight years of the Fraser government meant a return to the political agenda to recognise the land rights of the first Australians.

Whitlam had failed politically to enact the *Aboriginal Land Rights (Northern Territory) Act 1976* (Cth) (ALRA) before losing government, but Malcolm Fraser played a strong hand in ensuring that this law was implemented immediately by his administration in 1976. The Fraser version of the land rights law was only slightly short in meeting all important principles identified in the Woodward Report, the report of the Aboriginal Land Rights Commission, in 1974.

Woodward had insisted that Aboriginal people must have the right of veto over mining and major developments on our lands because, without such control, the people would not be able to exercise their rights and responsibilities over our territories. Even though the legislation did not contain the complete right of veto, and allowed a Minister of the Crown to have the final decision, the ALRA was the closest that Australian law has come to recognising the rights of Indigenous peoples.

The Hawke government said the proposed national land rights legislation, to be enacted in 1985, would carry five principles for national land rights. They were:
1. Aboriginal land to be held under inalienable freehold title;
2. protection of sacred sites;
3. Aboriginal control in relation to mining on Aboriginal land;
4. access to mining royalty equivalents; and
5. compensation for lost land to be negotiated.

Native title laws now in operation in Australia do not meet these principles.

INDIGENOUS PEOPLES AND INTERNATIONAL LAW

Australia prides itself on being a strong advocate of the 'rule of law'.[5] We have heard of late about Aboriginal and Torres Strait Islander policy being administered according to the rule of law. It is an interesting reference being used to justify heavy-handed policies against Aboriginal people who apparently offend Australian society's sensibilities.

However, the application of the rule of law, without respect for human rights, is not necessarily consistent with democratic principles. It is commonly viewed that the rule of law is:

> A legal principle, of general application, sanctioned by the recognition of authorities, and usually expressed in the form of a maxim or logical proposition. Called a 'rule', because in doubtful or unforeseen cases it is a guide or norm for their decision. The rule of law, sometimes called 'the supremacy of law', provides that decisions should be made by the application of known principles or laws without the intervention of discretion in their application.[6]

Kahn states:

> The predominant view is that the concept of 'rule of law' per se says nothing about the 'justness' of the laws themselves, but simply how the legal system operates. As a consequence of this, a very undemocratic nation or one without respect for human rights can exist with a 'rule of law'.[7]

Indigenous peoples around the world have pressed their case at international fora because the rule of law and democratic government do not necessarily guarantee the equal enjoyment of human rights by first peoples.

15. A long journey to climb the mountain

The United Nations adopted the Declaration on the Rights of Indigenous Peoples by an overwhelming vote in 2007. The Declaration was the culmination of twenty-five years of campaigning by Indigenous peoples from around the world for justice at the United Nations. The United Nations' attention has now turned to the application of the rights of Indigenous peoples.

In May 2009 the United Nations Permanent Forum considered its obligations under Article 42 of the Declaration, which states:

> The United Nations, its bodies, including the Permanent Forum on Indigenous Issues, and specialized agencies, including at the country level, and States shall promote respect for and full application of the provisions of this Declaration and follow up the effectiveness of this Declaration.

Following close examination of this Article, the Permanent Forum has adopted a general comment that sets out to clarify its role under Article 42 and, in doing so, elaborates on the status of the rights of Indigenous peoples under international law.[8] In this general comment the Permanent Forum asserts the rights of Indigenous peoples contained in the Declaration are already based in established international human rights instruments.

> The Declaration forms a part of universal human rights law…The human rights treaty bodies will need to refer to the Declaration, as their practice already indicates, whenever dealing with indigenous rights. The Declaration is…a general instrument of human rights.
>
> The Declaration is a human rights standard elaborated upon the fundamental rights of universal application and set in the cultural, economic, political and social context of Indigenous peoples…The human rights envisaged in the Declaration are the same human rights that have been recognized for the rest of humankind…A number of the articles are based on the human rights covenants and other conventions…[9]

While the general comment stops short of stating the Declaration is a binding instrument under international law, it does recognise that the Declaration does have some binding character. The general comment states the long-lasting negotiations over the final text of the Declaration resulted in 'a document expressing a broad common ground, which has now also been endorsed by the General Assembly'.[10] Therefore, in reality the Declaration is almost universally agreed upon and in this context is part of a growing 'rapprochement' (or harmonious relationship) between declarations and treaties.

I divert here slightly to point out that the Committee on Economic, Social and Cultural Rights did, in fact, recommend in its report on Australia, dated 22 May 2009, that Australia 'strengthen its efforts to guarantee the indigenous peoples' rights under articles 1 and 15 to enjoy their identity and culture'.[11] Article 1 in this case refers to the right of self-determination.

So far in 2009 I have attended sessions of three human rights treaty bodies to follow their concerns about Australia's treatment of the Aboriginal and Torres Strait Islander peoples. Let me tell you something about the position of each of these treaty bodies.

The CERD, using its 'urgent action' procedures in response to requests received from Australia, wrote to the Australian Government on 13 March 2009 to request an update by end of July on the Northern Territory intervention laws and Australia's compliance with the 'race convention' — adding to the still outstanding issues in relation to native title and land rights.

In 2005, at its last consideration of the periodic report from Australia, CERD asked Australia to submit its next periodic report by 30 October 2008. At the time of writing, that had not occurred. In its last report on Australia of 14 April 2005, CERD expressed strong views on the native title laws in Australia:

> The Committee recommends that the State party refrain from adopting measures that withdraw existing guarantees of indigenous rights and that it make every effort to seek the informed consent of indigenous peoples before adopting decisions relating to their rights to land. It further recommends that the State party reopen discussions with indigenous peoples with a view to discussing possible amendments to the Native Title Act and finding solutions acceptable to all…
>
> The Committee is concerned about information according to which proof of continuous observance and acknowledgement of the laws and customs of indigenous peoples since the British acquisition of sovereignty over Australia is required to establish elements in the statutory definition of native title under the Native Title Act. The high standard of proof required is reported to have the consequence that many indigenous peoples are unable to obtain recognition of their relationship with their traditional lands (art. 5)…
>
> The Committee wishes to receive more detailed information, including statistical data, on the extent to which such arrangements respond to indigenous claims over land. Information on achievements at State and Territory levels may also be provided.[12]

Similarly, the Human Rights Committee, in its report of 2 April 2009, expressed concern about the high cost, complexity and strict rules of evidence applying to claims under the NTA and expressed its regret about the lack of sufficient steps taken by the state party to implement the Committee's recommendations adopted in 2000.

In 2000 the Human Rights Committee had expressed its concern:

> that in many areas native title rights and interests remain unresolved and that the Native Title Amendments of 1998…limit the rights of indigenous persons and communities…and affects their interests in native title lands, particularly pastoral lands…The high level of exclusion and poverty facing indigenous persons is indicative of the urgent nature of these concerns. In particular, the Committee recommends that the necessary steps be taken to restore and protect the titles and interests of indigenous persons in their native lands, including by considering amending anew the Native Title Act, taking into account these concerns.[13]

In its report of April 2009, the Human Rights Committee requested Australia to continue its efforts to improve the operation of the native title system, in consultation with Aboriginal and Torres Strait Islander peoples.

The Committee on Economic, Social and Cultural Rights held meetings with the Government of Australia on 23 and 24 March 2009. Once again, I attended those meetings. The Committee on Economic, Social and Cultural Rights reported that:

> the Covenant [on Economic, Social and Cultural Rights] has not been incorporated into domestic law and that [Australia] has not yet adopted a comprehensive legal framework for the protection of the Covenant rights at the Federal level, despite the recommendations adopted by the Committee in 2000. Furthermore, the Committee regrets that judicial decisions make little reference to international human rights law, including the Covenant.[14]

The Committee called for effective judicial remedies for the protection of rights under the Covenant; that training programs be organised for the judiciary on the Covenant and the jurisprudence of the Committee.

On land rights, the Committee noted with concern:

> the high cost, complexity and strict rules of evidence applying to claims under the Native Title Act. It regrets the lack of sufficient steps taken by the State party to implement the Committee's recommendations adopted in 2000. [Australia] should continue its efforts to improve the

operation of the Native Title system, in consultation with Aboriginal and Torres Strait Islander Peoples.[15]

I conclude my comments on the human rights treaty body reports for this year by pointing out that I have been very selective about the quotations I have used. There is much more information in those reports and findings which warrant attention. I have used these instances to make clear four particular points.

First, Australia has international obligations regarding human rights law, and these obligations emerge from existing treaties signed by Australia. About this there can be no doubt.

The second point is that we, as the Aboriginal and Torres Strait Islander peoples, have been taken in by the government regarding our rights and the legal obligations to promote and protect our rights. In the pursuit of native title we have allowed ourselves to be subjected to a process, a supposedly fair legal process, where our interests were to be resolved without discrimination and under the principle of equality. Has the Government of Australia addressed the findings and recommendations of the human rights treaty bodies, not just one treaty body, but all relevant treaty bodies to which Australia has an obligation under international law that suggest that native title is in breach of our rights? Has the government made the necessary steps to inform us of our rights and of the findings of these bodies? Has the government consulted with us regarding reforms to the native title system?

The third point is that Aboriginal and Torres Strait Islander people are blinded and crippled by our lack of capacity to engage in human rights and legal reforms. I am not referring here to the information generated by the Australian Human Rights Commission, which has done a wonderful job under the leadership of Commissioner Tom Calma, to highlight the important issues. I am referring to the actions by government to strip us of our own institutions and to prevent us having access to means for autonomy. The native title representative body (NTRB) structures are not, for the most part, the structures of land councils. They do not function as land councils. They are structures that can be controlled by governments through legislation, funding and contracts. Many NTRBs — particularly along the eastern seaboard — have now been replaced by 'Native Title Services' and these Native Title Services are not even community-controlled organisations. They are custom-built by the government. While I have respect for many of the people I know who administer and work in these bodies, and there are a few people for whom I have no respect whatsoever, that is not the point. The point is that Aboriginal and Torres Strait Islander people are entitled to have capacity and control, and that means we must have access to our own institutions and to autonomous funding.

The fourth point, and the most critical, is that the current system is not achieving good outcomes in land rights. The native title debates have been so constrained that we have been left holding a process which does not work. It is a process that is proven to be racially discriminatory. It is a process removed from the principles of land rights but which has totally replaced the land rights agenda of the Aboriginal and Torres Strait Islander people. It is an inefficient, ineffective and ultimately manipulated process which draws everyone's attention and takes our mind off the results being achieved, or not achieved.

Having made these four very strong criticisms, I want to turn my attention to the legitimate human rights of the Aboriginal and Torres Strait Islander people in Australia.

THE DECLARATION AND LAND RIGHTS

The Government of Australia has expressed its solemn support for the Declaration.[16] In doing so, the government confirmed that the Declaration does not change any of the laws in Australia. However, it is misleading to refer to the Declaration as an aspirational document. 'Aspirational' can mean ambitious or ideal. The Declaration is neither of these things. The rights contained in the Declaration are very much meant to be implemented. The Declaration is a practical instrument designed in its construction to address the areas of racial discrimination, inequality and exploitation that have manifestly and consistently occurred against Indigenous peoples around the world.

I have already explained that the Declaration has a binding nature and that many of the rights in the Declaration are already legally binding under existing human rights treaties. Article 42 of the Declaration leaves no doubt that the Declaration is intended to have application.[17] This intention also is expressed in many United Nations resolutions, instruments and mechanisms including, inter alia, in the Durban Declaration and Programme of Action, the Durban Review Outcome Document, and the Second International Decade of the World's Indigenous Peoples and associated Programme of Action.[18]

In 1982 the United Nations accepted evidence that around the world there were populations, now identified as the Indigenous peoples of the world, who had common characteristics, and that these people were so marginalised and exploited by other dominating populations that it should be addressed as a matter of international concern.[19]

There are over 370 million Indigenous peoples living in up to eighty countries around the world. We survive on all continents except Antarctica, and we inhabit all biospheres from deserts to rainforests, from tundra to the tropics, from small islands to mountain tops. We are the holders of eighty percent of the cultural diversity in the world, including most of the six thousand languages of the world. We survive in those regions where the biodiversity has survived the ravages of the industrialised world. We are, ultimately, the protectors of that biodiversity and the environment and the climate.

Apart from these identifiers, we have characteristics that leave little doubt about our identities. Here are some of those.

a. We have a historical and traditional association with our territories that is spiritual and sustaining.
b. We have experienced colonisation of our territories and our resources.
c. We have a distinct identity and have been marginalised by the dominant society, in political, social, economic and cultural terms. We are usually at the bottom of the socioeconomic ladder.
d. We have a desire to continue our cultural distinctions and to have our future generations survive as a distinct culture based upon our values.

The most important thing to know about the Declaration, at least the most important from my experiences, is to know that most of the rights are related to the rights of 'peoples' rather than the rights of individuals. The Declaration is ultimately concerned with collective rights. I will not elaborate on that, suffice to say many of the rights cannot be exercised or enjoyed unilaterally by individuals.

Who are peoples in international law? This is a question that dominated the final stages of negotiations. For us, as Aboriginal peoples and Torres Strait Islanders, it is a critical question.

The United Nations is founded upon the interests of peoples, not governments as we might think. The Charter of the United Nations begins, 'we, the peoples of the world'. Many governments believe that it is the nation state that is the entity of the peoples. For example, the 'peoples of Ireland' are the entire population of Ireland and their 'right as peoples to self-determination' is exercised through the national government as the political institution of the peoples.

As the Aboriginal and Torres Strait Islander populations in Australia, I believe we have to consider, if not ultimately answer, the question, 'are we peoples?' Perhaps the Government of Australia has already answered that question, by saying we are all Australians together and therefore our right of self-determination exists in the form of the Australian Government, and our political rights are individual rights expressed through our participation in voting and other democratic procedures within Australia. Perhaps that is why the government often refers to us in official statements as merely Indigenous Australians.

The Declaration has, in my view, two central components: the right to self-determination and land rights. (Perhaps, we could argue that the right to non-discrimination is a third component but this only becomes relevant if equality and non-discrimination are not integral to the exercise of self-determination and land rights.)

For this paper I am concentrating on land rights, but let me first address some relevant aspects of self-determination. While Article 3 of the Declaration expressly states, 'Indigenous Peoples have the right to self-determination', the majority of the remaining forty-five articles really give further definition to the right of self-determination. For example, the articles address rights to:

a. autonomy or self-government (Articles 4, 37);
b. distinct political, legal, economic, social and cultural institutions (Article 5);
c. identity, dignity and non-discrimination (Articles 2, 7, 15, 22, 33);
d. protection against genocide or assimilation (Articles 7, 8);
e. control and ownership of culture, cultural property, ceremonies (Articles 12, 13);
f. ownership of traditional practices and traditional knowledge (Articles 24, 34, 36);
g. control of education, languages, media (Articles 14, 16);
h. representative institutions, choosing representatives, decision making and free, prior informed consent to developments and intrusions (Articles 18, 19, 20);
i. economic and social development (Articles 3, 21, 23, 32, 36).

These are all rights associated one way or another with collective interests of peoples and the exercise of self-determination.

Articles 25 to 32 in the Declaration relate to the rights of Indigenous peoples to our lands, territories including waters and seas, and resources, and to have control of development within those territories. These land rights are inherent rights derived from our identity as peoples and our status as first peoples in those territories. The rights contained in these eight articles (note that some other articles also relate to lands, such as Article 10) are very deliberately derived. Most of the rights contained in

Articles 25 to 32 are also defined in International Labour Organization (ILO) Convention 169.

ILO Convention 169, a convention concerning Indigenous and tribal peoples in independent countries, was adopted by the International Labour Organization in 1989. While Aboriginal and Torres Strait Islander delegates were closely involved in the drafting of this convention, they made a decision to walk away from the convention when it was finally adopted. Their reason was because the convention did not recognise that Indigenous peoples had the rights of peoples under international law.

Now that the Declaration has been adopted, it might be to our advantage to have the Government of Australia ratify ILO 169. Where the binding nature of the Declaration might be arguable, there is no doubt that ILO 169 is a legally binding document and recognises most of what we seek under a land rights model. I hope that we will be able to have national consultations on ratification of this convention.

Article 25 of the Declaration establishes the significance of the relationship between Indigenous peoples and our territories, stating, 'Indigenous peoples have the right to maintain and strengthen their distinctive spiritual relationship with their traditionally owned or otherwise occupied and used lands, territories, waters and coastal seas and other resources and to uphold their responsibilities to future generations in this regard'.

Article 26 establishes that Indigenous peoples have the right of ownership and control over their territories. It also establishes that governments should recognise and protect those rights.

Article 29 clarifies that Indigenous peoples are responsible for the protection and/or development of their territories and the governments do not have the capacity to interfere with those rights without the peoples' free, prior and informed consent. This right is further elaborated in Article 30, which prohibits our territories being used for military purposes without our consent. However, Article 30 incorporates a provision for governments to use the lands if 'justified by a significant threat to relevant public interest'. This point was hotly contested by Indigenous peoples' delegations, as it potentially leaves discretion to government and not Indigenous peoples as to interpretation of 'significant threat' or 'public interest'.

Article 31 expands the right of control over the resources of Indigenous peoples' territories by making it clear that intellectual property rights, traditional knowledge and genetic resources are under the ownership and control of the Indigenous peoples.

Article 32 deals with development of resources and lands in Indigenous peoples' territories. It makes it clear that any development, utilisation or exploitation of mineral, water or other resources on Indigenous peoples' territories cannot occur without their free, prior and informed consent.

For the most part, these articles that I have presented are easy to comprehend and understand. I believe they are beyond criticism and they establish quite clearly that complete ownership and control of the territories and the resources within those territories rests with the Indigenous peoples concerned, under a regime of self-determination by 'peoples'. However, these rights are not recognised in Australia.

I mentioned that the Declaration was written as a practical or pragmatic document to address the areas of discrimination and exploitation that have been experienced by the Indigenous peoples. Articles 27 and 28 are good examples of this aspect. Article 28 states:

> 1. Indigenous peoples have the right to redress, by means that can include restitution or, when this is not possible, just, fair and equitable compensation, for the lands, territories and resources which they have traditionally owned or otherwise occupied or used, and which have been confiscated, taken, occupied, used or damaged without their free, prior and informed consent.
>
> 2. Unless otherwise freely agreed upon by the peoples concerned, compensation shall take the form of lands, territories and resources equal in quality, size and legal status or of monetary compensation or other appropriate redress.

Our rights to have our territories returned, replaced or compensated is unambiguous in Article 28. Our experiences tell us that arrangements for redress in Australia have mostly turned out to be duds in practice. For example, the *Aboriginal Land Act 1991* (Qld) or the Aboriginal Land Fund have not been regarded as successful instruments for redress.

I remember that New Zealand had particularly strong objections to the use of the word 'redress'. Not surprisingly, the more that New Zealand objected to the term, the more we grew to like it. I understand that 'redress' is the correct term to be used in this context. That is, redress includes restitution, replacement and/or compensation. The right to redress also appears in Articles 8, 11, 20 and 32 of the Declaration.[20]

Article 27 addresses the circumstances where Indigenous peoples are in dispute with government and can only appeal to the government or a justice system which is biased:

> States shall establish and implement, in conjunction with indigenous peoples concerned, a fair, independent, impartial, open and transparent process, giving due recognition to indigenous peoples' laws, traditions, customs and land tenure systems, to recognize and adjudicate the rights of indigenous peoples pertaining to their lands, territories and resources, including those which were traditionally owned or otherwise occupied or used. Indigenous peoples shall have the right to participate in this process.

So, where are we in Australia with native title and our rights as Indigenous peoples to our territories and resources? Clearly change must occur. This is already incumbent upon government, as we can see under their international obligations. The real crunch (for the government) is that they are expected to reach a satisfactory outcome in partnership with the Indigenous peoples.

MABO — THE NEXT STEP

It has been over seventeen years since the High Court released its ruling on *Mabo*. Seventeen years since the High Court stated that the people of Mer are 'entitled as against the whole world to possession, occupation, use and enjoyment of the lands of the Murray Islands'.[21]

It has been over a decade since the Committee on the Elimination of Racial Discrimination first found that Australia's native title laws, as amended in 1998, were in breach of the International Convention on the Elimination of All Forms of Racial Discrimination.

It has been over four years since the United Nations adopted the Programme of Action for the Second International Decade of the World's Indigenous Peoples and:

a. called upon governments to launch a review of their national legislations to eliminate possible discriminatory provisions, with the full and effective participation of Indigenous experts;
b. recommended that national constitutions should recognise the existence of Indigenous peoples and make explicit reference to them, where relevant; and
c. recommended that governments should consider integrating traditional systems of justice into national legislations in conformity with international human rights law and international standards of justice.

It has been over two years since the United Nations adopted the Declaration.

Also, the Durban Review Conference, which examined the progress made since the World Conference on Racism in 2001, welcomed the adoption of the Declaration and urged states 'to take all necessary measures to implement the rights of Indigenous peoples in accordance with international human rights instruments without discrimination'.[22] And in September 2009 the Government of Australia announced its position of support for the Declaration.

Now, in Australia, it is time for us to take the next step arising from *Mabo*. It is time to evaluate the outcomes from the *Mabo* decision of the High Court and to analyse fundamental principles to ensure that we have eliminated racism entirely from the land rights system.

If Koiki Mabo were alive today he would be an angry man. The rights he won in the High Court have been eroded away by government, courts and socioeconomic pressures. The Australian culture — which we know as Aboriginal and Torres Strait Islander people — of take everything and give back nothing has survived the *Mabo* phenomenon of 1992.

The High Court of Australia was not prepared to discuss the issue of Indigenous peoples' sovereignty when Koiki Mabo's case went before it. The legitimacy of Crown sovereignty in Australia's legal system was stringently upheld. The issue of whether Aboriginal and Torres Strait Islander peoples ever legitimately lost our sovereignty was not directly dealt with in the *Mabo* case.

While I have steadfastly not used the word 'sovereignty' in my international dealings for the rights of Indigenous peoples, I have never been hesitant to assert the power of self-determination, a right held by Indigenous peoples.

It was interesting to hear Justice French bring public attention to the concept of a treaty between the Government of Australia and the Aboriginal and Torres Strait Islander peoples. The opinion of Justice French, if I understood him properly, is that a treaty can be concluded consistent with all domestic and international legal frameworks.

That is my opinion also. I refer to Article 37 of the Declaration that says, 'Indigenous peoples have the right to the recognition, observance and enforcement of treaties, agreements and other constructive arrangements concluded with States or their successors and to have States honour and respect such treaties, agreements and other constructive arrangements'.

SOME IDEAS OUT OF THE BOX

Let me now set out some ideas for consideration. I stress that these ideas may seem fanciful but are not so inconceivable if a serious attempt is to be made to address the shortcomings of the current system and implement the rights of Indigenous peoples in accordance with the standards that have now been internationally recognised.

1. The government should be prepared to enter into an agreement, or constructive arrangement (which I shall call a 'treaty'), and under this treaty the issue of our sovereignty as Aboriginal and Torres Strait Islander peoples shall be addressed to our satisfaction and to the satisfaction of the Australian Government. The agreement will focus upon the fundamental and essential rights that we hold as the Indigenous peoples. The Declaration provides the platform for those rights.
2. The agreement will establish just and fair procedures for adjudicating disputes between the Australian Government and the Aboriginal and Torres Strait Islander peoples. I can envisage here a process modelled upon the Waitangi Tribunal in New Zealand but where the final decision rests with an authority, in lieu of a Minister of the Crown, who is an Aboriginal or Torres Strait Islander person chosen by Aboriginal and Torres Strait Islander people.
3. In relation to our ownership of our territories, all territories held as Aboriginal territories should come under one title, a form of land title agreed between the Australian Government and the Aboriginal people. Similarly, all Torres Strait Islander territories, including the Torres Strait, shall come under one form of land title.
4. Disputes within Aboriginal territories or Torres Strait Islander territories between members of the Indigenous population should be resolved by an Indigenous institution specifically established for that purpose. This process will eliminate the need to disclose specific information of individuals to the Australian Government.
5. In all states and territories of Australia there shall be set a minimum area of territory to be identified as Aboriginal territory or Torres Strait Islander territory, but ensuring that the minimum is uniformly available across all local areas. The minimum amount would be negotiated. Statistics show that Aboriginal people in Western Australia, Northern Territory and South Australia have ownership or control over twenty-five percent of the total land mass. However, in the four eastern states, the Aboriginal or Torres Strait Islander people, who make up sixty-five percent of the total Indigenous population, only have control of three percent of the land. New South Wales, Australian Capital Territory, Victoria and Tasmania only have 0.4 percent of the land.

6. Associated with the program of redress for territories taken without the free, prior and informed consent, there should be compensation, including financial payments, made to Aboriginal and Torres Strait Islander people, through their institutions, for the past, present and ongoing exploitation of territories through mining, infrastructure development, bio-prospecting or other forms of wealth extraction.
7. Aboriginal governments in communities should have all the powers of self-determination and not be limited to local government functions or mainstream government. This means that essential services such as health, shelter, law enforcement and education should be delivered via Indigenous institutions. Accordingly, Indigenous systems of accountability and community engagement will be needed.

Having proposed these extraordinary ideas, let me tell you what is unsustainable in the present system.

UNSUSTAINABLE POLICIES

The government cannot continue to control our people through partisan politics, discriminatory regimes, incompetent bureaucrats, centralised controls, fringe policies and manifest neglect. Especially, there cannot continue to be an inadvertent long-term strategy to assimilate us as mainstream Australians.

There may well be people of Aboriginal descent or Torres Strait Islander descent who want to enjoy equality as Australians and are prepared to forego their identity in community with other Aboriginal and Torres Strait Islander people. However, those individuals should not be allowed to dictate policies for our people.

Many of us see for ourselves, our children and our future generations a continuation of our existence as the Aboriginal and Torres Strait Islander people of this land, with a distinct culture. We will always be the first peoples and custodians of this country.

We cannot afford for government to be confused between the two separate outcomes or allow the politicians and social commentators to use the two completely different aspirations to deny our right to self-determination as Indigenous peoples.

It is unacceptable that native title procedures have reverted to re-establish the concept of terra nullius for the convenience of developments and exploitations of Indigenous lands and resources.

Future acts and the right to negotiate are lesser rights than free, prior and informed consent. Any proposals for developments on our territories or exploitation of our resources must comply with the right of free, prior and informed consent.

Native title law and procedures are not the mechanisms to return control of our territories to us. Native title cannot continue to place the onus of proof upon us before we are able to exercise and enjoy our rights and freedoms.

The courts that sit in judgment on our cases must be trained in international law and human rights standards, particularly the rights of Indigenous peoples. The laws under which the courts preside must conform or be compatible with the rights of Indigenous peoples. Otherwise we need new structures for the administration of justice to the Aboriginal and Torres Strait Islander peoples.

As self-determining peoples we must have our own institutions to promote and protect our rights as Indigenous peoples. The NTRBs and native title service providers, as structures, are failing us, though they are not to blame for the shortcoming of the procedures. We need advocacy. We need opposition to the centric policies of government. We need a capacity to unite and fight. Unless this system changes, we will have no voice to negotiate effectively with government.

Once again I say it is time to take the next steps after *Mabo* to achieve our inherent rights as the first peoples of Australia.

In conclusion, I again pay my respects to Koiki Mabo and wonder how crazy this all sounds. Was it as crazy as it sounded in the early 1980s? I show my respects as best as I can with the message that I carry. It is time for the Australian Government to enter into negotiations with the Aboriginal and Torres Strait Islander people to reach agreement on land rights and the rights of Indigenous peoples.

16.
Native Title Conference, Gumbayynggir Country, 2005

MABO LECTURE
Addressing the economic exclusion of Indigenous Australians through native title

ADEN RIDGEWAY

We meet today on Gumbayynggir land — the land of my people.

Nyandi baaliga Jaingatti
Nyandi mimiga Gumbayynggir
Nya jawgar yaam Gumbayynggir

My father is Dhunghutti
My mother is Gumbayynggir
And, therefore, I am Gumbayynggir.

So I begin, by paying respect to my elders. Thank you to Bonita Mabo and members of the Mabo family; I offer you a particularly warm welcome to Gumbayynggir land. I am very privileged to be able to share this day with you and to reflect on the legacy that your late husband, Eddie Koiki Mabo, has left for all Australians. I am humbled to give this paper in the name of such a great man — a warrior for all Indigenous peoples and a great Australian — and to do so on the land of my own people.

THE CHALLENGE OF *MABO*

The High Court's decision in *Mabo v Queensland [No. 2]* (Mabo) in 1992 remains one of the most significant events in the relationship of Indigenous and non-Indigenous Australians.[1] The decision, along with the Deaths in Custody Royal Commission[2] and the commencement of the work of the Council for Aboriginal Reconciliation, came at a time when Australia had barely begun to grapple with the ramifications of our history.

Mabo was an important step in breaking through the 'great Australian silence', as Bill Stanner had described this malaise in the 1970s.[3]

It is probably trite to note that *Mabo* was the catalyst for the establishment of the native title claims process and the establishment of the Indigenous Land Fund, which continues today with over $1 billion in capital. However, notwithstanding the significant concerns that exist about the operation of the native title system, it is important to recognise that as a result of the *Mabo* decision many tribes have succeeded in having native title recognised either through the courts or through agreement-making processes. This is a significant part of the legacy of Koiki Mabo, and one which we sometimes overlook.

But I think that the most significant part of the legacy of Koiki Mabo is the challenge that he, and his co-plaintiffs David Passi and James Rice, created for all Australians. That challenge — which I actually think is a great gift — was the opportunity to transform our national identity by forging the way for a new, more inclusive Australia.

Mabo created the opportunity to acknowledge the impact of the past treatment of Indigenous people in relation to their traditional land, and then to also enable us to move forward together in a spirit of coexistence by providing a place for Aboriginal and Torres Strait Islander cultures in the fabric of the Australian nation.

The offer that stemmed from the *Mabo* decision was the opportunity for a new national unity which acknowledges and respects the past, celebrates and recognises the continuation of diverse Aboriginal and Torres Strait Islander cultures, and paves the way for a more respectful future in which the lives and destinies of Indigenous and non-Indigenous people alike are joined together, rather than pitted against each other in opposition.

Addressing this challenge is something that I have continually promoted during my time in the Senate. In my maiden speech to parliament I stated:

16. Addressing the economic exclusion of Indigenous Australians

> If reconciliation is to challenge, then it must remove the obstacles of exclusion and provide the vehicle by which we achieve proper recognition and National social cohesion…We must 'bulldoze' every obstacle to the inclusion of Australia's Indigenous people in National life.
>
> Our complaint is not so much about our condition…but that we have no recognition from the other people in this country. *Mabo* should never have been a cause for outrage at Indigenous success, it was simply the victory of belated justice over other's discontent and it should have given us the opportunity for talk on the higher ideal of justice rather than the mere question of property…No one should suggest that what I contemplate is the domination of one or the other — it is the struggle for recognition of rights and equality of opportunity.

It is a great tragedy that on the thirteenth anniversary of the *Mabo* decision we have to admit that the opportunity offered for such a transformation of our national identity has yet to be grasped. The challenge of *Mabo* remains to be met.

Now this may sound optimistic and some of you may prefer if I had said that the moment has passed and the opportunity provided by the *Mabo* decision has gone. But I don't believe that to be the case.

Koiki Mabo demanded justice and fought doggedly and with determination for it. He had to fight against the attempt of the Queensland Government in 1985 to extinguish native title before any Court had even recognised its existence. He could have given up then. But he didn't. He won that case and set an important precedent under the *Racial Discrimination Act 1975* (Cth).[4] He fought for twelve years for recognition of his rights — although tragically he did not live long enough to see the fruits of his struggle. He looked beyond the situation as it existed at the time, and demanded a just settlement. If I am to honour his legacy, then I must learn from his example that striving for justice is never futile — no matter the odds.

It is a simple fact that the taint of injustice is a heavy burden and will continue to weigh on the psyche of our nation until it is addressed.

ADDRESSING THE ECONOMIC EXCLUSION OF INDIGENOUS AUSTRALIANS

In this paper I want to talk about what I see as important stepping stones to creating a more inclusive Australian society. I am going to focus on just one aspect of the way forward, which has received a lot of media attention and public debate in the last twelve months. That is the issue of addressing the economic exclusion of Indigenous people in this country.

There are a number of aspects to this debate. First, we have seen a renewal of commitments from all governments to address the disadvantage that is faced by Indigenous peoples. This has particularly been so through various commitments made by the Council of Australian Governments and the work of the Productivity Commission in establishing and reporting on a national framework for addressing Indigenous disadvantage.

Second, we have seen the introduction of new arrangements for administering Indigenous affairs at the federal level. This is a process with more acronyms and jargon than a computer manual. It is based on principles of whole-of-government coordination, direct engagement and negotiation with Indigenous communities and, of course, that elusive concept of 'shared responsibility'.

Third, there has also been debate about the state of the native title system and whether it is achieving its goals. In particular, Indigenous people have expressed concern about the disconnect between the system as it is constructed and the realisation of economic outcomes.

Fourth, there is an interlinked debate about the inalienability of Indigenous communal land and whether this is the barrier to economic development for Indigenous people.

We have reached a critical stage in debates about these issues. The Howard government battered its ideological opponents into the ground and silenced opposition to its approach. The mainstreaming that took place through the new arrangements also saw the stepping up of efforts to silence independent voices, most obviously the abolition of the Aboriginal and Torres Strait Islander Commission (ATSIC).

There has also been an emphasis from the government on creating a distinction between service delivery and advocacy roles, achieved through restrictions in funding agreements and tendering out of services — both which are fairly benign-sounding processes that will be difficult to scrutinise and both of which have already begun to happen in relation to other issues such as the environment and services for migrants and refugees.

It has also been suggested that the government intends to reform the native title representative body provisions of the *Native Title Act 1993* (Cth) (NTA), to move to a service delivery model, devoid of any representational role.

Don't believe the rhetoric — any such move will be primarily about silencing criticism of the government and centralising control in government.

An ideological wet blanket has been placed over all debate on Indigenous issues. The result is a debate that is frequently crass, that takes place at such a rudimentary level that it overlooks basic lessons from the past, and is based on stereotypes of Indigenous people which are happily promoted through the media.

To give an example of the tenor of debate — almost all government activity is based on commitments to address Indigenous disadvantage. We are defined as 'disadvantaged citizens'. The goal is to provide us with 'the same opportunities as other Australians'.

The Ministerial Taskforce on Indigenous Affairs — one of the initiatives under the federal arrangements — had a charter which set out the commitments of the federal government. It highlighted a focus on practical measures in the areas of health, education, employment and family violence. It says:

> the taskforce recognises the importance to indigenous people of other issues such as cultural identity and heritage, language preservation, traditional law, land and 'community' governance. These are issues on which Indigenous people themselves should take the lead, with government supporting them as appropriate.

This illustrates perfectly the mindset of the government. It sees a distinction between addressing disadvantage on the one hand, and cultural issues on the other hand. It is a false dichotomy. The two are entwined.

A failure to recognise and embrace the cultural characteristics and the cultural capital that Indigenous people possess is one of the major barriers which excludes us. It limits our ability to participate. And it denigrates our greatest strength and asset — our culture.

Of course, we do want the same opportunities for our people as everyone else gets. Historically, we were not provided with services and access to tools that would equip us to succeed in mainstream society. But having the same opportunities is different from being the same. National inclusiveness is about creating space for our different cultures to coexist. Defining us as 'disadvantaged citizens' masks the structural and systemic barriers that have contributed to the situation we now find ourselves in. It enables the debate and proposed solutions to be grossly over-simplified.

We are not simply 'disadvantaged' people; we have been actively excluded from the economic life of the nation, discriminated against and marginalised. In looking to ways forward we should define our goal as creating opportunities for our inclusion in all forms of the economy — not simply as overcoming 'disadvantage'.

We need to be careful not to be co-opted into over-simplified debates about our needs which are based on language which is benign in appearance but loaded in meaning.

Let me provide a further example of why this is of concern. In June 2004 the Council of Australian Governments (COAG) adopted a National Framework of Principles for Government Service Delivery to Indigenous Australians. Through this framework all Australian governments committed 'to achieving better outcomes for Indigenous Australians, improving the delivery of services, building greater opportunities and helping Indigenous families and individuals to become self-sufficient'.[5]

It is based on six principles of sharing responsibility; harnessing the mainstream; streamlining service delivery; establishing transparency and accountability; developing a learning framework; and focusing on priority areas. They are important commitments that indicate an intention to address problems we have experienced with our federal system of government. But what is missing from these principles?

The 2004 principles in essence superseded COAG's 1992 principles which were known as the National Commitment to Improved Outcomes in the Delivery of Programs and Services for Aboriginal Peoples and Torres Strait Islanders (National Commitment). This National Commitment included the following guiding principles:

- empowerment, self-determination and self-management by Aboriginal peoples and Torres Strait Islanders;
- economic independence and equity being achieved in a manner consistent with Aboriginal and Torres Strait Islander social and cultural values;
- the need to negotiate with and maximise participation by Aboriginal peoples and Torres Strait Islanders through their representative bodies…and community-based organisations in the formulation of policies and programs that affect them.[6]

This is a more appropriate recognition of the importance of Indigenous culture and participation to addressing the economic marginalisation of Indigenous peoples. It demonstrates that the COAG commitments are narrower in focus and less inclusive of Indigenous concerns.

DEVELOPMENTS IN THE NATIVE TITLE SYSTEM — RESISTING INCLUSIVENESS

The native title system has played a role in maintaining the economic marginalisation of Indigenous people. The discussion at this conference in recent years has lamented the limitations that have been built into the native title system. The consequence of this is that Indigenous people are not benefiting as much as we could and should from native title.

This is primarily due to the amendments to the NTA in 1998, which were more concerned about limiting recognition of Indigenous peoples' rights and ensuring that non-Indigenous interests prevail in any contest.

It is also due to the inequalities that have been created administratively in the machinery of the native title system. The clearest example of this is the funding model for native title issues which demonstrably favours the courts and tribunal that oversee the system, along with the interests of third parties. The interests of native title claimants and representative bodies are left under-funded and flooded with demands from the rest of the native title system.

In recent years this has been added to by the regressive decisions of the High Court that have stripped native title of much of its content.[7] This is by, on the one hand, raising the bar for proof of native title unreasonably high and, on the other hand, making it easier to extinguish native title. Through these twin approaches the High Court has become a vehicle for confirming dispossession rather than setting the parameters for coexistence.

What these developments have in common is that they each treat native title and Indigenous people as antagonists. They do not promote inclusiveness but, instead, opposition. The interests of Indigenous people are cast as antithetical to the national interest. This is where governments have got it wrong. And I will return to the importance of this shortly.

Overall, the focus of the native title system is not on forging relationships with Indigenous peoples, but instead about resisting and minimising the recognition that is provided to our cultures and ongoing connection with land.

The COAG National Framework of Principles for Government Service Delivery to Indigenous Australians, adopted in June 2004, confirmed this approach. Under the principle of shared responsibility, all Australian governments agreed to cooperate 'between jurisdictions on native title, *consistent with Commonwealth native title legislation*'.[8]

The federal Attorney-General made clear what the implications of this were on several occasions: namely, that the Commonwealth will not sign off on any agreement or agree to any settlement of native title issues if it forms the view that Indigenous people are being provided with benefits above what the Commonwealth deems they are entitled to under the NTA.

The existence of a concept of 'non-native title outcomes' has to be one of the most damning indictments of the problems of the current system.

There is a need for greater scrutiny of the Commonwealth's approach to this issue. At a practical level it is difficult to understand why the federal government would not be willing to accept a negotiated settlement that is acceptable to the state and other interests.

It involves a reductive view of the agreement-making process which sees the purpose of negotiation as limited to achieving a quicker, less costly settlement with the same outcome as litigation *and nothing more*. But negotiation is about much more than this — it is about seeking mutually acceptable solutions which address the concerns of both sides. It disturbs me that all states and territories would be co-opted into the Commonwealth's approach through agreeing to this aspect of the COAG principles.

The strength of native title lay in the fact that Indigenous identity and economic development could be seen as complementary and inter-related, not contradictory and oppositional. The native title system has evolved through legislation, its administration and the courts in such a way that it works against economic inclusion and opportunities for Indigenous peoples.

COMMUNAL OWNERSHIP OF LAND AND ALIENABILITY

It is somewhat ironic that we now face a national debate about the possibility of alienating communal Indigenous land on the basis that such title — be it under land rights legislation or native title — has not contributed to economic improvement in Indigenous communities. This is an objective that the current native title system and the policies of governments have worked against!

This debate about communal ownership of land and whether it should be alienable goes to the core of the importance of the *Mabo* decision and the land rights debate prior to that.

In the Gove Land Rights case in 1971, Justice Blackburn found that the claimants who represented eleven clans had established 'a subtle and elaborate system' and a 'stable order of society' which constituted a 'system of law'; however, he also found that this system of law, based on communal title, had 'little resemblance' to Western notions of property law and so was incapable of recognition, in no small part because of its inalienability.[9]

In *Mabo* the High Court considered whether inalienable communal ownership of land was of such uniqueness that the common law was incapable of recognising it as a proprietary interest. Justice Brennan stated that 'it would be wrong…to point to the inalienability of land by that community and, by importing definitions of "property" which require alienability under the municipal laws of our society…to deny that the indigenous people owned their land'.[10]

Prime Minister Howard restarted a debate about inalienable title in April 2005 when he visited Wadeye in the Northern Territory, saying he believed there was a case for reviewing Aboriginal land title in the sense of looking more towards private recognition. He stated 'that all Australians should be able to aspire to owning their own home and having their own business: having title to something is the key to your sense of individuality; it's the key to your capacity to achieve and to care for your family'.[11] Subsequent debate has raised the option of government compulsorily acquiring Indigenous communal land to enable individual home ownership and economic development.

In the same interview, in Wadeye the Prime Minister also talked about how pleased he is that the Northern Territory Government and Warren Mundine 'support change in the native title approach'. This leaves us with an ambiguity about whether the Prime Minister was talking about reform to the *Aboriginal Land Rights (Northern Territory) Act* (ALRA) or native title.

Either way, Howard's comments illustrate a profound cross-cultural misunderstanding. His comments are drawn purely from a Western perspective that prizes individualism and make no attempt to understand the cultural perspectives of Indigenous peoples.

I don't often get the chance to do this, but I think the best response to the Prime Minister's comments is from Senator Vanstone, who stated in her address to the National Press Club in February this year that:

> We…need to understand the richness, diversity and strength of indigenous culture. We need to understand that when Indigenous Australians take on aspects of our culture they are not necessarily discarding their own. They are in fact, walking in two worlds. Sometimes it amazes me how many people expect Indigenous

> Australians to understand and take on our culture, when so few of us even bother to begin to understand theirs.[12]

It is worth recalling the findings of the 1998 Reeves Review of the ALRA, relating to the issue of inalienable title. Justice Reeves concluded that this is the most appropriate form of title for Aboriginal land, being the form of title that is most likely to protect the interests of Aboriginal people, including future generations, in their traditional lands.[13] The review also found that the inalienability of Aboriginal freehold title does not significantly restrict the capacity of Aboriginal Territorians to raise capital for business ventures.

Importantly, the Reeves Review also notes that the achievement of Aboriginal social and economic advancement through land rights was not an objective of the ALRA when it was introduced. He noted that 'slight attention' had been given to this when the ALRA was devised twenty years ago and that the attention on this objective now may reflect that the original objectives of the ALRA (that is, of granting traditional Aboriginal land to Aboriginal people, and recognising traditional Aboriginal interests in, and relationships to, land) have largely been met.[14]

This debate can therefore also be seen as an evolution of the land rights system and the movement of it to the next stage. But to suggest that the ALRA has failed for not having met this contemporary objective takes land rights out of its historical context and confuses the issues.

My view is that removing inalienable communal title to Indigenous land is not an option. I think the Prime Minister's comments were ill conceived and demonstrably lacking in understanding.

SOME OPTIONS FOR ADDRESSING THE ECONOMIC EXCLUSION OF INDIGENOUS AUSTRALIANS THROUGH NATIVE TITLE AND COMMUNAL LAND

We now have a good opportunity to put on the table options for overcoming the exclusion of Indigenous people from economic prosperity. This debate needs to include consideration of the role of traditional land, either under native title or land rights. As I stated earlier, my starting point for looking at how native title and other communal land can be utilised to achieve economic outcomes is that the underlying communal title must not be disturbed.

I believe that it is a furphy to suggest that communal ownership is *the* barrier to enabling economic development on Indigenous land, or that it prevents home ownership. There are a range of other factors that must be considered and addressed. This can be seen to be the case when we look to some schemes which exist on communal Indigenous land in other countries and consider some options that have been put forward in the Australian context. Some of these are modest and others are more radical and long term. At the level of the individual, we need to look at the saving capacity of Indigenous people and the accessibility of banking and financial services, particularly in rural and remote areas and on Indigenous land.

There is no mystery that what excludes Indigenous people from home ownership is a lack of financial resources. The lack of employment opportunities in communities, and long-term welfare dependency combined with poor health status, virtually guarantees inter-generational poverty with no ability to inherit and build wealth. The 2006 Census also shows the average Indigenous household income to be sixty-two percent of the average of non-Indigenous households. This figure drops to approximately forty percent in very remote areas.

There is also a significant lack of banking services creating a savings deficit in Indigenous communities. Over the last fifteen years, the process of deregulation of the financial sector has impacted significantly on the accessibility of services for Indigenous people due to the combination of the historical lack of equitable access to financial services and the continued low socioeconomic status of most Indigenous people.

The inaccessibility of banking services, including, for example, the lack of electronic banking methods, often leaves Indigenous people reliant on more expensive, informal financial services such as hoteliers, taxi drivers, stores and through practices such as 'book up'. These severely constrain the already limited ability of Indigenous people to save.

The lack of provision of basic financial services is one of the most significant contributors to the ongoing poverty of Indigenous people, particularly in remote areas. This issue often doesn't feature in policy debates about issues such as home ownership or creating economic independence for Indigenous people, but it should.

The House of Representatives Standing Committee on Economics, Finance and Public Administration argued in 1999 that banking services are essential services equal in importance to clean water, health care, education and telecommunications.[15] That is the priority with which this issue should be treated.

There are a number of innovative programs that currently exist which seek to build the savings capacity and the financial literacy of Indigenous people. For example:

- Tangentyere Council in Alice Springs runs a money management and bank shopfront, with the involvement of the likes of Westpac and Centrelink;
- the Fred Hollows Foundation has completed a trial with communities in the Katherine East region of a nutrition and financial literacy program, known as the *Money $tory*;
- in Cape York there is the Family Income Management Trials focused on family budgeting and banking; and
- in Redfern and the Grafton/Kempsey area, the Hillsong Emerge program offers micro-finance to Indigenous people for small business development.

A focus on financial literacy and micro-credit models is essential to address issues that are raised by the home ownership and economic development debate.

It may also be possible for the introduction of modest changes to other existing programs to address the concerns raised in this debate. For example, ATSIC ran an extremely successful home ownership program. This is now administered by Indigenous Business Australia. It is a self-sustaining program with a sizeable capital base. The program is not, however, available for housing on communal Indigenous land. One option may be to consider mechanisms for extending this scheme onto Indigenous land.

A related option, which might be possible through the Home Ownership Scheme or separately, has been suggested by the Central Land Council. They argue that models from the United States of America for housing schemes on Indian reservation land might be adaptable to the Australian situation. These include under the Indian Housing Block Grant Scheme and the *Housing Community Development Act* (1992). Through these, the government provides guarantees to facilitate lending to individuals or tribal groups.

An important benefit of this approach is that the government is not financing the housing themselves, although they are exposing themselves to potential liability. This opens up private sector capital to Indigenous communities where it is otherwise not available. This is of particular importance given the projected rapid growth of the size of the Indigenous population, which will outstrip available funds from government for housing and infrastructure needs. This creates an incentive for government to open up private sector involvement.

In terms of entrepreneurial activity on Indigenous land, it has often been reported that some of the main barriers that Indigenous people face relate to the lack of appropriate infrastructure in communities — ranging from roads and telecommunications through to appropriate banking and financial services.

Financial institutions still do not have a lot of experience in dealing with Indigenous people, and this can contribute to difficulties in obtaining loans and obtaining sufficient capital for economic ventures. In Canada the Bank of Montreal has developed a lending guide for reservation land which demystifies concerns about investing on Indigenous communal land. This is another simple mechanism that could be advanced in Australia to promote greater accessibility to capital for investment on Indigenous land.

But let me conclude by considering two bigger picture options to stimulate investment in remote and regional economies, and which could be applied on Indigenous communal land.

First is the Community Development Financial Institutions Fund (CDFI Fund) and New Markets Tax Credit Program run by the United States Treasury. The Tax Credit Program allows taxpayers to receive a credit against federal income taxes for making qualified equity investments in designated Community Development Entities (CDEs).

A CDE is a domestic corporation or partnership that is an intermediary vehicle for the provision of loans, investments or financial counselling in low-income communities. They provide small infusions of capital to low-income individuals and distressed communities for first-home buyers, financing community facilities, support for starting or expanding small businesses, loans to rehabilitate rental housing and so forth.

A CDE must demonstrate that they have a primary mission of serving or providing investment capital for low-income communities, and are accountable to residents of the communities that they serve.

The Tax Credit Program is part of the CDFI Fund, which aims at expanding the capacity of financial institutions to provide capital, credit and financial services in under-served markets.

An example under this scheme is the Navajo Partnership for Housing. This organisation finances home loans on Navajo land and runs a home-buyer education course, financial literacy programs and a program where they purchase, rehabilitate and then on-sell properties on Navajo land. From 1998 to 2005 they packaged or financed 210 loans and grants totalling $7.7 million.

The introduction of a scheme such as this would not be unduly costly. It would require, however, a solid investment of time to ensure that communities can experience the full benefits and lessons that flow from true partnerships. I would envisage a process such as this being in place for ten, perhaps even twenty to thirty, years.

Second, is a proposal raised by Jon Altman and Mike Dillon in a recent paper for the establishment of what they call an Indigenous Profit-related Investment Scheme.[16] This proposed scheme is based on an existing venture capital scheme administered by the Commonwealth, entitled the Innovation Investment Fund (IIF). The IIF was introduced in 1998 with a $220 million investment by the federal government which has been joined with private investment totalling $138 million.

What is proposed is 'that the federal government establishes a series of new funds for investment in partnership with Indigenous corporations in commercial development projects on Indigenous land'.[17] The government would have the role of investor and underwriting risk, as well as a role as a regulator. It would be a profit-contingent loan or capped public investment mechanism to finance development opportunities on Indigenous land.

The proposal involves the establishment of five funds with an initial outlay by the government of $100 million. Fund managers would then be selected by tender to manage the funds and would be required to raise or contribute ten to thirty percent of the capital. Each fund would invest in a number of commercial projects and be required to have a minimum Indigenous investment equity holding of at least thirty percent. The funds would run for ten years.

I commend this proposal to you as an innovative example of how government can more effectively support achieving economic independence for Indigenous communities on communally owned Indigenous land. At a total cost of $100 million over ten years, to be repaid where schemes succeed, there is no reason why government could not trial such a model.

Overall, what these options demonstrate is that there are significant opportunities for building genuine partnerships with Indigenous communities for economic development. Government can play a key role — not by seeking to undermine Indigenous title, but by exploring other options such as offering guarantees, tax breaks and other incentives for private investment.

Communities must be responsible for changing their situations themselves. There is now not much room left for charity, but lots of room for inclusion, partnerships and broadening the level of engagement between governments, private investors and Indigenous people.

CONCLUSION

Finally, I want to stress that the broader engagement is already occurring and nowhere is that more obvious, in the native title context, than in Indigenous Land Use Agreements (ILUAs). At the time of giving this paper there were over 170 ILUAs registered — one hundred of them in Queensland.[18] At the time of publication there will be over four hundred. Practical, flexible agreements like these are signs of communities moving forward.

If we return to the challenge of Mabo — that is *Mabo* the decision and Koiki Mabo, the man — we must remember that it is not about doing more of the same but it is about how we can do things differently.

In conclusion, I am pleased to have been able to participate in the national Native Title Conference. I think that it takes on increased significance in the post-ATSIC world.

This conference now stands as one of very few forums in which Indigenous people are able to get together annually to assess where we are at, to share information about successes, to identify systemic problems in the native title system, and to look to ways forward. So I want to leave you with a plea.

We need to give attention to the issue of how we will have a voice at a national level, and this conference is ideally placed to set some directions for governments by indicating with clarity what Indigenous people think about the current state of land law in this country.

I urge you to consider how a conference which is as well organised and patronised as this one could be better utilised to give voice to Indigenous concerns about native title. Already there is an Indigenous stream to the conference, and perhaps there could be a declaration or statement that emerges from this stream of the conference every year to provide an unambiguous and clear message to governments about these issues which affect us directly.

As important as it is, forums like these need to be more than academic talk-fests. Indigenous people need to take leadership of the process and be proactive.

I hope that I have left you with some ideas that can stimulate debate along these lines.

NOTES

Introduction: The legacy of Mabo's case
1. *Mabo v Queensland [No. 2]* (1992) 175 CLR 1.
2. *Members of the Yorta Yorta Aboriginal Community v Victoria* (2002) 214 CLR 422.
3. *Western Australia v Ward* (2002) 213 CLR 1.

1. Mabo Lecture: Asserting our sovereignty
1. Human Rights and Equal Opportunity Commission, *Aboriginal and Torres Strait Islander Social Justice Commission: First Report*, Canberra, 1993, p. 41.
2. United Nations Declaration on the Rights of Indigenous Peoples, G.A. Res. 61/295, Annex, U.N. Doc. A/RES:61/295 (Sept. 13, 2007), Article 3.
3. *Mabo v Queensland [No. 2]* (1992) 175 CLR 1.
4. See *Wik Peoples v Queensland* (1996) 187 CLR 184; *Ward v Western Australia* (1998) 159 ALR 483; *Mary Yarmirr and Others v Northern Territory and Others* (1998) 82 FCR 533 (Croker Island); *Gumana v Northern Territory of Australia* [2005] FCA 50 (Blue Mud Bay); *Bennell v State of Western Australia* (2006) 153 FCR 120 (Noongar); *Rubibi Community v State of Western Australia (No. 7)* [2006] FCA 459 (Yawuru).
5. See *Bennell v State of Western Australia* (2006) 153 FCR 120, at 83(g) (Wilcox J).
6. Human Rights and Equal Opportunity Commission, *Bringing Them Home: The 'Stolen Children' report*, Human Rights and Equal Opportunity Commission. 2005, <http://www.humanrights.gov.au/social_justice/bth_report/index.html> viewed 11 February 2010.
7. *Aboriginal Land Rights (Northern Territory) Act 1976* (Cth).
8. See M Dodson, 'Violence dysfunction Aboriginality', speech delivered at the National Press Club, Canberra, 11 June 2003.
9. M Dodson, 'Speech by Professor Mick Dodson', speech delivered at Taking the Next Steps luncheon, Melbourne, 25 July 2006.
10. J Howard, 'Speech by Prime Minister John Howard', speech delivered at Taking the Next Steps luncheon, Melbourne, 25 July 2006.
11. PBCs or Registered Native Title Bodies Corporate (RNTBCs) are required to be established and are determined at the time of a determination to hold or manage recognised native title on behalf of the common law native title holders, under s 55ff of the NTA.

2. Confessions of a native judge: Reflections on the role of transitional justice in the transformation of indigeneity
1. *Mabo v Queensland [No. 2]* (1992) 175 CLR 1.
2. *Wik Peoples v Queensland* (1996) 187 CLR 184.
3. Native title remained a live issue in New Zealand during much of this period, particularly in the two areas of fishing rights and title in the foreshore and seabed, but land claims dominated both Crown and Māori attention. Because of the historical recognition, in theory at least, of native title to land, the focus of modern land claims was the means by which those titles were extinguished during and after the colonial period.
4. Here Tawhiao has cleverly embedded multiple meanings into his words in a way for which the great philosophers of the Māori world were renowned. *Rengarenga* is pounded fern-root meal, a very humble food, but it is also used to describe things that are scattered about. He thus also imports the idea that the reality for him and

his people will be as a scattered remnant in the foreseeable future — literally, they will eat the fruits of their defeat. Similarly, *kawariki* is a swamp plant, but according to the Williams Dictionary it is also sometimes applied to children (*riki* means small). So it is possible that he also intended to mean that strength — *whakapakari* — would only come with succeeding generations.

5. PJ Keating, speech delivered at Australian launch of the International Year of the World's Indigenous Peoples, Redfern, 10 December 1992. Published in *Aboriginal Law Bulletin* 3(61), April 1993, pp. 4–5.
6. H Wootten, 'The humanities and the law' in I McCalman and A McGrath (eds), *Proof and Truth,* The Australian Academy of the Humanities, Canberra, 2003, pp. 15, 34.

3. Mabo Lecture: Where we've come from and where we're at with the opportunity that is Koiki Mabo's legacy to Australia

1. *Western Australia v Ward* (2002) 213 CLR 1 (*Miriuwung Gajerrong*); *Members of the Yorta Yorta Aboriginal Community v Victoria* (2002) 214 CLR 422 (*Yorta Yorta*).
2. *Mabo v Queensland [No. 2]* (1992) 175 CLR 1 (*Mabo*).
3. Note the *Eastern Kuku Yalanji* determination: *Walker on behalf of the Eastern Kuku Yalanji v Queensland* [2007] FCA 1907; *Western Yalanji* determination: *Riley v Queensland* [2006] FCA 72.
4. *Western Australia v Commonwealth* (1995) 183 CLR 373 (*NTA* case).
5. WEH Stanner, 'Some notes on Aboriginal law and its possible recognition', paper for Mr Justice Kirby, Law Reform Commission, AIATSIS, Canberra, c. 1978, MS 3752, Item 405; later published: 'Aboriginal "law" misunderstood', *Canberra Times*, 26 May 1980, pp. 20, 22.
6. *Mabo v Queensland [No. 2]* (1992) 175 CLR 1, at [48] (Brennan J) citing *In re Southern Rhodesia* [1919] AC 211 at 233–234.
7. *Mabo v Queensland [No. 2]* (1992) 175 CLR 1, at [41] (Brennan J).
8. *Mabo v Queensland [No. 2]* (1992) 175 CLR 1, at [40] (Brennan J) citing *Western Sahara (Advisory Opinion)* [1975] ICJR 12, at 39; at [53] (Brennan J).
9. *Delgamuukw v British Columbia* (1997) 3 SCR 1010, at [119], [122] & [124] (Lamer CJ).
10. ibid. at [80]–[81] citing *R v Van der Peet* (1996) 2 SCR 507 (emphasis removed) (references omitted).
11. *Members of the Yorta Yorta Aboriginal Community v Victoria* (2002) 214 CLR 422, at [8], [81] & [82] citing *Milirrpum v Nabalco Pty Ltd* (1971) 17 FLR 141, at 151–165.
12. *Mabo v Queensland [No. 2]* (1992) 175 CLR 1, at [50] (Deane & Gaudron JJ).
13. N Pearson, 'The High Court's abandonment of "the time-honoured methodology of the common law" in its interpretation of native title in Miriuwung Gajerrong and Yorta Yorta', speech delivered at the Sir Ninian Stephen Lecture, University of Newcastle Law School, 17 March 2003, <www.cyi.org.au/speeches.aspx> viewed 2 February 2010.
14. *Members of the Yorta Yorta Aboriginal Community v Victoria* (2002) 214 CLR 422, at [129]–[133] (McHugh J).
15. ibid., at [134].
16. *R v Van der Peet* (1996) 2 SCR 507, at [261] (McLachlin J).
17. *Members of the Yorta Yorta Aboriginal Community v Victoria* (2002) 214 CLR 422, at [75]–[76] (Gleeson CJ Gummow & Hayne JJ).
18. Pearson, above, n. 13, p. 29.

19. See High Court Transcripts P59/2000, 6 March 2001.
20. *Members of the Yorta Yorta Community v Victoria* [1998] FCA 1606.
21. ibid., at [25].
22. ibid., at [104].
23. ibid.

4. Native title is property

* Note that this paper is adapted from submissions made to the High Court on behalf of the Kimberley Land Council and the Gija and Malngin peoples in *Western Australia v Ward* (2002) 213 CLR 1. Walter Sofronoff QC contributed to and settled those submissions and so, indirectly, contributed to this paper.
1. *Mabo v Queensland [No. 1]* (1988) 166 CLR 186 (*Mabo [No. 1]*). Because of the operation of the *Racial Discrimination Act 1975* (Cth), s 10, which invoked the human right to own property and not be arbitrarily deprived of it, accorded by Article 5 of the International Convention on the Elimination of All Forms of Racial Discrimination and Article 17 of the Universal Declaration of Human Rights (1948).
2. *Western Australia v Ward* (2000) 99 FCR 316. Postscript: *Western Australia v Ward* (2002) 213 CLR 1.
3. Gleeson CJ, Gaudron, Kirby and Hayne JJ in *Yanner v Eaton* (1999) 201 CLR 351, at 366, quoting K Gray and SF Gray, 'The idea of property in land' in S Bright and J Dewar (eds), *Land Law: Themes and perspectives,* Oxford University Press, Oxford, 1998, pp. 15–16.
4. *Yanner v Eaton* (1999) 201 CLR 351, at [17]. Note also that 'Property is not a block of cheese…' as described by Gummow J in the course of argument being put by Walter Sofronoff QC in *Yanner v Eaton*.
5. K Gray, 'Property in thin air', *Cambridge Law Journal* 50(2), 1991, pp. 251, 299.
6. K Gray and SF Gray, *Elements of Land Law* (3rd edn), Butterworths, London, 2001, pp. 94, 96.
7. *Western Australia v Ward* (2000) 99 FCR 316, at 354–356 referring to K Gray & SF Gray, above, n. 3, p. 27.
8. K Gray and SF Gray, above, n. 3, p. 113, referring to *Western Australia v Ward* (2000) 99 FCR 316, per Beaumont and von Doussa JJ at [187] and [189] and *Minister of State for the Army v Dalziel* (1944) 68 CLR 261, at 285 per Rich J.
9. K Gray and SF Gray, above, n. 6, pp. 115, 118.
10. *Yanner v Eaton* (1999) 201 CLR 351, at [269]–[270] (emphasis added), quoting K Gray and SF Gray, above, n. 3, p. 27.
11. Gummow J in *Wik Peoples v Queensland* (1996) 187 CLR 184, at 169, relying on various dicta in *Mabo v Queensland [No. 2]* (1992) 175 CLR 1 from Brennan J at 58, 66–67 and Deane and Gaudron JJ at 89.
12. See *Native Title Act 1993* (Cth), s 223(1).
13. *Mabo v Queensland [No. 2]* (1992) 175 CLR 1, at 207.
14. See Beaumont and von Doussa JJ in *Ward v Western Australia* (1998) 159 ALR 483, at [207]–[208].
15. K McNeil, 'The relevance of traditional laws and customs to the existence and content of native title at common law' in K McNeil (ed.), *Emerging Justice? Essays on Indigenous rights in Canada and Australia,* Native Law Centre, University of Saskatchewan, Canada, 2001, pp. 416, 420; N Pearson, 'Concept of native title at common law' in *Land Rights — Past, present and future: Conference papers,* Canberra,

16–17 August 1996, Northern Land Council and Central Land Council, Darwin and Alice Springs, p. 118; G Meyers, 'The content of native title: questions for the Miriuwung Gajerrong appeal' in *Land, Rights, Laws: Issues of native title,* Native Title Research Unit, AIATSIS, Canberra, vol. 2, Issues Paper No. 7, 2000, p. 3.

16. McNeil, above, n. 15, pp. 6–17; relying on *Mabo v Queensland [No. 2]* (1992) 175 CLR 1, per Brennan J at 51–52, Deane and Gaudron JJ at 86, Toohey J at 184–192, 194–195, 207–214.
17. McNeil, above, n. 15, pp. 29–30, relying on *Mabo v Queensland [No. 2]* (1992) 175 CLR 1 per Brennan J at 61, Deane and Gaudron JJ at 110, Toohey J at 192; a view adopted by Beaumont and von Doussa JJ in *Western Australia v Ward* (2000) 99 FCR 316, at 212–213; see Meyers, above, n. 15, p. 5.
18. McNeil, above, n. 15, p. 11, referring to Brennan J in *Mabo v Queensland [No. 2]* (1992) 175 CLR 1, at 22.
19. McNeil, above, n. 15, p. 10; see also N Pearson, above, n. 15, p. 4.
20. McNeil, above, n. 15, pp. 24–27, relying on Gummow J in *Yanner v Eaton* (1999) 201 CLR 351, at [278] and *Fejo v Northern Territory of Australia* (1998) 195 CLR 96, and K McNeil, above, n. 15, pp. 39–40, referring to Merkel J in *Yarmirr v Northern Territory* (1998) 156 ALR 370, at 495.
21. McNeil, above, n. 15, p. 43, relying on Gummow J in *Yanner v Eaton* (1999) 201 CLR 351 and Merkel J in *Yarmirr v Northern Territory* [1999] FCA 1668.
22. North J in *Western Australia v Ward* (2000) 99 FCR 316, at [792].
23. Lee J in *Ward v Western Australia* (1998) 159 ALR 483, at 507; and Lamer CJ in *Delgamuukw v British Columbia* [1997] 3 SCR 1010, at [137].
24. *Mabo v Queensland [No. 2]* (1992) 175 CLR 1, at 58.
25. ibid., at 61.
26. ibid., at 75 (Brennan J).
27. ibid., at 22 (Brennan J).
28. *Western Australia v Ward* (2000) 99 FCR 316, at [534].
29. *Ward v Western Australia* (1998) 159 ALR 483, at 508.
30. *Mabo v Queensland [No. 2]* (1992) 175 CLR 1, at 88.
31. ibid., at 58, 60 (Brennan J); Deane and Gaudron JJ at 88, 110; and Mason CJ and McHugh J at 15–16.
32. *Fejo v Northern Territory of Australia* (1998) 195 CLR 96, at 731; per Gleeson CJ, Gaudron, McHugh, Gummow, Hayne and Callinan JJ and per Lee J *Ward v Western Australia* (1998) 159 ALR 483, at 507.
33. *Western Australia v Ward* (2000) 99 FCR 316, at [96].
34. ibid., at [106]–[108].
35. ibid., at [99]. See also *Yanner v Eaton* (1999) 201 CLR 351, [269]–[270].
36. K Gray & SF Gray, above, n. 6, p. 113, referring to *Western Australia v Ward* (2000) 99 FCR 316, at [187], [189] (Beaumont and von Doussa JJ); and *Minister of State for the Army v Dalziel* (1944) 68 CLR 261, at 285 (Rich J).
37. *Contra* Beaumont and von Doussa JJ in *Western Australia v Ward* (2000) 99 FCR 316, at [106].
38. *Western Australia v Ward* (2000) 99 FCR 316, at [106]–[108]. See *In re Southern Rhodesia* [1919] AC 211, at 233–234.
39. *Western Australia v Ward* (2000) 99 FCR 316, at [784].
40. *Mabo v Queensland [No. 1]* (1988) 166 CLR 186, at 213–214; *Mabo v Queensland [No. 2]* (1992) 175 CLR 1, at 110–111, 136, 138, 193, 195–196; *Western Australia v Commonwealth* (1995) 183 CLR 373, at 423; *Wik Peoples v Queensland* (1996) 187 CLR 184, at 242–243.

41. *Mabo v Queensland [No. 1]* (1988) 166 CLR 186, at 213, 223.
42. Cf *Sorby v The Commonwealth* (1983) 46 ALR 237; *Pyneboard Pty Ltd v Trade Practices Commission* (1993) 45 ALR 609.
43. *Hamilton v Oades* (1989) 166 CLR 486, at 495.
44. *Delgamuukw v British Columbia* (1993) 104 DLR (4th) 470 at [529]; quoted with approval in the joint judgment of the High Court in *Western Australia v The Commonwealth* (1995) 183 CLR 373, at 433.
45. *Wik Peoples v Queensland* (1996) 187 CLR 184, at 126, 201, 225, 243.
46. *Ward v Western Australia* (1998) 159 ALR 483, at 507–509 (Lee J); *Western Australia v Ward* (2000) 99 FCR 316, at [844]–[861] (North J).
47. *Western Australia v The Commonwealth* (1995) 183 CLR 373, at 422; *Ward v Western Australia* (1998) 159 ALR 483, at 508 (Lee J).
48. *Western Australia v The Commonwealth* (1995) 183 CLR 373, at 422; *Ward v Western Australia* (1998) 159 ALR 483, at 508 (Lee J); see also *Wik Peoples v Queensland* (1996) 187 CLR 184, at 133 (Toohey J), 86 (Brennan CJ), 135 (Gaudron J), 185 (Gummow J) and 221 (Kirby J), where it is emphasised that the focus is upon the 'rights conferred' by the doing of the act.
49. *United States v Santa Fe Pacific Railroad Co* (1941) 314 US 339, 347; *Ward v Western Australia* (1998) 159 ALR 483, at 508 (Lee J). Lee J noted that for extinguishment to occur under the 'adverse dominion' test there must be (i) a clear and plain expression of intention of the parliament to bring about extinguishment by adverse dominion; (ii) an act which demonstrates the exercise of permanent adverse dominion in accordance with the legislation; and (iii) actual use of the land pursuant to the tenure which is permanently inconsistent with the continued existence of native title.
50. *Ward v Western Australia* (1998) 159 ALR 483, at 508–509; Brennan J in *Mabo v Queensland [No. 2]* (1992) 175 CLR 1, at 68, 70; *Wik Peoples v Queensland* (1996) 187 CLR 184, at 166 (Gaudron J), 203 (Gummow J).
51. *Wik Peoples v Queensland* (1996) 187 CLR 184, at 85–86.
52. *Ward v Western Australia* (1998) 159 ALR 483, at [67]–[73]. The High Court expressly rejected the adverse dominion test, preferring the idea of Crown acquisition for inconsistent purpose: *Western Australia v Ward* (2002) 213 CLR 1.
53. See *Mabo v Queensland [No. 1]* (1988) 166 CLR 186.
54. See *Fejo v Northern Territory of Australia* (1998) 195 CLR 96.
55. *Western Australia v Ward* (2000) 99 FCR 316, at [82]. They apply that conclusion and suggest that a permanently extinguishing effect may relate to rights in relation to a pre-existing pastoral lease.
56. *Fejo v Northern Territory of Australia* (1998) 195 CLR 96.
57. *Wik Peoples v Queensland* (1996) 187 CLR 184, at 133 (Toohey J, speaking with the concurrence of Gaudron, Gummow and Kirby JJ).
58. See *Wik Peoples v Queensland* (1996) 187 CLR 184, Toohey J at 128, Gaudron J at 154, Gummow J at 186–90 and Kirby J at 233–5.
59. *Mabo v Queensland [No. 2]* (1992) 175 CLR 1, at 50. There, Brennan J had said that a reversion expectant on the expiry of the term of a statutory 'lease' of the kind then under consideration expanded the Crown's radical title to a *plenum dominium*.
60. *Wik Peoples v Queensland* (1996) 187 CLR 184, at 94.
61. *Western Australia v Ward* (2000) 99 FCR 316, at [125]–[143].
62. ibid., at [90], [109].
63. *Mabo v Queensland [No. 2]* (1992) 175 CLR 1, at 169.

Notes

64. *Wik Peoples v Queensland* (1996) 187 CLR 184, at 132.
65. *Ward v Western Australia* (1998) 159 ALR 483, at 509–510.
66. *North Ganalanja Aboriginal Corporation & Waanyi People v Queensland* (1996) 185 CLR 595.
67. *Ward v Western Australia* (1998) 159 ALR 483, at 508 (Lee J) referring to Lamer CJ in *Delgamuukw v British Columbia* (1993) 104 DLR (4th) 470, at [240]–[241].
68. See Lee J in *Ward v Western Australia* (1998) 159 ALR 483, at 510.
69. Meyers, above, n. 15, p. 3, relying on Lee J in *Ward v Western Australia* (1998) 159 ALR 483, at 508. Meyers at p. 4 concludes that the opinion of Beaumont and von Doussa JJ supports the proposition that there can be no partial extinguishment of possessory native title. He does not, however, explain why or cite a passage from which that conclusion can be derived.
70. *Wik Peoples v Queensland* (1996) 187 CLR 184, at 86.
71. See *Mabo v Queensland [No. 2]* (1992) 175 CLR 1, at 68 (Brennan J), 110 (Deane and Gaudron JJ).
72. ibid., at 69.
73. *Wik Peoples v Queensland* (1996) 187 CLR 184, at 133.
74. *Fejo v Northern Territory of Australia* (1998) 195 CLR 96, at 737.
75. *Western Australia v Ward* (2002) 213 CLR 1.
76. *Western Australia v Ward* (2000) 99 FCR 316, at 207.
77. ibid., at 316.
78. ibid., at 405.
79. ibid., at 329, 454, 456–470.
80. ibid., at 316.
81. ibid., at 446.
82. ibid., at 329, 641.
83. *Lardil and other Peoples v Queensland* [2001] FCA 414 (11 April 2001). See also French, this volume, Chapter 6.
84. *Lardil and other Peoples v Queensland* [2001] FCA 414 (11 April 2001), [45].
85. *Fejo v Northern Territory of Australia* (1998) 195 CLR 96 at [128].
86. K Gray & SF Gray, above, n. 6, p. 96.
87. *Western Australia v Ward* (2000) 99 FCR 316, [104].
88. *Fejo v Northern Territory of Australia* (1998) 195 CLR 96, at 126, 128.
89. Brennan J in *R v Toohey; Ex parte Meneling Station Pty Ltd* (1982) 158 CLR 327 and Beaumont and von Doussa JJ in *Western Australia v Ward* (2000) 99 FCR 316, at [104].
90. *Mabo v Queensland [No. 2]* (1992) 175 CLR 1, Order.
91. *Mabo v Queensland [No. 2]* (1992) 175 CLR 1, at 208–9 (Toohey J).
92. See *Mining Act 1978* (WA), s 85(3).
93. *Delgamuukw v British Columbia* (1993) 104 DLR (4th) 470, at [117], [155]–[157] and [185], also La Forest J at 196.
94. *Delgamuukw v British Columbia* (1993) 104 DLR (4th) 470, at [158], referring to *United States v Santa Fe Pacific Railroad Co* (1941) 314 US 339.
95. *Ward v Western Australia* (1998) 159 ALR 483, at 510. See also M Tehan, 'Co-existence of interests in land: a dominant feature of the common law', *Land, Rights, Laws: Issues of native title*, Native Title research Unit, AIATSIS, Issues Paper No. 12, January 1997, p. 4.
96. McNeil, above, n. 15, p. 8, refers to fn 17 in K McNeil, *Common Law Aboriginal Title*, Clarendon Press, Oxford, 1989.

97. *Mabo v Queensland [No. 2]* (1992) 175 CLR 1, at 189–90.
98. The use by Meyers of the concept of 'exclusive occupation' is also appropriately to be understood in that way.

5. A curious history of the *Mabo* litigation

1. Galarrwuy Yunupingu, 'Mabo Lecture', Native Title Conference 2006: Tradition and Change; Culture and Commerce, Darwin, Northern Territory, 24–26 May 2006.
2. E Pownall, *The Australia Book*, (illus. M Senior), The House of John Sands, Sydney, 1952; Black Dog Books, Fitzroy, Vic., 2008.
3. Brennan J in *Walden v Hensler* (1987) 163 CLR 561, at 565.
4. *Mabo v Queensland [No. 2]* (1992) 175 CLR 1.
5. L Strelein, *Compromised Jurisprudence: Native title cases since Mabo*, Aboriginal Studies Press, Canberra, 2006, p. 1.
6. See M Connor, *The Invention of Terra Nullius: Historical and legal fictions on the foundation of Australia*, Macleay Press, Paddington, NSW, 2005.
7. ibid., p. 2.
8. *Mabo v Queensland [No. 2]* (1992) 175 CLR 1, at 66.
9. *In re Southern Rhodesia* [1919] AC 211, at 233.
10. *Milirrpum v Nabalco Pty Ltd* (1971) 17 FLR 141.
11. *Mabo v Queensland [No. 2]* (1992) 175 CLR 1, at 99–100.
12. ibid., at 145.
13. ibid., at 120.
14. *Fejo v Northern Territory* (1998) 195 CLR 96.
15. Tim Fischer, Deputy Prime Minister and Minister for Trade, quoted in J Brough, 'Wik draft threat to native title', *Sydney Morning Herald*, 28 June 1997, p. 3.
16. *Mabo v Queensland [No. 2]* (1992) 175 CLR 1, at 138–139.

6. The role of the High Court and the recognition of native title: Address in honour of Ron Castan QC AM

* A version of this paper was published in the University of Western Australia Law Review: R French, 'The Role of the High Court in the recognition of native title', 30 *UWA Law Review* 129, 2001-2

1. R Castan, 'Land, memory and reconciliation', keynote address at Indigenous–Jewish Forum on Land, Memory and Reconciliation, Monash University, November 1998, p. 3.
2. WEH Stanner, 'After the Dreaming: Black and White Australians – An Anthropologist's View', The Boyer Lectures (1969) 18, at 53.
3. Castan, above, n. i, p. 6.
4. *Wik Peoples v Queensland* (1996) 187 CLR 1, at 182 (Gummow J).
5. R Castan, 'Native land title in Australia: reflections on Mabo', address to Annual Dinner of Australian Jewish Democratic Society, 1993.
6. G Yunupingu, 'Letter from black to white', *Land Rights News* 2(6), 1976, p. 9.
7. Federal Court Rules O 78 r 32. Postscript: the *Native Title Amendment Act 1998* (Cth) reverted to application of the normal rules of evidence. However, this position has again been reconsidered with proposed amendments to the *Evidence Act 1995* (Cth).
8. *Milirrpum v Nabalco Pty Ltd* (1971) 17 FLR 141.
9. *Cooper v Stuart* (1889) 14 App Cas 286.

10. ibid., at 291.
11. *MacDonald v Levy* (1833) 1 Legge 39, at 45.
12. *Attorney General v Brown* (1847) 1 Legge 312; *Williams v Attorney General (NSW)* (1913) 16 CLR 404.
13. *In re Southern Rhodesia* [1919] AC 211.
14. ibid., at 233–234.
15. *Amodu Tijani v The Secretary, Southern Nigeria* [1921] 2 AC 399, at 403.
16. *Milirrpum v Nabalco Pty Ltd* (1971) 17 FLR 141, at 267.
17. *The Administration of the Territory of Papua and New Guinea v Daera Guba* (1973) 130 CLR 353, at 458 (Gibbs J); see also at 397 (Barwick CJ).
18. Castan, above, n. i, p. 1.
19. ibid., p. 2.
20. ibid., p. 7.
21. Aboriginal Land Rights Commission, *Second Report, April 1974*, Parliamentary Paper No. 69, Parliament of the Commonwealth of Australia, Canberra, 1975.
22. Report on Yingaunarri (Old Top Springs) Mudbura Land Claim — AGPS, Canberra, 1980, at [70].
23. *Pitjantjatjara Land Rights Act 1981* (SA), *Land Act (Aboriginal and Islander Land Grants) Amendment Act 1982* (Qld), *Maralinga Tjarutja Land Rights Act 1984* (SA), *Aboriginal Land Rights Act 1984* (NSW), *Aboriginal Land Act 1991* (Qld), *Torres Strait Islander Land Act 1991* (Qld). *The Aboriginal Land (Lake Condah and Framlingham Forest) Act 1987* was passed by the Commonwealth Government on the request of the Victorian Government to grant freehold title to a corporation of elders who had proven their clan's traditional relationship to the land. There is otherwise no general provision for statutory grants of Aboriginal land rights in Victoria.
24. CD Rowley, *Recovery: The politics of Aboriginal reform,* Penguin Books, Australia, 1986, p. 84.
25. Castan, above, n. v.
26. *R v Toohey; Ex parte Attorney General (NT)* (1980) 145 CLR 374.
27. *R v Toohey; Ex parte Northern Land Council* (1981) 151 CLR 170.
28. *R v Toohey; Ex parte Stanton* (1982) 44 ALR 94.
29. *R v Toohey; Ex parte Meneling Station Pty Ltd* (1982) 158 CLR 327.
30. *R v Kearney; Ex parte Northern Land Council* (1984) 158 CLR 365.
31. *R v Kearney; Ex parte Japanangka* (1984) 158 CLR 395.
32. *R v Kearney; Ex parte Jurlama* (1984) 158 CLR 426.
33. *Minister for Aboriginal Affairs v Peko Wallsend* (1986) 162 CLR 24.
34. *Attorney General (NT) v Kearney* (1985) 158 CLR 500.
35. *Northern Land Council v The Commonwealth* (1986) 161 CLR 1.
36. *Northern Land Council v The Commonwealth (No. 2)* (1987) 75 ALR 210.
37. *Attorney General (NT) v Maurice* (1986) 161 CLR 475.
38. *Attorney General (NT) v Hand* (1991) 172 CLR 185.
39. *Commonwealth v Northern Land Council* (1993) 176 CLR 605.
40. *R v Toohey; Ex parte Meneling Station Pty Ltd* (1982) 158 CLR 327, at 355.
41. *R v Toohey; Ex parte Attorney General (NT)* (1980) 145 CLR 374, at 392.
42. *R v Toohey; Ex parte Meneling Station Pty Ltd* (1982) 158 CLR 327, at 358.
43. *Northern Land Council v Commonwealth* (1987) 75 ALR 210, at 215.
44. *Koowarta v Bjelke-Petersen* (1982) 153 CLR 168.
45. ibid., at 200 (Gibbs CJ); 245 (Aickin J concurring); 251 (Wilson J).
46. ibid., at 217 (Stephen J).

47. ibid., at 218 (Stephen J); see also 227 (Mason J); 238–239 (Murphy J) and 258 (Brennan J).
48. ibid., at 186 (Gibbs CJ, Aickin J agreeing); 209 (Stephen J); 244 (Wilson J).
49. ibid., at 242.
50. *Commonwealth v Tasmania* (1983) 158 CLR 1.
51. ibid., at 159.
52. ibid., at 242.
53. An account of the proceedings may be seen in R Castan and B Keon-Cohen, 'Mabo and the High Court: A reply to S.E.K. Hulme QC', *Victorian Bar News*, no. 87, 1993, p. 47.
54. *Queensland Coast Islands Declaratory Act 1985* (Qld),s. 3
55. *Mabo v Queensland [No. 1]* (1988) 166 CLR 186, at 213 (Brennan, Toohey and Gaudron JJ).
56. ibid., at 218-219.
57. Castan, above, n. v.
58. R Castan, *Australian Catharsis: Coping with native title,* Jewish Ozzies Inter.Net — Selected Articles, B'nai B'rith Oration, 1993, <http://www.join.org.au/articles/ntitle.htm> viewed 11 February 2010.
59. *Mabo v Queensland [No. 2]* (1992) 175 CLR 1.
60. ibid., at 76 (Brennan J); 216 (Toohey J).
61. ibid.
62. ibid., at 57, 69 (Brennan J, Mason CJ and McHugh J agreeing); 81 (Deane and Gaudron JJ); 184 and 205 (Toohey J).
63. ibid., at 60 and 61 (Brennan J); 81, 82, 86–87 (Deane and Gaudron JJ); 187 (Toohey J).
64. ibid., at 64 (Brennan J); 111, 114 and 119 (Deane and Gaudron JJ); 195–196 and 205 (Toohey J).
65. ibid., at 59–60 and 70 (Brennan J); 86 and 110 (Deane and Gaudron JJ); 188 (Toohey J).
66. ibid., at 59 (Brennan J); 110 (Deane and Gaudron JJ).
67. ibid., at 52 and 62 (Brennan J); 85–86 and 88, 119–110 (Deane and Gaudron JJ).
68. ibid., at 60 and 70 (Brennan J); 88 and 110 (Deane and Gaudron JJ).
69. ibid., at 60 (Brennan J); 110 (Deane and Gaudron JJ).
70. ibid., at 61 (Brennan J); 110 (Deane and Gaudron JJ); 192 (Toohey J).
71. ibid., at 63, 69 and 73 (Brennan J); 111–112 (Deane and Gaudron JJ).
72. ibid., at 42.
73. For discussion see SJ Anaya, *Indigenous Peoples in International Law* (2nd edn), Oxford University Press, New York, 2004, pp. 15–26.
74. *Adeyinka Oyekan v Musendiku Adele* [1957] 1 WLR 876, at 880.
75. *Mabo v Queensland [No. 2]* (1992) 175 CLR 1, at 109.
76. *Wik Peoples v Queensland* (1996) 187 CLR 1, at 179–180.
77. *Mabo v Queensland [No. 2]* (1992) 175 CLR 1, at 178.
78. ibid., at 51.
79. ibid.
80. *Western Australia v Ward* (2000) 170 ALR 159, at 221 (Beaumont and von Doussa JJ).
81. *Mabo v Queensland [No. 2]* (1992) 175 CLR 1, at 85.
82. ibid., at 89.
83. ibid, at 178-179.
84. ibid.

85. ibid., at 70.
86. *Wik Peoples v Queensland* (1996) 187 CLR 1, at 126 (emphasis added).
87. *Fejo v Northern Territory of Australia* (1998) 195 CLR 96.
88. ibid., at 128. (emphasis added).
89. ibid., at 131.
90. N Pearson, 'The concept of native title at common law' in G Yunupingu (ed.), *Our Land is Our Life: Land rights — past, present and future,* University of Queensland Press, St Lucia, 1997. See also the discussion by Professor P Patton of the University of Sydney Philosophy Department, 'The translation of Indigenous land into property: the mere analogy of English jurisprudence', *Parallax* 6(1), 2000, pp. 25–38.
91. *Lardil and other Peoples v State of Queensland* (2001) 108 FCR 453, at 470.
92. *Western Australia v Commonwealth* (1995) 183 CLR 373.
93. The cases were heard together and dealt with in the same judgment.
94. *Western Australia v Commonwealth* (1995) 183 CLR 373, at 452-453.
95. ibid., at 422.
96. ibid., at 459.
97. ibid., at 461.
98. ibid., at 462.
99. ibid., at 463.
100. ibid.
101. *North Ganalanja Aboriginal Corporation v State of Queensland* (1996) 185 CLR 595.
102. ibid., at 613-614.
103. ibid., at 614.
104. ibid.
105. ibid.
106. ibid.
107. ibid.
108. ibid., at 616-617.
109. ibid., at 617.
110. *Northern Territory v Lane* (1995) 59 FCR 332; *Kanak v National Native Title Tribunal* (1995) 132 ALR 329.
111. *Brandy v Human Rights and Equal Opportunity Commission* (1995) 183 CLR 245.
112. *Wik Peoples v Queensland* (1996) 187 CLR 1.
113. ibid., at 86 (Brennan CJ, Dawson and McHugh JJ agreeing), 124 (Toohey J); 186 (Gummow J); 238 (Kirby J).
114. ibid., at 237.
115. ibid., at 184.
116. *Kartinyeri v Commonwealth* (1998) 195 CLR 337.
117. *Fejo v Northern Territory of Australia* (1998) 195 CLR 96.
118. ibid., at 125 — a comment based upon the NTA as it stood prior to the 1998 amendments.
119. ibid.
120. ibid., at 128.
121. ibid.
122. ibid., at 131, citing *Mabo v Queensland [No. 2]* (1992) 175 CLR 1, at 63 (Brennan J).
123. *Yanner v Eaton (1999) 201 CLR 351.*
124. ibid., at 373, citing K Gray and SF Gray, 'The idea of property in land' in S Bright and J Dewar (eds), *Land Law: Themes and perspectives,* Oxford University Press, Oxford, 1998, p. 27.

125. ibid.
126. ibid., at 383.
127. *Western Australia v Ward* (2002) 213 CLR 1.
128. *Yarmirr v Northern Territory* (2001) 208 CLR 1.
129. *Patrick Stevedores Operations No. 2 Pty Ltd v Maritime Union of Australia* (1998) 195 CLR 1, at 16.
130. *Wik Peoples v Queensland* (1996) 187 CLR 1, at 133.

7. Hypothesising social native title

1. The author's evolved views can be found in D Ritter, *The Native Title Market*, UWA Press, Perth, 2009, and D Ritter, *Contesting Native Title*, Allen & Unwin, Sydney, 2009.
2. *Mabo v Queensland [No. 2]* (1992) 175 CLR 1.
3. H Wootten, 'Native title in a long perspective: a view from the eighties', paper presented at the Native Title Representative Bodies Conference, Geraldton, 3 September 2002, p. 3, <http://www.aas.asn.au/publications/Conference%202002/Hall%20Wootten%20AAS%20paper.pdf> viewed 11 February 2010.
4. See D Smith, 'Representative politics and the new wave of native title organisations' in J Finlayson and DE Smith (eds), *Native Title: Emerging issues for research, policy and practice*, Research Monograph No. 10, Centre for Aboriginal Economic Policy Research, Australian National University, Canberra, 1995, p. 68.
5. Now Chief Justice French of the High Court of Australia.
6. M Dodson and L Strelein, 'Australia's nation-building: renegotiating the relationship between Indigenous peoples and the state', *University of New South Wales Law Journal* 24(3), 2001, pp. 826, 835.
7. *Ward v Western Australia* (2002) 191 ALR 1, at [234] (Gleeson CJ, Gaudron, Gummow and Hayne JJ).
8. C Scholtz, 'Land claims: a negotiated option', *Limits & Possibilities of a Treaty Process in Australia*, AIATSIS Seminar Series, 27 August 2001, p. 4.
9. See *Ward v Western Australia* (2002) 191 ALR 1, at [14]–[20] (Gleeson CJ, Gaudron, Gummow and Hayne JJ).
10. ibid., at [21].
11. *Fejo v Northern Territory of Australia* (1998) 195 CLR 96, at 759.
12. *Waanyi People, North Ganalanja Aboriginal Corporation, Bidanggu Aboriginal Corporation* [1995] NNTTA 4 (14 February 1995).
13. See R French, 'The role of the High Court and the recognition of native title: address in honour of Ron Castan QC AM', paper presented at the Native Title Conference, Townsville, 28 August 2001; also see this volume, Chapter 6.
14. This has been much written about. See, for example, W Jonas, *Native Title Report 2001*, Human Rights and Equal Opportunities Commission, Sydney, January, 2002.
15. ibid., p. 11.
16. Most obviously, such as the International Convention on the Elimination of All forms of Racial Discrimination, opened for signature 21 December 1965 (entered into force 4 January 1969).
17. *National Native Title Tribunal 1995/96 Annual Report*, 45.
18. *North Ganalanja Aboriginal Corporation & Waanyi People v Queensland* (1996) 185 CLR 595, at [26] (Brennan CJ, Dawson, Toohey, Gaudron and Gummow JJ).

19. H Wootten, 'Finding the future: Indigenous Australians in the 21st century', paper presented at *Nulloo Yumbah Lectures*, Inaugural Lecture, University of Central Queensland, Rockhampton, 1 May 2002, p. 17.
20. D Watson, *Recollections of a Bleeding Heart: A portrait of Paul Keating PM*, Knopf, Sydney, 2002, p. 112. (The reference to Watson was topical: he had given one of the after-dinner speeches at the conference.)

8. Symbolism and function: From native title to Indigenous self-government

★ Previously published in M Langton, M Tehan, L Palmer and K Shain (eds), *Honour among Nations: Treaties and negotiations with Indigenous people,* Melbourne University Press, Melbourne, 2004.

1. *Western Australia v Ward* (2002) 213 CLR 1.
2. *Mabo v Queensland [No. 2]* (1992) 175 CLR 1.
3. *Members of the Yorta Yorta Aboriginal Community v Victoria* (2002) 214 CLR 422.
4. N Pearson, 'Where we've come from and where we are at with the opportunity that is Koiki Mabo's legacy to Australia', Mabo Lecture, presented to the Native Title Conference 2003: Native Title on the Ground, Alice Springs, 3 June 2003; also this volume, Chapter 3.
5. P Macklem, 'Distributing sovereignty: Indian nations and equality of peoples', *Stanford Law Review* 45, 1993, pp. 1311, 1325.
6. *Western Australia v Ward* (2002) 213 CLR 1, at [18].
7. ibid., at [64]: implicit in this construction is an acknowledgment by the Court that the observance of laws and customs is separate from the existence of those laws. A failure to exercise a right does not result in the loss of the right.
8. ibid., at [14].
9. ibid., at [88]–[89].
10. See N Pearson, 'Communal native title', principles discussed at the Cape York Land Council Seminar on 'The legal concept of native title', Cairns, 21–23 July 2000, *Native Title Newsletter*, no. 5/2000, p. 3. In his view, rights arise because of the fact of prior occupation; Pearson points to K McNeil, 'Aboriginal title and Aboriginal rights: what's the connection?', *Alberta Law Review* 36(1), 1997, p. 117. This view was explicitly rejected by the High Court in *Western Australia v Ward* (2002) 213 CLR 1, at [93]; see also N Pearson, 'Land is susceptible of ownership' in M Langton et al. (eds), above, n. 1.
11. A Cape York Heads of Agreement was signed in 1996 by Indigenous organisations and peak industry and environmental groups. The agreement was heralded as an historic land use protocol that would set a precedent for negotiated settlements of land use issues across the country. Original signatories were the Cape York Land Council and the Peninsula Regional Council of ATSIC, the Cattlemen's Union, the Australian Conservation Foundation and the Wilderness Society. In 2001 the Cape York Agreement was revisited and the State of Queensland became a party. The Balkanu Cape York Development Corporation, and the Cairns and Far North Environment Centre, also signed.
12. P Agius, J Davies, R Howitt and L Johns, 'Negotiating comprehensive settlement of native title issues: building a new scale of justice in South Australia', *Land, Rights, Laws: Issues of Native Title*, AIATSIS, vol. 2, Issues Paper No. 20, December 2002, p. 4.

13. See P Agius and R Howitt, 'Different visions, different ways: lessons and challenges from the native title negotiations in South Australia', paper presented to the Native Title Conference 2003: Native Title on the Ground, Alice Springs, 3–5 June 2003.
14. The large-scale state-wide negotiations are supported by local authority structure across the state. Native title claimants have organised Native Title Management Committees for each of their claims and meet state-wide as the South Australian 'Congress' of NTMCs to negotiate over common issues. The Congress has also agreed on priorities and pilot negotiations to progress towards substantive incremental outcomes.
15. Agius et al., above, n. 12, p. 2.
16. For discussion, see Agius and Howitt, above, n. 13, p. 8.
17. In August 1999 Queensland entered into a state-wide consultation protocol, *Building Reconciliation*, between the Queensland Government and the Queensland Indigenous Working Group, the latter representing the native title representative bodies in the state. The Queensland Government and Indigenous representative bodies chose to focus on a consultation protocol.
18. The parties to the *Statement of Commitment* are the Government of Western Australia, represented by the Premier and the Minister for Indigenous Affairs, Aboriginal and Torres Strait Islander Commission, the WA Native Title Working Group, the WA Aboriginal Community Controlled Health Organisation and the Aboriginal Legal Service of WA.
19. *Ngalpil v Western Australia* [2001] FCA 1140.
20. Parliament of Western Australia, *Budget Papers 2003–04*, vol. 2, p. 992.
21. *James (on behalf of the Martu People) v Western Australia* [2002] FCA 1208.
22. See D Hawgood, 'Imagine what could happen if we worked together: shared responsibility and a whole of government approach', paper presented to the Native Title Conference 2003: Native Title on the Ground, Alice Springs, 3–5 June 2003.
23. M Jones, R Cook and D Pearce, 'One claim or many? From native title to nation building', paper presented to the Native Title Conference 2003: Native Title on the Ground, Alice Springs, 3–5 June 2003.
24. The negotiations over the settlement were interrupted by litigation in the Single Noongar claim. The resulting Full Federal Court decision in *Bodney v Bennell* (2008) 167 FCR 84 forced the parties back to the negotiating table and renewed commitments to settling the claim by agreement have been made.
25. Section 86F of the Native Title Act provides that some or all parties to a native title application may negotiate to settle the application through an agreement that involves matters other then native title.
26. N Pearson, 'Aboriginal law and colonial law since Mabo', in C Fletcher (ed.), *Aboriginal Self-determination in Australia*, Aboriginal Studies Press, Canberra, 1994, p. 157.
27. ibid.
28. *Western Australia v Ward* (2002) 213 CLR 1, at [561] (McHugh J).
29. ibid., at [970] (Callinan J).
30. J Webber, 'Constitutional poetry: the tension between symbolic and functional aims in constitutional reform', *Sydney Law Review* 21, 1999, pp. 260, 265.
31. ibid., pp. 262, 267.
32. See, for example, *Mabo v Queensland [No. 2]* (1992) 175 CLR 1, at 109 (Deane and Gaudron JJ), who described the decision as 'a retreat from injustice'.

Notes

33. *De Rose v State of South Australia* [2002] FCA 1342.
34. Pearson, above, n. 4.

9. Societies, communities and native title

* This paper was previously published in *Land, Rights, Laws: Issues of Native Title*, Native Title Research Unit, AIATSIS, Canberra, vol. 4, no. 1, August 2009.

† I thank Wendy Asche for her comments and suggestions on an earlier version of this paper. I also thank two anonymous reviewers for their thoughts.

1. K Palmer, 'Anthropology and applications for the recognition of native title', *Land, Rights, Laws: Issues of Native Title* 3(7), 2007, pp. 2–3, 5. See also D Trigger, 'Anthropology in native title court cases: mere pleading, expert opinion or hearsay?' in S Toussaint (ed.), *Crossing Boundaries: Cultural, legal, historical and practice issues in native title*, Melbourne University Press, Melbourne, 2004, pp. 24–33; and see generally S Toussaint (ed.), *Crossing Boundaries: Cultural, legal, historical and practice issues in native title*, Melbourne University Press, Melbourne, 2004.
2. Palmer, above, n. 1, p. 14. See *Jango v Northern Territory* [2006] FCA 318.
3. P Burke, *Law's Anthropology: From ethnography to expert testimony in three native title claims*, PhD thesis, Department of Archaeology and Anthropology, Australian National University, 2006.
4. J Morton, 'Sansom, Sutton and Sackville: three expert anthropologists?', *Anthropological Forum* 17(2), 2007, pp. 70–173. See also B Sansom, '*Yulara* and future expert reports in native title cases', *Anthropological Forum* 17(1), 2007, pp. 71–92.
5. Morton, above, n. 4, p. 171.
6. ibid.
7. ibid.
8. Noted by J Sackville in *Jango v Northern Territory (No. 2)* FCA 1004, 314; see Palmer, above, n. 1, pp. 13–15.
9. *Members of the Yorta Yorta Aboriginal Community v State of Victoria* (2002) 214 CLR 422.
10. ibid., p. 50.
11. L Strelein, *Compromised Jurisprudence: Native title cases since Mabo*, AIATSIS, Canberra, 2006, p. 90.
12. *Northern Territory v Alyawarr* (2005) 145 FCR 135, 78, quoted in *Griffiths v Northern Territory of Australia* [2006] FCA 903, at [513].
13. *Rubibi Community v State of Western Australia* (No. 5) [2005] FCA 1025, at [8]; The Yawuru claimants relied on *Members of the Yorta Yorta Aboriginal Community v State of Victoria* (2002) 214 CLR 422, at 439 [29], 444–445 [47] and 445 [49].
14. *Neowarra v State of Western Australia* (2003) 134 FCR 208, at [61].
15. Strelein, above, n. 11, p. 104 citing *Members of the Yorta Yorta Aboriginal Community v Victoria* (2002) 214 CLR 422, at 445–446, 450.
16. An example is a paper by S Holcombe, 'The sentimental journey: a site of belonging. A case study from Central Australia', *TAJA* 15(2), 2004, pp. 163–84. The author shows that the term 'community' has a 'deep genealogy' in the social sciences.
17. K Maddock, *The Australian Aborigines: A portrait of their society*, Allen Lane Penguin Press, London, 1974.
18. CD Rowley, *The Destruction of Aboriginal Society*, Australian National University Press, Canberra, 1970.
19. I Keen, *Aboriginal Economy and Society: Australia at the threshold of colonisation*, Oxford University Press, Melbourne, 2004.

20. ibid., pp. 2–5. Examples of the use of the word in titles of academic papers are not common. MC Howard wrote on 'Aboriginal society in south west Australia': MC Howard, 'Aboriginal society in south-western Australia' (1979) in RM and CH Berndt (eds), *Aborigines of the West: Their past and their present*, University of Western Australia, Perth, 1980, pp. 90–9, and Kolig used the word in the titles of at least four papers that I have come across: E Kolig, 'Post-contact religious movements in Australian Aboriginal society', *Anthropos* 82, 1987, pp. 251–9; E Kolig, *Dreamtime Politics: Religion, world view and utopian thought in Australian Aboriginal society*, Dietrich Reimer Verlag, Berlin, 1989, although in the first two citations the word qualified either 'European' or 'Australian'.
21. J Beattie, *Other Cultures. Aims, methods and achievements in social anthropology*, Cohen & West, London, 1964, pp. 34–5.
22. ibid., p. 56.
23. ibid., pp. 58–9.
24. M Herzfeld, *Anthropology: Theoretical practice in culture and society*, Blackwell, Oxford, 2001, p. 133.
25. ibid.
26. ibid. Herzfeld provides no citation for this quotation, although he provides references to five of Escobar's works in the bibliography.
27. J Weiner, 'Anthropology vs. ethnography in native title: a review article in the context of Peter Sutton's *Native Title in Australia*', *TAPJA* 8(2), 2007, p. 154.
28. P Sutton, *Native Title in Australia: An ethnographic perspective*, Cambridge University Press, Port Melbourne, 2003, p. 42.
29. ibid., pp. 99–107.
30. RM and CH Berndt, *A World that Was: The Yaraldi of the Murray River and the Lakes, South Australia*, UBC Press, Vancouver, 1993, p. 19.
31. See Strelein, above, n. 11, pp. 104–05, 135–7 for a discussion and some examples in the legal context.
32. Sutton, above, n. 28, p. 88.
33. ibid.
34. ibid., pp. 89–92.
35. AR Radcliffe-Brown, 'The social organisation of Australian tribes', *Oceania* 1(1–4), 1930–31, pp. 445–55; Sutton, above, n. 28, p. 46.
36. WE Roth, *Ethnological Studies among the North-West-Central Queensland Aborigines*, Government Printer, Brisbane, 1897. Facsimile edition 1984, *The Queensland Aborigines,* vol. 1. Hesperian Press, Perth, p. 41.
37. Sutton, above, n. 28, pp. 92–8.
38. ibid., p. 95.
39. ibid., p. 96; N Peterson, 'The natural and cultural areas of Aboriginal Australia' in N Peterson (ed.), *Tribes and Boundaries in Australia*, Australian Institute of Aboriginal Studies, Canberra, 1976, pp. 50–71.
40. RM Berndt, 'The concept of the "tribe" in the Western Desert of Australia', *Oceania* 30, 1959, p. 104.
41. ibid., p. 92.
42. ibid., p. 84.
43. ibid., p. 104.
44. ibid., p. 105.
45. ibid. I thank an anonymous reviewer for pointing out this contribution to the idea of a 'society' provided by RM Berndt.

Notes

46. RM Berndt, 'Territoriality and the problem of demarcating sociocultural space' in N Peterson (ed.), above, n. 39, pp. 145–6.
47. ibid.
48. Horton's map of Aboriginal Australia (Horton D, *Aboriginal Australia Map*, Aboriginal Studies Press, Canberra, 1994) was based on Tindale's map of Tribal boundaries (NB Tindale, *Tribal Boundaries in Aboriginal Australia*, South Australian Museum, Adelaide, 1974).
49. For a comprehensive summary of this issue, see A Rumsey 'Language and territoriality' in M Walsh and C Yallop (eds), *Language and Culture in Aboriginal Australia*, Aboriginal Studies Press, Canberra, 1993.
50. See, for example, AP Elkin, *The Australian Aborigines: How to understand them*, Angus & Robertson, Sydney, 1945, 22 ff.; NB Tindale, *Aboriginal Tribes of Australia*, University of California Press, Berkley, 1974, pp. 30–3.
51. DS Davidson, *An Ethnic Map of Australia*, reprinted from the proceedings of the *American Philosophical Society* 79(4), 1938, p. 649. Generally later called the local descent group (Berndt, above, n. 40, pp. 102–03); also called the 'country group' (Keen, above, n. 19, p. 277, Sutton, above, n. 28, pp. 54–66).
52. ibid.
53. Keen, above, n. 19, p. 234; see also MC Howard, *Nyoongah Politics: Aboriginal politics in the south-west of Western Australia*, PhD thesis, University of Western Australia, 1976, pp. 17–19 for a similar view.
54. Berndt, above, n. 40, pp. 91–5.
55. Rumsey, above, n. 48, pp. 191–5.
56. P Monaghan, *Laying Down the Country: Norman B. Tindale and the linguistic construction of the north-west of South Australia*, PhD thesis, University of Adelaide, 2003, p. xi.
57. ibid., p. 149.
58. Keen, above, n. 19, pp. 134–5.
59. ibid., p. 135.
60. ibid., p. 6.
61. ibid.
62. Rumsey, above, n. 48, p. 191.
63. ibid., pp. 201–04.
64. There are examples of successful native title applications that have included members of more than one language-speaking group. Miriuwung and Gajerrong (*Ward v Western Australia* (1998) 159 ALR 483), *Neowarra v Western Australia* (2003) 134 FCR 208 and *Griffiths v Northern Territory of Australia* [2006] FCA 903 are examples.
65. W McGregor, 'A survey of the languages of the Kimberley Region — Report from the Kimberley Language Resource Centre', *Australian Aboriginal Studies* 2, 1988, p. 97.
66. M Walsh, 'Language ownership: a key issue for native title' in J Henderson and D Nash (eds), *Language and Native Title*, Aboriginal Studies Press, Canberra, 2002, p. 233.
67. P Sutton and A Palmer, *Daly River (Malak Malak) Claim*, Northern Land Council, Darwin, 1980.
68. *Griffiths v Northern Territory of Australia* [2006] FCA 903, at 6, 377.
69. *Neowarra v Western Australia* (2003) 134 FCR 208, at 386.
70. Sansom has disagreed, arguing in relation to the Yulara ethnography that 'earliest sources are best' (Sansom, above, n. 4, p. 79). It was a view challenged by some other

anthropologists (Burke, above, n. 3, p. 164; K Glaskin, 'Manifesting the latent in native title litigation', *Anthropological Forum* 17(2), 2007, p. 167 and Morton, above, n. 4, p. 172).

71. See, for example, NB Tindale, 'Distribution of Australian tribes: a field survey', *Royal Society of South Australia* 64(1), 1940; Tindale, above, n. 49.
72. Indeed, Bates tells us that along the line that marked the circumcising people of the south west of Western Australia from the neighbours to the north and east, 'On the borders of this line, right through to its north-western point, the local groups appear to become mixed'. D Bates, edited by Isobel White, *The Native Tribes of Western Australia*, National Library of Australia, Canberra, 1985, p. 45.

10. Self-determination and Indigenous nations in the United States: International human rights, federal policy and Indigenous nationhood

1. Self-determination, and its meaning, is approached differently by scholars. The political mandate of self-determination 'has…come to mean…in cases of cession and annexation, it is peoples, not governments, who are to dispose of the territory they inhabit…peoples are entitled to a say in the conduct of government…peoples and nations are entitled to freedom from external oppression, particularly of the colonial variety'; MC Lâm, *At the Edge of the State: Indigenous peoples and self-determination,* Transnational Publishers, New York, 2000, p. 110, citing A Cassese, *Self-determination of Peoples: A legal reappraisal*, Cambridge University Press, New York, 1995, p. 11; '…[S]elf-determination is identified as a universe of human rights precepts concerned broadly with peoples, including Indigenous peoples, and grounded in the idea that all are equally entitled to control their own destinies.' SJ Anaya, *Indigenous Peoples in International Law* (2nd edn), Oxford University Press, New York, 2004, p. 98. 'In essence, self-determination is understood to occur whenever a people freely determines its own political status.' TD Musgrave, *Self Determination and National Minorities*, Oxford University Press, New York, 1997, p. 2.
2. The same language is contained in both the International Covenant on Economic, Social and Cultural Rights, Art. 1, and the International Covenant on Civil and Political Rights, Art. 1. Lâm, above, n. 1, p. 123.
3. ibid., p.110, citing Cassese, above, n. 1, p. 11.
4. ibid., pp. 92–3.
5. ibid., p. 97.
6. ibid., p. 98.
7. ibid., p. 97.
8. ibid., p. 98.
9. United Nations Draft Declaration on the Rights of Indigenous Peoples, Anaya, above, n. 1, p. 207. The Declaration was adopted by the General Assembly of the United Nations on 13 September 2007. See *United Nations Declaration on the Rights of Indigenous Peoples, GA Res. 61/295, Annex, U.N. Doc. A/RES:61/295 (Sept. 13, 2007)* (The Declaration).
10. Anaya, above, n. 1, p. 209; The Declaration's provision on self-determination reads the same as the Draft Declaration's Article 3. Article 4 of the Declaration and Article 46(1) are important articles which frame internal and external expressions of sovereignty.

    Article 4 reads: 'Indigenous peoples, in exercising their right to self-determination, have the right to autonomy or self-government in matters relating to their internal and local affairs, as well as ways and means for financing their autonomous functions.'

Article 46(1) reads: 'Nothing in this Declaration may be interpreted as implying for any State, people, group or person any right to engage in any activity or to perform any act contrary to the Charter of the United Nations or construed as authoring or encouraging any action which would dismember or impair, totally or in part, the territorial integrity or political unity of sovereign and independent States.'

11. Lâm, above, n. 1, p. 70.
12. See The Declaration, above, n. 9.
13. Lâm, above, n. 1, pp. 63–76. Of no surprise to anyone, even in its audacity, the United States voted against the adoption of the Declaration on the Rights of Indigenous Peoples in the United Nations (UN) General Assembly on 13 September 2007. The CANZUS (Canada, Australia, New Zealand, United States) bloc was the sole dissenter, however; the Declaration was adopted by 144 nations, with 11 abstaining. See The Declaration, above, n. 9; see also, S Wiessner, 'Indigenous sovereignty: a reassessment in light of the UN Declaration on the Rights of Indigenous Peoples', *Vanderbilt Journal of Transnational Law* 41(4), 2008, p. 1141 (discussing the legal scope of Indigenous sovereignty under the Declaration as necessarily including the authentic claims and aspirations of Indigenous peoples and recognising that Indigenous concepts of sovereignty differ from Western ideas of self-government); AG Organick, *Listening to Indigenous Voices: What the UN Declaration on the Rights of Indigenous Peoples means for U.S. Tribes*, ExpressO, 2009, <http://works.bepress.com/aliza_organick/1> viewed 28 January 2010 (exploring the CANZUS bloc's vote against the Declaration, including Australia's subsequent adoption of the Declaration on 3 April 2009).
14. F Cohen, *Handbook of Federal Indian Law* (1982 edn), Michie Bobbs-Merrill, Charlottesville, VA, 1982, pp. 233–5 (citing *Cherokee Nation v State of Ga.*, 30 US 1, 8 L. Ed. 25 (1831); see also F Cohen, *Handbook of Federal Indian Law* (2005 edn), LexisNexis, Newark, NJ, p. 207. Cohen's *Handbook of Federal Indian Law*, a leading treatise on federal Indian law, was substantially revised and updated in 2005 to reflect the developments in the field since the 1982 edition and is now supplemented. Citations to both editions are provided.
15. Cohen (1982 edn), above, n. 14, pp. 231–2, citing *U.S. v Wheeler*, 435 US 313, at 322–23 (1978) and *Oliphant v Suquamish Indian Tribe (Oliphant)*, 435 US 191 (1978); Cohen (2005 edn), above, n. 14, p. 206.
16. Cohen (1982 edn), above, n. 14, pp. 217–20 (plenary power subject to constitutional limitations and must be tied rationally to trust obligations of Congress); Cohen (2005 edn), above, n. 14, p. 413 (plenary power not absolute but subject to constitutional, Indian law canons of construction, trust relationship, developing norms of international law).
17. *Indian Self-Determination and Educational Assistance Act* of 1975, 88 Stat. 2203 (codified at 25 USC ss 450–450n, 455–458e). Congress commits 'to the maintenance of the Federal Government's unique and continuing relationship with and responsibility to the Indian people through the establishment of a meaningful Indian self-determination policy which will permit an orderly transition from Federal domination of programs for and services to Indians to effective and meaningful participation by the Indian people in the planning, conduct, and administration of those programs and services'. Sections 2, 3, 88 Stat. at 2203 (codified at 25 USC ss 450–450a).
18. FP Prucha, *The Great Father*, vols I and II, 1995, p. 8. 'There was little doubt in the minds of the Europeans (pace those who used the noble savage concept to condemn evils in their own society) that savagism was an inferior mode of existence and must give way to civility (civilization).'

19. HP Glenn, *Legal Traditions of the World: Sustainable diversity in law*, Oxford University Press, Oxford, UK, 2007 (Glenn 2007). Now in its third edition, some attributions in this article are to the first publication, which appeared in 2000 (Glenn 2000). Citations to the 2000 edition are made where the language is not exactly the same as the 2007 edition.
20. Glenn 2000, above, n. 19, p. 57, citing E Goldsmith, *The Way: An ecological world view*, Random Century, London, 1992; Glenn 2007, above, n. 19, p. 60.
21. Glenn 2007, above, n. 19, p. 60.
22. ibid.
23. ibid.
24. ibid., p. 61.
25. ibid.
26. ibid.
27. ibid.
28. ibid.
29. ibid., p. 62.
30. ibid.
31. ibid.
32. ibid., p. 63.
33. Glenn 2000, above, n. 19, p. 60.
34. Glenn 2007, above, n. 19, pp. 63–4.
35. This comment is in reference to the Pueblo of Isleta Appellate Court. I serve as an Associate Justice of the Appellate Court with two Isleta elders and two Isleta lawyers. See, generally, C Zuni Cruz, 'Indigenous Pueblo culture and tradition in the justice system: maintaining Indigenous language, thought and law in judicial review', *Land, Rights, Laws: Issues of native title*, Issue Paper no. 23, Native Title Research Unit, AIATSIS, Canberra, 2003.
36. Glenn 2007, above, n. 19, p. 64.
37. See, generally, Zuni Cruz, above, n. 35.
38. Glenn 2007, above, n. 19, p. 64.
39. ibid., p. 66.
40. Glenn 2000, above, n. 19, p. 63.
41. Glenn 2007, above, n. 19, p. 67.
42. ibid.
43. ibid., p. 69.
44. ibid.
45. ibid., p. 70.
46. ibid., p. 71 citing K M'Baye, 'African conception of law' in *The Legal Systems of the World and Their Common Comparison and Unification*, vol. II, 1975, pp. 138–9 (African law 'ignorant of law as a weapon placed in the individual's hands', Africans giving 'no importance to individual rights').
47. ibid., p. 73.
48. ibid., p. 75.
49. Glenn 2000, above, n. 19, p. 71.
50. Glenn 2007, above, n. 19, p. 78.
51. ibid.
52. ibid., p. 79, citing and quoting 'Tradition was the storehouse of a Tribal people's *knowledge of themselves as a people* and a guide to how they should act' (emphasis added). R White, *Middle Ground*, Cambridge University Press, New York, 1991, p. 57.

Notes

53. Glenn 2007, above, n. 19, p. 80.
54. ibid.
55. Prucha, above, n. 18, p. 647, citing 'Rules for the courts of Indian offenses', 10 April 1883.
56. Cohen 1982 edn, above, n. 14, p. 139; Cohen 2005 edn, above, n. 14, p. 82.
57. See, for example, LA French, *The Winds of Injustice, American Indians and the U.S. Government*, Garland Publishing Co., New York, 1994, pp. 45–60 (brief discussion of the removal and allotment policies as they impacted selected Tribes).
58. *Indian Reorganization Act* of 1934 (*Wheeler-Howard Act*), 48 Stat. 984 (codified at 25 USC s.461 et seq.).
59. Cohen 1982 edn, above, n. 14, p. 140. 'Off-reservation federal boarding schools were founded in 1879. Reformists thought them an ideal method of assimilation, since Indian youth were completely removed from the family and from the barbarism of tribal life.' Cohen 2005 edn, above, n. 14, p. 82; see also *Indian Child Welfare Act* 1978, 92 Stat. 3069, '…Congress finds that an alarmingly high percentage of Indian families are broken up by the removal, often unwarranted, of their children from them by nontribal public and private agencies and that an alarmingly high percentage of such children are placed in non-Indian foster and adoptive homes and institutions…'
60. Cohen 1982 edn, above, n. 14, pp. 139–41; Cohen 2005 edn, above, n. 14, pp. 82–3.
61. Cohen 1982 edn, above, n. 14, pp. 128–9; Cohen 2005 edn, above, n. 14, p. 77.
62. *Mabo v Queensland [No. 2]* (1992) 175 CLR 1. 'In the result, six members of the Court (Dawson J dissenting) are in agreement that the common law of this country recognises a form of native title which, in the cases where it has not been extinguished, reflects the entitlement of the Indigenous inhabitants, *in accordance with their laws or customs*, to their *traditional lands*…' (emphasis added) (Mason, CJ).
63. *Delgamuukw v British Columbia* (1997) 3 SCR 1010 (*Delgamuukw*). '*Delgamuukw* is a victory for Aboriginal people as it requires governments to recognize and respect Aboriginal title, Aboriginal law and oral histories', in L Mandell, 'The *Delgamuukw* decision' in L Strelein and K Muir (eds), *Native Title in Perspective, Selected Papers from the Native Title Research Unit 1998–2000*, Native Title Research Unit, AIATSIS, Canberra, 2000, p. 199; 'Aboriginal title is now very well defined as a broad and substantial interest in land, capable of sustaining Aboriginal people in a contemporary society. Aboriginal title also embraces Aboriginal laws that have sustained Aboriginal people on the land for centuries and which can sustain future generations', Mandell, p. 206; see also pp. 216–17 (acceptable evidence of past laws, past occupation, present physical occupation, and change of use not affecting future restraint on use as proof of Aboriginal title), citing *Delgamuukw*, 3 SCR ([148], [149], [153], [154]).
64. 'The task of the Court is to identify those laws and customs which regulated the lives of the forebears of the present members of the applicants prior to European settlement which are currently acknowledged and observed.' G Neate, 'Three lessons for Australia from *Delgamuukw v British Columbia*' in L Strelein and K Muir (eds), above, n. 63, p. 227, citing *Yarmirr and Others v Northern Territory of Australia and Others* (1998) 82 FCR 533, at [85]; see also Mandell, above, n. 63, pp. 216–17 (evidence of past laws acceptable as proof of Aboriginal title), citing *Delgamuukw*, 3 SCR [148] (Lamer CJ).
65. '…and where it exists there is necessarily very persuasive pre-existing information to explain and justify it.' Glenn, above, n. 19, p. 71. 'In summary, contrary to

assertions made by the government that Aboriginal title is "vague and uncertain" and "pertaining only to the continuation of traditional activities", Aboriginal title is now very well defined as a broad and substantial interest in land, capable of sustaining Aboriginal people in a contemporary society. Aboriginal title also embraces Aboriginal laws that have sustained Aboriginal people on the land for centuries and which can sustain future generations.' Mandell, above, n. 63, p. 206. In a sense this is reflected in *Delgamuukw's* recognition of the past, present and change not inconsistent with future use being tied up in the proof of Aboriginal title. Mandell, above, n. 63, pp. 215–17.

66. *Oliphant*, 435 US 191; *Duro v Reina*, 495 US 676, 110 S. Ct. 2053 (1990) (*Duro*); *Nevada v Hicks*, 533 US 353 (2001).

67. *Oliphant*, 435 US 191, at 211 'These considerations [extending tribal law over aliens and strangers; over the members of a community separated by race and tradition, from the authority and power which seeks to impose upon them the restraints of an external and unknown code; which judges them by a standard made by others and not for them and tries them, not by their peers, nor by the customs of their people, nor the law of their land, but by a different race, according to the law of a social state of which they have an imperfect conception] applied here to the non-Indian rather than Indian offender, speak equally strongly against the validity of respondents' contention that Indian Tribes, although fully subordinated to the sovereignty of the United States, retain the power to try non-Indians according to their own customs and procedure' referring to the considerations in *Ex Parte Crow Dog*, 109 US 556 (1883) in which the Court ruled 'federal courts had no jurisdiction to try Indians who had offended against fellow Indians on reservation land'. *Oliphant*, 435 US 191 at 210.

68. *Duro*, 495 US 676 at 693. 'The special nature of the tribunals at issue makes a focus on consent and the protections of citizenship most appropriate. While modern tribal courts include many familiar features of the judicial process, they are influenced by the unique customs, languages, and usages of the Tribes they serve. Tribal courts are often "subordinate to the political branches of tribal governments," and their legal methods may depend on "*unspoken practices and norms*"', citing Cohen, 1982 edn, above, n. 14, pp. 334–5 (emphasis added).

69. 'We hesitate to adopt a view of tribal sovereignty that would single out another group of *citizens*, non-member Indians, for trial by political bodies that do not include them. As *full citizens*, Indians share in the territorial and political sovereignty of the United States.' *Duro*, 495 US at 693 (emphasis added). 'By submitting to the overriding sovereignty of the United States, Indian tribes therefore necessarily give up their power to try non-Indian *citizens* of the United States except in a manner acceptable to Congress. This principle would have been obvious a century ago when most Indian tribes were characterised by a "want of fixed laws [and] of competent tribunals of justice."' H. R. Rep. No. 474, 23d Cong., 1st Sess., 18 (1834). 'It should be no less obvious today, even though present-day Indian tribal courts embody dramatic advances over their historical antecedents.' *Oliphant*, 435 US at 210 (emphasis added).

70. See *Duro*, 495 US 676.

71. '…[S]ince at least the writings of Locke in the seventeenth century, our concept of custom has not been a very charitable one. This is reflected in recent western concepts of law, which come very close to eliminating custom entirely as a source of normativity. Custom became with Locke, "the defacto habits acquired by

engaging in the practices and institutions of one's society, from the most primitive and least reflective to the most civilized and enlightened"…Tradition is just doing things over and over again. The same can be said of custom. The rational tradition does this, however, by divorcing custom from its justification, from the reasons and information which lead to its ongoing performance.' Glenn 2000, above, n. 19, pp. 69–70.

72. 'Although some modern tribal courts "mirror American courts" and "are guided by written codes, rules, procedures, and guidelines", tribal law is still frequently unwritten, being based instead "on the values, mores, and norms of a Tribe and expressed in its customs, traditions, and practices," and is often "handed down orally or by example from one generation to another."' AP Melton, 'Indigenous justice systems and Tribal society', *Judicature* 79(3), 1995, pp. 126, 130–1. The resulting law applicable in tribal courts is a complex 'mix of tribal codes and federal, state, and traditional law,' National American Indian Court Judges Assn., *Indian Courts and the Future* 43 (1978), which would be unusually difficult for an outsider to sort out. *Nevada v Hicks* (2001) 533 US 353, at 384–385.

73. 'We recognize that some Indian tribal court systems have become increasingly sophisticated and resemble in many respects their state counterparts. We also acknowledge that with the passage of the *Indian Civil Rights Act* of 1968, which extends certain basic procedural rights to anyone tried in Indian Tribal Court, many of the dangers that might have accompanied the exercise by tribal courts of criminal jurisdiction over non-Indians only a few decades ago have disappeared… But these are considerations for Congress to weigh in deciding whether Indian Tribes should finally be authorized to try non-Indians.' *Duro*, 435 US 191, at 212.

74. *Wheeler-Howard Act*, above, n. 58, 48 Stat. 984.

75. *General Allotment Act* 1887 (*Dawes Act*), 24 Stat. 388 (codified as amended at 25 USC ss 331–334, 339, 341, 342, 348, 349, 354, 381).

76. Cohen, 1982 edn, above, n. 14, p. 140; Cohen, 2005 edn, above, n. 14, p. 82.

77. *Wheeler-Howard Act*, above, n. 58, 48 Stat. 984; see also Cohen, 1982 edn, above, n. 14, at 238–239 (Indian governments reached their low point between the 1870s and 1920s).

78. Cohen, 1982 edn, above, n. 14, p. 149. (Boilerplate constitutions were prepared by the Bureau of Indian Affairs (BIA) based on federal constitutional and common law rather than tribal custom); Cohen, 2005 edn, above, n. 14, p. 87.

79. F Pommersheim, 'A path near the clearing: an essay on constitutional adjudication in Tribal courts', *Gonzaga Law Review* 27, 1991, pp. 393, 396 (BIA model constitutions omitted protections of Bill of Rights and doctrine of separation of powers, omissions that Tribes are now criticised for).

80. See, generally, RB Porter, 'Strengthening Tribal sovereignty through government reform: what are the issues?', *Kansas Journal of Law and Public Policy*, winter, 1997, p. 72 (Porter 1997a) (discussing the impact of colonisation on Tribal government dysfunction); see also, RB Porter, 'Strengthening Tribal sovereignty through peacemaking: how the Anglo-American legal tradition destroys Indigenous societies', *Columbia Human Rights Law Review* 28, 1997, p. 235 (Porter 1997b) (discussing Seneca civil war and the consequences of transformation of Indigenous dispute resolution associated with the adoption of the Anglo-American legal tradition).

81. See, generally, C Zuni Cruz, 'Tribal law as Indigenous social reality and separate consciousness-[re]incorporating customs and traditions into Tribal law', *Tribal Law Journal* 1, 2000, <http://tlj.unm.edu/tribal-law-journal/articles/volume_1/zuni_cruz/index.php> viewed 26 February 2010.

82. *Indian Civil Rights Act* of 1968, 82 Stat. 73, 77 (codified as amended at 25 USC s 1301 et seq.).
83. Pommersheim, above, n. 79, text at fn. 15 (a number of Tribes, including Rosebud Sioux Tribe, adopted Bill of Rights in 1966, prior to enactment of *Indian Civil Rights Act*); see also, Pueblo of Isleta Constitution, Art. III (Art. III, Rights of Members, included in original constitution adopted in 1942).
84. R Yazzie, 'Law school as a journey', *Arkansas Law Review* 46, 1993, p. 271.
85. ibid.
86. Porter 1997b, above, n. 80, p. 235.
87. ibid., p. 284.
88. ibid.
89. ibid., p. 293.
90. *Morton v Mancari*, 417 US 535, at 537–538 (1974) (*Morton*), <http://laws.findlaw.com/us/417/535.html>, 'Section 12 of the *Indian Reorganization Act*, 48 Stat. 986, 25 USC s 472, provides "The Secretary of the Interior is directed to establish standards of health, age, character, experience, knowledge, and ability for Indians who may be appointed, without regard to civil-service laws, to the various positions maintained, now or hereafter, by the Indian Office, in the administration of functions or services affecting any Indian Tribe. Such qualified Indians shall hereafter have the preference to appointment to vacancies in any such positions."'
91. *Morton*, 417 US at 538. 'In June 1972, pursuant to [25 USC s.472], the Commissioner of Indian Affairs, with the approval of the Secretary of the Interior, issued a directive (Personnel Management Letter No. 72–12) (App. 52) stating that the BIA's policy would be to grant a preference to qualified Indians not only, as before, in the initial hiring stage, but also in the situation where an Indian and a non-Indian, both already employed by the BIA, were competing for a promotion within the Bureau.'
92. ibid.
93. ibid., at 535.
94. 'Since 1934, the BIA has implemented the preference with a fair degree of success. The percentage of Indians employed in the Bureau rose from 34% in 1934 to 57% in 1972…The Commissioner's extension of the preference in 1972 to promotions within the BIA was designed to bring more Indians into positions of responsibility and, in that regard, appears to be a logical extension of the congressional intent.' ibid., at 545.
95. ibid., at 541–542, 554–555 (preference viewed as promoting self-government).
96. B Clavero, 'Overlapped constitutionalism: Indigenous people and non-Indigenous law between Mexico and the United States', in possession of the author, New Mexico.
97. ibid.
98. ibid., p. 2.
99. ibid., pp. 37–8. 'The very right to self-determination for Indigenous peoples or, to put it in the other way, Indian sovereignty can be taken quite more seriously to its fullest extent by international law than through State Constitutions.'
100. Perhaps things come full circle here. One of José R Martínez Cobo's most important conclusions in his study for the UN Commission on Human Rights of the discrimination experienced by Indigenous peoples was 'that the discrimination against Indigenous peoples was fundamentally tied to their lack of self-determination'. He also concluded 'that externally imposed assimilation was a form of discrimination' and proposed 'that the right of Indigenous peoples to cultural

distinctiveness, political self-determination, and a secure resource base should be formally declared by the United Nations'. See Lâm above, n. 1, pp. 42–3, citing the *Study of the Problem of Discrimination against Indigenous Populations*, U.N. Doc. E/CN.4/Sub.2/1986/7 and Add.1–3.
101. Lilla Watson, Gangulu people (located in northern Queensland, Australia).
102. Cipriano Manuel, Santa Rosa village, Tohono O'odham Nation (located in southern Arizona, United States).

11. Legal personality and native title corporations: The problem of perpetual succession

1. These practical and inherent problems have been identified during the conduct of research by Frith on native title corporations and by Langton on agreements with Indigenous people. The authors acknowledge the financial support for this research from the Australian Research Council (Linkage Projects LP0561857 and LP0211472) and the Industry Partners, Rio Tinto Ltd and the Department of Families, Community Services, Housing and Indigenous Affairs. We also acknowledge and are grateful for the assistance of the former manager of this research project, Odette Mazel.
2. See *Native Title Act 1993* (Cth) ss 55–57. The powers and functions of Prescribed Bodies Corporate are set out in the *Native Title (Prescribed Bodies Corporate) Regulations 1999* (Cth) (PBC Regulations). PBCs are required under the regulations to incorporate under the *Corporations (Aboriginal and Torres Strait Islander) Act 2006* (Cth) and are therefore regulated by that legislation.
3. Once the corporation is approved by the Court it is entered on the National Native Title Register as a 'Registered Native Title Body Corporate' (RNTBC): NTA s 193.
4. JS Fingleton, 'Native title corporations', *Land, Rights, Laws: Issues of Native Title*, no. 2, Native Title Research Unit, AIATSIS, Canberra, 1994, p. 2.
5. ibid.
6. ibid., p. 3.
7. ibid., p. 3.
8. C Mantziaris and D Martin, *Native Title Corporations: A legal and anthropological analysis*, Federation Press, Leichhardt, 2000, p. 114.
9. See NTA pt 11 for the statutory provisions governing the operation and function of NTRBs.
10. K McNeil, 'Aboriginal title as a constitutionally protected property right', in Owen Lippert (ed.), *Beyond the Nass Valley: National implications of the Supreme Court's Delgamuukw decision*, Fraser Institute, Vancouver, 2000, pp. 59–60.
11. Department of Families, Community Services and Indigenous Affairs, Land Branch, *Guidelines for Support of Prescribed Bodies Corporate*, Canberra, 2007.
12. Australian Government, *Structures and Processes of Prescribed Bodies Corporate*, 27 October 2006, p. 6.
13. See Agreements, Treaties and Negotiated Settlements Project, <http://www.atns.net.au> viewed 11 February 2010.
14. *Mabo v Queensland [No. 2]* (1992) 175 CLR 1, at 70, 110, 192 recognises that laws and customs of Indigenous people may undergo change; see also *Yanner v Eaton* (1999) 201 CLR 351, at [277].

15. *Harrington-Smith on behalf of the Wongatha People v State of Western Australia (No. 9)* (2007) 238 ALR 1.
16. R Mohr, 'Law and identity in spatial contests', *National Identities* 5(1), 2003, pp. 53–66.
17. *Saibai People v Queensland* [1999] FCA 158.
18. *Congoo v Queensland* [2001] FCA 868.
19. *Brown v Western Australia* [2001] FCA 1462; *Brown v Western Australia* (No. 2) [2003] FCA 556.
20. Hopevale Congress Aboriginal Corporation RNTBC and Gulf Region Aboriginal Corporation RNTBC.
21. For example, De Rose Hill — Ilpalka Aboriginal Corporation RNTBC; Western Yalanji Aboriginal Corporation RNTBC; Western Desert Lands Aboriginal Corporation (Jam Ukurnu-Yapalikunu) RNTBC.
22. For example, Kunin (Native Title) Aboriginal Corporation RNTBC (see *Rubibi Community v Western Australia* [2001] FCA 607; (2001) 112 FCR 409).
23. For example, Wanjina-Wunggurr (Native Title) Aboriginal Corporation RNTBC (see *Neowarra v Western Australia* (2003) 134 FCR 208).
24. For example, Miriuwung and Gajerrong # 1 (Native Title Prescribed Body Corporate) Aboriginal Corporation RNTBC (see *Ward v Western Australia* [1998] FCA 1478; (1998) 159 ALR 483).
25. See K Doohan, *Making Things Come Good: Relations between Aborigines and miners at Argyle*, Back Room Press, Broome, 2008; see also Aboriginal and Torres Strait Islander Social Justice Commissioner, Australian Human Rights Commission, *Native Title Report 2006*, Ch. 5.
26. *Sampi v Western Australia* [2005] FCA 777, at [34]. This aspect of the decision was not dealt with on appeal: *Sampi v Western Australia* [2010] FCAFC26.
27. See for example, *Rubibi Community v Western Australia (No. 6)* (2006) 226 ALR 676, at [16]–[18]; *Rubibi Community v Western Australia (No. 7)* [2006] FCA 459, at [16]–[18].
28. *James v State of Western Australia* [2007] WASCA 18, at [16]–[17].
29. See 'Determination of prescribed body corporate. *Ngalpil v Western Australia* [2003] FCA 1098 per Carr J, 9 October 2003', *Native Title Hot Spots*, National Native Title Tribunal; see also 'Determination of prescribed body corporate. *Brown v Western Australia (No. 2)* [2003] FCA 556 per French J, 4 June 2003', *Native Title Hot Spots*, National Native Title Tribunal.
30. *Sampi v Western Australia* [2005] FCA 777, at [14], [33].
31. See NTA ss 190–190C.

13. Achieving real outcomes from native title claims: Meeting the challenges head on

1. *Mabo v Queensland [No. 2]* (1992) 175 CLR 1.
2. R McClelland, 'Negotiating native title forum', speech delivered at the Negotiating Native Title Forum, Brisbane, 29 February 2008, at [6], <http://www.attorneygeneral.gov.au/www/ministers/mcclelland.nsf/Page/Speeches_2008_FirstQuarter_29February2008-NegotiatingNativeTitleForum> viewed 11 February 2010.
3. ibid., at [15], see also [12]–[14].
4. ibid., at [18], see also [68].
5. ibid., at [4], [5], [67].

Notes

6. ibid., at [5].
7. ibid., at [26], [60].
8. ibid., at [26].
9. ibid., at [21], [23], [61].
10. J Macklin, 'Beyond *Mabo*: Native title and closing the gap', speech delivered at the 2008 Mabo Lecture, James Cook University, Townsville, 21 May 2008, <http://www.nswbar.asn.au/circulars/macklin.pdf> viewed 11 February 2010.
11. ibid.
12. ibid.
13. J Macklin, 'Opening address', speech delivered at the Sustainable Indigenous Communities Forum, Minerals Council of Australia, Canberra, 27 May 2008, pp. 5, 11, <http://www.jennymacklin.fahcsia.gov.au/internet/jennymacklin.nsf/content/sustainable_indig_comm_27may08.htm> viewed 11 February 2010.
14. Aboriginal and Torres Strait Islander Social Justice Commissioner, *Native Title Report 2007*, Human Rights and Equal Opportunity Commission, Sydney, 2008, p. 4, <http://www.hreoc.gov.au/social_justice/nt_report/ntreport07/pdf/ntr2007.pdf> viewed 11 February 2010.
15. ibid., p. 4.
16. ibid., p. 2.
17. ibid., p. 5.
18. *Rubibi Community v State of Western Australia (No. 7)* [2006] FCA 459, at [164], [169].
19. Aboriginal and Torres Strait Islander Social Justice Commissioner, above, n. 14, pp. 13, 23.
20. 107 applications where the determination covers the entire application area and 28 applications where the determination covers part of the application area.
21. The NNTT produces a map of the location of areas covered by determinations of native title: <http.www.nntt.gov.au>.
22. The NNTT produces a map of the locations of areas covered by registered ILUAs: <http.www.nntt.gov.au>.
23. The NNTT produces a map of the geographic extent of the areas covered by claimant applications and determinations of native title: <http.www.nntt.gov.au>.
24. See National Native Title Tribunal, *Annual Report 2006–2007*, National Native Title Tribunal, Perth, p. 20.
25. *Aboriginal Land Rights (Northern Territory) Act 1976*, s 3(1).
26. Aboriginal Land Commissioner, *Report for the Year Ended 30 June 2007*, Aboriginal Land Commissioner, Darwin, at [38]–[40], and Appendix 1.
27. ibid., at [19], see also [13]–[17].
28. See NTA ss 47, 47A, 47B.
29. See NTA ss 47, 47A, 47B.
30. *Bodney v Bennell* (2008) 167 FCR 84, at [148].
31. ibid., at, [168].
32. ibid., at [171]–[174].
33. ibid., at [175]–[179]; for the practical effect of this for the Perth metropolitan claim, see [180]–[190].
34. For example, see *James (on behalf of the Martu People) v Western Australia* [2002] FCA 1208, at [11], *James on behalf of the Martu People v Western Australia* (No. 2) [2003] FCA 731.
35. *Western Australia v Ward* (2002) 213 CLR 1.
36. *Members of the Yorta Yorta Aboriginal Community v Victoria* (2002) 214 CLR 422.

Notes

37. Other significant judgments were not delivered by the High Court until late 2001 (*Commonwealth v Yarmirr* (2001) 208 CLR 1) or 2002 (*Wilson v Anderson* (2002) 213 CLR 401).
38. See *Webb v Western Australia* [2007] FCA 1342, *Button Jones (on behalf of the Gudim People) v Northern Territory of Australia* [2007] FCA 1802.
39. NTA s 136F.
40. NTA ss 138A–138G.
41. NTA s 203BF.
42. NTA s 303BK(3).
43. Including referral for the purpose of mediating the resolution of the overlaps, see NTA s 86B(5).
44. NTA ss 138A–138G.
45. NTA ss 136GC–136GE.
46. NTA ss 136D, 86D(1).
47. See NTA ss 203B–203BK for the functions and powers of representative bodies.
48. Kalkadoon People #4 (QUD579/05).
49. Yulluna People (QUD6012/99) and Yulluna People #2 (QUD6004/02); Native Title Directions Hearing, Rockhampton, 12 November 2007, transcript p. 2; Russell David Tatow & Ors on behalf of the Iman People #2 (QUD6162/1998).
50. NTA s 223(1).
51. NTA s 86A(1).
52. See R Farrell, J Catlin and T Bauman, *Getting Outcomes Sooner: Report on a native title connection workshop, Barossa Valley, 2007*, National Native Title Tribunal and AIATSIS, 2007, <http://ntru.aiatsis.gov.au/major_projects/connectionpdfs/getting_outcomes_sooner.pdf> viewed 11 February 2010.
53. McClelland, above, n. 2, at [30].
54. Macklin, above, n. 10, at p. 6.
55. ibid.
56. M Ferguson, Speech to the Minerals Council of Australia Minerals Week Conference, Department of Resources, Energy and Tourism, Canberra, 28 May 2008, <http://www.minerals.org.au/__data/assets/pdf_file/0004/28156/Speech_to_Minerals_Council_-_28.5.08.pdf> viewed 11 February 2010.
57. McClelland, above, n. 2, at [13].
58. ibid., at [33].
59. ibid., at [29].
60. *Lovett on behalf of the Gunditjmara People v Victoria* [2007] FCA 474, at [37].
61. ibid.
62. ibid., at [38].
63. For example, the shortage of experts and no straightforward way to make them more readily available, the delay and cost of securing reports, competing arguments about connection to specific areas.
64. McClelland, above, n. 2, at [34]–[38].
65. NTA s 86F(1).
66. NTA s 86F(1).
67. NTA s 86F(2).
68. McClelland, above, n. 2, at [5].
69. ibid., at [45]–[47], [49].
70. ibid., at [59], [60].
71. ibid., at [26].

Notes

72. ibid., at [26].
73. ibid., at [10].
74. South Australian Native Title Resolution Program 2007–2008, p. 2.
75. Department of Natural Resources and Water, *Annual Report 2006–07*, Queensland Government, 2007.
76. K Rudd, 'Apology to Australia's Indigenous peoples', House of Representatives, *Debates,* 13 February 2008, pp. 167–73, <http://www.aph.gov.au/Hansard/reps/dailys/dr130208.pdf> viewed 11 February 2010.
77. ibid.
78. ibid.
79. ibid.
80. NTA s 200.
81. NTA s 84A.
82. McClelland, above, n. 2, at [5].
83. ibid., at [17].
84. ibid., at [5].
85. ibid., at [33].
86. ibid., at [38].
87. ibid., at [63].
88. ibid., at [45]–[47].
89. ibid., at [48].
90. ibid., at [62].
91. ibid., at [26].
92. See *Risk v Northern Territory* (2007) 240 ALR 75, at [4]–[8], [182].
93. See NTA s 225(c).
94. *Munn v Queensland* (2001) 115 FCR 109.
95. NTA s 84(3)(a)(iii). The phrase 'interest, in relation to land or waters' is defined in s 253.
96. NTA s 84(5). These new provisions apply only to applications lodged on or after the 'commencing day' of the relevant amendments: *Native Title Amendment Act 2007*, Item 78.
97. NTA s 136DA(1)
98. NTA ss 78(2)(b), 108(3)(a).
99. NTA s 84(8).
100. For example, at a regional directions hearing on 11 December 2007, Spender ACJ, in response to notices of motion filed by the North Queensland Land Council Aboriginal Corporation, made self-executing orders in relation to seven claimant applications involving nineteen respondents.
101. Section 183 of the NTA prohibits the Attorney-General from providing assistance to government Ministers, native title holders or claimants, and claimants for compensation in relation to native title. Their funding is dealt with under Div. 4, Pt 11 of the Act.
102. Commonwealth Government, *Guidelines on the Provision of Financial Assistance by the Attorney-General under the Native Title Act 1993*, 2006, ss 36–38, <http://www.ag.gov.au/www/agd/rwpattach.nsf/VAP/(3A6790B96C927794AF1031D9395C5C20)~Guidelines+on+the+Provision+of+Financial+Assistance+by+the+Attorney-General+under+the+Native+Title+Act+1993.pdf/$file/Guidelines+on+the

+Provision+of+Financial+Assistance+by+the+Attorney-General+under+the+Native+Title+Act+1993.pdf> viewed 11 February 2010.
103. ibid., ss 43–46.
104. ibid., s 19.
105. ibid., ss 81–83.
106. ibid., ss 96–98.
107. ibid., s 9.2.2.
108. *Wik Peoples v Queensland* [2000] FCA 1443, at [5].
109. ibid., at [7], [8].
110. ibid., at [9].
111. *Attorney-General of the Northern Territory v Ward* (2003) 134 FCR 16, introductory statement of the Court (Wilcox, North and Weinberg JJ).
112. *Rubibi Community v Western Australia (No. 7)* [2006] FCA 459, at [166].
113. ibid.
114. ibid., at [167].
115. ibid., at [168].
116. For example, see *Members of the Yorta Yorta Aboriginal Community v Victoria* [1998] FCA 1606, at [130]; *De Rose v South Australia* [2002] FCA 1342, at [89], [144].
117. For example, see *Ward v Western Australia* (1998) 159 ALR 483, at 639; *Smith v Western Australia* (2000) 104 FCR 494, at [27].
118. McClelland, above, n. 2, at [39].
119. ibid., at [49].
120. ibid., at [64].
121. National Native Title Tribunal, *Native Title Agreement-making in Australia: A guide to National Native Title Tribunal practice* (2nd edn), National Native Title Tribunal, 2005, p. 15, at [2.4.1].
122. ibid.
123. *Attorney-General of the Northern Territory v Ward* (2003) 134 FCR 16, introductory statement of the Court, per Wilcox, North and Weinberg JJ.
124. See *Frazer v Western Australia* (2003) 128 FCR 458, at [24].
125. *Ngalpil v Western Australia* [2001] FCA 1140, at [30].
126. *Brown v Western Australia* [2001] FCA 1462, at [12].
127. McClelland, above, n. 2, at [63].
128. As Justice French noted: 'Mediation is necessarily consensual. No party can be directed to reach agreement about a pending application or any part of it.' *Franks v Western Australia* [2006] FCA 1811 at [37].
129. NNTT, *Mediation Guidelines: Guidelines for the behaviour of parties and their representatives in mediation in the National Native Title Tribunal*, 2007
130. NNTT, *Procedural Direction No. 2 of 2007*, National Native Title Tribunal, 26 September 2007, at [4], <http://www.nntt.gov.au/Applications-And-Determinations/Procedures-and-Guidelines/Documents/Procedural%20Direction%202007/Procedural%20Direction%202%20of%202007.pdf> viewed 11 February 2010.
131. Those parties may object to the Court making a determination in the terms sought. In deciding whether to make the consent determination, the Court must take into account any objections from those parties. See NTA s 87A(5).
132. NTA s 64(1B), (1C).
133. NTA ss 190(3)(a), 190A(1A).
134. NTA s 136B(1A).
135. NTA s 136CA.

Notes

136. See *Franks v Western Australia* [2006] FCA 1811.
137. NTA s 136GC(1), (2), (4).
138. NTA s 136GC(3).
139. NTA s 136GC(6).
140. *Native Title Amendment Bill* 2006, Explanatory Memorandum at [2.136].
141. NTA s 136GC(7).
142. NTA s 136GD.
143. NTA s 136GC(9).
144. NTA s 136GE(3).
145. NTA s 136GE(1).
146. NTA s 136GE(2).
147. If a native title application inquiry is being held, the NNTT cannot conduct a review at the same time in relation to the same area: NTA s 138E(2). NNTT, Procedural Direction No. 6 of 2007 sets out the procedures to be followed by the President and members of the NNTT.
148. NTA s 138B(1), (2).
149. NTA s 138D.
150. NTA s 156(7).
151. NTA s 141(5).
152. NTA s 154A.
153. NTA s 138E(1).
154. NTA s 138F(1), (2).
155. NTA s 138F(3).
156. NTA s 163A.
157. NTA s 164.
158. NTA s 86(2). NNTT, *Procedural Direction No. 7 of 2007* sets out the procedures to be followed by the President and members of the NNTT when deciding whether and how to conduct an inquiry.
159. NTA ss 62(2)(a) and (b), 190B(2).
160. NNTT, *Procedural Direction No. 9 of 2007,* National Native Title Tribunal, 24 December 2007, at [13], [19]–[21], <http://www.nntt.gov.au/Applications-And-Determinations/Procedures-and-Guidelines/Documents/Procedural%20Direction%202007/Procedural%20Direction%209%20of%202007.pdf> viewed 11 February 2010.
161. ibid., at [13], [21]–[24].
162. Subject to the operation, if any, of ss 47, 47A or 47B of the NTA to areas of land within the claim area.
163. NNTT, above, n. 160, at [36]–[40].
164. See NTA ss 136GC–136GE (reviews), ss 138A–138G, 163A (inquiries) and Procedural Direction No. 6 of 2007.
165. NNTT, above, n. 160, at [25]–[28]. NNTT Procedural Direction No. 5 of 2007, 'Reference to the Federal Court of the question whether a party should cease to be a party to a proceeding', sets out the procedures to be followed by members of the NNTT.
166. NTA s 86E(2).
167. NTA s 136G(3A). Note: such a report may only be provided if the President considers that it would assist the Court in progressing proceedings.
168. NNTT, Procedural Direction No. 8 of 2007 deals with regional mediation progress reports and regional work plans.

169. See the annual reports of the NNTT.
170. See NTA s 86F.
171. See NTA ss 30(3), 39(1)(a)(i).
172. McClelland, above, n. 2, at [5], [6], [17], [22], [26].
173. ibid., at [17], [22], [24].
174. ibid., at [13], [16], [24], [26], [33], [36]–[46], [64].
175. Macklin, above, n. 10, p. 6.
176. See Gurang Regional Directions Hearings, Rockhampton, 1 May 2008, transcript of proceedings, pp. 4, 25 per Dowsett J; Central Queensland Regional Directions Hearings, Townsville, 26 November 2007, transcript of proceedings, p. 11 per Dowsett J.
177. See Gurang Regional Directions Hearings, Rockhampton, 1 May 2008, transcript of proceedings, pp. 2–3.
178. See GMI Regional Directions Hearings, Mount Isa, 29 April 2008, transcript of proceedings, pp. 2, 32, 39.
179. NTA s 86C.
180. NTA s 84C.
181. Federal Court of Australia, Notices to practitioners and litigants (Native Title) issued by the Chief Justice, 1: Conduct of native title proceedings in the Federal Court of Australia, 2007 (revoked 25 September 2009).
182. ibid.
183. NTA s 86BA(2).
184. See *Button Jones (on behalf of the Gudim People) v Northern Territory of Australia* [2007] FCA 1802.
185. *King v Northern Territory* [2007] FCA 944, (2007) 162 FCR 89; *King v Northern Territory* [2007] FCA 1498.
186. For example, see *Frazer v Western Australia* (2003) 128 FCR 458, 198 ALR 303.
187. See *Harrington-Smith v Western Australia (No. 6)* [2003] FCA 663.

14. Who's driving the agenda?

1. *Mabo v Queensland [No. 2]* (1992) 175 CLR 1.
2. *Yarmirr v Northern Territory* (2001) 208 CLR 1.
3. Australian Joint Statement to UN Permanent Forum on Indigenous Issues, Eighth Session, New York, 18–29 May 2009.
4. United Nations Human Rights Committee, Ninety-fifth session, New York, 16 March–3 April 2009, Consideration of Reports Submitted by States Parties, Under Article 40 of the Covenant, Concluding observations of the Human Rights Committee: AUSTRALIA, CCPR/C/AUS/CO/5 (7 May 2009).
5. Committee on Economic, Social and Cultural Rights, Forty-second session, Geneva, 4–22 May 2009, Consideration of Reports Submitted by States Parties Under Articles 16 and 17 of the Covenant, Concluding Observations of the Committee on Economic, Social and Cultural Rights, Australia, at [32].
6. J Drape, 'NT govt to focus funds on 20 communities', *Sydney Morning Herald*, 19 May 2009.
7. Australia, House of Representatives, *Debates*, 12 May 2009, p. 3461 (Dreyfus MP).
8. ibid., p. 3459 (Oakeshott MP).
9. ibid., p. 3743 (Butler MP).
10. ibid.
11. Australia, House of Representatives, *Debates*, 14 May 2009, p. 3879 (Melham MP).

12. ibid., p. 3886 (Haase MP).
13. ibid., p. 3886 (The Hon. McClelland MP, Attorney-General).
14. R Oakeshott, *Oakeshott Moves Amendment to Native Title Act*, media release, 12 May 2009.
15. Australia, House of Representatives, *Debates*, 14 May 2009, p. 3888 (The Hon McClelland MP, Attorney-General).
16. ibid., p. 3880 (Melham MP).

15. Mabo Lecture: A long journey to climb the mountain

1. Australian Joint Statement to UN Permanent Forum on Indigenous Issues, Eighth Session, New York, 18–29 May 2009.
2. Les Malezer, Statement by the Chairman, Global Indigenous Caucus to the United Nations General Assembly, 13 September 2007.
3. *Mabo v Queensland [No. 2]* (1992) 175 CLR 1.
4. UN Committee on the Elimination of Racial Discrimination (CERD), *Report of the UN Committee on the Elimination of Racial Discrimination: Fifty-fourth session (1–19 March 1999), Fifty-fifth Session (2–27 August 1999)*, 29 September 1999, A/54/18, <http://www.unhcr.org/refworld/docid/45c30b260.html> viewed 3 February 2010.
5. A Sykes, 'The "rule of law" as an Australian constitutionalist promise', *Murdoch University Electronic Journal of Law* 9(1), March 2002, <http://www.murdoch.edu.au/elaw/issues/v9n1/sykes91.html> viewed 2 March 2010.
6. HC Black, *Black's Law Dictionary* (5th edn), West Publishing Company, St Paul, MN, 1979, p. 1196.
7. P Kahn, *The Reign of Law*, Yale University Press, London, 2002, pp. 151–3.
8. General Comment E/C.19/2009/L.3.
9. ibid., at [7]–[8].
10. ibid., at [9].
11. *Consideration of Reports Submitted by States Parties under Articles 16 and 17 of the Covenant* [33] UN Doc E/C.12/AUS/CO/4 (2009).
12. *Consideration of Reports Submitted by States Parties under Article 9 of the Convention*, UN Doc CERD/C/AUS/CO/14 (2005).
13. *Concluding Observations of the Human Rights Committee: Australia*, [498–528], UN Doc A/55/40, (2000).
14. *Consideration of Reports Submitted by States Parties under Article 40 of the Covenant*, UN Doc CCPR/C/AUS/CO/5 (2009).
15. ibid.
16. *United Nations Declaration on the Rights of Indigenous Peoples,* G.A. Res. 61/295, Annex, UN Doc A/RES/61/295 (13 Sept. 2007), (Declaration), <http://www.un.org/esa/socdev/unpfii/en/drip.html> viewed 1 February 2010; for Australia's support of the Declaration, see Australian Human Rights Commission, 'United we stand — Support for United Nations Indigenous rights declaration a watershed moment for Australia', media release, 3 April 2009, <http://www.hreoc.gov.au/about/media/media_release/2009/21_09.html> viewed 1 February 2010.
17. Article 42 of the Declaration states: 'The United Nations, its bodies, including the Permanent Forum on Indigenous Issues, and specialized agencies, including at the country level, and States, shall promote respect for and full application of the provisions of this Declaration and follow up the effectiveness of this Declaration.'

18. United Nations, *Durban Declaration and Plan of Action*, adopted at the World Conference against Racism, Racial Discrimination, Xenophobia and Related Violence, 8 September 2001, <http://www.unhcr.org/refworld/docid/3db573314.html> viewed 1 February 2010; UN Office of the High Commissioner for Human Rights, *Outcome Document of the Durban Review Conference*, 24 April 2009, <http://www.unhcr.org/refworld/docid/49f584682.html> viewed 1 February 2010; United Nations General Assembly, *Second International Decade of the World's Indigenous Peoples*, UN Doc A/Res/59/174, 20 December 2004, <http://daccess-dds-ny.un.org/doc/UNDOC/GEN/N04/486/70/PDF/N0448670.pdf> viewed 1 February 2010; United Nations General Assembly, *Programme of Action for the Second International Decade of the World's Indigenous Peoples*, UN Doc A/60/270, 18 August 2005, <http://daccess-dds-ny.un.org/doc/UNDOC/GEN/N05/464/96/PDF/N0546496.pdf> viewed 1 February 2010.
19. JM Cobo, Special Rapporteur of the United Nations Sub-Commission on the Prevention of Discrimination and Protection of Minorities, *Study of the Problem of Discrimination against Indigenous Populations*, UN Doc E/CN.4/ Sub.2/1986/7.
20. Article 8 — redress for forced assimilation or destruction of culture; Article 11 — redress for loss of cultural property taken without consent; Article 20 — redress for people deprived of their means to subsistence and development; Article 32 — redress for exploitation of minerals, water or other resources.
21. *Mabo v Queensland [No. 2]* (1992) 175 CLR 1, Order.
22. Outcome document of the Durban Review Conference, Geneva, 20–24 April 2009, at [73].

16. Mabo Lecture: Addressing the economic exclusion of Indigenous Australians through native title

1. *Mabo v Queensland [No. 2]* (1992) 175 CLR 1.
2. E Johnston, *Royal Commission into Aboriginal Deaths in Custody: National report*, AGPS, Canberra, vols. 1–5, 1991.
3. WEH Stanner, 'The great Australian silence', in *After the Dreaming* (Boyer Lectures), Australian Broadcasting Commission, Sydney, 1969.
4. *Mabo v Queensland [No. 1]* (1988) 166 CLR 186.
5. COAG, *National Framework of Principles for Government Service Delivery to Indigenous Australians*, 2004, <http://www.fahcsia.gov.au/sa/indigenous/pubs/general/bilateralagreements/Pages/national_framework_principles.aspx> viewed 10 February 2010.
6. COAG, *National Commitment to Improved Outcomes in the Delivery of Programs and Services for Aboriginal Peoples and Torres Strait Islanders*, 1992, at [4.1]–[4.5], <http://www.alga.asn.au/policy/indigenous/nationalCommitment.php> viewed 10 February 2010.
7. See *Western Australia v Ward* (2002) 213 CLR 1 and *Members of the Yorta Yorta Aboriginal Community v Victoria* (2002) 214 CLR 422.
8. COAG, *National Framework of Principles for Government Service Delivery to Indigenous Australians*, 1992, <http://www.fahcsia.gov.au/sa/indigenous/pubs/general/bilateralagreements/Pages/national_framework_principles.aspx> viewed 10 February 2010.
9. *Milirrpum v Nabalco Pty Ltd* (1971) 17 FLR 141.
10. *Mabo v Queensland [No. 2]* (1992) 175 CLR 1, at [53].
11. M Grattan, 'Howard tilts at title fight', *The Age*, 10 April 2005.

12. A Vanstone, 'Address to the National Press Club by the Minister for Immigration and Multicultural and Indigenous Affairs', Canberra, 23 February 2005, <http://www.kooriweb.org/foley/news/vanstone1.html> viewed 11 February 2010.
13. J Reeves, *Building on Land Rights for the Next Generation: Report of the review of the Aboriginal Land Rights (Northern Territory) Act 1976*, AGPS, Canberra, 1998, <http://www.austlii.edu.au/au/journals/AILR/1999/6.html> viewed 11 February 2010.
14. ibid.
15. Parliament of the Commonwealth of Australia, *Regional Banking Services: Money too far away*, Report from the House of Representatives Standing Committee on Economics, Finance, and Public Administration, CanPrint Communications Pty Ltd, Canberra, 1999.
16. JC Altman and MC Dillon, *A Profit-related Investment Scheme for the Indigenous Estate*, CAEPR Discussion Paper No. 270/2004, Australian National University, Canberra, 2004, <http://www.anu.edu.au/caepr/Publications/DP/2004_DP270.pdf> viewed 11 February 2010.
17. ibid., pp. 6–7.
18. There are now 411 registered ILUAs, 212 in Queensland.

INDEX

Aboriginal and Torres Strait Islander Commission, 2, 39, 260, 290, 298
Aboriginal and Torres Strait Islander Social Justice Commissioner, 199, 253, 254, 264–265
Aboriginal Economy and Society (Keen), 144
Aboriginal Land Commissioner, 83, 84–85, 205
Aboriginal land councils *see* land councils
Aboriginal Land Fund, 281
Aboriginal Land Fund Commission, 87
Aboriginal Land Rights Commission *see* Woodward Royal Commission
Aboriginal Land Rights (Northern Territory) Act 1976 (Cth), 15, 82–87, 271, 295–296
   comparison with *Native Title Act*, 75–76, 204
   land claims process, 204–205
   Reeves review, 296
Aboriginal sites, 85, 89, 189–190
Aboriginal society *see* 'society' (terminology)
Aboriginal territory (proposed), 284
Aboriginal title (Canada), 44–45, 66–67 *see also* native title
acculturation, 8, 181–182
Adeyinka Oyekan v Musendika Adele [1957], 94, 95
administrative tribunals, 76
adversarial system, 27–28, 50
adverse dominion, 59–61
agreements, 116, 136, 175, 177–178
   administrative costs of, 195
   ILUAs, 108, 130–132, 137, 172, 177, 182, 201, 247, 301
   under *Native Title Act*, 130–135, 186–197
   with native title and non-native title outcomes, 221–228
   treaty (proposed) between Australian Government and Aboriginal and Torres Strait Islander peoples, 283–284
   where there is legal uncertainty, 235–236
ALRA *see Aboriginal Land Rights (Northern Territory) Act 1976* (Cth)
Altman, Jon, 259, 300
Amodu Tijani v The Secretary, Southern Nigeria [1921], 81, 95
Anaya, James, 258
anthropology, 6, 139–158, 176, 178–179
Argyle Diamond Mine agreement, 177–178, 187, 189
assimilation, 163, 164–165
ATSIC *see* Aboriginal and Torres Strait Islander Commission

Attorney-General, 1, 8, 198–199, 218, 219, 221, 222, 225, 228–229, 234, 236, 248, 263–264, 294
Attorney-General's Department, 185–186, 208, 232, 239–240
Australia Book (Pownall), 69
Australian Aborigines (Maddock), 144
Australian Constitution, 88–89, 91, 98, 100
Australian government *see* Commonwealth government
Australian Human Rights Commission, 276–277 *see also* Human Rights and Equal Opportunity Commission
Australian Law Reform Commission on the Recognition of Aboriginal Customary Laws, 95
Australian Mining Industry Council, 37
autonomy *see* regional autonomy; self-determination

Badimia people's declaration of principles for engagement with resource developers, 121, 125–126
banking services, 297–299
Basten, J, 3, 4
Beattie, J, 145
Beaumont, J, 55, 57–58, 60, 61–62, 64–65, 66
Benham, James, 108, 109
Berndt, RM, 147, 150
bijuralism, 6–7, 175–176, 177–179, 181–182
Bill of Rights (USA), 165
Blackburn, J, 72, 80–81, 294–295
Blue Mud Bay mob, 14
bodies corporate, defined, 170 *see also* Prescribed Bodies Corporate
'boundaries' concept, 150–152, 155–156
Brandy v Human Rights and Equal Opportunity Commission, 104, 107
Brennan, Frank, 74
Brennan, J, 42, 43, 71, 86, 89
   on courts, 113
   on extinguishment, 96–97
   Mabo [No. 1], 91
   Mabo [No. 2], 56, 59–60, 61, 62, 63, 72–73, 93, 95, 295
   on race power, 89–90
   on traditional ownership, 85–86
   Walden v Hensler, 70
   Western Australia v Commonwealth (1995), 100–101
   Wik, 60, 62, 63
Bringing Them Home report, 15

Index

broadcasting, 20–21
Browse Gas, 186–187
bundle of rights concept, 57–58, 62–65
Bureau of Indian Affairs (USA), 167–168
Burke, Paul, 139
Butler, Mark, 262
Byers, Sir Maurice, 88, 89

Callinan, J
   Fejo, 109
   Ward, 136
   Yanner, 112
Calma, Tom, 8, 10, 11, 199, 276
Canada, 42, 44–45, 94, 163, 176, 195, 299
Cape York Land Council, 34
Cape York, Qld, 130
Carr, J, 180, 236
Castan, Ron, 78–79, 82, 84, 87–92, 100, 103, 105, 109, 113, 115
Centre for Aboriginal Economic Policy Research, 42
CERD *see* Committee on Elimination of Racial Discrimination
certainty, 37–38, 51
chthonic law, 160–169
Clark, Geoff, 39
Clavero, Bartholemé, 168
COAG *see* Council of Australian Governments
coastal regions, 186–188, 190 *see also* offshore resources; offshore waters
coexistence, 36, 59, 61, 65, 66–67, 106–107, 113–114
collective action *see* working together
colonial legal and political systems, 14, 70, 79, 81, 94
   German (New Guinea), 82
   impact on Indigenous people, 28–29
colonisation, 69, 80–81, 92
commitment, 29–31
Committee on Economic, Social and Cultural Rights (UN), 258, 274, 275–276
Committee on Elimination of Racial Discrimination (UN), 39, 271, 282
common law and native title, 46–48, 51, 58, 67–68, 72, 92–93, 270
common law rights, 37, 38–39, 42–44
   discourse and publications on, 41–42
Commonwealth Constitution, 88–89, 91, 98, 100
   empowered to make laws for Indigenous Australians, 15, 88
   external power, 88–89
   race power, 87–92, 100, 102, 108
Commonwealth government, 14
   encouraged opposition to recognition of native title, 15
   laws validated by NTA, 99
   role in native title system, 228–229, 276
   and Tangentyere land, 16
   working with (challenges), 185–186
Commonwealth of Australia *see* Commonwealth Constitution; *see* Commonwealth government
Commonwealth v Tasmania (1983), 89, 100, 102
Commonwealth v Yarmirr (2001), 112
   see also Croker Island people
communal title, 8–9, 54, 55–57, 72, 172–173, 290, 294–297
'community' (terminology), 6, 139, 141–158
   anthropological criteria, 144
   in Australian Aboriginal studies, 145–146
   legal criteria, 143–144
community benefit from agreements, 196–197
community development, 123, 184–185, 188–189, 197
compensation, 91, 96, 98–99, 100, 108, 285
   achievements in Kimberley, 188–189, 196
   denied, 27, 70, 83, 90
   in determinations, 200
   New Guinea, 82
   principle in proposed national land rights legislation, 272
   and UN Declaration, 257, 281
connection with land, 4, 62, 72, 76, 128–130, 219–221
   establishment of, 206–207
   inquiry and review, 241–244
   nature of recognition in common law, 94–98
   severed by non-Indigenous law, 111–112
Connor, Michael, 70–71, 75
consent determinations, 104–105
Constitution of Australia, 88–89, 91, 98, 100
consulting industry, 41
Cooper v Stuart, 80–81
Council of Australian Governments
   principles for service delivery to Indigenous Australians, 292, 293–294
   whole-of-government processes, 133–134, 137–138
courts, Brennan on, 113 *see also* Federal Court; High Court
Croker Island people, 14
   see also Yarmirr
'Cult of Disremembering', 79
cultural awareness initiatives, 191
'cultural bloc' concept, 147–148
cultural cohesion (model for society), 153
cultural sites *see* Aboriginal sites

Dambimangari people, 190
Davidson, DS, 149–150, 151
Dawson, J, 72–73, 75, 86, 100–101
De Jersey, Paul, 88
De Rose v State of South Australia [2002], 137
Deane J, 46, 86, 89
   Mabo [No. 2], 56, 63, 72–73, 94, 95
   Tasmanian Dam case, 102
   Western Australia v Commonwealth (1995), 100–101
declarations, 120–121
Delgamuukw decision, 44–45, 66–67, 172–173
demography, 25
Department of Families, Housing, Community Services and Indigenous Affairs, 208, 239–240
Department of Prime Minister and Cabinet, 75
determinations, 170–171, 185, 186, 200–201
   Martu, 133, 134
   partial, 237–238
   Tjurabalan, 133–134
   trends and forecast, 202–205
   variations, 235–236
Dillon, Mike, 300
discrimination *see* racial discrimination
Dodson, Mick, 10–11, 118, 257
Dowsett, J, 215, 249
Dreyfus, Mark, 262
Drummond, J, 233
Duro v Reina, 164

economic development, 76–77, 187–191, 297–300
economic exclusion of Indigenous Australians, 289–292, 296–301
economic independence, 8–9, 297–300
education, Western versus Indigenous, 166, 169
electorate, 25, 27 *see also* public reaction
employment preference for Indigenous people (USA), 167–168
engagement
   negotiation tips, 191–195
   principles for engagement with resource developers, 125–126
equality/inequality *see* non-discrimination principle; racial discrimination; self-determination
equity in ventures/developments, 188, 190–191, 196, 223, 299, 300
Escobar, Arturo, 145
ethnography, 145–146, 149–150, 152, 154–155, 178

evidence, Federal Court rules, 80
evidence of traditional ownership *see* native title claims: standards of proof
'exclusivity', 64–67, 133–134
executive acts *see* legislative or executive acts of extinguishment
Expert Mechanism on the Rights of Indigenous Peoples, 257, 258
external affairs power of Commonwealth, 88–89
extinguishment, 61–62, 73–74, 76, 92, 96–98, 99, 111
   areas of Australia, 205–206, 221–222
   Brennan, J on, 96–97
   and Crown grants, 74
   doctrine of, 14, 129
   in *Fejo*, 97
   and freehold title, 109–111
   general principles, 59
   as metaphor, 65–66
   modes of, 101–102
   New Zealand, 27
   NTA 1998 amendments, 108
   NTA definition, 97–98
   partial, 52, 62–65, 99
   principle, 101
   protection against, 37–38
   statutory, 98, 108
   tests of, 59–61, 105

FAIRA *see* Foundation for Aboriginal and Islander Research Action
Fauna Conservation Act 1974 (Qld), 111
Federal Court, 104–105, 108, 202, 208
   on connection to claimed area, 206
   grouped claims, 251
   and native title outcomes, 233–234, 235, 246–251
   rules for giving evidence, 80
   Ward decision *see Western Australia v Ward* (2000)
Federal government *see* Commonwealth government
fee simple *see* grant in fee simple
Fejo v Northern Territory of Australia (1998), 61, 62, 63, 65, 66, 74, 97, 108–111, 119
Ferguson, Martin, 218
fiduciary duty, 85, 86, 106
financial management and benefit-sharing, 196–197
financial resources
   innovative programs, 298–299
   lack of, 297 *see also* funding

Index

financial services, 297–299
Fingleton, JS, 170
fishing and hunting rights, 20, 111, 261, 302
foreshore and seabed, title in (NZ), 27, 302
  see also offshore waters
Foundation for Aboriginal and Islander Research Action, 269–270
Fraser government, 271
freehold title, 66, 99, 188, 272
  and extinguishment, 61, 63, 109–111
French, J, 3, 4, 65, 88, 117, 119, 180, 236, 263, 283
funding
  administrative costs of agreements, 195
  for negotiation and engagement, 192–193
  Prescribed Bodies Corporate, 174, 178
  see also financial resources

Gajerrong people *see* Miriuwung Gajerrong people
gas fields, 186–187, 188, 259 *see also* resources
Gaudron, J, 46, 48
  Fejo, 109
  Mabo [No. 1], 91
  Mabo [No. 2], 56, 63, 72–73, 94, 95
  Western Australia v Commonwealth (1995), 100–101
  Wik, 60, 61, 113
  Yanner, 53, 111
genealogies, 179–180
Gibbs, CJ, 90
Gleeson, J
  Fejo, 109
  Ward, 127
  Yanner, 53, 111
  Yorta Yorta, 45–46, 47, 48
Glenn, H Patrick, 161–162
globalisation of Australian law, 88, 93
Gordon River, Tasmania, 89
Gove Land Rights case (*Milirrpum v Nabalco*), 72, 73, 82, 294–295
governance arrangements for PBCs, 174–175, 176, 178
government *see* Commonwealth government; state and territory governments
grant in fee simple, 60, 61, 63, 66
  and extinguishment, 97, 101, 109–111
Gray, K and SF, 53, 58, 65
'Great Australian Silence', 79
Griffiths v Northern Territory of Australia [2006], 153
Gummow, J
  Fejo, 109
  Wik, 60, 61, 79, 94, 106, 113

Yanner, 112
Yorta Yorta, 45–46, 47, 48

Haase, Barry, 263
Hanger, Ian, 88
Hawke government, 271–272
Hayne, J
  on *Fejo*, 109
  on *Yanner*, 53, 111
  on *Yorta Yorta*, 45–46, 47, 48
Herzfeld, Michael, 145
High Court
  members of *Fejo* Court, 109
  members of *Mabo* Court, 86
  role in native title recognition, 78–114
High Court decisions
  concerning Tribunal consent determinations, 104–105
  Courts' responses to native title cases, 42–48
  land rights litigation, 84–87
  language of, 3, 73–74
  limits to achievement, 112–114
  Mabo see *Mabo v Queensland [No. 2]* (1992)
  Miriuwung Gajerrong see *Miriuwung Gajerrong* decision
  Wik see *Wik Peoples v Queensland* (1996)
  Yanner v Eaton see *Yanner v Eaton*
  Yorta Yorta see *Yorta Yorta* decision
history and historians, 70
'horde' concept, 149, 151
Horner, Phillipa, 75
House of Representatives Standing Committee on Economics, Finance and Public Administration, 297
housing/home ownership programs, 298–299
Howard, John, 17, 295
Howard government, 74–75, 290
human rights, 8, 120, 121, 159–160, 256–260, 272–276 *see also* racial discrimination
Human Rights and Equal Opportunity Commission, 104 *see also* Australian Human Rights Commission
Human Rights Committee (UN), 258, 275
Human Rights Council (UN), 258
hunting rights *see* fishing and hunting rights

identity, 29–31
identity labels (native title groups), 177
IHRNA *see* Indigenous Human Rights Network of Australia
ILO *see* International Labour Organization
ILUA *see* Indigenous Land Use Agreements
In re Southern Rhodesia, 42–44, 58, 71–72, 73, 81, 95

Index

inconsistency, 59–61, 62, 76, 105
Indian Civil Rights Act 1968 (USA), 165
Indian nations (USA), 160–169, 299
Indian Reorganization Act (USA), 164, 167
Indigenous Affairs Advisory Committee (WA), 132–133
Indigenous Australians
    areas of Australia owned/controlled, 284
    economic exclusion of, 289–292, 296–301
    law and customs *see* traditional law and custom
    non-Indigenous relations with, 137
    representative bodies, 8, 40, 255, 260–261 *see also* land councils; native title corporations; native title representative bodies
    responses to *Mabo* decision, 40–42
    social and cultural organisation, 42–44
Indigenous communities
    declarations of sovereignty, 120–121
    economic independence, 8–9, 297–300
    greed and conflict, 11, 40–41
    mechanisms for involvement in land management/jurisdiction, 135
    negotiation tips, 191–195
    principles for engagement with resource developers, 125–126
    relationships with government (NZ), 31
    services for *see* service provision to Indigenous communities
    'society'/'community' terminology, 139–158
    working with Commonwealth government (challenges), 185–186
Indigenous Human Rights Network of Australia, 260
Indigenous Land Corporation, 76
Indigenous Land Fund, 288
Indigenous Land Use Agreements, 108, 130–132, 137, 172, 177, 182, 201, 247, 301
Indigenous languages *see* language and language groups
Indigenous law
    Australia *see* traditional law and custom
    USA *see* traditional law (Indian nations, USA)
Indigenous peoples, 278
    Australia *see* Indigenous Australians
    international forums, 257–258, 274–275
    rights in international law, 88, 120, 159–160, 258–260, 272–277, 278–282
    USA, 160–169
    see also United Nations Declaration on the Rights of Indigenous Peoples
Indigenous Peoples' Organisations of Australia, 259

Indigenous policy, 11, 27–28, 219, 225, 254–256, 261–266, 283–286, 290–293
interdependence, 29–31
International Convention on the Elimination of All Forms of Racial Discrimination, 39, 271, 282
International Covenant on Civil and Political Rights, 258international credibility and standing, 25
international forums, 256–257, 274–275
International Labour Organization Convention 169, 280
international law, 88, 120, 159–160, 258–260, 272–277, 278–282
Invention of Terra Nullius (Connor), 70–71, 75
investment, 298–300

'jural native title', 118–124 *see also* native title
jural right, 3, 5, 53–54, 55, 57–58, 62–63, 111

Kahn, P, 272
Keating, Paul, 25, 124
Keen, Ian, 144, 150–151
Kija people, 177, 189, 191
Kimberley Land Council, 7, 183–197, 259
Kimberley Nickel Mines, 191
Kimberley region, WA, 130, 133–134, 152, 183–197
Kirby, J, 48
    Fejo, 119
    Wik, 61, 105–106, 110, 113
    Yanner, 53, 111
KLC *see* Kimberley Land Council
knowledge, Western versus Indigenous, 166, 169
Koolan Island, 190
Koowarta v Bjelke–Petersen (1982), 87–88, 100

Lamer CJ (Canada), 66–67, 172
land, connection with *see* connection with land
Land Act 1962 (Qld), 87
land claims
    New Zealand, 20, 302
    Northern Territory, 204–205
land councils, 172, 174, 192 *see also* Kimberley Land Council
land ownership concepts, 43–44 *see also* property
land rights, 36
    Aboriginal/Torres Strait Islander territory (proposed), 284
    land justice, 9, 11, 36 *see also* 'transitional justice'
    legislation proposed, 271–272

Index

litigation (NT), 84–87 see also *Aboriginal Land Rights (Northern Territory) Act 1976* (Cth)
new forms of title (proposed), 12, 284
state statutes, 83, 261, 281
statutory, 82–87
and UN Declaration, 277–282
see also native title
Land Rights Act of 1976 *see Aboriginal Land Rights (Northern Territory) Act 1976* (Cth)
Land (Titles and Traditional Usage) Act 1993 (WA), 37, 99–100
language and language groups, 147–153
Indigenous languages broadcasting, 21
and 'tribes' concept, 148–150
Lardil and other Peoples v Queensland [2001], 65, 98
Larrakia Development Corporation, 76–77
Larrakia people, 108–109
Law Council of Australia, 263
leadership, 9–10, 16, 29
lack of, 40–41
leases, 37, 60–62, 99, 105–108, 112, 113
Lee, Tony, 116
Lee, J, 56–57, 59–61, 62, 64, 67
legal discourse, 41–42
legal industry, 41
legal pluralism, 176 *see also* bijuralism
legislative drafting, 75
legislative or executive acts of extinguishment, 59–60, 62
legitimacy *see* moral legitimacy
local government, 133, 134

Mabo, Eddie, 2, 14, 20, 33, 36, 268–269, 289
Mabo v Queensland [No. 1] (1988), 90–92
Mabo v Queensland [No. 2] (1992), 14, 25, 33–48, 58, 64, 69–77, 91, 92–98, 127, 128, 270, 288, 295
exclusivity, 66, 67
extinguishment, 59–60, 62–64
interest in land, 52, 54–56, 72 *see also* connection with land
limitations of 'recognition', 78–114
members of *Mabo* Court, 86
occupancy, 67
politics and perceptions, 74–75
possessory title, 54
property, 67–68
recognition of common law native title, 92–98, 270
responses to, 37–48, 74–75, 283, 288–289
weaknesses, 76–77
Macklin, Jenny, 199, 218, 248 *see also* Minister for Families, Housing, Community Services and Indigenous Affairs
MacLeod, Bobby, 267
Maddock, Ken, 144
Malezer, Les, 8, 39
Mantziaris, C, 170–171
Māori fisheries litigation, 20
Māori King's 'rebellion', 20, 23–24
Māori Land Court, 27
Māori language broadcasting, 21
Māori opposition to colonisation, 20
Māori Party, 27
Māori population, 25
Maralinga lands, 171
Marks, Greg, 39
Martin, D, 170–171
Martu people, 100, 133–134, 137
Mason, J, 86, 89
Mabo [No. 2], 93
Western Australia v Commonwealth (1995), 100–101
McClelland, Robert, 198–199, 218, 219, 221, 222, 225, 228–229, 234, 236, 248, 263–264
McGregor, Bill, 152
McHugh, J
Fejo, 109
Mabo [No. 2], 93
Ward, 136
Western Australia v Commonwealth (1995), 100–101
Yorta Yorta, 46
McIntyre, Greg, 3
McLachlin, J, 47
McNeil, Kent, 42, 67, 172–173
mediation, 108, 121–122, 202, 207, 213–218, 224, 235–243, 245 *see also* National Native Title Tribunal; negotiation
Melham, Daryl, 263, 264
Members of the Yorta Yorta Aboriginal Community v Victoria (2002), 33, 35, 45–48, 51, 127, 128, 129, 141–143
Meriam people, 14, 33, 36, 54, 55–56, 66, 90, 92, 262 *see also Mabo v Queensland [No. 1]* (1988); *Mabo v Queensland [No. 2]* (1992)
Merkel J, 143, 199, 234
Milirrpum v Nabalco Pty Ltd, 72, 73, 82, 294–295
miners *see* resource developers
mines and mining, 37, 85, 86, 190, 196–197
mining leases, 37, 99, 106–108, 112
Minister for Families, Housing, Community Services and Indigenous Affairs, 1, 8, 199, 218, 248
Minister for Resources and Energy, 218

Index

Ministerial Taskforce on Indigenous Affairs, 291
Miriuwung Gajerrong decision, 3, 33, 35, 48, 63, 112, 119, 127, 128, 129, 136
Miriuwung Gajerrong people, 14, 177–178, 188–189, 233
Mohr, R, 176
Monaghan, P, 150
moral legitimacy, 9, 22–23
  price of, 22, 25–26
Morton, J, 139
Morton v Mancari, 167
Moynihan, J, 56, 73
municipal government *see* local government
Murphy, J, 73, 89–90
Murray Islands people *see* Meriam people

'nation', use and meaning of term, 145–146, 147
National Aboriginal and Torres Strait Islander representative body *see* representative body (proposed)
national Indigenous representative body, 8, 40, 255, 260–261, 266
National Indigenous Working Group, 74–75
National Native Title Council, 256, 265
National Native Title Tribunal, 21, 42, 99, 104–105, 108, 109–110, 121–122, 202, 208, 238–246, 250–252 *see also* mediation
native title
  benefits of recognition, 210–212
  as a bundle of rights, 57–58, 62–65
  claims *see* native title claims
  coexistence, 36, 59, 61, 65, 66–67, 106–107, 113–114
  and common law, 46–48, 51, 58, 67–68, 72, 92–93, 270
  communal title, 54, 55–57, 72, 172–173, 290, 294–297
  declarations, 120–121
  defined/described, 54, 65, 215
  discourse on common law meaning, 41–42
  and discrimination *see* racial discrimination
  economic value, 6, 7, 12, 44, 50, 76
  exclusivity, 64–67, 133–134
  extinguished *see* extinguishment
  High Court contribution, 78–114 *see also* High Court
  interest in land, 55–57
  judgment content, 113
  'jural native title', 4–5, 118–124
  limits of, 2–3, 128–129
  New Guinea, 82
  New Zealand, 20–32

non-discrimination principle, 3, 12, 42–43, 73–74, 91, 99, 276, 279
occupancy-based doctrine, 130
principles, 92–93
prior to *Mabo*, 80–92
process *see* native title processes
property concepts, 52–68
recognition (nature and rules of), 94–98, 101, 111 *see also* native title processes
responses to *Mabo* decision, 37–48, 74–75, 283, 288–289
revival/non-revival, 4, 12, 61–62, 109–111
social native title, 118–124
surviving rights, 21, 28
symbolism and function, 137–138
system *see* native title processes
see also Indigenous policy; land rights
Native Title Act 1993 (Cth), 14, 34, 37–40, 74–75
  administration of *see* native title processes
  amendments, 38, 40, 49, 74–75, 107–108, 130–131, 202, 238–239, 262, 271
  comparison with *Aboriginal Land Rights (NT) Act*, 75–76, 204
  objectives, 98–99, 270–271
  Prescribed Bodies Corporate, 170–182
  reform challenges, 49–51, 184
  relationship with RDA, 102
  s 21, 130
  s 47A, 74
  s 47B, 74
  s 223(1), 42, 46–48, 57, 128
  strengths and failings, 37–40, 75, 198–200
  WA challenge, 37, 99–102
Native Title Act case *see Western Australia v Commonwealth* (1995)
Native Title Amendment Act 1998 (Cth), 74–75
Native Title Amendment Bill 2009 (Cth), 262–263
native title and land rights laws, 261–264
  see also Native Title Act 1993 (Cth)
native title claims, 34–35, 76, 137, 198–252
  applications at May 2008, 201–202
  death of claimants, 180, 213
  determinations *see* determinations
  grouped claims, 251
  Kimberley Land Council strategy, 185–186
  mediation, 108, 121–122, 202, 207, 213–218, 224, 235–243, 245
  non-native title outcomes, 121–122, 294
  opposition to recognition of native title, 7, 14–15, 34–35, 37, 84–89, 137–138
  outcomes sought
    all parties, 232–238

Index

claimants, 209–214
  claimants representatives, 214–218
  other respondents, 229–232
  overlapping claims, 207–208, 213–214, 244–245
  parties to, 38–39, 180, 213, 230–231, 245
  regional management, 216–217, 239–241, 250
  resources and funding, 39, 214–215, 217–218, 231–232, 246, 251
  standards of proof, 12, 45–46, 51, 55, 129–130, 207, 213, 215, 263–264, 286
  trends and forecast, 202–205
  see also native title processes
Native Title Conference 2002, 115–117
native title corporations, 6–7, 170–182 see also Prescribed Bodies Corporate
native title holding groups, 14, 17–18, 177–180 see also Prescribed Bodies Corporate
native title legal and consulting industry, 41
native title processes, 2, 7–8, 40, 41, 48–50, 76, 98–99, 108, 180–181, 293–294
  agreement-making, 116, 130–135, 136, 221–228, 235–236 see also agreements
  anthropology and, 139–158
  Commonwealth government role, 228–229, 276
  comparison with NT land claims process, 75–76, 204
  costs, 48–49, 127
  deficiencies and opportunities, 8, 11–12, 49–51, 116–117, 127, 198–200, 205–209, 262–264, 277, 285–286
  Federal Court role, 246–251
  government role, 218–229
  integrated system, 208–209
  participants, 208
  reporting and analysis, 245–246
  Waanyi case, 103–105, 109–110
  see also native title corporations; Prescribed Bodies Corporate
Native Title Report, 199, 265
native title representative bodies, 172, 174, 184, 208, 213–218, 290
negotiation, 7, 191–195 see also agreements; mediation
Neowarra see Wanjina–Wororra community
Nevada v Hicks, 164
New Guinea, 82
New South Wales (colony), 80–81
New South Wales (state)
  alternative settlements, 226
  land rights statutes, 83
  native title applications, 201–202

New Zealand, 20–32, 94, 281
Newcastle Waters case, 251
Ngaanyatjarraku, Shire of, 133, 134
Ngai Tahu people, 20
Ngalpil v Western Australia, 180
NIWG see National Indigenous Working Group
non-discrimination principle, 3, 12, 42–43, 73–74, 91, 99, 276, 279 see also human rights; racial discrimination
non-Indigenous Australians' responses
  to *Mabo* decision, 5, 35–36
  to statutory land rights for Aboriginal people, 83–84
non-native title outcomes, 121–122, 294
Noongar people, 14–15, 133, 134–135, 137, 206
North Ganalanja Aboriginal Corporation & Waanyi People v Queensland (1996), 62, 102, 103–105, 109–110, 122
North, J, 53, 58, 59, 64, 263
Northern Queensland, 34
Northern Territory, 14
  Fejo case, 108–111
  land claims, 204–205
  land rights litigation, 84–87
  native title applications, 201–202
  see also *Milirrpum v Nabalco Pty Ltd*

Oakeshott, Rob, 262, 263
occupancy, 55–57, 63, 67, 130, 243–244
O'Faircheallaigh, Ciaran, 186
Office of Parliamentary Counsel, 75
offshore resources, 186–187
offshore waters, 37, 112, 279
Olney, J, 51
Operation of Native Title Representative Bodies report, 174
oral tradition, 79–80, 162, 164
Ord Stage Two project, 188–189, 193
  see also Miriuwung Gajerrong
Orr, Robert, 75
'Outcomes and Possibilities' Conference 2002, 115–117
ownership see land ownership; land rights

Papua and New Guinea (Territory), 82
Parihaka movement, 23–24
Parliamentary Joint Committee on Native Title and Torres Strait Islander Land Account, 174, 217
Parliament's response to *Mabo* decision, 37–40, 74–75
partial extinguishment, 52, 62–65, 99

343

passive resistance, 24
pastoral leases, 60–62, 99, 105–107, 112, 113
paternalism, 167
Patrick Stevedores Operations No. 2 Pty Ltd v Maritime Union of Australia, 113
PBCs *see* Prescribed Bodies Corporate
Pearson, Noel, 2, 3, 5, 6, 9, 12, 98, 128, 130, 135, 138
perpetual succession, 173, 175–176, 178–182
Perth metropolitan area, 206
Pilbara region, WA, 133–134
Pitjantjatjara, 150, 171
policy *see* Indigenous policy
politics, 25–26, 27, 74–75, 115–116
Pownall, Eve, 69
practical commitment *see* commitment
preference provisions for Indigenous people, in employment, 167–168
Prescribed Bodies Corporate, 17–18, 171–182
    funding and governance, 174–175, 178
    number and diversity, 177
    requirements, 171, 176–177
price of legitimacy *see* moral legitimacy
Privy Council, 42, 71, 80–81, 94, 95
property, 3, 52–68
    concepts of, 53–54
    and terra nullius, 81
public reaction
    to *Mabo* decision, 5, 35–36
    to Māori rights, 25, 27
    to statutory land rights for Aboriginal people, 83–84

Queensland, 14
    agreement-making, 130
    Koowarta case, 87–89
    land rights statutes, 83, 261, 281
    Mabo litigation *see Mabo v Queensland [No. 1]* (1988); *Mabo v Queensland [No. 2]* (1992)
    native title applications, 201–202
Queensland Coast Islands Declaratory Act 1985, 90

R v Van der Peet (1996), 45, 47
race power of Commonwealth, 87–92, 100, 102, 108
racial discrimination, 168–169, 282–283
    international concern for human rights, 39, 88
    and native title legislation, 39–40, 42–44, 271
    terra nullius, 3, 78
    see also human rights; non-discrimination principle
Racial Discrimination Act 1975 (Cth), 38, 39–40, 87–92, 102, 289
    and state law, 91–92
    validity challenge, 87–89
Radcliffe-Brown, AR, 147
radio, 20–21
Ranger Project Area, Kakadu, NT, 85
'reconciliation', 44–46
'redress', 281, 285
Reeves J, 296
referendum of 1967, 15
regional autonomy, 130, 133–135 *see also* self-determination
regional management of claims, 216–217, 239–241, 250 *see also* native title claims; native title processes
representative body (proposed), 8, 40, 255, 260–261, 266
resource developers, principles for engagement with, 125–126
resources, 5–6, 76
    development of, 186–187
    ownership of, 5–6, 52
    royalties, 75–76
    use/taking of, 5–6, 56, 57, 66
Reynolds, Henry, 70
Ridgeway, Aden, 2, 8–9
Rights in Water and Irrigation Act 1914 (WA), 64
Roth, WE, 147
Rowley, CD, 83–84, 144
royalties (minerals and resources), 75–76
Rubibi claim, 143, 234
Rumsey, A, 150, 151

sacred sites *see* Aboriginal sites
Sampi v Western Australia [2005], 180
Sansom, B, 139
seabed, title in (NZ), 27, 302 *see also* offshore waters
self-determination, 6, 10, 11, 135–136, 255–256, 283, 285–286
    right of, 13–18, 120, 159–160, 276–277, 279
    US Indigenous nations, 159–169
self-government, 133, 134, 135, 136
self-sufficiency, 167–168
service provision to Indigenous communities
    COAG principles, 292, 293–294
    failures in, 260
    impact of development, 187
    inaccessibility of services, 297–299
    whole-of-government approaches, 133–134, 135
'setting things right' *see* social native title
Shire of Ngaanyatjarraku, 133, 134
Skoien, Tony, 88
Slattery, Brian, 42

Index

social impacts of development, 187
social native title, 4–5, 118–124
social problems, 169, 189
'society' (terminology), 6, 139, 141–158
    anthropological criteria, 144–145, 154
    legal criteria, 141–144, 145
    models of, in Australian Aboriginal studies, 146–154
    models of, used by anthropologists, 157–158
    in NTA context, 154–158
South Australia
    alternative settlements, 226
    land rights statutes, 83, 261
    opposition to native title claims, 137
    state-wide ILUA, 132–133
South West Aboriginal Land and Sea Council, 133, 134–135
In re Southern Rhodesia, 42–44, 58, 71–72, 73, 81, 95
sovereignty, 42–43, 70–71, 81, 92–93, 111, 129, 135–136, 216, 283
    Indigenous declarations of, 120–121
Special Rapporteur on the situation of human rights and fundamental freedoms of Indigenous people, 257–258
Stanner, Bill, 41, 79
state and territory governments
    agreements under *Native Title Act*, 130–135
    ministerial meetings, 219
    opposition to recognition of native title, 7, 14–15, 34–35, 37, 84–89, 137–138
    role in native title system, 225–228, 229
state and territory laws, 37, 83, 91–92, 98, 99–100, 181, 261
Statement of Commitment (WA government), 132–133
statutory extinguishment, 99, 108
statutory land rights, 82–87
Stephen, Sir Ninian, 88
Stolen Generations apology, 22–23
Stolen Generations report, 15
Strelein, Lisa, 70, 74, 118, 142
sui generis character, 94–95, 98, 172
Sumner, Lord, 58, 71–72, 81
Sundberg, J, 153
Supreme Court of Canada, 44–45, 47
Sutton, Peter, 146, 147, 152
symbolism, 5, 11–12, 25–26, 137–138

Tainui raupatu settlement, 20
Tangentyere land, 16
Taranaki confiscation claims, 20
Tasmanian Dam case, 89, 100, 102
Tawhiao (Māori King), 20, 23–24

Te Whiti o Rongomai, 24
television and radio, 20–21
terra nullius
    doctrine of, 80–82
    and *Mabo*, 70–71, 75
    meanings, 71, 73
    as racism, 3, 78
    re-establishment of, 285
    rejection of, 42–43, 93–94
    reliance on notion of, 21
'territorial boundaries' concept, 150–152, 155–156
tests of extinguishment, 59–61, 105
Thayorre people, 14, 105–106
third-party interests, 38–39 *see also* native title claims: parties to
Timber Creek society, 153
Tindale, NB, 148, 150, 155–156
Tjamu Tjamu Corporation, 177
Tjurabalan Native Title Land Aboriginal Corporation, 180
Tjurabalan people, 133–134, 137, 190–191
Tohu Kakahi, 24
Toohey, J, 86
    on *ALRA*, 83
    Mabo [No. 1], 91
    Mabo [No. 2], 54, 67, 94, 95
    Wik, 61, 62, 63, 97, 113
Torres Strait Islander territory (proposed), 284
tourism, 187–188
traditional law and custom, 6, 42–44, 55–57, 65, 74, 96, 119, 124, 128–130
    and colonial law, 14
    evidentiary basis for, 178–179
    expressions of, 79–80
    Fejo, 110
    and native title corporations, 175–182
    New Guinea, 82
    statutory land rights, 83–85
    and terra nullius doctrine, 81–82
    transmission, 180
traditional law (Indian nations, USA), 161–169
Traditional Owners, 16, 17–18, 76, 84–85, 86, 125–126, 193–197, 266
'transitional justice', 2, 9–10, 21–32
treaties, international *see* international law
treaty (proposed) between Australian Government and Aboriginal and Torres Strait Islander peoples, 283–284
Treaty of Waitangi, 20, 21, 23 *see also* Waitangi Tribunal
Treaty of Waitangi (Fisheries Claims Settlement) Act 1992 (NZ), 20
tribal settlements (NZ), 20

Index

'tribe', use and meaning of term, 145–146, 147, 148–152
Tribes (Indian nations) *see* Indian nations (USA)

United Nations Committee on Economic, Social and Cultural Rights, 258, 274, 275–276
United Nations Committee on Elimination of Racial Discrimination, 39, 271, 282
United Nations Declaration on the Rights of Indigenous Peoples, 8, 160, 254, 256–259, 268, 269–270, 273, 277–282
United Nations Human Rights Committee, 258, 275
United Nations Human Rights Council, 258
United Nations Permanent Forum on Indigenous Issues, 257
United States, 159–169, 299
usufructuary rights, 54, 82, 95, 111–112

Vanstone, Amanda, 295
venture capital, 300 *see also* economic development; investment
Victoria
 alternative settlements, 8, 226
 state-wide framework agreements, 132
vision, 29–31, 197
von Doussa J, 55, 57–58, 60, 61–62, 64–65, 66

Waanyi case, 62, 102, 103–105, 109–110, 122
Waitangi Tribunal, 20, 21, 284 *see also* Treaty of Waitangi
Walden v Hensler, 70
Wanjina–Wunggurr community, 153
Ward v Western Australia (1998), 56–57, 59–61, 64, 67
Watson, Lord, 80–81
wealth, basis of, 16–17
Webber, Jeremy, 137
Weber Plains, 193
Weinberg J, 142–143, 153
Western Australia, 14–15, 37, 95, 99–102, 112
 agreement-making, 130, 132–135, 186–197
 alternative settlements, 226
 native title applications, 201–202
 see also Kimberley Land Council; Kimberley region; Western Desert region
Western Australia v Commonwealth (1995), 99–102
Western Australia v Ward (2000), 52, 53, 55, 57–58, 61, 62, 64–65
Western Australia v Ward (2002), 3, 33, 35, 48, 63, 112, 119, 127, 128, 129, 136
Western Desert region, 133, 147–148, 150, 177
whole-of-government approaches, 133–134, 135, 137–138, 219
Wik people, 14
Wik Peoples v Queensland (1996), 60, 61–63, 105–107, 110, 113, 233
Williams, Joe, 2, 5, 9–10
Woodside, 187, 259
Woodward Royal Commission, 82–83, 87, 271
Wootten, Hal, 28, 116–117, 123
working together, 11, 15–16, 25, 27, 184, 187, 197, 286
World Heritage Properties Conservation Act 1983 (Cth), 89
Wororra people, 100

Yalanji people's claim, 34
Yamatji Land and Sea Council, 125–126
Yamatji Marlpa Land Council, 117
Yanner v Eaton, 53, 55, 57, 58, 111–112
Yarmirr decision, 112; *Yarmirr* sea rights claim, 254
Yawuru people, 14, 143
Yazzie, Robert, 166
'yes, but' principle, 22–23
Yorta Yorta decision, 33, 35, 45–48, 51, 127, 128, 129, 141–143
Yorta Yorta people, 15, 51
Yulara case, 139, 140
Yunkuntjatjara people, 137
Yunupingu, Galarrwuy, 79–80